ARTIFACT IN
BEHAVIORAL RESEARCH

SOCIAL PSYCHOLOGY

A series of monographs, treatises, and texts

Edited by

Leon Festinger   and   Stanley Schachter

Jack W. Brehm, A Theory of Psychological Reactance. 1966

Ralph L. Rosnow and Edward J. Robinson (Eds.), Experiments in Persuasion. 1967

Jonathan L. Freedman and Anthony N. Doob, Deviancy: The Psychology of Being Different. 1968

Paul G. Swingle (Ed.), Experiments in Social Psychology. 1968, 1969

E. Earl Baughman and W. Grant Dahlstrom, Negro and White Children: A Psychological Study in the Rural South. 1968

Anthony G. Greenwald, Timothy C. Brock, and Thomas M. Ostrom (Eds.), Psychological Foundations of Attitudes. 1968

Robert Rosenthal and Ralph Rosnow (Eds.), Artifacts in Behavioral Research, 1969

ARTIFACT IN BEHAVIORAL RESEARCH

Edited by

Robert Rosenthal
DEPARTMENT OF SOCIAL RELATIONS
HARVARD UNIVERSITY
CAMBRIDGE, MASSACHUSETTS

and

Ralph L. Rosnow
DEPARTMENT OF PSYCHOLOGY
TEMPLE UNIVERSITY
PHILADELPHIA, PENNSYLVANIA

 ACADEMIC PRESS New York and London 1969

ACADEMIC PRESS, INC.
111 Fifth Avenue, New York, New York 10003

United Kingdom Edition published by
ACADEMIC PRESS, INC. (LONDON) LTD.
Berkeley Square House, London W1X 6BA

LIBRARY OF CONGRESS CATALOG CARD NUMBER: 74-84254

PRINTED IN THE UNITED STATES OF AMERICA

To the memory of

Edwin G. Boring

PREFACE

The effort to understand human behavior must itself be one of the oldest of human behaviors. But for all the centuries of effort, there is no compelling evidence to convince us that we do understand human behavior very well. Instead, there are the unsolved behavioral problems of mental illness, racism, and violence, of both the idiosyncratic and institutionalized varieties, to bear witness to how much there is we do not yet know about human behavior. In the face of the urgency of the questions waiting to be answered it should not be surprising that behavioral scientists, and the publics that support them, should suffer from a certain impatience. That impatience is understandable; but perhaps from time to time we need remind ourselves that we have not really been in business for very long.

The application of that reasoning and of those procedures which together we call "the scientific method" to the understanding of human behavior is of relatively very recent origin. What we have learned about human behavior in the short period, say from the founding of Wundt's laboratory in Leipzig in 1879 until now, is out of all proportion to what we learned in preceding centuries. The success of the application of "scientific method" to the study of human behavior has given us new hope for an accelerating return of knowledge on our investment of time and effort. But most of what we want to know is still unknown. The application of what we think of as scientific method has not simplified human behavior. It has perhaps shown us more clearly just how complex it really is.

In contemporary behavioral research it is the research subject we try to understand. He serves as our model of man in general or at least of a certain kind of man. We know that his behavior is complex. We know it because he does not behave exactly as does any other subject. We know it because sometimes we change his world ever so slightly and observe his behavior to change enormously. We know it because sometimes we change his world greatly and observe his behavior to change not at all. We know it because the "same" careful experiment conducted in one place at one time often yields results very different from one conducted in another place at another time. We know his complexity because he is so often able to surprise us with his behavior.

Much of the complexity of human behavior may be in the nature of the organism. But some of this complexity may derive from the social nature of behavioral research itself. Some of the complexity of man as we know it from his model, the research subject, may reside in the fact that the subject usually knows perfectly well that he is to be a research subject and that this role is to be played out in interaction with another human being, the investigator.

That portion of the complexity of human behavior which can be attributed to the social nature of behavioral research can be conceptualized as a set of artifacts to be isolated, measured, considered, and, sometimes, eliminated. This book is designed to consider in detail a number of these artifacts. The purpose is not simply to examine the methodological implications, though that is an important aspect, but also to examine some of the substantive implications. It may be that all "artifacts," when closely examined, teach us something new about a topic of substantive interest.

The introductory chapter, which was written by our late colleague Edwin G. Boring, provides a perspective on artifact and a discussion of the nature of experimental control. The following six chapters are a series of position papers by researchers who have been actively engaged in systematic exploration of various antecedents of artifact in behavioral research, and each writer summarizes the findings in his respective area. Those six essays, in the order of their presentation, are by William J. McGuire on suspiciousness of intent, Robert Rosenthal and Ralph L. Rosnow on volunteer effects, Robert E. Lana on pretest sensitization, Martin T. Orne on demand characteristics, Rosenthal on experimenter expectancy effects, and Milton J. Rosenberg on evaluation apprehension. The final chapter, by Donald T. Campbell, takes into account the separate contributions and tells us something of the future prospects for behavioral research.

In organizing this volume, the editors have been guided by Herbert Hyman's comment that the demonstration of systematic error may well mark an advanced state of a science.

> All scientific inquiry is subject to error, and it is far better to be aware of this, to study the sources in an attempt to reduce it, and to estimate the magnitude of such errors in our findings, than to be ignorant of the errors concealed in the data. One must not equate ignorance of error with the lack of error. The

lack of demonstration of error in certain fields of inquiry often derives from the nonexistence of methodological research into the problem and merely denotes a less advanced stage of that profession.*

The editors thank Academic Press for their patience and continued interest throughout the two and one-half year evolution of this book. To our contributors—Boring, Campbell, Lana, McGuire, Orne, and Rosenberg—we are indebted for their thoughtful and thought-provoking essays. Our task was greatly facilitated by separate grants to each of us from the Division of Social Sciences of the National Science Foundation.

Edwin G. Boring, who passed away on July 1, 1968, wrote once of the sense of inadequacy of the individual scholar to available information at any moment of his existence and of the feeling sometimes of being overwhelmed by the complexity of nature.

> That would explain Kepler's looking for a geometrical generalization to explain the planets in the solar system, would give a sound basis for the need for all generalization in science. And nowadays we no longer hope to learn about everything that's in nature, but only about everything that's already been published about nature, and ultimately we sink, gasping . . . Still, I am content to live in this age. Titchener once said that he would have liked to live in the age when one man could know everything, and that was quite long ago. We must accustom ourselves to an age in which one man never knows more than just enough to use for a given purpose.†

How fortunate our age was to have Edwin G. Boring. We take pride in dedicating this book to his memory.

January 29, 1969

Robert Rosenthal

Ralph L. Rosnow

* Hyman, Herbert H. *Interviewing in social research.* Chicago: University of Chicago Press, 1954. P. 4.

† Personal communication, November 1, 1967.

CONTENTS

ARTIFACT IN BEHAVIORAL RESEARCH

Chapter 1

PERSPECTIVE:
Artifact and Control

Edwin G. Boring

Harvard University

I. THE CONCEPT OF CONTROL

If x, then y. That is the formula for John Stuart Mill's method of agreement. The independent variable is x and the dependent y. It says that x is a sufficient condition of y, and the experimental establishment of this relation has sometimes been thought to be the aim of science.

The statement is, however, not enough. It must be coupled with *if not–x, then not–y,* and the two formulas together constitute Mill's joint method of agreement and difference, establishing the independent variable, x, as both the sufficient and the necessary condition of y. It is essential to add the method of difference to the method of agreement in order to establish x as necessary to y as well as sufficient. (See Mill, 1843, Bk. III, chap. 8.) In short *not–x* is the control, for x is a necessary condition only if it be shown that y does not occur without it. In this sense Mill was a good expositor for the concept of control, although he did not use the term. (On the history of control, see Boring, 1954; 1963, 111–125.)

The principle had not been overlooked before Mill. When Pascal in 1648 planned the experiment for measuring the weight of the air by having a barometer carried 3000 feet up to the top of the Puy-de-Dome so as to show the loss of atmospheric pressure at the greater height, he provided also for a second barometer which was kept at the foot

1

of the mountain and was found to remain unchanged. (Pascal, 1937, 97–112; Cohen, 1948, 71f; Conant, 1951, 39; Boring, 1954, 577f; 1963, 115.) It was really a control. The independent variable was the height, the dependent variable was the atmospheric pressure, and the procedure was the joint method of agreement and difference—two centuries before Mill had named it and laid down the rules.

Actually it is the use of the method of difference, that is to say, of control, that puts rigor into science. A fact *is* a difference. Something is this and not that. Any observed value has meaning only in relation to some frame of reference, and any quantity only in respect of the scale in which it is set. Lana (Chapter 4) makes this point in his paper in the present volume. The method of concomitant variations, which Mill gave as a separate method, is really an elaboration of his method of difference, for every pair of values of x and y is placed in relation to every other x–y pair from which the first pair differs. The paradigm for concomitant variations is $y = f(x)$ and its determination is the scientific ideal. The joint methods of agreement and difference, *if x, then y* and *if not–x, then not–y*, are really only one pair of cases in the method of concomitant variations, where x is some positive value and also zero. In short, experimental science is the determination of functional relationships of the nature of $y = f(x)$ by the observation of concomitant variations. A fact is a difference, and ideally the use of control is always implied.

All this becomes clearer if we see what happens when we have no control. History depends for its general laws on the method of agreement and ordinarily lacks control because the initial term of an historical causal relationship is not truly an independent variable. To establish inductively a generality by repetition of an observable relationship, one has to wait in history on the recurrence of an x by what is called "chance" (a synonym for the inscrutable ignorance of prognostic causality). One cannot control historical sequence, and there are comparable examples to be found in other descriptive nonexperimental sciences like astronomy, geology and some branches of biology.

A. Four Meanings

The word *control* originally meant *counter-roll,* a master list against which any subsequent special list could be checked and if necessary corrected. Thus the term came to mean a check and so restraint in order to induce or maintain conformity. To control is now to guide. In science the word has had four meanings, successively adopted and all still useful.

(1)   Control has long been used in the sense of maintaining *constancy of conditions* and also for checking an experimental variable to see if it is adhering to its stated or intended specifications. The artifacts with which this volume is primarily concerned are mostly of this kind. The independent variable of $y = f(x)$ is contaminated, often unwittingly, by additional unspecified determinants that affect y. This is the oldest scientific meaning of the word *control,* one which the discussions of the present volume re-emphasize.

(2)   In the late nineteenth century the use of the *control experiment* or control test came into psychology and to a lesser extent into biology, although not always with that name. For instance, the Hipp chronoscope was calibrated by a "control hammer," a heavy pivoted hammer which was released electrically, and in falling tripped successively two switches, wired in with the chronoscope so that the time of the hammer's fall from one switch to the other was measured. Since less variability could be expected of the fall-hammer than of the chronoscope, the hammer was used to calibrate the chronoscope. A number of successive falls constituted a "control series" from which the variable and constant errors of the chronoscope could be computed. (Wundt, 1874, 772; 1911, III, 367.)

Control tests, called "puzzle experiments" (*Vexirversuche*) were used in the early measurements of the cutaneous two-point threshold. The separation of the compass points placed upon the skin was varied and the observer reported whether he felt one or two. Here the artifact that Titchener called the stimulus-error tends to make trouble. If the subject knows that two points are always being placed on his skin, it becomes difficult for him to report a unitary perceptual pattern because he knows that two points are being applied (Boring, 1921, 465–470; 1963, 267–271). Especially is this difficulty present in naive subjects, like McDougall's primitive people in the Torres Straits who wanted to show off their fineness of perception (McDougall, 1903, 141–223, esp. 189–193). To control this error, single points are mixed in with the double and that control works well to measure the skill with which the subject can discriminate single from double stimuli. It is not, however, wholly successful in obtaining a description of the perceptual pattern, for the reason that very often a single point does give a very good dual perception. A control of this second type can be vitiated by a failure of control of the first type, for the stimulations by a single point are not always the same. Some unknown factor in this independent variable remains uncontrolled in the sense that it has been left free to vary and does vary. It has been suggested that this variation could be caused by the presence or absence of multiple inner-vation at the point stimulated (Kincaid, 1918; Boring, 1954, 579f; 1963, 116f, also on multiple innervation, Boring, 1916, 89–93).

At the end of the century Müller and Pilzecker (1900) published their elaborate investigation on the use of the method of right associates in the study of memory. They used principal series (method of agree-ment) and comparison series (method of difference), what we should nowadays call the experimental and control series.

The use of the control test, experiment, or series became almost stan-dard in the twentieth century, and the growth of behavioral psychology in which discrimination plays the fundamental role in assessing the psy-chological capacities of the subject has practically put the word *control* out of common usage, for a discrimination is the observation of a differ-ence and Mill's joint method is now standard. Lana's discussion (Chap-ter 4) of the use of the pretest in social research shows both the impor-tance of control and the manner in which it often introduces an artifact by changing the experimental status of the subject before the crucial test.

(3) The use of the *control group* avoids the difficulty of the pretest artifact by introducing another difficulty. The control group and the experimental group are independent, since they are constituted of differ-ent noncommunicating organisms, but, being different, they are not iden-tical and one cannot tell certainly how nearly identical they are. You may match the two groups, individual for individual, litter-mates of the same body-weight if the subjects are animals, twins if the subjects are human, or you can make the groups of great size hoping that there is a law of large numbers that will perform the magic of reducing any inscrutable difference to a negligible amount, yet you remain in the dilemma of complementarity. You have gained independence at the ex-pense of assured equivalence.

One early example (Hankin, 1890) of the use of a control group is an experiment demonstrating the effective immunization of mice against tetanus. The immunized mice lived when inoculated and the controls died. The experiment is convincing because the difference be-tween a live mouse and a dead one is so large. An acceptable level of confidence that a dead mouse is not alive can be reached without the calculation of a critical ratio for how nearly dead the live mice are or how much life still inheres in the dead ones. This kind of com-parison is so easily conceived that it would seem that earlier examples of the use of a control group ought to exist.

In psychology the use of the control group came in with the study of the transfer of training where a pretest to establish a base of skill also provided some early practice, learning which could not readily be separated from the formal practice of the experimental group, the effect of which was what was being measured. It is desirable to give a pretest in skill A to both an experimental and a control group, and then to give formal practice in skill B to the experimental group while the control group is being left unpracticed. After that, both groups can be tested and compared for improvement in A to see if practice of the experimental group in B led it to more improvement in A than had been furnished by the pretest for the control group. Thorndike and Woodworth (1901, esp. 558) are the first to have introduced this conception into the study of transfer, but their use of it was trivial. The earliest carefully designed study was by Winch (1908), a study which just happens to have been made in the same year that Gosset (1908) published his paper on how to determine the significance of differences between groups by converting the critical ratio into a t-value. The two developments ran along neck and neck—the use of control groups and the statistical techniques for quantifying the confidence you should feel for the significance of the differences between such groups (the R. A. Fisher confidences). This kind of artifact, due to the impossibility of showing that the differences between the groups is negligible, is not an artifact that this book considers, so we may leave the topic there. Since some of the progress of science occurs by the discovery and correction of the many kinds of artifacts, it would seem that science still has a considerable future.

(4)   The fourth scientific use of the concept of control is irrelevant here. It is the reversion to the early use of the term that we find in Skinner's use of the notion of the control and *shaping of behavior* (Skinner, 1953). It is applied to what may be an intentional production of artifacts and has such social uses as the psychotherapy of behavioral deviations or the eradication of ignorance. Education itself is, of course, an artifact as man promotes it for his fellows. That is what Rousseau thought when he extolled the "noble savage."

II. THE PROBLEM OF ARTIFACT

Now let us turn more specifically from the understanding of control to the problem of the artifact. Most of the discussion in this volume is concerned with the constancy and specification of experimental conditions. These requirements raise questions of controls of type 1, the discovery and specification of extraneous conditions—for the most part social in nature—that affect the experimental variables. There is always the hope that, once understood, they can be eliminated or at least be made subject to correction. The experimenter's expectations and personality (Rosenthal, Chapter 6), subjects' personality (Rosenthal and Rosnow, Chapter 3), their awareness of the experimenter's intent (McGuire, Chapter 2), or their concern that they are being evaluated (Rosenberg, Chapter 7) may affect the results. The degree to which such factors inhere in the conditions of the experiment needs to be known, so that the ways to avoid their influences can come under consideration. (For an earlier discussion of these matters, see Rosenthal, 1965.)

Certainly one of the most scientifically important sources of error in experimentation lies in the indeterminacy of the specification of the variables. Consider the independent variable. *If x, then y,* and *if not–x, then not–y.* But what is *x?* Mill, the logician, did not have to consider that. To a logician, *x* is *x,* but to a scientist *x* is a variable, identified in words which may easily mean one thing at one time and another at another, or different things in different laboratories or at different periods of history. We have already seen that a single point touching the skin is not always the same stimulus. It may be felt as one, yet sometimes as two (a *Vexirfehler*).

Take the specific energy of nerves which was well validated by Johannes Müller in 1826 and 1838 and then discredited about seventy-five years later (Boring, 1942, 58–74). How could that have come about? The experiments were all right. Stimulation of the nerve of any one of the five senses gives rise to the quality appropriate to that sense. The discrediting discovery was the finding that even sensory nerves are passive conductors that deliver qualitatively identical messages. Perhaps this difficulty seems semantic now, but it was very real at the time. Sense-physiologists had been talking for many years about what it is that the nerves conduct: animal spirits, *vis viva, vis nervosa.* Müller was making the point that the sensorium does not perceive directly the external world, but only what the nerves bring to it. What each of the five nerves brings is patently different. *Vis* (force) and *energy* were not clearly distinguished in 1826 or 1838. If each of the five kinds of nerve brings something different to the brain, the five have different specificities, different "energies". What Müller almost forgot—actually he did not quite forget it but he did not take it seriously—was that the nerves have another specificity that lies not in what they conduct. They have specificity of projection, and the specificity of perceived quality is the specificity of the connections that the sensory nerves make in the brain. The crucial difference lies not in the nature of the conduction but in whither conduction leads, and it took more than half a century to right this error.

The Wever–Bray effect when it was first discovered furnished another example of the mistaken identity of a variable, this time not the x or y of the observation but a physiologically intervening variable. When electronic amplification came in before 1930, it became possible for these investigators to put electrodes on the auditory nerve of a cat, amplify the voltage, speak to the cat, and hear the sounds in a loud-speaker over the circuit of amplification. This was a dramatic finding, though Wever and Bray reported it with great care and circumspection (Wever and Bray, 1930). Presently it was discovered that the amplified potentials were not from the impulses of the VIIIth nerve but were induced by the electrical events involved in the action of the organ of Corti in the cochlea (Davis and Saul, 1931; Davis, Derbyshire, Lurie, and Saul, 1934; Boring, 1942, 420–423, 434–436). Both discoveries were important as bearing upon the electrical nature of receptor response, but the first belief that the finding supported the frequency theory of hearing was due to an incorrect specification of the variables.

As a matter of fact the experimental variable is ever so much more complex than is ordinarily supposed, and often the discovery of its nature is a scientific event of considerable importance. For instance, one is seldom sure about the true nature of a stimulus until research has accomplished the analysis. Such was Newton's discovery of the stimulus for color and especially of the surprisingly complex stimulus for white. Galileo's discovery of the stimulus for pitch not only put the psychology of tone in readiness for development but also made possible the scientific management of music. The psychology of smell has been long deferred because the nature of its stimulus remained unknown (Boring, 1942, 448). John Dewey in his famous paper on the reflex arc made the point that the stimulus cannot be presumed but has to be discovered (Dewey, 1896, 370; Boring, 1950, 554). The true stimulus is often an invariant known only as the result of careful research. For instance, the stimulus for apparent visual size under the rule of size constancy and Emmert's law is the linear size of the retinal image of the perceived object divided by the distance of the object from the observing eye, for that is the invariant (Boring, 1942, 292; 1952, 144–146). A great deal of the progress of science has depended upon the discovery of such invariants (Stevens, 1951, 19–21).

In social research the independent variable is less often called a stimulus but its specification as an invariant is just as important. Hypnosis furnishes us good examples of insufficiently specified initial determinants. When research on hypnosis is being undertaken, the independent variable is the experimenter's suggestion and the dependent variable the subject's behavior, but it is a mistake to think that the experimenter's words are all of the suggestion. "Bring me that rattlesnake," says the experimenter of a live coiled rattlesnake behind invisible glass, and the subject complies until prevented by the glass (Rowland, 1939). Would he have done so had there been no glass? Perhaps, but the "demand" made upon him, to use Martin Orne's term, was more than the verbal instruction. It included the knowledge that this was an experiment, that you do not get truly injured in an experiment, that there is an experimenter and a university looking out for you. The demand characteristic is much broader than it is explicit. Martin Orne (Chapter 5) shows how the essays in this book deal with instructional demands upon the subject's behavior, instructions that are enormously amplified by special cues of which in many cases the subject is unaware. The independent variable is insufficiently specified.

III. A DILEMMA

Now, how is the correctness of the specification of the experimental variables to be protected from all these predisposing additions, conscious and unconscious, that the subject adds, often from his knowledge about the experimental situation, to the intended explication of the independent variable? The answer would seem to lie in keeping the subject ignorant of what is going on, but that is difficult. In this respect a group control is better than a control experiment, because the one group has no communication with the other, but this advantage is offset by the fact that one cannot be sure that the two groups are comparable. Are animals better subjects because they do not know the difference between an experiment and real life? Not always. There was H. M. Johnson's dog whose threshold for pitch discrimination turned out to be the same as Johnson's because the dog watched Johnson's face and wanted to please (Johnson, 1913, 27–31). The skilled horse, Clever Hans, also watched his master and sought to please (Pfungst, 1911, 1965). It would be better to secure ignorance by not working in a laboratory nor letting the subjects know that they are subjects or that there is an experimenter. That limitation may, however, put you in the position of the historian or the astronomer, limited to the method of agreement without a control. You cannot tell the subject to do this or that without giving away the artificiality of the situation, and, if the intended part of the observation is known to be artificial, other artifacts are almost sure to squeeze in. The investigators whose observation resulted in the publication of *When Prophecy Fails* infiltrated a fanatical group in order to note what happens when an assured conviction is frustrated (Festinger, Riecken and Schachter, 1956), but such work is only gross preliminary taxonomy. One would like to get more rigorous facts by the use of experimentation.

The choice between laboratory control and the free uncontrolled behavior of natural phenomena is no new dilemma. Let us for a moment go back seventy-five or even only fifty years to the time when introspection was the principal method of the new experimental psychology. In those days secrecy was the rule about the experiments. Students did not talk about procedures and observations with one another. There was no general discussion of work in progress—except perhaps at the intimate meetings of the little Society of Experimental Psychologists, when graduate students who were subjects in an experiment were excluded from the room when the experiment was being discussed. Procedure without knowledge was the rule, and there was in force as strong an ethic about discussion of current experiments as there was later about classified war material. Did secrecy work? It must have been helpful. Nowadays, some subjects are undergraduates hired from outside the laboratory; yet gossip spreads in any student group. Perhaps the chief evidence that hypotheses influenced results in the old days lies in the fact that introspection never settled the question of the nature of feeling—as to whether feeling is an independent quality or a kind of sensation and, if so, what kind, as to whether feeling can or cannot become the object of attention and how it is observed if it cannot enter the clear focus of attention. There was always in this crucial introspective matter, a suspicion that laboratory atmosphere—local hypotheses—influenced the findings. No one could produce proof, but right there lies one of the reasons why introspection faded out for lack of confidence—at least systematic experimental introspection lapsed although not the use of psychophysical judgments.

All in all we are left with a dilemma. The experimental method is science's principal tool: $y = f(x)$ is the goal. Control is necessary and is used even when it is not recognized as such. Every fact is at bottom a difference, and the method of concomitant variations emphasizes this relational characteristic about facts. Nevertheless, in the specification of a variable one always remains uncertain as to how exhaustive the description is. Artifacts adhere implicitly to specification and, when they are discovered, ingenuity may still be unable to circumvent them. When they are not discovered, they may persist for a year or a century and eventually turn out to be the reason why a well-established fact is at long last disconfirmed. For this reason scientific truth remains forever tentative, subject always to this possible eventual disconfirmation. But that is no new idea, is it?

REFERENCES

Boring, E. G. Cutaneous sensation after nerve-division. *Quarterly Journal of Experimental Physiology*, 1916, **10**, 1–95.

Boring, E. G. The stimulus-error. *American Journal of Psychology*, 1921, **32**, 449–471.

Boring, E. G. *Sensation and perception in the history of experimental psychology*. New York: Appleton-Century, 1942.

Boring, E. G. *A history of experimental psychology*. 2nd ed. New York: Appleton-Century-Crofts, 1950.

Boring, E. G. Visual perception as invariance. *Psychological Review*, 1952, **59**, 141–148.

Boring, E. G. The nature and history of experimental control. *American Journal of Psychology*, 1954, **67**, 573–589.

Boring, E. G. *History, psychology, and science: selected papers*. R. I. Watson and D. T. Campbell (Eds.), New York: Wiley, 1963.

Cohen, I. B. *Science, servant of man*. Boston: Little, Brown, 1948.

Conant, J. B. *On understanding science*. New Haven: Yale University Press, 1951.

Davis, H., and Saul, L. J. Action currents in the auditory tracts of the mid-brain of the cat. *Science*, 1931, **74**, 205f.

Davis, H., Derbyshire, A. J., Lurie, M. H., and Saul, L. J. The electrical response of the cochlea. *American Journal of Physiology*, 1934, **107**, 311–332.

Dewey, J. The reflex arc concept in psychology. *Psychological Review*, 1896, **3**, 357–370.

Festinger, L., Riecken, H. W., and Schachter, S. *When prophecy fails*. Minneapolis: University of Minnesota Press, 1956.

Gosset, W. S. ("Student"). The probable error of a mean. *Biometrika*, 1908, **6**, 1–25.

Hankin, E. H. A cure for tetanus and diphtheria. *Nature*, 1890, **43**, 121–123.

Johnson, H. M. Audition and habit formation in the dog. *Behavior Monographs*, 1913, **2**, no. 3, serial no. 8.

Kincaid, Margaret. An analysis of the psychometric function for the two-point limen with respect to the paradoxical error. *American Journal of Psychology*, 1918, **29**, 227–232.

McDougall, W. Cutaneous sensation. *Reports of the Cambridge Anthropological Expedition to Torres Straits*. 1903, **II**, 141–223. Cambridge, England.: Cambridge University Press.

Mill, J. S. *A system of logic, ratiocinative and inductive, being a connected view of the principles of evidence and the method of scientific investigation*. 1843. Reprint: London: Longmans, Green, 1930.

Müller, G. E., and Pilzecker, A. Experimentelle Beiträge zur Lehre vom Gedächtniss. *Zeitschrift für Psychologie*, Ergbd. **I.** Leipzig: Barth, 1900.

Pascal, B. 1648. Trans.: *The physical treatises of Pascal: the equilibrium of liquids and the weight of the mass of the air*. New York: Columbia University Press, 1937.

Pfungst, O. *Clever Hans* (*The horse of Mr. von Osten*). 1907. Trans. 1911. Reprint: R. Rosenthal (Ed.), New York: Holt, Rinehart and Winston, 1965.

Riecker, A. Versuche über den Raumsinn der Kopfhaut. *Zeitschrift für Biologie*, 1874, **10**, 177–201.

Rosenthal, R. Introduction. In Pfungst, 1965, op. cit. supra., ix–xlii.

Rowland, L. W. Will hypnotized persons try to harm themselves or others? *Journal of Abnormal and Social Psychology*, 1939, 34, 114–117.

Skinner, B. F. *Science and human behavior*. New York: Macmillan, 1953.

Solomon, R. L. An extension of control group design. *Psychological Bulletin*, 1949, 46, 137–150.

Stevens, S. S. *Handbook of experimental psychology*. New York: Wiley, 1951.

Thorndike, E. L., and Woodworth, R. S. The influence of improvement in one mental function upon the efficiency of other functions. *Psychological Review*, 1901, 8, 247–261, 384–395, 553–564.

Vierordt, K. v. Die Abhänigkeit der Ausbildung des Raumsinnes der Haut von Beweglichkeit der Körperteile. *Zeitschrift für Biologie*, 1870, 6, 53–72.

Wever, E. G., and Bray, C. W. The nature of the acoustic response: the relation between sound frequency and the frequency of impulses in the auditory nerve. *Journal of Experimental Psychology*, 1930, 13, 373–387.

Winch, W. H. The transfer of the improvement of memory in school-children. *British Journal of Psychology*, 1908, 2, 284–293.

Wundt, W. *Grundzüge der physiologischen Psychologie*. 1st ed. Leipzig: Engelmann, 1874.

Wundt, W. *Grundzüge der physiologischen Psychologie*. 6th ed. III, Leipzig: Engelmann, 1911.

Chapter 2

SUSPICIOUSNESS OF EXPERIMENTER'S INTENT

William J. McGuire

University of California, San Diego

I. INTRODUCTION

It is a wise experimenter who knows his artifact from his main effect; and wiser still is the researcher who realizes that today's artifact may be tomorrow's independent variable. Indeed, even at a given time, one man's artifact may be another man's main effect. The essentially relativistic and ambiguous criterion for calling a variable an "artifact" is well illustrated by the topic on which we focus in this chapter, namely, suspiciousness of the experimenter's manipulatory intent. However, we shall begin by using the case of response sets to illustrate the transitory nature of the "artifact" status. Response sets serve better to show the stages by which a variable passes from artifact to theoretical focus since, as an older topic of study, they serve to illustrate the total career of an artifact more fully than does the more current "suspiciousness" problem. After discussing the career of artifacts in general, we shall devote a section to considering the current artifactual status of suspiciousness of experimenter's intent. This section will consider the antecedent variables that give rise to such suspiciousness and which therefore might be contaminated by it. A fourth section will review some of the theoretical housings in which current research on suspiciousness of experimenter's intent research is embedded. Finally, we shall consider the ethical problem of deception which is inextricably involved in any discussion of suspiciousness of experimenter's manipulatory intent.

13

Any full consideration of how suspiciousness of the experimenter's intent operates in psychological research would quickly broaden to include rubrics such as guinea pig reactions, placebos, faking good, awareness, etc., each of which carries in its train a long history of experimental investigation. In the mainstream of American experimental psychology, starting at its source back in the nineteenth century, it has been taken for granted that the subject should be kept unaware of the purpose of the experiment, even when it dealt with such unemotional issues as visual acuity or the serial position effect. It must be admitted that this routine secretiveness has not been universal, and some experimenters have even used themselves as observers and subjects in the areas of psychophysics and rote memorization (Ebbinghaus immediately comes to mind in this regard). An informal recollection of this undisguised research in which the experimenter serves as his own subject inclines me to believe that the results that were obtained in this flagrant manner have replicated remarkably well under covert conditions. Nevertheless, hiding from the subject the true purpose of one's experiment has become normative in psychological research. Ignorance is achieved either by noninformation or by misinformation. I suspect that one could discover such ludicrous cases as in, say, the rote memorizing area, where an experimenter who was investigating the serial position effect told his subjects that he was studying the effect of knowledge of results, while an investigator testing a hypothesis about knowledge of results informed his subjects that he was studying the serial position effect. The already existing "Minsk–Pinsk" joke fortunately relieves us from the felt need for the laborious scholarly investigation that would be needed to document this illustration. Inevitably there is growing concern regarding the probability and effect of a growing suspiciousness regarding experimenter's intent by subjects drawn from heavily-used populations, such as the college sophomore.

To some of us who have striven with more zeal than success to interest the student in the introductory classes (from whom the experimental subjects are drawn) in the results of much of the general experimental psychology research, the extent of our secretiveness compulsion in such areas as psychophysics and verbal learning might seem quite unnecessary. The problem seems more one of apathy than overcuriosity. If the student in the classroom seems so unmoved by the beauty of such a relationship as that between rate of presentation and shape of the serial position curve even when the instructor exhibits it to him framed in an enhancing theoretical architecture, why do we feel that special care is necessary to keep the same individual from actively suspecting what we are looking for when he participates as a subject in the laboratory and perhaps reacts so atypically that the results will not be generalizable to a naive population. Yet I suspect it was the great felt need for using unsuspecting subjects that has promoted some of the practices in American experimental psychology which seem a little peculiar to the layman. For example, our predilection for using nonhuman subjects, our avoidance of research on certain humanly gripping problems, our use of highly artificial laboratory situations, our avoidance of phenomenological explanatory concepts, etc., have all been partially motivated by our assumption that good research can be done only to the extent that the subject is unaware of the purpose of the investigation.

While our secretiveness might seem excessive in such traditional areas as rote learning, one is inclined to take the need for deception more seriously in the case of social and personality research. One might have had only minor worries about the generalizability of research regarding serial position curves even if our data came from subjects who suspected that this was indeed what we were studying. There seems more grounds for worry that disclosure might cause serious loss of generalizability in other areas such as operant verbal conditioning and attitude change research. In this chapter we shall concentrate on this latter line of research, but before focussing on this question of the extent to which awareness (or suspiciousness) of persuasive intent distorts the results of an attitude change experiment, we shall in the next section outline what we believe to be the life history of an artifact in general, illustrating the sequential stages through which it passes in terms of the "response bias" artifact.

II. THREE STAGES IN THE LIFE OF AN ARTIFACT

A review of the progress of psychological interest in a wide variety of artifacts would, we believe, reveal a natural progression of this interest through the three stages of ignorance, coping, and exploitation. At first, the researchers seem unaware of the variable producing the artifact and tend even to deny it when its possibility is pointed out to them. The second stage begins as its existence and possible importance become undeniable. In this coping phase, researchers tend to recognize and even overstress the artifact's importance. They give a great deal of attention to devising procedures which will reduce its contaminating influence and its limiting of the generalizability of experimental results. The third stage, exploitation, grows out of the considerable cogitation during the coping stage to understand the artifactual variable so as to eliminate it from the experimental situation. In their attempt to cope, some researchers almost inevitably become interested in the artifactual variable in its own right. It then begins to receive research attention, not as a contaminating factor to be eliminated, but as an interesting independent variable in its own right. Hence, the variable which began by misleading the experimenter and then, as its existence became recognized, proceeded to terrorize and divert him from his main interest, ends up by provoking him to new empirical research and theoretical elaboration.

The suspiciousness of persuasive intent artifact has only begun to reach this third stage. Hence, in this section we will illustrate the three stages by recounting the career of its somewhat older sibling in the artifact family, response biases. The preoccupation with response sets and styles developed about five years earlier than that in the awareness of persuasive intent issue, and now has reached a stage that allows a fuller illustration of the total life cycle. This brief consideration of the response bias artifact will also help to give our present discussion some perspective, and illustrate our claim that this three-stage career is a common one for artifacts, not peculiar to the suspiciousness of experimenter intent artifact that mainly concerns us in this chapter.

A. The Ignorance Stage

Once the existence of an artifact becomes known, its baleful influence is essentially at an end. Thus the part of its life span during which it achieves its notoriety is essentially an anticlimax. Its deleterious effect on the development of a field of knowledge occurs during the long period of ignorance prior to its achieving the explicit attention of researchers. It is then that it leads the psychologist to draw false conclusions from data, to elaborate or trim his theories in inappropriate ways, and to design new research in ways more likely to confuse than clarify the issue. To those of us who have elected an intellectual vocation, it is gratifying to consider that once we start worrying about an artifact rather than ignoring it, while our peace may be at an end, so also is its harmful impact on the development of knowledge.

Still, there seems to be a considerable inertia about admitting the existence of an artifact. While we are all ready enough to grant that progress inevitably involves upsetting the ongoing routine of things and disturbing the peace, one is always reluctant to admit that his *modus operandi* involves an artifact. It tends to become a question of whose peace is being disturbed. While our superordinate goal is the discovery of truth, we are reluctant to give up the subordinate goal of believing that our past research was heading inexorably toward such discovery. Hence, it seems necessary that an artifact be discovered and rediscovered several times before it becomes a sufficiently public scandal so that some bright young men seize upon it as a device to pry their elders out of their ruts and find a place in the sun for themselves. Like much else that disturbs and advances a field of knowledge currently, the discovery of artifacts seems to be the work of the associate professors.

Our illustrative artifact of response bias exhibits the difficulty of the discovery process. That it took the field so long to become interested in this artifact seems strange for a number of reasons. In the first place, it is a sufficiently obvious problem so that it occurs to the layman, and must have suggested itself constantly, at least preconsciously, to those engaged in testing enterprises. Moreover, so much of psychological research involves ability or personality testing that opportunities to stumble upon such an artifact were constantly available. With the almost stifling amount of current research on response biases, it is hard to believe there was ever a time when the field was not preoccupied with them. As a matter of fact, though, not even several explicit considerations of its existence stirred up any great amount of research interest. Thus, the demonstration by Lorge (1937) and by Lentz (1938) of an acquiescence response set in personality tests seems to have stirred up little interest until a decade passed. It is undoubtedly Cronbach (1941, 1942, 1946, 1950) who deserves to be called "the father of the response set." Since he called attention to the role of response biases, research interest in this area has grown progressively. It is perhaps significant of a psychological reality in the history of science that he dealt primarily with response biases in abilities tests, where they are more manageable. It was in this manageable area that the possible importance of the artifact was first admitted and attention paid to it. Lorge was sounding the alarm, in connection with response biases in personality tests, where they are somewhat more difficult to cope with, and not surprisingly he found the field little attuned to the drum he was beating. In the personality tests area, we are faced with more difficult response biases such as social desirability, while with abilities tests the discussion is more confined to acquiescence or position biases that can be somewhat more easily handled by mechanical adjustments in the wording of questions or of the ordering of responses. By the late 1940's, however, even those working in the personality area admitted the importance of controlling for "faking good" tendencies. At least those who were working with the MMPI realized this problem (Ellis, 1946; Meehl and Hathaway, 1946; Gough, 1947). This resurgence of intent in the social desirability artifact, which has been maintained (or overmaintained) until the present, followed ten years of silence after the earlier reports by Steinmetz (1932) and by Kelly, Miles, and Terman (1936) of the existence and importance of this response bias artifact in personality measurement.

B. The Stage of Coping

Once a field has admitted the existence of an artifact, as occurred in the case of response biases in the 1940's, researchers in the area devise methods of coping with it so that it does not make the results of experimentation ambiguous or less generalizable. Sophistication in achieving this aim tends to pass through several successive steps during the coping phase. Three of these, rejection, correction, and prevention, can be illustrated in the case of response sets.

1. Detection and rejection as a mode of coping. The most primitive form of coping with an artifact is to detect in which subjects it is operative beyond a certain (arbitrarily determined) amount, and then to reject the data from all the subjects above and accept at face value the data from subjects not above this threshold. Behind this strategy there lurks the double-fallacies that there is a magic sieve which can skim off the noise and leave the information behind; and that this can be done by simple dichotomization. Still, it must be admitted that research is the art of the possible and that we must often compromise by using less-than-perfect methodological tactics. If we will grant that some subjects are more susceptible to the artifactual process than others, then there is a certain logic of desperation in this tactic of rejecting the data from all subjects who exhibit it beyond a certain arbitrarily set amount, and ignoring it in the subjects who do not exceed this preset amount. In this way one hopes to avoid major contamination by the artifact, while admitting that some information is thrown away with the rejected subjects while some artifactualness remains in those subjects who did not exhibit the contamination beyond the preset amount.

There are various alternative procedures used in this detection and rejection mode of coping. MMPI research furnishes good examples of the use of three of these: catch scales, response counts, and discrepancy scores. Early in the development of this standardized personality inventory, a number of subscales were introduced in order to catch response sets. The most widely used of these are undoubtedly the F, the K, and L scales (though additional scales to catch malingering, social desirability, etc., were all developed by the nineteen-fifties). The notion is that anyone who answers too many questions in a way that is inconsistent, exceedingly rare, too good to be true, etc., should be rejected as manifesting too much response bias to furnish a usable protocol.

The response count procedure is closely akin to the use of catch scales. This simply involves counting up the number of responses in a certain category, for example, the number of "?" responses, to detect noncommit-

ment response sets or the number of "yes" responses to check for acquiescence response bias. Here again, when one detects subjects exceeding
a certain arbitrarily set level in the use of the response category, their
protocols are rejected.

A third tactic employing the detection and rejection mode of coping
is the use of discrepancy scores. In general, the several discrepancy
approaches involve partitioning the items that measure a given variable,
for example, the schizophrenic measure on the MMPI, into two subsets,
one of which is made up of obvious items and the other of more subtle
items. Subjects are then rejected as trying to conceal their symptoms
if the discrepancy between the subtle and the obvious subscores exceed
a certain preset amount. Alternatively, the use of simulated patterns,
based on the responses of subjects who have been asked "to fake good,"
is used to detect and reject subjects whose protocols reflect an unac-
ceptably high need to appear healthy.

2. *The correction mode of coping.*   The detection and rejection procedures which we just considered had an obvious arbitrariness to them
which made them less than ideal as methods for eliminating the effects
of the artifact. The use of an arbitrary cutoff point leaves in a considerable amount of the artifactual variance and eliminates a fair amount
of the variance due to the factor under investigation. Inevitably, this
primitive stage is succeeded by a more sophisticated approach to the
problem which we here call the "correction" procedure. The experimenter using this tactic attempts to retain all of the data collected and
adjust each person's scale score for the amount of artifactual variance
that contaminates his responses. A classic example of this adjustment
procedure is given by the K scale of the MMPI. The subscale is here
used, not as a device for detecting and rejecting certain protocols, but
as a suppression scale score which furnishes a correction factor for each
person's score, hopefully tailored to his amount of artifactual variance.

Other examples of correction procedures involve the use of control
groups or conditions. For example, we might determine a person's feelings about a subject matter area by giving him a reasoning, retention
or perception task involving material from that area and calculating
how much his score is affected by motivated distortion, after correcting
the raw score for his capacity at this type of task on neutral materials.
These correction procedures typically involve elaborate statistical
adjustments.

3. *Prevention modes of coping.*   The more we learn about the correction modes, the more hypersensitive they seem to be to the validity
of the scales. For example, it can be demonstrated that unless our predictor scale correlates at least .70 with the criterion, it is better to develop

an additional predictor scale than to develop a suppressor scale to correct the original one (Norman, 1961). In view of the tedium and the indifferent success of the correction modes, it is not uncommon to find that attempts to cope with an artifact develop from an adjustment stage to a prevention stage. These prevention tactics involve use of one or another procedure that avoids the artifact's occurring or at least its contaminating our obtained scores.

In the case of response sets, the prevention approach has taken several forms. One procedure is to use counterbalanced scales, such as keying the items so that "yes" and "no" responses equally often indicate possession of the trait. A second procedure is the use of ipsatizing procedures. These sometimes take the form of *a priori* ipsatizing as in the use of forced-choice items. In our opinion it is preferable that they take the form of *a posteriori* ipsatizing as, for example, pattern analysis. A third prevention approach involves utilizing experimental procedures which minimize the likelihood of occurrence of the artifact. For example, one might attempt to minimize the extent of response biases such as noncommitment, acquiescence, and social desirability, by anonymous administration or by explicit instructions to the respondent. A fourth method for preventing response biases such as social desirability is to use subtly worded items or other disguising procedures.

As this second or "coping" stage in the career of an artifact reaches its height, we find methodological *tours de force* with experimenters using all three tactics. They devise administration and scoring procedures that tend to eliminate the response artifact, adjust the scores for such detectable artifactual variance as remains, and eliminate a few of the subjects showing an excessive degree of artifact-proneness. By the time that this elaborate coping response is evoked, one is likely to find that the artifact has already reached the third stage of its career, its apotheosis into an independent variable in its own right.

C. The Exploitation Stage

It is rather heartwarming to observe that in the final stage in the career of an artifact, the variable comes into its own. The ugly duckling becoming the Prince Charming which gives rise to a new line of research. Not only in the case of the artifact considered in this chapter—suspiciousness of experimenter's intent—but in the artifacts considered in several other chapters of the present volume, we find variables which, long considered annoying artifacts to be eliminated, ultimately become independent variables of considerable theoretical interest in their own right. For example, in Chapter 4 we see Lana's depiction of how the use of "before" tests developed from the methodological device to reduce the impact of initial individual differences to a sensitization variable of intrinsic interest; or we find in Chapter 6 Rosenthal's account of how the influence of the experimenter's expectations on the obtained results developed from being a worrisome contamination to the status of a research program on nonverbal communication and social influence.

The case of response bias, which we are using to illustrate this account of the career of an artifact, shows the typical happy ending. Variables like social desirability (Crowne and Marlowe, 1964) or acquiescence (Couch and Keniston, 1960) are now considered interesting individual difference characteristics in their own right, rather than merely contaminants to be eliminated from our personality scales. We even find attempts such as that of Messick (1960) to map out personality space entirely in terms of what were once regarded only as biases to be eliminated before such an enterprise could get underway.

In the case of the suspiciousness artifact to which we devote the remainder of our discussion in this chapter, research interest has only recently entered the third phase. A necessary preliminary to the efficient investigation of an independent variable, or even of an artifact, is that we gain experimental control over it so that the experimenter is able to manipulate it. In the next section we will consider a dozen or so procedures by which the extent of the subject's suspiciousness of the experimenter's intent can be manipulated. Almost all of these procedures were developed for other reasons than the manipulation of the subject's suspiciousness, which indeed is the reason why such suspiciousness was initially considered an artifact. As our interest in the suspiciousness variable enters the third phase, the availability of so many procedures for manipulating is quite useful. Hence what is, during the second stage of an artifact's career, considered its deplorable pervasiveness, becomes, in the third phase, a considerable convenience in its study. While the suspiciousness problem is a pervasive one in research, to provide focus for our discussion, all our examples of procedures for manipulating this suspiciousness will be taken from the special area of attitude change and social influence.

III. ANTECEDENTS OF THE AWARENESS OF PERSUASIVE INTENT

In attitude change research, the experimenter traditionally pretends to the subject that his research deals with another topic. If he is studying the effect of peer pressure on conformity, he might employ visual stimuli and represent his study as an investigation of sensory acuity. If he is studying the impact of persuasive messages on beliefs, the experimenter might say he is studying reading comprehension ability and represent the persuasive message as the test material. It seems to be taken for granted that if one admitted the persuasive intent of the communication, the subjects' behavior could not be interpreted and generalized to the behavior of the naive subjects to whom our theories of persuasion are supposed to apply. Hence, any sign that the subject is suspicious of the persuasive intent of the experimenter is likely to elicit alarm. There is consequently cause for concern that in at least eleven lines of attitude change research there is reason to suspect that the experimental manipulation, in addition to (or instead of) varying whatever it is intended to vary, might also be affecting the subject's suspiciousness of persuasive intent. Any relationship which is found might be due, not to the originally theorized effect of the manipulation, but to its impact on the subject's suspiciousness. Some of these possibly artifactual manipulations involve how the source is represented to the subject; others have to do with the contents of the persuasive message; and still others concern the experimental procedures. We shall consider each of these classes of work in turn, discussing their possible artifactual components.

We are here considering suspiciousness of persuasive intent as a second stage artifact, that is, a contaminating factor in our experiments which we deplore and attempt to eliminate. As interest in this variable develops to the third stage of independent variable in its own right, our evaluative reaction to its pervasiveness undergoes a change. The fact that it might be affected by all eleven of these types of manipulations then becomes a convenience for studying it and a sign of its importance. Its pervasiveness is then seen as increasing its attractiveness for study, rather than as an endemic contaminant that drives us to despair.

A. Effect of Source Presentation on Subject's Suspiciousness

A number of variables having to do with how the source is represented to the subject might affect the subject's suspiciousness of persuasive intent. One such variable is the extent to which the introduction is such that the subject is led to perceive that the source has some profit to gain from his position's being accepted. A second involves whether or not the source is represented as realizing that the subject is an audience for his message. Whether the source's presentation is represented as having occurred in the context of a debate or as a noncontroversial presentation is a third such variable. A fourth situation of this type involves the primacy-recency issue, and concerns whether the source presents his message first and therefore to a naive audience, or comes only after they have been exposed to the opposition side and are sensitized to controversiality. We shall consider each of these lines of work as they bear on the question of suspiciousness of persuasive intent. It should be noted that this suspiciousness is an intervening variable. Hence to understand its operation we must answer two questions. To what extent do these antecedent conditions actually affect suspiciousness of persuasive intent? And given that suspiciousness is affected, to what extent is the ultimate dependent variable of opinion change (or whatever) further affected?

1. Perceived disinterestedness of the source. A number of studies have involved varying the introductory description of the source in such a way that he is represented to some of the subjects as having something to gain from their agreement with his point of view, while for other subjects he is made to appear more disinterested in the point about which he is arguing. It seems reasonable to assume that the former procedure will produce greater suspiciousness of the source's intent to persuade. For example, a given speech advocating more lenient treatment of juvenile delinquents is judged to be fairer and produces more opinion change when the speaker is identified as a judge or a member of the general public, than when he is identified as someone himself involved in juvenile offenses (Kelman and Hovland, 1953). There is, however, evidence to suggest that the differential persuasiveness of these sources is due to their status difference rather than their differential intent to persuade. Thus Hovland and Mandell (1952) used a speech favoring currency devaluation and attributed it, for half the subjects, to an executive in an importing firm who would stand to profit financially from such devaluation; while for the other half of the subjects, the speaker was represented as a knowledgeable but disinterested academic economist. The speech was judged considerably fairer when it came from this latter, disinterested source but it was equally effective in changing opinions regardless of the source. Put together, the results of the two experiments suggest that by proper portrayal of source disinterestedness one can manipulate suspiciousness of intent to persuade but this differential suspiciousness does not seem to eventuate in any attitude change differential unless the source's status is also varied. In practice, the source variables of disinterestedness, expertise, and status will often be contaminated and so the results of varying any one of them must be interpreted carefully lest the contamination of the characteristic produce misleading results. At any rate, these "disinterestedness" manipulations provide little support at present for the assumption that suspiciousness of the source's persuasive intent reduces the amount of opinion change he effects.

2. Source's purported perception of his audience. We might assume that the subject will be more suspicious of the persuasive intent of the source if he is made to perceive that the source knows he is listening than if he believes that he is overhearing the source without the latter's knowledge. Walster and Festinger (1962) did indeed find that women are more likely to be persuaded by a given conversation if they think they are inadvertently overhearing it rather than when they feel the speakers are aware that they are listening, though this difference was found only with highly involving topics. Subsequent work by Brock and Becker (1965) indicated that the greater effectiveness of overheard communication was even further limited, requiring that the sources argue both in the direction which the audience wants to hear and also on an involving issue. Mills and Jellison (1967) interpreted this limitation of the difference to arguments in desirable directions as indicating that a source is more likely to be judged sincere when he argues in a direction which he knows undesirable to his audience. They found in line with this interpretation that students are more influenced by a speech favoring raising truck license fees if they are told it has originally been given to truck drivers (for whom it would be arguing in an undesirable direction) than when told it has been delivered to railway men (who would have found its conclusion desirable). Walster, Aronson, and Abrahams (1966) also found that a source has more impact when he is perceived as arguing against his own best interest.

This set of experiments could be interpreted as indicating that a given message is persuasive to the extent that its source is not perceived as trying to persuade. However, a more precise interpretation would seem to be that the source is more persuasive when he is perceived to be urging an opinion in which he sincerely believes. Hence, if the crucial variable here is to be called suspiciousness, it seems that it is suspiciousness of insincerity rather than suspiciousness of persuasive intent that is crucial.

3. Perceived disputatiousness of the source. The orthodox suspiciousness theorizing would suggest that if the source is represented as having given the message in a controversial setting it will evoke more suspiciousness of persuasive intent and therefore less attitude change impact, than if purportedly given a noncontroversial setting. Sears, Freedman, and O'Connor (1964) report that subjects respond differently when they anticipate a confrontation of speakers in a debate situation from when they are led to expect simply two uncoordinated opposed speeches. In anticipation of the clear-cut debate, the more highly committed subjects tend to polarize and the less committed subjects to moderate their initial opinions. Somewhat relevant, though nonsupportive, to the suspiciousness hypothesis are the results of Irwin and Brockhaus's (1963) study comparing the effectiveness of two speeches favoring the telephone company, an educational type talk, versus one more explicitly asking for the subject's approval. The educational one was judged as more interesting, but one more directly appealing for approval produced more favorableness to A. T. & T. While this difference has been interpreted as indicating that the more explicit advocacy of the company produces more effect, it seems to us that the conditions were such that the differences could have been due to more personally relevant appeals used in the disputatious version, or to the distracting effect of the information in the educational version. Further evidence that overt disputatiousness and partisanship might actually enhance attitude change impact by clarifying the source's point is indicated by a study in which Sears (1965) presented material favoring the defense or prosecution in a juridical proceeding and found that this material had more persuasive impact when it was clearly identified as coming from a defense or a prosecution lawyer than when it purportedly came from a neutral lawyer, even though the latter was rated as more trustworthy.

4. Order of presentation as affecting suspiciousness. The primacy-recency variable becomes involved in the suspiciousness question since, as Hovland, Janis, and Kelley (1953) conjectured, the first side in debate would have the advantage of seeming less controversial than the second, particularly with a noncontroversial issue and in a situation not clearly defined in advance as a debate. An audience would be more inclined to interpret the first side's presentation as a rounded view of the topic, but when they received the second side it would be much clearer to them that they were now hearing a one-sided viewpoint on an issue where other views were quite possible. In this formulation, primacy effects in persuasion are attributed to the subject's greater suspiciousness of persuasive intent while listening to the second side. Hovland (1957) finds some suggestive support for this notion in his impression that primacy effects are more pronounced in situations where a single communicator presents both sides than when each side is presented by a different communicator.

This suspiciousness hypothesis predicts main order primacy effects and more manageably, a number of interactions between order of presentation and other variables in the communications situation as they affect opinion change. These interaction variables include the controversiality and the familiarity of the issue, the use of suspicion-arousing pretests, etc. We have reviewed this literature in some detail elsewhere (McGuire, 1966, 1968) as has Lana in his chapter in this book and elsewhere (Lana, 1964). In general, the experimental results seem to defy description by the suspiciousness hypothesis. As regards main effect, primacy effects may be somewhat the more common, but recency effects are far from rare. The interactions between the order variable and others, such as issue controversiality, go in the direction opposite to that required by the suspiciousness hypothesis in some studies while confirming it in others. Overall, the primacy-recency results offer little support for the orthodox formulation that suspiciousness of persuasive intent dampens persuasive impact.

B. Suspicion-arousing Factors Having to do with Message Style and Content

Above we considered ways in which source presentation might arouse suspiciousness of persuasive intent and thus purportedly affect the persuasive impact of the message. In this section we shall consider how the content and style of the message might give rise to such suspicions. One such possible variable is whether the conclusion is drawn explicitly within the message, as opposed to being left for the subject's own inferring. Another content variable which might give rise to suspicion is whether the opposition arguments are completely ignored or taken into consideration within the persuasive message. Still another possible message factor which might give rise to such suspicion is the extremity of the position which is urged. Finally, we shall consider such stylistic characteristics as the dynamism of the delivery as it might affect suspiciousness of persuasive intent. As has already been seen in the case of source factors, the results regarding message factors which we shall review here give surprisingly little support to the notion that arousal of suspiciousness tends to reduce persuasive impact.

1. Explicitness of conclusion drawing. The belief that a conclusion is more persuasive if the person derives it for himself (rather than having it announced to him by the source, however prestigeful) has been current at least since the beginning of the psychoanalytic movement and nondirective therapy in general. Freud indicated that he abandoned hypnotherapy with its stress on therapist suggestion, in favor of psychoanalysis with its stress on the patient's active participation in the discovery of the bases of his problems, in part because of the incredulity with which many of the therapist-drawn conclusions were received by the patient. Indeed, psychoanalytic theorists have developed an epistemology as well as a therapy based on the notion that its insights require personal experience and self-analysis, rather than simply external presentation, in order to obtain credence and comprehensibility. There are, of course, other theoretical reasons for advocating that the patient participate actively in the drawing of conclusions regarding the nature of his problem. Any theory of therapy which depended on such concepts as abreaction, emotional catharsis, rapport, transference, etc., would tend to encourage the patient's active participation in the therapeutic process even aside from credibility factors. However, the notion that the patient is more likely to believe the therapist's interpretation of his problem if he himself actively participates in the arrival at the conclusion, rather than having the conclusion presented to him passively, provides at least part of the motivation for urging nondirective therapy.

The empirical results give little support for this notion that a message is more persuasive if it leaves the conclusion to be drawn by the subject. The early work by Janis and King (1954; King and Janis, 1956) did seem to indicate that a subject was more persuaded by actively improvising a speech, rather than by passively reading or listening to a comparable speech. However, subsequent research has cast considerable doubt on the persuasive efficacy of active improvisation, as reviewed recently by McGuire (1968). The Hovland and Mandell (1952) study indicated that allowing the subject to draw the conclusion for himself, far from being more efficacious, actually produced far less opinion change than when he had the conclusion passively presented to him. A number of other studies have likewise failed to indicate that a message which allows the subject to draw the conclusion for himself, and thus would presumably arouse less suspiciousness of persuasive intent, was more persuasive than was a more explicit conclusion drawing (e.g. Cooper and Dinerman, 1951).

What we seem to have here is a situation in which any enhanced effectiveness due to the increased credibility that is produced by the subdued, implicit-conclusioned message through its lesser arousal of suspiciousness, is more than cancelled by its loss of effectiveness due to the subject's failure to get the point. We have been arguing frequently of late that most of the difficulty in persuading the audience (both in laboratory experiments and in naturalistic mass media situations) derives from the difficulty of getting the apathetic audience to attend to and comprehend what we are saying, rather than in overcoming its resistance to yielding to our arguments. The barrier is provided by intellectual indolence, rather than by motivated resistance. It seems quite possible that those who do in fact actually draw for themselves the conclusion of the implicit message may be more persuaded thereby; but it is more apparent that very few do in fact avail themselves of the opportunity actively to draw the conclusion or rehearse the arguments (McGuire, 1964). It is also probable that there is a gradual "filtering down" of the persuasive impact from the explicit premises to the implicit conclusion with the passage of time (Cohen, 1957; Stotland,

Katz, and Patchen, 1959; McGuire, 1960, 1968). A cognitive inertia may prevent the need for cognitive consistency from manifesting its full effect on remote issues immediately after the message. The studies cited suggest that with the passage of time these logical ramifications are increasingly discernible in the belief system, as the initial inertia is gradually overcome. Even over time, however, the impact of the implicit message only catches up with, rather than surpasses, that of the explicit message.

2. *Treatment of the opposition arguments.* We might expect that the treatment of the opposition's arguments would have some influence on the obviousness of our intent to persuade, and thus affect the persuasive efficacy of our message. A message which is completely one-sided, ignoring the existence of opposition arguments of which the subject may be quite aware, should seem more biased and blatantly attempting to persuade than would a message which took into account the opposition arguments by mentioning them and attempting to deal reasonably with them. Yet the World War II studies in the Army indoctrination program indicated that neither the one-sided nor the "two-sided" message had an overall greater persuasive impact, where the former presented the arguments for one's own side and ignored completely the opposition arguments while the latter presented one's own side but at least mentioned and sometimes refuted the opposition arguments (Hovland, Lumsdaine, and Sheffield, 1949). In fact, the latter was not even perceived as more fair a presentation, the impression of objectivity being, if anything, in the reverse direction. This peculiarity may have derived from the peculiar condition that the "two-sided" message ignored one of the most salient opposition arguments, while refuting less salient ones. It may be that to elicit the appearance of objectivity by the mention of the opposition arguments, one loses more credibility than he gains unless he is careful to mention all of the salient counterarguments. As far as the direct persuasive impact of refuting versus ignoring the opposition is concerned, the results seem to indicate that counterarguments which the subjects are likely to think of spontaneously are best refuted and those which would not arise spontaneously are best ignored if one wishes to achieve maximum persuasive impact. Hence, less intelligent subjects and those who are closer in their initial position to the conclusion being urged tend to be more influenced by messages which ignore the opposition arguments; while refuting the opposition argument tends to be more effective with subjects of higher intelligence and those further in the opposition as regards their initial opinions. Refuting, rather than ignoring, the opposition arguments does seem to be superior in developing resistance to subsequent counterattacks. The superior immunizing efficacy of mentioning and refuting (rather than ignoring) opposition

arguments has been demonstrated by Lumsdaine and Janis (1953), Mc-Guire (1964), Tannenbaum (1966), and others. It should be noted in the present connection, however, that the suspiciousness of persuasive intent mechanism does not seem to play any major part in the immunizing efficacy of considering the opposition arguments. The evidence currently seems to indicate that resistance conferral derives from the motivating threat which the mention of the opposition argument arouses. It is conceivable, though, that the subsequent persuasive attack is less effective also because the prior mention of its arguments makes the subject more suspicious of its persuasive intent.

3. *Extremity of message position.* Suspiciousness of persuasive intent would seem to occur with greater probability as the position espoused in the message became more and more extreme. In so far as this suspiciousness factor is concerned, increasing the discrepancy between position urged in the message and the subject's initial position should progressively reduce the persuasive impact. It would be naive, however, to disregard the likelihood that other processes mediate the relationship between message discrepancy and the amount of opinion change. For example, Anderson and Hovland (1957) postulate that a reverse relationship obtains such that amount of attained opinion change is an increasing function of amount of change urged. This position is plausible since when a discrepancy is quite small the amount of change produced would be relatively minor even if the message was completely effective, while with large discrepancies, even a partly effective message could produce a considerable absolute change. These considerations have led a number of theorists to posit an overall nonmonotonic relationship between amount of obtained change and amount of urged change (Osgood and Tannenbaum, 1955; Sherif and Hovland, 1961), with maximal opinion change occurring at intermediate discrepancies.

This theoretical formulation that, as discrepancy becomes quite large it produces sufficient suspiciousness of persuasive intent to overcome the effect postulated in the Anderson and Hovland proportional model, is quite plausible but empirical work has shown that it occurs only at very extreme ranges of discrepancy. Over a surprisingly wide range, the monotonic relationship holds such that the greater the discrepancy the greater the induced change. It is true though that some experimenters who persevered to the extent of producing extremely wide discrepancies have succeeded in demonstrating a reversal in effectiveness as the position urged became quite extreme (Hovland, Harvey and Sherif, 1957; Fisher and Lubin, 1958; Whittaker, 1964, etc.). As might be expected from these suspiciousness explanations, the turn-down is most likely to occur with low credible sources (Bergin, 1962; Aronson,

Turner, and Carlsmith, 1963) and with ambiguous issues (Insko, Murashima and Saiyadain, 1966), and where commitment to one's initial position is high (Freedman, 1964; Greenwald, 1964; Miller, 1965). The turn-down is probably least likely to occur where the subject experiences a great deal of evaluation apprehension (Zimbardo, 1960) which is discussed more fully in Rosenberg's chapter in this book.

As compared with most of the lines of research we have been considering, the evidence for the straightforward suspiciousness hypothesis (that as the position urged becomes more extreme, suspiciousness of persuasive intent increases and persuasiveness decreases) is fairly encouraging. Still, it should be noted that it takes rather surprising degrees of extremity before any such effect is manifested.

4. *Style of presentation.* It seems likely that suspiciousness of persuasive intent can be aroused, not only by the content of the message, but also by the style in which it is presented. A dynamic style of presentation seems more likely to arouse such suspicion than does a more subdued style; more conjecturally, an elegantly worded and presented speech might seem more suspicious than an improvised informal style.

As regards the intensity of presentation variable, Hovland, Lumsdaine, and Sheffield (1949) found no differences either in attitude change or in perceived intent to persuade between two forms of an argumentative presentation used with U.S. Army personnel in World War II, a dynamic documentary style presentation and a subdued narrator style. Greater attention to this intensity of style variable is given by researchers in the speech area than in psychology. Bowers (1964) has attempted to determine the components of judged intensity of language. Both he (Bowers, 1963) and Carmichael and Cronkhite (1965) have found some very slight tendency (not reaching conventional levels of significance) for the more intense speech to produce less attitude change. One study suggests that the use of metaphors may be a special case of language intensity in this regard. Bowers and Osborn (1966) find that highly metaphorical speech, which is judged to constitute a more intense style, produces more attitude change. Possibly metaphor constitutes a special type of intensity in this regard because, as Aristotle and Cicero suggested, it increases the perceived intelligence of the speaker. If so, the mechanism involved in the metaphorical affect might be perceived source competence rather than perceived intent to persuade.

It seems reasonable, if not quite compelling, to assume that an informal extemporaneous-seeming presentation would not arouse suspiciousness of intent to persuade quite as saliently as would a more polished and organized presentation. Hence, one would predict that the source employing this latter, more polished style will be perceived more suspiciously and will be less efficacious in producing opinion change. However, a number of counteracting processes would also seem to be operative in connection with this variable. The more polished style would also be likely to produce a greater comprehension of the message content and would tend to raise the perceived competence of the speaker (Sharp and McClung, 1966). Addington (1965) found no difference in opinion change impact as a function of how many mispronunciations had been introduced into the speech. Miller and Hewgill (1964) found that other inelegancies of speech, such as pauses, did produce a lower perceived competence of the source but did not affect his perceived trustworthiness. In this area of research, differences in the mediating processes (such as the perception of source characteristics and message comprehension) which were produced by the stylistic variables did not seem to eventuate in any impressive amount of opinion change differentials.

C. Experimental Setting as a Factor Arousing Suspiciousness

In this section we turn from intrinsic communication variables (such as source and message factors) to a consideration of how extrinsic factors deriving from the experimental setting might affect suspiciousness and, consequently, attitude change. We shall consider such variables as the clarity with which the situation is depicted as a psychological experiment, the use of an attitude pretest which might arouse suspiciousness that one's persuasibility is being investigated, and the introduction of explicit warnings that the experiment deals with persuasibility. It is in this area that we have the most clear-cut examples of how a procedure or variable which initially attracts attention purely for methodological reasons begins to gain theoretical interest in its own right.

1. Revealing the experimental content. It seems likely that the subject will become more suspicious of the persuasive intent of the messages presented in attitude change research if we reveal to him that he is taking part in an experiment. McGinnies and Donelson (1962) had their subjects read messages to other subjects which advocated a negative attitude towards ecclesiastical matters. It was revealed to half of these subjects that their own attitudes were under investigation. They found some slight evidence that this revelation did reduce the persuasive impact of the message for initially opposed subjects but only in some sub-groups. On the other hand, Silverman (1968) found greater compliance with the message in situations that were clearly designated to the subject as psychological experiments, in keeping with the "demand character" notion considered in more detail in Orne's chapter in this volume. This interpretation receives further support from the fact that this greater conformity in the revelation condition occurred to a greater extent with subjects who had to identify themselves and with female subjects.

Further evidence on this point is given by studies of the effect of "debriefing." Deliberate deception in experiments gives rise to the felt necessity on the part of most experimenters who use deception to employ also a "debriefing" or "catharsis" treatment at the end of their experiment. During this final procedure, the true purposes of the experiment are explained to the subject, and the deceptions employed are pointed out to him, along with the reasons why they were employed. We shall return to the ethical considerations in the final section of this chapter; here we shall focus on the theoretical aspects. There has long been some concern that participation in deception experiments and going through these debriefing procedures produces suspicious, experiment-wise persons who are unsuited to serve as subjects in subsequent experiments because this acquired sophistication will cause them to behave in a way unrepresentative of the more naive population to whom the results are to be generalized. It does seem plausible that the revelation during prior debriefing about the deception used in the earlier experiment will make the subject suspicious about what is going on in subsequent experiments and hence harder to persuade. However, the results to date provide little substantiation for this reasonable concern. Fillenbaum (1966) finds that the performance of the "faithful" subject who has been exposed to prior deceptions yields results little different from those of the more naive subjects. Indeed, though both previously deceived and naive subjects included a sizable number of suspicious persons, suspiciousness did not seem to affect their experimental performance in any important way. Brock and Becker (1966) find that prior participation in a deception experiment with debriefing produces surprisingly little effect on performance in a subsequent test experiment, even when it follows immediately afterwards. Only when the test experiment and the prior debriefing experiment were made ostentatiously similar was performance found to be affected in a substantial way. This work is quite reassuring (or disappointing, depending on one's initial attitude) regarding the possible contaminating effect of the subject's suspiciousness of the experimenter's true purpose in the experiment. Not only do manipulations which seem quite likely to arouse subjects' suspicion fail to produce any noticeable change in the obtained relationship, but even when one does internal analyses separately for suspicious and non-suspicious subjects, the two groups yield surprisingly similar relationships about the hypothesis in question.

In my own research on attitude change, where I usually represent the persuasive communications as part of a test of reading comprehension, we rather routinely introduce near the end of the experiment a questionnaire of some subtlety designed to detect any suspicions regarding the true nature of the experiment. Subjects can then be partitioned on the basis of their responses to high and low suspiciousness of persuasive intent. In many experiments we have analyzed the data separately for the sub-group of subjects who seem to indicate at least a moderately good grasp of the true nature of the experiment, which tends to include about 15% of the total sample. So far, we have never found significant differences between suspicious and non-suspicious subjects as regards the effects of any of the important variables. Hence, we have never had to face the anguishing decision as to whether or not we should eliminate from our experiments a particularly suspicious subject, which, as we indicated in a previous section of this paper, is an inadequate methodological solution for the problem and also tends to raise more problems of generalizability than it resolves. Judging from the uniformity of our own results, we suspect that many other researchers have had the same reassuring experience when they performed a similar internal analysis.

2. *Pretests as a suspicion arouser.* The subject's suspiciousness that we are investigating his persuasibility in a disguised attitude change experiment seems more likely to arise if we employ a pretest than if we use an after-only design, particularly when the pretest involves an undisguised opinionnaire administered just prior to the persuasive messages. We face here a classical question of experimental design involving the efficiency of "before-after" versus "after-only" designs (Hovland, Lumsdaine, and Sheffield, 1949) and the inclusion of control groups (Solomon, 1949). The current state of this question is reviewed in detail in Lana's chapter of this volume on "Pretest Sensitization." To oversimplify somewhat the conclusion to be drawn from the pretest experimentation as regards the current suspiciousness issue, it seems to us that there is evidence from this work of a rather slight depressing effect of using a pretest, as one would expect on the basis of the straightforward suspiciousness hypothesis that the pretest arouses suspicion and therefore reduces the amount of opinion change induced. There are, however, a few experiments in which a test actually enhances the main effect of the manipulation, as one might predict on the basis of a "demand character" interpretation (as discussed more fully in Orne's chapter of this volume). And quite frequently, the pretest is found to produce no main effect at all.

Even if we do tentatively accept the working hypothesis that pretests arouse suspicion, which then slightly decreases the main effect of our independent variables, the methodological anguish that such a main effect should provoke can be quite low. We have indicated elsewhere (McGuire, 1966, 1968) that a serious problem of interpretation would occur only if we find that the pretest interacts with our main independent variable. Studies in which there is an interaction between this design feature and the independent variable are exceedingly rare. Hence, it seems likely that we will be misled, at most, by failing to detect some relationships because of use of a pretest, rather than being misled into finding the "wrong" kind of relationship that would not be generalizable to a more naive, unpretested population.

3. *Effects of forewarning of persuasive intent.* The most straightforward procedure for investigating the effect of suspiciousness on the amount of opinion change produced would seem to be designing an experiment with a well-disguised attitude change induction, and then explicitly stating the persuasive intent of the communications to half the subjects while the remainder of the subjects are given a quite different plausible explanation of the materials to be read. We would then expect, in line with the orthodox suspiciousness notion, that the informed subjects made aware of the persuasive intent of the messages would come forearmed and premotivated to resist the predesignated belief-discrepant communications. Rather slight support is given to this common sense notion in several experiments. On the basis of internal analyses within some subsets of subjects, Allyn and Festinger (1961) report that teenage subjects were more influenced by an anti-driving speech when they were led to believe it was being presented to them to study how well they could judge the personality of the speaker rather than to assess their opinions. However, the results from the total subject sample did not confirm this orthodox prediction at the conventional level of significance. McGuire and Papageorgis (1962) found that a forewarning of an impending persuasive attack on certain cultural truisms accepted by the subjects indirectly strengthened their resistance to these attacks when they were given an opportunity to study defensive material in advance. However, the forewarning itself did not directly enhance the resistance to the persuasive message when no defensive material intervened. Hastorf and Piper (1951) also failed to detect any resistance to suggestion produced by explicitly reminding the subjects that they had answered a pretest and should give similar answers on the post-test after receiving some normative feedback. Wright (1966) likewise finds no significant across-conditions superiority of a direct over an indirect influence attempt, though he finds some suggestion that when coming from a liked partner, the indirect message is somewhat more effective.

Brehm's (1966) reactance theory leads to the notion that the subject will tend to respond to a source's attempt at persuasion with a "boomerang" response when the attempt is too blatant. Perhaps the study that comes nearest to indicating any strong resistance-conferral effect of warning is that by Freedman and Sears (1965), and even their results seem somewhat dependent upon the time parameters, and the same might be said of the Kiesler and Kiesler (1964) study.

This body of research on the effects of explicit warning of persuasive intent has been frustratingly elusive as regards its implications. There does seem to be a relationship begging to be found, and yet it seems to be hiding out in only certain cells of our experimental design. That it so seldom shows up as an across-condition significant effect, suggests that, while in some cells the warning reduces the persuasive impact, under other conditions the warning enhances impact. The source of such powerful interactions may be found in the demand character of the experiment and in the attractiveness of the source, as the research which we will discuss below seems to indicate.

In general, the results of these many lines of research considered in this section are not particularly alarming as regards the possible artifactual nature of results obtained under conditions that might make the subject suspicious of the experimenter's intent. It might be, of course, that some of the experimental variables did not actually manipulate in any dramatic way the degree of suspiciousness. However, we have seen a number of cases in which the independent variable did seem to manipulate suspiciousness to a considerable extent, and still no overall main effect in terms of differential opinion change eventuated. In a few cases, there was a diminution of communication effectiveness after suspicion was aroused; in the vast number of experiments, no overall significant difference occurred as a function of suspiciousness; and in a few experiments, arousing suspiciousness actually increased the amount of change. Furthermore, such effects of warning as have been found tend to be main effects which are annoying rather than misleading. Evidence for the more worrisome interaction effects are almost nonexistent. As regards the main effect, where there is evidence of enhanced resistance, it is still unclear what is the mechanism by which suspiciousness reduces attitude change. Does it operate by giving the person a chance to marshall his defenses; or by making it more difficult for him to yield to the outside influence without suffering more loss of self-esteem than he is willing to countenance; or by some other mechanism? Furthermore, we have been forced to suspect that under a number of conditions suspiciousness of intent actually enhances persuasive impact of the message. Again, the mechanism question arises. Such a result could be obtained in various ways, for example by clarifying the demand character of the experiment, or by the channeling of his ingratiation or cooperative motives, etc. In the following section we shall turn to a consideration of what are some of the theoretical formulations that seem called for.

IV. THEORETICAL HOUSINGS OF THE
SUSPICIOUSNESS VARIABLE

In the previous section we looked somewhat askance at the suspiciousness variable, regarding it somewhat as a poor relation whose advent spelled trouble. In this section we shall look at the suspiciousness variable in a more positive way, asking what interesting processes it might involve and what opportunities for theoretical elaboration and refinement it might offer. We shall first consider some matters of definition to clarify the question regarding just what the subject is supposed to be suspicious about in order for the hypothesized effect to occur, and what areas of behavior suspiciousness is supposed to affect. After dealing with the definitional problem, we shall turn to a consideration of the various mediating factors which seem possibly to be involved with the suspiciousness variable, and which could result in either enhancing or diminishing the persuasive impact of experimental messages. We shall then consider much more briefly some of the temporal considerations and individual difference factors that seem involved in the suspiciousness effects.

A. The Problem of Definition

That in the previous section we considered as many as eleven rather separate lines of research purportedly giving rise to suspiciousness of experimenter's intent should lead us to expect that this suspiciousness variable is not a completely homogeneous concept. Hence, some conceptual clarification seems called for here if the results of the suspiciousness variable are not to be unnecessarily confusing. First we shall consider the question of what the person is supposed to be suspicious about in order that the predicted effect occurs. We shall then point out some needed distinctions regarding the several different dependent variables that suspiciousness purportedly affects.

1. Suspiciousness of what?   In the introductory section of this chapter we pointed out that the suspiciousness variable is practically coterminous with the awareness variable, and hence arises pervasively over the whole range of psychological research. To ask about the effect of "suspiciousness of experimenter's intent" is to ask what is the effect of awareness of what is going on in the experiment. We pointed out that currently in psychology this awareness issue has arisen particularly is regard to the work on verbal conditioning and in the area of attitude change and that we would confine our discussion to the latter. Even within the narrow realm of attitude change experiments, several further distinctions are useful to avoid unnecessary confusions. For example, in the experiments involving forewarning of persuasive intent, Papageorgis' (1967) work indicates we should distinguish between situations in which the person is simply warned that the (unspecified) communication which he is about to hear is designed to persuade him as compared with situations in which he is also warned regarding the precise issue and the side which is to be developed by the message.

Still another distinction which seems necessary to facilitate generalization of laboratory results to the real world is the distinction between being aware that the communicator is trying to persuade oneself and being aware that one's persuasibility is being studied. For example, the former obtains in most naturalistic situations to which we would want to generalize our laboratory results on attitude change, in that the person is at least preconsciously aware that the material with which he is being presented was designed to influence his beliefs and behavior. For example, the average audience being exposed to an advertising presentation, a political speech, a disputation with a friend, etc., is more than a little suspicious that the material with which he is being presented is designed to influence him. Hence, when in the laboratory we strain our intellectual and moral resources in order to design some elaborate deception which will hide from the subject the persuasive nature of the material, we are paradoxically making it more difficult to generalize to the naturalistic situation, even though the researcher frequently justifies the deception as necessary for extrapolation to the real world. Are we then making a peculiar logical error in calling suspicious laboratory situations artifactual, rather than regarding situations in which the subject's suspicions are allayed by deceptions as the artifactual ones?

Behind our conventional thinking in this area, there seems to lie the assumption that it is particularly essential to prevent the subject's becoming aware that his persuasibility is being studied, since this awareness would seriously affect his behavior and it is not operative in the naturalistic situation. Hence, to make his attitude change behavior more comparable between laboratory and naturalistic setting, we try by deception to divert his suspiciousness into some other channel. This strategy represents a peculiar and devious compromise. In the natural setting, the person is suspicious of the persuasive intent of the communication that is being presented to him but he is not at all suspicious that his reactions to it are being studied. To achieve comparability in the laboratory, we design the situation so that the subject suspects neither that the material presented was designed to persuade him nor that his persuasive reaction is being studied. Without the deception, he would be suspicious both that the material was designed for persuasive purposes and that his own persuasibility is being measured. It can be seen that both the deception experiment and the undisguised experiment deviate from the naturalistic situation in one crucial manner. Perhaps some re-examination is necessary as to whether the typical two-fold deception experiment is any closer to the naturalistic situation to which we wish to generalize than is the somewhat more tolerable (intellectually and morally) fully undisguised experiment. Even more clearly, the situation seems to call for the study of each of these dimensions of awareness separately and in combination, rather than choosing one or the other for exclusive study or, worse, confounding the two.

So far we have seen that there are several levels of awareness: is the subject aware that the material was designed to persuade him, is he aware of the issue and side on which it will argue, and is he aware that his attitudinal or behavioral response to the message is being evaluated? There is an even higher level of awareness of persuasive intent, since we can ask further whether the subject is aware of the particular hypothesis being investigated. For example, the experiment might be designed to test the hypothesis that there is a nonmonotonic, inverted-U shaped relationship between fear arousal and the persuasive impact of the message. The subject could be aware of all the points so far discussed (for example, that the experiment involves persuasion, that it deals with the advocacy of automobile seatbelts, and that the extent to which he is influenced by the material presented to him will be measured) and yet he might be quite unaware of the particular hypothesis about fear appeals. Hence we could produce still higher degrees of awareness of the experimenter's intent by making differentially clear to him the independent variable in the experiment, its hypothesized relationships to the dependent variable, and the level of the independent variable to which he himself is being exposed. Research results have been unclear about the effect of suspiciousness in general, and also about the differential effects of suspiciousness of these different aspects of the experiment, two deficiencies that are probably interrelated.

2. *Clarification of the dependent variables.* Since suspiciousness of persuasive intent constitutes a mediating variable in most of the theorizing into which it enters, we must be concerned with "checking our manipulations" as well as with measuring our dependent variable. Thus,

if we are testing how communications with implicit versus explicit conclusions affect opinion change via the mediation of suspiciousness of
persuasive intent, we must not only measure the dependent variable
of opinion change but also we should have some direct measure of
the purported mediating suspiciousness. In some of the research discussed
in the previous section, where suspiciousness of persuasive intent was
indeed theorized to be operative, there was such a check on the purported mediator. However, in many of the studies cited, suspiciousness
of persuasive intent rose as a possible artifact suggested by later commentators and in these cases there usually was no such direct measure
of this purported process. Where the predicted relationship does hold
between the antecedent manipulation and the amount of opinion change,
but the direct measure of the suspiciousness does not show any difference
as a function of the manipulation, the doubt is raised regarding whether
this process does indeed enter into the relationship. However, we might
alternatively wonder if our measure of this mediator, usually a self-report
instrument devised without too much consideration (one tends to worry
less about constructing this incidental "check" than about measuring
the dependent variable) is indeed adequate to pick up fluctuations in the
suspiciousness. Where this suspicion mediator is found to vary in
the appropriate direction, the question remains whether this variation is
adequate in amount to account for the obtained difference on the dependent variable of opinion change. A covariance analysis could test whether
the relationship between the antecedent manipulation and opinion
change remains significant, even when we adjust for the variance due to
suspiciousness. Here again we would probably draw any conclusions
only tentatively, since it is unlikely that we would have any considerable
confidence in the quantitative precision of our measuring instrument
for suspiciousness.

At least three quite different dependent variables have been used
in testing how suspiciousness of persuasive intent affects the subject's
persuasibility. In some studies (McGuire and Millman, 1965; Papageorgis, 1967) the dependent variable has been the direct impact
on opinions of the warning of persuasive intent, even before the persuasive communications are actually presented. In most studies the dependent variable is the effect of the warning on the persuasive impact
of the message when it is actually presented (Allyn and Festinger, 1961;
Freedman and Sears, 1965). Still other studies (McGuire and Papageorgis, 1962) have investigated the extent to which the suspicion of impending persuasive attack enhances the immunizing efficacy of a prior
defense presented before the forewarned attack occurs. These three
dependent variables would not be expected to yield exactly the same

relationships, and so ignoring the distinction among them is likely to lead to some confusion. More important, analyzed in conjunction, they can help considerably in clarifying the processes involved, since the several mechanisms associated with suspiciousness affect these different dependent variables in somewhat different ways, allowing us to tease out and evaluate the several factors involved.

B. Possible Mechanisms for Suspiciousness Effects

Suspiciousness of persuasive intent could have an effect on the amount of opinion change produced via any of a number of mechanisms. The operation of some of these would enhance the persuasive impact while others should mitigate it. Still others seem able to operate in either direction. We shall first consider three mechanisms associated with suspiciousness that are likely to enhance the person's resistance to persuasion. One of these is that suspiciousness of impending attack should motivate the person to absorb and generate defensive arguments for his own position. A second such factor is that he would, having been warned of an impending attack, be more likely to rehearse actively his defense. A third consideration is that a forewarning would constitute something of a challenge to his self-esteem to demonstrate his ability to stand up for his own beliefs.

Fourth, fifth, sixth, and seventh considerations suggest that suspiciousness may well have the opposite effect of enhancing the persuasiveness of the message when it comes. Assuming that the subject was responding to some kind of perceived demand to go along with whatever the experiment entails, making him aware of its persuasive intent would tend to increase the amount of opinion change he would show. If he was trying to ingratiate himself for some reason with the source, any awareness of the persuasive intent should have a similar enhancing effect. Also, since the main obstacle to persuasive effect is often the subject's failure to perceive accurately the point of the message, being made aware of its purpose should enhance its impact on him. Finally the awareness of persuasive intent brings home to the person that there exists the source, often a person of some status, who holds a view opposite to his own and this would generate conformity pressures even prior to the communication.

Two other mechanisms which may be involved and whose operation is more ambiguous are set and distraction. Either one of these could be produced by suspiciousness of persuasive intent, and either one could operate by enhancing or diminishing the persuasive impact of the message. In the sections that follow we shall consider each of these nine possible associated mechanisms in turn.

1. Suspiciousness as motivating preparatory defense. McGuire and Papageorgis (1961, 1962) postulated that people tend to underestimate the vulnerability of their beliefs (at least those which they perceive as cultural truisms) and are little motivated spontaneously to develop a defense or even to absorb effectively the bolstering arguments that are presented to them. In a series of studies (McGuire, 1964) it has been demonstrated in accord with this motivational deficit notion that the prior presentation of various kinds of threats to the belief is efficacious in making beliefs more resistant to subsequent strong attacks. However, the type of threat most relevant to the present discussion, forewarning that the forthcoming communication will constitute a persuasive attack on the given belief, is efficacious in enhancing resistance only if presented in conjuncion with belief-bolstering material, indicating that both motivation and help in developing a defense must be supplied. The belief bolstering material plus the suspicion arousing threat was more efficacious than the belief bolstering material alone (McGuire and Papageorgis, 1962).

2. Defense, rehearsal consequent on forewarning. Another possible source of resistance to persuasion occasioned by a suspicion of impending attack is that such a forewarning increases the likelihood that the believer will rehearse his belief defenses and thus be better prepared to refute the suspected attack when it comes. That a rehearsal opportunity is important in the resistance-conferring effect of promoting suspiciousness of impending attack is suggested by the studies varying the temporal interval between the threat and the actual arrival of the attack. Freedman and Sears (1965) have shown that a forewarning of impending attack is more efficacious if it comes ten rather than two minutes prior to the attack. McGuire (1962, 1964) has demonstrated that prior mention of weakened attacking arguments or the requirement of active participation in defending one's beliefs has an accumulative effect over time, for a period of several days at least, in conferring resistance. There is some suggestion that the rehearsal factor which would produce a delayed reaction resistance effect in the case of active participation (McGuire, 1964) occurs also as regards the persistence of opinion change (Watts, 1967).

3. Suspiciousness as enhancing one's personal commitment to one opinion. It was argued by McGuire and Millman (1965) that making the believer suspicious that a forthcoming communication constitutes an attack on his belief tends to engage his self-esteem more explicitly in his response to the communication. The notion here is that people tend to behave so as to maintain their self-esteem and that in our society there are many situations in which yielding to a persuasive communication would be damaging to one's self-regard, for example when the issue is a matter of taste or when the source is disreputable, or when one is clearly committed publicly (or at least in one's own mind) to one's initial position. Since suspiciousness that the communication is designed to persuade puts one's self-esteem on the line, it might be predicted that the person who is made suspicious will be resistant to the attack when it comes. Actually, the McGuire-Millman (1965) study was designed to test a hypothesis about a different mode of coping with self-esteem needs in the face of an impending persuasive attack. They predicted (and found) that forewarned subjects actually lowered their beliefs on matters of taste on which they had not explicitly committed themselves, in advance of a suspected attack. In this case the forewarning actually weakened the belief, our interpretation being that the believer spontaneously moves his belief in the direction of the impending attack so that he can tell himself afterward that he felt the same way all the time, rather than was influenced by the persuasive message. It should be noted, however, that while under the conditions of the McGuire–Millman study (suspicion of an impending attack weakening the belief) the situation could have been designed so that self-esteem considerations would have produced greater resistance to the attack.

4. Suspiciousness and message perception. We have been stressing here and elsewhere that in most persuasion situations, in the laboratory and in the natural environment as well, we do not confront an audience attentively alert and resolute to resist our arguments, a notion that seems to be the point of departure for more than a little theorizing about persuasibility. Rather, the audience tends to be rather apathetic with little felt need to resist such arguments as get to them but not much inclined to pay attention to the message either. According to our analysis of the situation, the ineffectiveness of persuasive communication more often derives from poor message reception than from unyieldingness to such part of it as is received by the audience.

Insofar as this conceptualization has general validity, awareness of the persuasive intent of the message would actually augment its opinion change impact. Defining prior to message reception just what the communication is designed to achieve in the way of attitude change could be looked upon as an introductory summary that facilitates message reception (Hovland, Lumsdaine, Sheffield, 1949). Theorists are becoming increasingly aware that persuasive communication situations are looked upon by the audience more as a problem to be solved than as an intrusion on their autonomy to be resisted (Bauer, 1966).

5. Suspiciousness as clarifying demand character. Since Orne in

Chapter 5 of this volume discusses the role of "demand character" in determining the outcome of psychological experiments, we need discuss this matter only briefly here, as it bears on the suspiciousness of persuasive intent issue. The usual psychological subject is a fairly co-operative individual. Sometimes he comes to our laboratory voluntarily (giving rise to problems that are considered more fully by Rosenthal and Rosnow in Chapter 3 of this volume) but even when he comes simply to earn a fee or to fill a course requirement, he tends to enter the experiment in a fairly compliant mood. We would venture a guess that perhaps nine out of every ten subjects in psychological experiments would prefer to help rather than hinder the experimenter. The experimenter, being associated with the university faculty tends to be a fairly benevolent and prestigeful figure to the college students who constitute the majority of our subjects. The student population, perhaps even more than the general population at large, is made up of reasonable, well disposed individuals who value research and are disposed to "help" the experimenter according to their lights in the conduct of this experimentation.

Hence any indication in the experimental situation which arouses the subject's suspiciousness of the persuasive intent of the communication would tend to enhance the amount of opinion change produced. The cooperative subject is likely to assume that if the experimenter presents him with a persuasive message he intends that the audience be persuaded by it. The effect of such enhanced compliance on the part of suspicious subjects responding to what they perceive as the demand character of the experiment would be a main effect, such that opinion change would be enhanced across most experimental conditions. Occasionally, we might use experimental conditions such that the suspiciousness would lead the subject to cooperate in some way other than increased compliance. Such situations are more worrisome, since then the suspiciousness would tend to interact with our main independent variable rather than simply to add a constant to the persuasive impact across conditions. An earlier distinction which we made regarding what the subject is suspicious of is relevant here. If the subject is merely suspicious that the intent of the communication is to persuade him, the result should be simply to add a constant to the amount of change produced. If however he is suspicious that a certain hypothesis is being tested, the effect is more worrisome, since he might be complying with what he feels is demanded of him in a way that would make the result difficult to generalize to the population at large which is not responding to any such sophisticated demand character.

6. *Suspiciousness and source attractiveness and power.* Many theo-

rists have pointed out that in the laboratory and in the natural environment people behave in accord with an "exchange" theory such that, if one person conforms to the other's persuasive communication, the other incurs an obligation to do a reciprocal favor for the first person. An implication of this exchange theory in the present context is that increasing the subject's suspiciousness that the persuasive communication is designed to persuade him will, under specifiable conditions of source valence, increase rather than diminish its persuasive impact. Two relevant lines of current work come to mind in this connection. The ingratiation work by Jones (1964) would indicate that when an inferior is confronted by the demands of a more powerful source (a set of conditions frequently operative in the laboratory as well as in natural persuasion situations) he can by judicious compliance on selected issues build up "credit" with the power figure which could serve him well later. Hence, where the subject is inclined to use conformity as an ingratiation tactic, arousing his suspiciousness of persuasive intent will only increase his attitude change.

While history may have demonstrated that for controlling the minds and behavior of man, it is better to be feared than loved, love also wists the way to the hearts and minds of men. Mills and Aronson (1965) have deomonstrated that a communicator who makes clear his desire to influence the subject's opinion is more persuasive than one who does not so arouse suspiciousness of persuasive intent, but only when this source is attractive. Where the communicator was unattractive, suspiciousness had little effect on the amount of change produced. In a subsequent study Mills (1967) finds that suspiciousness of persuasive intent enhances the opinion change impact with an attractive source and diminishes it with an unattractive source. The psychodynamics involved here indicate again that it is naive to assume that suspiciousness will routinely result in diminished effectiveness.

7. *Suspiciousness and the communication of consensus.* McGuire and Millman (1965) explained the anticipatory belief-lowering effect of an announcement of an impending attack on one's belief as due to a self-esteem preserving tactic. Specifically, one moved one's belief in the direction of the suspected influence prior to the communication so that one would not have to admit to having been influenced by it. This anticipatory belief lowering following the announcement of an impending persuasive attack has been replicated in other laboratories. However, Papageorgis (1967) has demonstrated that this self-esteem explanation may be superfluous. He has demonstrated that the "anticipatory" belief lowering occurs after simply announcing that the other person holds the divergent belief, even when there is no implication that he is about

to present the subject with a persuasive communication. Whether there is an additional impact via the self-esteem mechanism when the subject is also told that this other person is about to present him with a persuasive communication remains to be tested. Some suggestion that the self-esteem explanation may also be responsible for the effect is given by the interaction with type of issue which was obtained in McGuire and Millman (1965).

8. *Suspicion as establishing* einstellung. Arousing the person's suspicion of the persuasive nature of an impending communication should induce in him a preparatory set that would influence the way in which he perceives the message when it comes and hence its impact on his belief system. Elsewhere (McGuire, 1966), we have considered the evidence for and against this *einstellung* hypothesis that has been contributed by research on the primacy-recency issue in attitude change research. The implication of this formulation in the present instance is rather ambiguous. Given that suspiciousness of persuasive intent establishes an expectation as to what the content of the message will be, it is hard to predict whether this preparatory set will result in assimilation or contrast in the person's perception of the content when it actually comes. The Sherif–Hovland (Sherif and Hovland, 1961; Sherif, Sherif and Nebergall, 1965) formulation would suggest that assimilation tends to occur (along with increased opinion change) when the message is close to the subject's own position; while when the message is more discrepant, the contrast effect (and lessened opinion change) results. The appropriate prediction is even more difficult to make in the present case since we are dealing, not with the subject's own position as the reference point, but with his suspicion-aroused opinion of where the message will be. There is some weak evidence (Ewing, 1942) that a subject who suspects that he is about to hear a quite discrepant communication would tend to perceive the given mesage as more discrepant from his own position than actually it was. On the other hand, there seems to be an overall tendency in human perception to distort information toward, rather than away from, one's own position as a secular trend which is imposed across the operation of other distortion tendencies.

9. *Suspiciousness and distraction.* Allyn and Festinger (1961) manipulated suspiciousness of persuasive intent by disguising the communication as a test of the subject's ability to judge the speaker's personality in one condition, while in the other condition its persuasive intent was revealed. Subsequently, Festinger and Maccoby (1964) argued that the crucial factor here was not the suspiciousness aroused by the revelation of persuasive intent but rather the distraction produced by the personality judgment task. (Since the original effect was quite slight by conven-

tional statistical standards, a wise commentator has aptly written of it with amused patience that, "seldom has so slight an effect been made to bear so heavy a burden of explanation.") In the later study, Festinger and Maccoby (1964) report that when their audience was distracted from the persuasive sound track by an irrelevant amusing film, it showed more attitude change than when they watched a film appropriate to the sound track. Freedman and Sears (1965), however, find little evidence for the distraction effect over and above the effect of warning. McGuire (1966) has conjectured that such effect of the film as may have obtained in the Festinger and Maccoby study was perhaps produced by the pleasant hedonic feeling resulting from its entertaining nature, rather than by the distraction's lowering of the audiences' defenses, as Festinger and Maccoby conjectured. That a given message is more persuasive if the audience hears it in a pleasant mood has been demonstrated by Janis, Kaye, and Kirschner (1965) and by Dabbs and Janis (1965).

McGuire (1966) has argued further that it would be surprising if distraction did indeed enhance the persuasive impact of a message. The prediction of such an enhancement rests on the notion that the audience tends to be waiting and ready to defend themselves against the coming onslaught unless they are distracted so that it reaches them with their defenses down. As we have mentioned at several points in this chapter and elsewhere, we entertain the contrary notion that audiences are typically apathetic, disinclined to attend to the message sufficiently for it to affect them, but disinclined also to resist such of its arguments as reach them. Since what is in shortest supply is motivation and ability to comprehend the message content sufficiently to be affected by it, it seems to us that the distraction would rather weaken than enhance its persuasive impact. Perhaps some resolution of this difference of opinion is found in the work by Rosenblatt (1966; Rosenblatt and Hicks, 1966) which suggests a nonmonotonic relationship between distraction and persuasive effectiveness, with maximum impact occurring with a moderate amount of distraction. He also finds some confounding between distraction and the subject's suspiciousness. We anticipate that the current movement in psychology towards the concept of the organism as an information processing machine will probably sustain this line of research for some time to come. Indeed, we would venture the prediction that this information-processing theme which is developing in psychology will cause more attention to be paid to the reception mediator, as opposed to the yielding mediator, in determining the relationship of such independent variables as suspiciousness to opinion change.

C. Temporal Considerations Regarding Suspiciousness

The relationship of suspiciousness of persuasive intent to amount of opinion change seems highly dependent on time parameters. We shall review the results of research on the effects of varying the interval between the warning and the attack and also the interval between the attack and the measurements of opinion change effect.

1. The warning-attack interval. A number of studies have indicated that the warning is effective only if it precedes the actual attack. Thus, McGuire (1964) shows that a forewarning of an impending attack increases the immunizing efficacy of a prior defense if it is presented before the defense, but that it has little or no efficacy if the warning comes after the defense. Kiesler and Kiesler (1964) report that an attribution designed to arouse suspiciousness of persuasive intent is effective in reducing the impact of the message if it is presented at the beginning but not if it comes at the end of that message. Greenberg and Miller (1966) find in three replications that if a source is identified as a person of low credibility prior to the presentation of the message, the message has less persuasiveness than when the source is not identified; but there is no retroactive effect such that the low credibility attribution diminishes the impact when it occurs only after the message has been presented.

There is further evidence that the warning must not only precede rather than follow the message, but that it should precede the message by some finite time period in order to exhibit its maximum effectiveness. Thus, McGuire (1964) has shown that the resistance conferral produced by having the believer participate in a worrisome active defense shows up more fully against an attack which comes a week later than an attack which follows the defense immediately. He has also shown (McGuire, 1962) that a "refutational" defense which mentions some threatening counterarguments develops its immunizing efficacy increasingly for several days subsequent to its initial presentation. Hence, resistance is greater to an attack that follows this threatening defense by two days than to one which follows it immediately. Freedman and Sears (1965) found that a warning was more efficacious in reducing opinion change if it preceded the attacking message by ten, rather than two, minutes.

2. Interval between attack and measurement of effect. Both the temporal effect just discussed and the one to which we turn here assume an inertia in the cognitive apparatus, such that effects produced by experimental intervention or by persuasive communications in the natural environment manifest themselves only gradually over time. Hence, an immediate post manipulation measure might indicate relationships rather different from those revealed by delayed measures of effect. Above, we conjectured that suspicion of persuasive intent does produce strain in the person but the effect of this strain becomes manifest only as the person has sufficient time and ingenuity to act on the induced motivation. The same gradualism considerations have something of a reciprocal effect when we consider the dampening effect of suspiciousness on opinion change when it is allowed time to be operative. We have in mind that the suspiciousness at the time of the message reception constitutes the "discounting cue" in the Hovland sleeper-effect formulation (Hovland and Weiss, 1951; Kelman and Hovland, 1953). If this analysis is correct, we would expect that suspiciousness of persuasive intent would reduce the immediate opinion change impact but as time passes, allowing the association between the discounting suspiciousness cue and the convincing message content to weaken, the full impact of the persuasive message would begin to mainfest itself. Related delayed action effects in persuasion have been more fully discussed elsewhere (McGuire, 1968).

D. Individual Differences in Suspiciousness

It often happens in the history of the psychological research on any issue that after it has been studied as an across-subject variable for a certain period, attention is turned to individual differences in its manifestation. First individual differences are investigated as they moderate the effect of the variable and then the investigation begins to focus on interaction between the variable and the personality or other individual difference characteristics. Since we started our discussion in this chapter with an overview of the career of an artifact through the stages of ignorance, coping, and exploitation, it is only appropriate that we conclude our discussion of the substantive issues raised by the suspiciousness of persuasive intent variable with a discussion of individual differences in the operation of this factor.

It seems rather evident that people will vary as regards the extent to which our manipulation arouses their suspiciousness. These individual differences involve both ability and motivational variables. For example, quite early in the research on overt versus covert conclusion drawing in the message (which we considered above) attention was turned to the possible role of audience intelligence in moderating any such effect (Cooper and Dinerman, 1951; Hovland and Mandell, 1952; Thistlethwaite, deHaan and Kamenetzky, 1955) with rather weak evidence for any such ability interaction. More positive evidence in line with the suspiciousness notion was given by the World War II findings (Hovland, Lumsdaine, and Sheffield, 1949) that a message which mentioned the opposition arguments was more effective than one which ignored them if we consider the more intelligent army personnel rather than the less intelligent.

Besides the question of individual differences in responsiveness to a deliberate manipulation of suspiciousness, there is the question of idiosyncrasies in the spontaneous arousal of suspiciousness in experimental situations, a topic that has begun to receive attention from Stricker and his colleagues (Stricker, 1967; Stricker, Messick and Jackson, 1966). They find considerable situational variance in the amount of suspiciousness aroused but an appreciable degree of across-situational generality of suspiciousness for individuals. In their studies males show more suspiciousness than females and they also report some tendency for males to show a positive relationship between need for approval and suspiciousness. This would seem to reverse the finding by Rosenthal, Kohn, Greenfield, and Carota (1966) that subjects scoring high on social approval show less awareness of the response-reinforcement contingencies in verbal conditioning situations. However, the resolution may reside in a distinction between suspiciousness and willingness to report suspiciousness. With the focusing of interest on individual difference characteristics as they interact with suspiciousness-arousing manipulations, the latter variable has achieved full status as a respectable psychological issue in its own right, rather than as an artifact to be overcome. The next step should be the demonstration that the effects produced by this erstwhile artifact should themselves be attributed to an artifact yet to be discovered.

V. DECEPTION AND SUSPICIOUSNESS: THE ETHICAL DIMENSION

Without experimenter deception, the issue of suspiciousness would never arise. Hence, the methodological and theoretical problems raised by the suspiciousness issue imply that there is already an ethical problem. Kelman (1965, 1967) particularly has called attention to the ethical problems involved specifically in experimenters' use of deception. The present time seems to be one of rising ethical anxieties among many involved in behavioral science research and, perhaps even more, in lay observers of this research. Some would feel that as unsavory as the use of deception is, there is even greater cause for moral concern in other practices in behavioral science research such as invasion of privacy, harmful manipulation, etc. Paradoxically, deception is sometimes employed to circumvent these more serious concerns, as when Milgram (1963, 1965) deceived the subject into thinking that he was hurting another person rather than allowing him actually to do so.

The argument that worse things are done in behavioral science than deceiving subjects offers cold comfort to the researcher suffering moral qualms. Hence, we shall confine ourselves in the present chapter to discussing deception apart from other ethical issues, since it is the one intrinsically involved in the question of suspiciousness of persuasive intent. It seems undeniable that there is some moral cost in the use of deception in experimental situations. Perhaps few can feel distaste for willful deception more than we scientists, for whom the discovery of truth constitutes the basic moral imperative which lies at the core of our vocation. Most of us feel at least a slight moral revulsion, aesthetic strain, and embarrassment when deceiving a subject in order to create an experimental situation, even when we feel that our deception is in the service of the discovery of a higher and more lasting truth. Even our more crass fellow researchers, who sometimes act as if they enjoy and relish every experimental deception they ever practiced, do show a sign of healthy moral unease in their sharing our compulsion to remove the deception by a suitable debriefing or catharsis explanation at the end of the experiment. The almost universal use of such a postexperimental revelation of the deceptions is particularly impressive evidence of the felt ethical concern, since such a revelation introduces another source of artifact about which researchers worry, namely, the communication of the true purpose of the experiment by earlier participants to later ones (Zemack and Rokeach, 1966). The data therefore become contaminated with the suspiciousness artifact which our deception was used to avoid. Some bases for feeling this moral unease over deceiving one's fellow man, even in an experimental situation in the service of truth, have been discussed more fully by Kelman (1965, 1967). We shall simply state here our opinion that the experimenter who denies he feels any moral qualms about the use of deception in experiments is deceiving himself.

While we emphatically insist that the use of deception does involve a moral cost, we equally emphatically insist that it might be necessary to pay this cost and continue to use deception rather than to cease our research. We must first admit here that our notion of ethics involves quantitative considerations, a stand which some of our more absolutistic fellow intellectuals might regard as vulgar. We deny that a practice which involves a moral cost must ipso facto be avoided. Admittedly with more resignation than enthusiasm, we are willing to employ a cost-utility analysis in the ethical evaluation of our behavioral alternatives, as our economist colleagues are applying it to the problems of adminstrative decision making and program budgeting. We are willing to admit that we are arguing that the signal for stopping a practice is not the discovery that it has a moral cost, but that it has a greater moral cost relative to its moral utility than have other available courses of behavior.

It seems to us that the alternatives to using deception in our experiments are to find some way of pursuing the line of research without the use of deception or of giving up the line of research. Let us consider each of these in turn. It has been argued that certain research cannot be done unless the subject is deceived as regards the experimental purpose. In an earlier section of this chapter we exhibited an undisguised description of such an experiment to indicate the patent absurdity of taking the subject fully into the experimenter's confidence and expecting to find generalizable results. Some might argue that we can disguise the intent of our experiment without the use of deception. For example, we might provide no information to the subject regarding the true purpose of the experiment. The use of active deception is not simply hiding the true intent but providing false information so as to mislead the subject into suspecting another purpose. This practice probably originated in the realization that many subjects will find it psychologically necessary to generate some explanation for what is involved in the experiment in which they are participating. If they are not deceived by a plausible alternative explanation provided by the experimenter, they will derive their own explanation (which may be correct or incorrect as regards the actual purpose, but in either case might equally contaminate the results in unknown ways and reduce their generalizibility). Even if the experimenter not only withholds explanation but explicitly requires the subjects not to try to figure out what the experiment is about, many, even with the best of good will, might be unable to restrain their conjecturing about its purpose. Hence, simply not revealing to the subject the purpose of the experiment will perhaps not be as effective in eliciting generalizable results as will actively deceiving him by presenting him with a false purpose. Furthermore, leaving the subject in ignorance or allowing him to deceive himself as to the purpose of the experiment might be felt by some moralists to itself present an ethical problem and to skirt perilously on the fringe of active deception.

A diametrically opposed method of carrying on the research without the use of deception is to be blatantly outspoken about the nature of the experiment, as regards various levels discussed in a previous section, and enlisting the subject as an active collaborator in the investigation. Such a procedure usually involves some form of role-playing, such that the subject is in effect told what the experiment is about and then asked to adopt the role of subject by behaving as he feels a subject who is actually in the situation would probably behave. The role-playing procedure has been used to good effect by Rosenberg and Abelson (1960) and Kelman (1967) and the role-playing is not necessarily linked to a full disclosure of the experimental purpose. An interesting variant is the "observer" procedure used in Bem's (1967) radical behavioral technique.

In a role-playing procedure, instead of deceiving the subject into thinking that he is lying to a fellow student in return for a one dollar or a 20 dollar "bribe" and then testing him to see how much he believes his own lie, the subject can be asked to imagine that he is telling the lie for one dollar or for 20 dollars and then asked to indicate how much he would probably believe the lie if he had actually told it under the several conditions. This role-playing procedure is particularly attractive in that it avoids, not only deception, but some of the other ethically troublesome procedures such as involving the subject in psychologically harmful acts. Despite this moral attractiveness of the role-playing procedure, and even though some of the recent studies in this line of work indicate that similar results are obtained from the role-players and "observers" as from actual subjects, we have little confidence that this role-playing procedure will constitute a final solution that will eliminate the deception problem from the psychologist's list of woes. We feel intuitively that over the wide range of psychological problems, this "public opinion polling" approach of having the quasi-subjects tell us how the experiment would probably come out had we done it will prove quite limited. Still, until its limits are explored it seems a feasible line of research to pursue. We expect that the success of Kelman and Bem in their lines of research will encourage other investigators to take up the exploration.

Should all attempts to circumvent the deception problem and still continue the research fail, there remains the alternative of ceasing the research altogether. While we feel that considerable effort is worthwhile in order to carry on our research without deception, we ourselves value our research sufficiently so that, rather than give it up altogether, we would think it worthwhile to pay the moral cost of deceiving subjects as to the nature of the experiment, provided we explain to the subject at the end of the experiment the various deceptions to which he was exposed and our reasons for utilizing them. In general, we listen with little enthusiasm to the argument that research that cannot be done without deception should be given up altogether. The alternative of giving up a line of research is one that too many of our colleagues have found too easy to take for us to entertain such behavior on the part of our still-working colleagues with any enthusiasm.

For psychologists who are actually engaged in research, we regard the solution of ceasing work the least attractive of the alternatives open to them. On the contrary, we feel that the most besetting moral evil in the psychological community today is indolence. Were we to list the moral problems of psychology, we would cite those who are doing experiments which involve deception far below those who are doing too few experiments or none at all as a source of ethical concern. The besetting offense that we find in the psychological profession, as in so many other sectors of the middle class, is not malfeasance but nonfeasance. It seems to us that the angel of death is likely to come upon more of our colleagues in idleness than in sin. We hope that methodological and moral concern over the problem of deception and subject's suspiciousness will not be used to add to the ranks of the self-unemployed.

REFERENCES

Addington, D. W. Effect of mispronunciations on general speaking effectiveness. *Speech Monographs,* 1965, **32**, 159–163.

Allyn, Jane and Festinger, L. The effectiveness of unanticipated persuasive communication. *Journal of Abnormal and Social Psychology,* 1961, **62**, 35–40.

Anderson, N. H. and Hovland, C. I. The representation of order effect in communication research. *In* C. I. Hovland (Ed.) *The order of presentation in persuasion.* New Haven: Yale University Press, 1957, 158–169.

Aronson, E., Turner, Judith, and Carlsmith, M. Communicator credibility and communicator discrepancy as determinants of opinion change. *Journal of Abnormal and Social Psychology,* 1963, **67**, 31–36.

Bauer, R. A. A revised model of source effect. Presidential address of the Division of Consumer Psychology, American Psychological Association Annual Meeting, Chicago, Ill., Sept. 1965.

Bem, D. Self-perception: an alternative interpretation of cognitive dissonance phenomena. *Psychological Review,* 1967, **74**, 183–200.

Bergin, A. E. The effect of dissonant persuasive communications on changes in a self-referring attitude. *Journal of Personality,* 1962, **30**, 423–436.

Bowers, J. W. Language intensity, social introversion and attitude change. *Speech Monographs,* 1963, **30**, 345–352.

Bowers, J. W. Some correlates of language intensity. *Quarterly Journal of Speech,* 1964, **50**, 415–420.

Bowers, J. M. and Osborn, M. M. Attitudinal effects of selected types of concluding metaphors in persuasive speech. *Speech Monographs,* 1966, **33**, 147–155.

Brehm, J. *Reactance theory.* New York: Academic Press, 1966.

Brock, T. C. and Becker, L. A. Ineffectiveness of "overheard" counterpropaganda. *Journal of Personality and Social Psychology,* 1965, **2**, 654–660.

Brock, T. C. and Becker, L. A. "Debriefing" and susceptibility to subsequent experimental manipulation. *Journal of Experimental Social Psychology*, 1966, **2**, 314–323.

Carmichael, C. W. and Cronkhite, G. L. Frustration and language intensity. *Speech Monographs*, 1965, **32**, 107–111.

Cohen, R. A. Need for cognition and order of communication as a determinant of opinion change. *In* Hovland, C. I. (Ed.) *Order of presentation in persuasion.* New Haven: Yale University Press, 1957, 79–97.

Cooper, Eunice and Dinerman, Helen. Analysis of the film "Don't Be A Sucker": a study of communication. *Public Opinion Quarterly*, 1951, **15**, 243–264.

Couch, A. and Keniston, K. Yeasayers and naysayers: Agreeing response set as a personality variable. *Journal of Abnormal and Social Psychology*, 1960, **60**, 151–174.

Cronbach, L. J. An experimental comparison of the multiple true-false and the multiple-choice tests. *Journal of Educational Psychology*, 1941, **32**, 533–543.

Cronbach, L. J. Studies of acquiescence as a factor in true-false tests. *Journal of Educational Psychology*, 1942, **33**, 401–415.

Cronbach, L. J. Response sets and test validity. *Educational and Psychological Measurement*, 1946, **6**, 475–494.

Cronbach, L. J. Further evidence on response sets and test design. *Educational and Psychological Measurement*, 1950, **10**, 3–31.

Crowne, D. P. and Marlowe, D. *The approval motive.* New York: Wiley, 1964.

Dabbs, J. M. and Janis, I. L. Why does eating while reading facilitate opinion change? An experimental inquiry. *Journal of Experimental Social Psychology*, 1965, **1**, 133–144.

Ellis, R. S. Validity of personality questionnaires. *Psychological Bulletin*, 1946, **43**, 385–440.

Ewing, R. A study of certain factors involved in changes of opinion. *Journal of Social Psychology*, 1942, **16**, 63–88.

Festinger, L. and Maccoby, N. On resistance to persuasive communications. *Journal of Abnormal and Social Psychology*, 1964, **68**, 359–366.

Fillenbaum, S. Prior deception and subsequent experimental performance: the "faithful" subject. *Journal of Personality and Social Psychology*, 1966, **4**, 537.

Fisher, S. and Lubin, A. Distance as a determinant of influence in a two-person serial interaction situation. *Journal of Abnormal and Social Psychology*, 1958, **56**, 230–238.

Freedman, J. L. Involvement, discrepancy, and opinion change. *Journal of Abnormal and Social Psychology*, 1964, **69**, 290–295.

Gough, H. G. Simulated patterns on the MMPI. *Journal of Abnormal and Social Psychology*, 1947, **42**, 215–225.

Greenberg, B. L. and Miller, G. R. The effect of low credibility source on message acceptance. *Speech Monographs*, 1966, **33**, 127–136.

Greenwald, H. The involvement-discrepancy controversy in persuasion research. Unpublished Ph. D. dissertation, Columbia University, New York, 1964.

Hastorf, A. H. and Piper, G. W. A note on the effect of explicit instructions on prestige suggestion. *Journal of Social Psychology*, 1951, **33**, 289–293.

Hovland, C. I. Summary and implications. *In* Hovland, C. I. (Ed.) *Order of presentation in persuasion.* New Haven: Yale University Press, 1957, 129–157.

Hovland, C. I., Harvey, O. J., and Sherif, M. Assimilation and contrast effects in communication and attitude change. *Journal of Abnormal and Social Psychology*, 1957, **55**, 242–252.

Hovland, C. I., Janis, I. L., and Kelley, H. H. *Communication and Persuasion.* New Haven: Yale University Press, 1953.

Hovland, C. I., Lumsdaine, A. A., and Sheffield, F. D. *Experiments on mass communications.* Princeton, N.J.: Princeton University Press, 1949.

Hovland, C. I. and Mandell, W. An experimental comparison of conclusion-drawing by the communicator and by the audience. *Journal of Abnormal and Social Psychology,* 1952, **41**, 581–588.

Hovland, C. I. and Weiss, W. The influence of source credibility on communication effectiveness. *Public Opinion Quarterly,* 1951, **15**, 635–650.

Insko, C. A., Murashima, F., and Saiyadain, M. Communicator discrepancy, stimulus ambiguity and difference. *Journal of Personality,* 1966, **34**, 262–274.

Irwin, J. V. and Brockhaus, H. H. The "teletalk project": a study of the effectiveness of two public relations speeches. *Speech Monographs,* 1963, **30**, 359–368.

Janis, I. L., Kaye, D., and Kirschner, P. Facilitating effects of "eating-while-reading" on responsiveness to persuasive communications. *Journal of Personality and Social Psychology,* 1965, **1**, 181–186.

Janis, I. L. and King, B. T. The influence of role-playing on opinion change. *Journal of Abnormal and Social Psychology,* 1954, **49**, 211–218.

Jones, E. E. *Ingratiation.* New York: Appleton-Century-Corfts, 1964.

Kelly, E. L., Miles, Catherine C., and Terman, L. Ability to influence one's score on a typical paper and pencil test of personality. *Character and Personality,* 1936, **4**, 206–215.

Kelman, H. C. Manipulation of human behavior—an ethical dilemma for the social scientist. *Journal of Social Issues,* 1965, **21**, 31–46.

Kelman, H. C. Human uses of human subjects, the problem of deception in social psychological experiments. *Psychological Bulletin,* 1967, **67**, 1–11.

Kelman, H. C. and Hovland, C. I. "Reinstatement" of the communicator in delayed measurement of opinion change. *Journal of Abnormal and Social Psychology,* 1953, **48**, 327–335.

Kiesler, C. A. and Kiesler, Sara B. Role of forewarning in persuasive communications. *Journal of Abnormal and Social Psychology,* 1964, **68**, 547–549.

King, B. T. and Janis, I. L. Comparison of the effectiveness *vs.* nonimprovised role-playing in producing opinion changes. *Human Relations,* 1956, **9**, 177–186.

Lana, R. E. Three interpretations of order effect in persuasive communications. *Psychological Bulletin,* 1964, **61**, 314–320.

Lentz, T. F. Acquiescence as a factor in the measurement of personality. *Psychological Bulletin,* 1938, **35**, 659.

Lorge, I. Gen-like: halo or reality? *Psychological Bulletin,* 1937, **34**, 545–546.

Lumsdaine, A. A. and Janis, I. L. Resistance to "counterpropaganda" produced by one-sided and two-sided "propaganda" presentation. *Public Opinion Quarterly,* 1953, **17**, 311–318.

McGinnies, E. and Donelson, Elaine. Knowledge of experimenter's intent and attitude change under induced compliance. Dept. of Psychology, University of Maryland, 1963, (Mimeo).

McGuire, W. J. A syllogistic analysis of cognitive relationships. *In* C. I. Hovland and M. J. Rosenberg (Eds.) *Attitude organization and change.* New Haven: Yale University Press, 1960, 65–111.

McGuire, W. J. Persistence of the resistance to persuasion induced by various types of prior belief defenses. *Journal of Abnormal and Social Psychology,* 1962, **64**, 241–248.

McGuire, W. J. Inducing resistance to persuasion: some contemporary approaches. *In* Berkowitz, L. (Ed.) *Advances in Experimental Social Psychology.* Vol. 1. New York: Academic Press, 1964, 191–229.

McGuire, W. J. Attitudes and opinions. *In* Farnsworth, P. *Annual Review of Psychology.* Vol. 17. Palo Alto, Calif. Anual Review Press, 1966, 475–514.

McGuire, W. J. Attitudes and attitude change. *In* Lindzey, G. and Aronson, E. (Eds.) *Handbook of social psychology.* Reading, Mass.: Addison-Wesley, 1968, 136–314.

McGuire, W. J. and Millman, Susan. Anticipatory belief lowering following forewarning of a persuasive attack. *Journal of Personality and Social Psychology,* 1965, **2**, 471–479.

McGuire, W. J. and Papageorgis, D. The relative efficacy of various types of prior belief-defense in producing immunity against persuasion. *Journal of Abnormal Social Psychology,* 1961, **62**, 327–337.

McGuire, W. J. and Papageorgis, D. Effectiveness of forewarning in developing resistance to persuasion. *Public Opinion Quarterly,* 1962, **26**, 24–34.

Meehl, P. E. and Hathaway, S. R. The K– factor. *Journal of Applied Psychology,* 1946, **30**, 525–564.

Messick, S. Dimensions of social desirability. *Journal of Consulting Psychology,* 1960, **24**, 279–287.

Milgram, S. Behavioral study of obedience. *Journal of Abnormal and Social Psychology,* 1963, **67**, 371–378.

Milgram, S. Liberating effects of group pressure. *Journal of Personality and Social Psychology,* 1965, **1**, 127–134.

Miller, N. Involvement and dogmatism as inhibitors of attitude change. *Journal of Experimental Social Psychology,* 1965, **1**, 121–132.

Miller, G. R. and Hewgill, M. A. The effects of variations in nonfluency in audience ratings of source credibility. *Quarterly Journal of Speech,* 1964, **50**, 36–44.

Mills, J. Opinion change as a function of the communicator's desire to influence and liking for the audience. Dept. of Psychology, University of Missouri, Columbia, Mo. 1967, (Mimeo).

Mills, J. and Aronson, E. Opinion change as a function of communicator's attractiveness and desire to influence. *Journal of Personality and Social Psychology,* 1965, **1**, 173–177.

Mills, J. and Jellison, J. M. Effect on opinion change of how desirable the communication is to the audience the communicator addressed. *Journal of Personality and Social Psychology,* 1967, **6**, 98–101.

Norman, W. I. Problem of response contamination in personality assessment. Personality Laboratory, Lackland A. F. Base, Texas, ASD–TN–61–43, May, 1961.

Osgood, C. E. and Tannenbaum, P. H. The principle of congruity in the prediction of attitude change. *Psychological Review,* 1955, **62**, 42–55.

Papageorgis, D. Anticipation of exposure to persuasive message and belief change. *Journal of Personality and Social Psychology,* 1967, **5**, 470–496.

Rosenberg, M. J. and Abelson, R. P. An analysis of cognitive balancing. *In* C. I. Hovland and M. J. Rosenberg (Eds.) *Attitude organization and change.* New Haven: Yale University Press, 1960, 112–163.

Rosenblatt, P. C. Persuasion as a function of varying amounts of distraction. *Psychonomic Science,* 1966, **5**, 85–86.

Rosenblatt, P. C. and Hicks, J. M. Pretesting, forewarning, and persuasion. Paper read at Midwestern Psychological Association Annual Convention, Chicago, Illinois, May, 1966.

Rosenthal, R., Kohn, P., Greenfield, Patricia M., and Carota, N. Data desirability, experimenter expectancy, and the results of psychological research. *Journal of Personality and Social Psychology*, 1966, 3, 20–27.

Sears, D. O. Opinion formation on controversial issues. Dept. of Psychology, University of California, L.A., June 18, 1965, (Mimeo).

Sears, D. O., Freedman, J. L., and O'Connor, E. F. The effects of anticipated debate and commitment on the polarization of audience opinion. *Public Opinion Quarterly*, 1964, 28, 615–627.

Sharp, H. and McClung, T. Effect of organization on the speaker's ethics. *Speech Monographs*, 1966, 33, 182–183.

Sherif, M. and Hovland, C. I. *Social Judgment*. New Haven: Yale University Press, 1961.

Sherif, Carolyn W., Sherif, M., and Nebergall, R. E. *Attitude and Attitude Change*. Philadelphiia: Saunders, 1965.

Silverman, I. Role-related behavior of subjects in laboratory studies in attitude change. *Journal of Personality and Social Psychology*, 1968, 8, 343–348.

Solomon, R. L. An extension of control group design. *Psychological Bulletin*, 1949, 46, 137–150.

Stotland, E., Katz, D., and Patchen, M. The reduction of prejudice through the arousal of self-thought. *Journal of Personality*, 1959, 27, 507–531.

Steinmetz, H. C. Measuring ability to fake occupational interest. *Journal of Applied Psychology*, 1932, 16, 123–130.

Stricker, L. J. The true deceiver, *Psychological Bulletin*, 1967, 68, 13–20.

Stricker, L. J., Messick, S. and Jackson, D. N. Suspicion of deception: implications for conformity research. *Journal of Personality and Social Psychology*, 1967, 5, 379–389.

Tannenbaum, P. H. The congruity principle revisited: studies in the reduction, induction and personalization of persuasion. *In* Berkowitz, L. (Ed.) *Advances in Experimental Social Psychology*. Vol. 4. New York: Academic Press, 1966.

Thistlethwaite, D. L., de Haan, H., and Kamenetzky, J. The effects of "directive" and "nondirective" communication procedures on attitudes. *Journal of Abnormal and Social Psychology*, 1955, 51, 107–113.

Walster, Elaine, Aronson, E., and Abrahams, D. On increasing the persuasiveness of a lower-prestige communicator. *Journal of Experimental Social Psychology*, 1966, 2, 325–342.

Walster, Elaine and Festinger, L. The effectiveness of "overheard" persuasive communications. *Journal of Abnormal and Social Psychology*, 1962, 65, 395–402.

Watts, W. A. Relative persistence of opinion change induced by action compared to passive participation. *Journal of Personality and Social Psychology*, 1967, 5, 4–15.

Whittaker, J. O. Parameters of social influence in the autokinetic situation. *Sociometry*, 1964, 27, 88–95.

Wright, P. H. Attitude change under direct and indirect interpersonal influence. *Human Relations*, 1966, 19, 199–211.

Zemack, R. and Rokeach, M. The pledge to secrecy: a method to assess violations. *American Psychologist*, 1966, 21, 612.

Zimbardo, P. G. Involvement and communication discrepancy as determinants of opinion conformity. *Journal of Abnormal and Social Psychology*, 1960, 60, 86–94.

Chapter 3

THE VOLUNTEER SUBJECT*

Robert Rosenthal

and

Ralph L. Rosnow

Harvard University

Temple University

There is a long-standing fear among behavioral researchers that those human subjects who find their way into the role of "research subject" may not be entirely representative of humans in general. McNemar (1946, 333) put it wisely when he said, "The existing science of human behavior is largely the science of the behavior of sophomores." Sophomores are convenient subjects for study, and some sophomores are more convenient than others. Sophomores enrolled in psychology courses, for example, get more than their fair share of opportunities to play the role of the research subjects whose responses provide the basis for formulations of the principles of human behavior. There are now indications that these "psychology sophomores" are not entirely representative of even sophomores in general (Hilgard, 1967), a possibility that makes McNemar's formulation sound unduly optimistic. The existing science of human behavior may be largely the science of those

* Preparation of this chapter, which is an extensive revision of an earlier paper published in *Human Relations* (Rosenthal, 1965), was facilitated by research grants GS-714, GS-1741 and GS-1733 from the Division of Social Sciences of the National Science Foundation. We want to thank our many colleagues who helped us by sending us unpublished papers, unpublished data, and additional information of various kinds. These colleagues include Timothy Brock, Carl Edwards, John R. P. French, Donald Hayes, E. R. Hilgard, Thomas Hood, Gene Levitt, Perry London, Roberta Marmer, A. H. Maslow, Ray Mulry, Lucille Nahemow, John Ora, Jr., David Poor, David Rosenhan, Dan Schubert, Duane Schultz, Peter Suedfeld, Jay Tooley, Allan Wicker, Abraham Wolf, and Marvin Zuckerman.

sophomores who both (a) enroll in psychology courses and (b) volunteer to participate in behavioral research. The extent to which a useful, comprehensive science of human behavior can be based upon the behavior of such self-selected and investigator-selected subjects is an empirical question of considerable importance. It is a question that has received increasing attention in the last few years (e.g., London and Rosenhan, 1964; Ora, 1965; Rosenhan, 1967; Rosenthal, 1965).*

The problem of the volunteer subject has been of interest to many behavioral researchers, and evidence of their interest will be found in the pages to follow. Mathematical statisticians, those good consultants to behavioral researchers, have also interested themselves in the volunteer problem (e.g., Cochran, Mosteller, and Tukey, 1953). Because of their concern we now know a good deal about the implications for statistical procedures and statistical inference of having drawn a sample of volunteers (Bell, 1961). The concern with the volunteer problem has had for its goal the reduction of the nonrepresentativeness of volunteer samples so that investigators may increase the generality of their research results (e.g., Hyman and Sheatsley, 1954; Locke, 1954). The magnitude of the problem is not trivial. The potential biasing effects of using volunteer samples has been clearly illustrated recently. At one large university, rates of volunteering varied from 10 per cent to 100 per cent. Even within the same course, different recruiters visiting different sections of the course obtained rates of volunteering varying from 50 per cent to 100 per cent (French, 1963). At another university, rates of volunteering varied from 26 per cent to 74 per cent when the same recruiter, extending the same invitation to participate in the same experiment, solicited female volunteers from different floors of the same dormitory (Marmer, 1967).

Some reduction of the volunteer sampling bias may be expected from the fairly common practice of requiring psychology undergraduates to spend a certain number of hours serving as research subjects. Such a requirement gets more students into the overall sampling urn, but without making their participation in any given experiment a randomly determined event. Students required to serve as research subjects often have a choice among alternative experiments. Given such a choice, will brighter (or duller) students sign up for an experiment on learning? Will better (or more poorly) adjusted students sign up for an experiment

---

* Most of the interest has been centered on the selection of human subjects, which is our concern here, but there are similar problems of the selection and representativenss of those animal subjects that find their way into behavioral research (e.g., Beach, 1950, 1960; Christie, 1951; Kavanau, 1964, 1967; Richter, 1959).

on personality? Will students who view their consciousness as broader (or narrower) sign up for an experiment that promises an encounter with "psychedelicacies"? We do not know the answers to these questions very well, nor do we know whether these possible self-selection biases would make any difference in the inferences we want to draw.

If the volunteer problem has been of interest and concern in the past there is good evidence to suggest that it will become of even greater interest and concern in the future. That evidence comes from the popular press and the technical literature and it says to us: In the future you, as an investigator, may have less control than ever before over the kinds of human subjects who find their way into your research. The ethical questions of humans' rights to privacy and to informed consent are more salient now than ever before (Bean, 1959; Clark, *et al.*, 1967; Miller, 1966; Orlans, 1967; Rokeach, 1966; Ruebhausen and Brim, 1966; Wicker, 1968; Wolfensberger, 1967; Wolfle, 1960). One possible outcome of this unprecedented soul-searching is that the social science of the future may, due to internally and perhaps externally imposed constraints, be based upon propositions whose tenability will come only from volunteer subjects who have been made fully aware of the responses of interest to the investigator. However, even without this extreme consequence of the ethical crisis of the social sciences, we still will want to learn as much as we can about the external circumstances and the internal characteristics that bring any given individual into our sample of subjects or keep him out.

Our purpose in this chapter will be to say something of what is known about the act of volunteering and about the characteristics that may differentiate volunteers for behavioral research from nonvolunteers. Subsequently we shall consider the implications of what we think we know for the representativeness of the findings of behavioral research and for the possible effects on the results of experiments employing human subjects.

I. THE ACT OF VOLUNTEERING

Finding one's way into the role of the subject is not a random event. The act of volunteering seems to be as reliable a response as the response to many widely used tests of personality. Martin and Marcuse (1958), employing several experimental situations, found reliabilities of the act of volunteering to range from .67 for a study of attitudes toward sex to .97 for a study of hypnosis. Such stability in the likelihood of volunteering raises a question as to whether there may not also be stability in the attributes associated with the likelihood of volunteering. Several relatively stable attributes that show promise of serving as predictors of volunteering will be discussed later in this chapter. In this section we shall discuss the less stable, more situational determinants of volunteering.

It is no contradiction that situational determinants can be powerful even in view of the reliability of the act of volunteering. In studies of the reliability of volunteering, situational determinants tend to be relatively constant from the initial request for volunteers to the subsequent request, so that the role of situational determinants is artificially diminished. Unavailable at present, but worth collecting, are data on volunteering as a simultaneous function of personal characteristics of volunteers and situational determinants of volunteering.

A. Incentives to Volunteer

Not surprising is the fact than when potential subjects fear that they may be physically hurt, they are less likely to volunteer. Subjects threatened with electric shocks were less willing to volunteer for subsequent studies involving the use of shock (Staples and Walters, 1961). More surprising perhaps is the finding that an increase in the expectation of pain does not lead concomitantly to much of an increase in avoidance of participation. In one study, for example, 78 per cent of college students volunteered to receive very weak electric shocks, while almost that many (67 per cent) volunteered to receive moderate to strong shocks (Howe, 1960). The difference between these volunteering rates is of only borderline significance ($p < .15$). The motives to serve science and to trust in the wisdom and authority of the experimenter (Orne, this volume), and to be favorably evaluated by the experimenter (Rosenberg, this volume), must be strong indeed to have so many people willing to tolerate so much for so little tangible reward. But perhaps in Howe's (1960) experiment the situation was complicated by the fact that there was more tangible reward than usual. The rates of volunteering which he obtained may have been elevated by a $3.00 incentive that he offered in return for participation. The subjects who volunteered for electric shocks may also have been those for whom the $3.00 had more reward value. Volunteers showed a significantly greater ($p = .001$) "need for cash" than did nonvolunteers. Need for cash, however, was determined after the volunteering occurred, so it is possible that the incentive was viewed as more important by those who had already committed themselves to participate by way of justifying their commitment to themselves.

As the intensity of the plea for participation increases, more subjects are likely to agree to become involved. For an experiment in hypnosis, adding either a lecture on hypnosis or a $35 incentive increased the rate of volunteering among student nurses about equally (Levitt, Lubin, and Zuckerman, 1962). On intuitive grounds one can speculate that students should perceive $35 as more rewarding than a lecture, so possibly the student nurses in this study were responding to the heightened intensity of the request for volunteers. Perhaps the more important it seems to the subject that his participation is to the recruiter, the higher will be the rate of volunteering. That certainly seems to be the case among respondents to a mail questionnaire who, though they did not increase their participation when personalized salutations and true signatures were employed by the investigator, markedly increased their participation when special delivery letters were employed (Clausen and Ford, 1947). Consistent results were also obtained by Rosenbaum (1956), who found that a great many more subjects were willing to volunteer for an experiment on which a doctoral dissertation hung in the balance than if a more desultory request was made.

Volunteering also seems to become more likely as it becomes the proper, normative, expected thing to do. If other subjects are seen by the potential volunteer as likely to consent, the probability increases that the potential volunteer also will consent to participate (Bennett, 1955; Rosenbaum, 1956; Rosenbaum and Blake, 1955). And, once the volunteer has consented, it may be that he would find it undesirable to be denied an opportunity actually to perform the expected task. Volunteers who were given the choice of performing a task (a) that was more pleasant but less expected or (b) one that was less pleasant but more expected, tended relatively more often to choose the latter (Aronson, Carlsmith, and Darley, 1963).

Sometimes it is difficult to distinguish among appeals of increased intensity, appeals that give the impression that volunteering is very much the expected thing to do, and appeals that offer almost irresistable inducements to participation. More subjects volunteer when they get to miss a lecture as a reward, and a great many more volunteer when they get to miss an examination (Blake, Berkowitz, Bellamy and Mouton, 1956). Being excused from an exam seems to be such a strong inducement that subjects tend to volunteer without exception even when it means that they must raise their hands in class to do it. Under conditions of less extreme incentive to volunteer, subjects seem to prefer less public modes of registering their willingness (Blake et al., 1956) unless almost everyone else in the group also seems willing to volunteer publicly (Schachter and Hall, 1952). Bennett (1955), however, found no relationship between volunteering and the public versus private modes of registering willingness to participate.

Schachter and Hall (1952) have performed a double service for students of the volunteer problem. They not only have examined the conditions under which volunteering is more likely to occur but also the likelihoods that subjects recuited under various conditions will actually show up for the experiment to which they have verbally committed their time. The results are not heartening. Apparently it is just those conditions that increase the likelihood of a subject's volunteering that increase the likelihood that he will not show up when he is supposed to. This should serve to emphasize that it is not enough even to learn who will volunteer and under what circumstances. We will also need to learn which people show up, as our science is based largely on the behavior of those who do. At least in the case of personality tests there is evidence from Levitt, Lubin, and Brady (1962) to suggest that "no-shows" (i.e., volunteers who never show up) are psychologically more like nonvolunteers than they are like "shows" (i.e., volunteers who show up as scheduled).

B. Subject Involvement

The proposition that subjects are more likely to volunteer the more they are involved or the more they have to gain finds greater support in the literature on survey research than in the literature on laboratory experiments. Levitt, Lubin, and Zuckerman (1959), for example, found no differences between volunteers and nonvolunteers for hypnosis research in their attitudes towards hypnosis. Attitudes of their student nurse subjects were measured by responses to the "hynotist" picture of the TAT. In contrast, Zamansky and Brightbill (1965) found that male undergraduate volunteers for hypnosis research rated the concept of "hypnosis" more favorably ($p = .05$) than did nonvolunteers. These same authors also found that subjects who were more susceptible to hypnotic phenomena tended to rate the concept of "hypnosis" more favorably (Brightbill and Zamansky, 1963; Zamansky and Brightbill, 1965). Subjects for hypnosis research, therefore, may select themselves not only for their view of hypnosis but also for their susceptibility to hypnosis. Direct evidence for this possibility has been presented by Boucher and Hilgard (1962).

It seems reasonable to speculate that college students majoring in psychology would be more interested in behavioral research than would nonpsychology majors. In an experiment on sensory deprivation twice as many psychology majors volunteered to participate than did non-psychology majors (Jackson and Pollard, 1966). Among the motives given for volunteering, curiosity was listed by 50 per cent of the subjects, financial incentive ($1.25 per hour) by 21 per cent, and being of help to "Science" by a surprisingly low 7 per cent. The main reason for not volunteering, given by 80 per cent of those who did not volunteer, was that they had no time available.

In support of these results are those of Rosen (1951). His request to undergraduates to take the Minnesota Multiphasic Personality Inventory (MMPI) met with greater success among students who were more favorably disposed toward psychology and behavioral research. Similarly, Ora (1966) found his volunteers for psychological research to be significantly more interested in psychology than were his nonvolunteers. The greater interest and involvement of volunteers as compared to nonvolunteers also is suggested in the work of Green (1963). He found that when subjects were interrupted during their task performance, nonvolunteers recalled fewer of the interrupted tasks than did volunteers. Presumably the volunteers' greater involvement facilitated their recall of the tasks that they were not able to complete.

It was noted earlier that it is in the literature on survey research that one finds greatest support for the involvement-volunteering relationship. Thus, the more interested a person is in radio and television programming, the more likely he is to answer questions about his listening and viewing habits (Belson, 1960; Suchman and McCandless, 1940). When questions were asked in the 1930's about the use of radio in the classroom, it was discovered that nonresponders tended to be those who did not own radios (Stanton, 1939).

College graduates are about twice as likely to respond to a mail questionnaire as college drop-outs (Pace, 1939). Shuttleworth (1940) found that those college graduates who responded more promptly to questionnaires had an appreciably lower rate of unemployment (0.5%) than did those who were slower to respond (5.8%). Similar results have been reported by Franzen and Lazarsfeld (1945), Gaudet and Wilson (1940), and Edgerton, Britt, and Norman (1947), all of whom conclude that responders tend to be those individuals who are more interested in the topic under study. A particularly striking example of this relationship can be found in the research of Larson and Catton (1959). Questionnaires were sent to 700 members of a national organization. Of those responding to the first request only 17 per cent of the respondents were thoroughly inactive and presumably disinterested members. Of those members who did not reply even after three requests, about 70 per cent were inactive, presumably disinterested individuals.

Sometimes it is not so much a matter of the general interest of the individual as it is his specific attitude toward the issue under discussion that determines whether he will be self-selected into the sample. Matthysse (1966) wrote follow-up letters to research subjects who had been exposed to pro-religious communications. He found that the subjects who replied to his letter were more often those individuals who regarded religious questions as more important, i.e., attached greater importance to the question of the existence of God. Siegman (1956), recruiting subjects for Kinsey-type interviews found that 92 per cent of those undergraduates who volunteered to be interviewed advocated sexual freedom for women, while only 42 per cent of those who did not volunteer advocated such freedom. Data obtained by Benson (1946) suggested that when public policy is under discussion, respondents may be over-represented by individuals with strong feelings against the proposed policy—a kind of political protest vote.

Survey literature is rich with suggestions for dealing with these potential sources of bias. One practical suggestion offered by Clausen and Ford (1947) follows directly from the work on involvement. It was discovered that a higher rate of response was obtained if, instead of one topic, a number of topics were surveyed in the same study. People seem to be more willing to answer a lot of questions if at least some of the questions are on a topic of interest to them. Another, more standard technique is the follow-up letter or follow-up phone call that reminds the subject to respond to the questionnaire. However, if the follow-up is perceived by the subject as a bothersome intrusion, then, if he responds at all, his response may reflect an intended or unintended distortion of his actual beliefs. The person who has been reminded several times to fill out the same questionnaire may not approach the task in the same way he would if he were asked only once.

There is some evidence from Norman (1948) and from Wallin (1949) which suggests that an increase in the potential respondent's degree of acquaintanceship with the investigator may lead to an increase in the likelihood of the individual's cooperation. Similarly, an increase in the perceived status of the investigator may lead to an increase in the rate of cooperation (Norman, 1948; Poor, 1967). Increases in the acquaintanceship with the investigator and in the investigator's status may, therefore, reduce the volunteer bias, but there is a possibility that one bias may simply be traded for other biases. Investigators who are better acquainted with their subjects or who have a higher perceived status may obtain data from their subjects that is different from data obtained by investigators less well-known to their subjects or lower in perceived status (Rosenthal, 1966). We may need to learn with which biases we are more willing to live, which biases we are better able to assess, and which biases we are better able to control.

C. The Phenomenology of Volunteering

Responding to a mail questionnaire is undoubtedly different from volunteering for participation in a psychological experiment (Bell, 1961), yet there are likely to be phenomenological similarities. In both cases the prospective data-provider, be he "subject" or "respondent," is asked to make a commitment of his time for the serious purposes of the data-collector. In both cases, too, there may be an explicit request for candor, and almost certainly there will be an implicit request for it. Perhaps most important, in both cases the data-provider recognizes that his participation will make the data-collector wiser about him without making him wiser about the data-collector. Within the context of the psychological experiment, Riecken (1962) has referred to this as the "one-sided distribution of information." On the basis of this uneven distribution of information the subject-respondent is likely to feel an uneven distribution of legitimate negative evaluation.*

From the subject's point of view, the data-collector may judge him to be maladjusted, stupid, unemployed, lower class or in possession of any one of a number of other negative characteristics. The possibility of being judged as any of these might be sufficient to prevent someone from volunteering for either surveys or experiments. The data-provider, on the other hand, can, and often does, negatively evaluate the data-collector. He can call the investigator, his task, or his questionnaire inept, stupid, banal, and irrelevant but hardly with any great feeling of confidence as regards the accuracy of this evaluation. After all, the data-collector has a plan for the use of his data, and the subject or respondent usually does not know this plan, though he is aware that a plan exists. He is, therefore, in a poor position to evaluate the data-collector's performance, and he is likely to know it.

Riecken (1962) has postulated that one of the major aims of the subject is to "put his best foot forward." It follows that in both survey and experimental research, the volunteer subject may be the individual who guesses that he will be evaluated favorably. Edgerton, Britt, and Norman (1947) found that contest winners were more likely than losers to respond helpfully to a follow-up questionnaire relevant to their achievement. These same authors convincingly demonstrated the consistency of their results by summarizing work which showed, for example, that (a) parents of delinquent boys are more likely to respond to questionnaires about the boys if the parents have nice things to say, (b) college professors who hold minor and temporary appointments

---

* For a full discussion of the importance to the subject of feeling evaluated by the behavioral scientist who studies him, see Chapter 7 by Milton Rosenberg.

are not so likely to reply usefully to job-related questionnaires, and (c) patrons of commercial airlines are more prompt to return questionnaires about airline usage than non-patrons. Locke (1954) found married respondents more willing than divorced respondents to be interviewed about their marital adjustment. None of these findings deny the interest hypothesis advanced by Edgerton, Britt, and Norman (1947). Indeed, additional evidence, some of which was cited earlier, can simply be interpreted as demonstrating that greater interest in a topic leads to a higher response rate. Nevertheless, on the basis of Riecken's (1962) analysis and in light of the empirical evidence cited here, we may postulate that another major variable which contributes to the decision to volunteer is the subjective probability of subsequently being favorably evaluated by the investigator. It is trite but necessary to add that this formulation requires more direct empirical test.

II. CHARACTERISTICS OF VOLUNTEERS

We have discussed some of the less stable characteristics of the volunteer subject that are specifically related to the source and nature of the invitation to volunteer. Now let us consider more stable characteristics of volunteers. We shall proceed attribute by attribute. In principle it would have been desirable to perform such an analysis separately for each type of subject population investigated and for each type of experiment or survey conducted. However, the variations of outcomes of different studies of volunteer characteristics within even a given type of subject sample and within even a given area of research were sufficiently great that it seemed a prematurely precise strategy, given the state of the data.

A. Sex

The variations in the results of studies of volunteer characteristics are well-illustrated when the characteristic investigated is the subject's sex. Belson (1960), Poor (1967), and Wallin (1949) reported no sex differences associated with the rate of volunteering in their survey research projects, nor did Hilgard, Weitzenhoffer, Landes, and Moore (1961), Hood (1963), London (1961), and Schachter and Hall (1952) in their experimental laboratory projects. However, for every study that does not find a relationship between volunteering and sex of the respondent, there is one or more that supports such a relationship. Table I summarizes the results of 12 such studies. Eight of the studies discovered that females volunteered more than males, while the remaining

TABLE I

VOLUNTEERING RATES AMONG MALES AND FEMALES

Author	Task	Percentage volunteering Females	Males	Two-tail p of difference
MORE VOLUNTEERING BY FEMALES				
Himelstein (1956)	Psychology experiment	65%	43%	.02
Newman (1956)	Perception experiment	60%	39%	.02
Newman (1956)	Personality experiment	59%	45%	.25
Ora (1966)	Psychology experiments	66%	54%	.001
Rosnow & Rosenthal (1966)	Perception experiment	48%	13%	.02
Rosnow & Rosenthal (1967)[a]	Psychology experiment	27%	10%	.005
Schubert (1964)	Psychology experiment	60%	44%	.001
Wicker (1968)	Questionnaire	56%	38%	.10
MORE VOLUNTEERING BY MALES				
Howe (1960)	Electric shock	67%	81%	.05
Schultz (1967b)	Sensory deprivation	56%	76%	.06
Siegman (1956)	Sex interview	12%	42%	.02
Wilson & Patterson (1965)	Psychology experiment	60%	86%	.005

[a] Unpublished data. The experiment on which these data are based is described later in the present chapter.

four studies found the inverse relationship. Those studies for which women are more likely to volunteer seem to have in common that they requested subjects to participate in rather standard or unspecified psychological experiments.* The exceptions are the studies by Schachter and Hall (1952) and Wilson and Patterson (1965). The former study asked for volunteers for a study of interpersonal attraction and found no sex differences in rates of volunteering. The latter study employed a vague request for volunteers to which the New Zealand male undergraduates responded more favorably than females.

The experiments by Hilgard et al. (1961) and London (1961) had requested volunteers for hypnosis and neither had found any sex differences in volunteering. London did find, however, that among those subjects who were "very eager" to participate, males predominated. For the hypnosis situation London felt that women were less likely to show such eagerness because of a greater fear of loss of control. Perhaps being very eager to be hypnotized, willing to be electrically shocked

* Related to these results are those obtained by Rosen (1951) and Schubert (1964), both of whom found males more likely to volunteer for standard experiments if they showed greater femininity of interests.

(Howe, 1960), and sensation-deprived (Schultz, 1967b), and ready to answer questions about sex behavior (Siegman, 1956) reflect the somewhat greater degree of unconventionality that is more often associated in our culture with males than with females.*

If one were to attempt to summarize the findings thus far, one might hypothesize that in behavioral research (a) there is a likelihood of females volunteering more than males if the task for which participation is solicited is perceived as relatively standard and (b) there is a likelihood of males volunteering more than females if the task is perceived as unusual. Some modest support for this hypothesis comes from the research of Martin and Marcuse (1958). Volunteers were solicited for four experiments—one in learning, a second on personality, a third involving hypnosis, and a fourth for research on attitudes toward sex. Female volunteers were overrepresented in the first three experiments, those which could be described as relatively more standard. Male volunteers were overrepresented in the sex study.

The joint effects on volunteering rates of subjects' sex and nature of the task for which participation is solicited are probably complicated by other variables. For example, Coffin (1941) long ago cautioned about the complicating effects of the investigator's sex, and one may wonder along with Coffin and Martin and Marcuse (1958), about the differential effects on volunteer rates among male and female subjects of being confronted with a male versus a female Kinsey interviewer as well as the differential effects on eagerness to be hyponotized of being confronted with a male versus a female hypnotist.

Our interest in volunteers is based on the fact that only they can provide us with the data the nonvolunteers have refused us. But not all volunteers, it usually turns out, provide us with the data we need. To varying degrees in different studies there will be those volunteers who fail to keep their experimental appointment. These "no-shows" have been referred to as "pseudovolunteers" by Levitt, Lubin, and Brady (1962) who showed that on a variety of personality measures pseudovolunteers are less like volunteers, and more like the nonvolunteers who never agreed to come in the first place. Other studies also have examined the characteristics of experimental subjects who fail to keep their appointments. Frey and Becker (1958) found no sex differences between subjects who notified the investigator that they would be absent versus those who did not notify him. Though these results argue against a sex difference in pseudovolunteering, it should be noted that the entire

---

* Consistent with this interpretation is the finding by Wolf and Weiss (1965) that, relative to female subjects, male subjects showed the greater preference for isolation experiments.

experimental sample was composed of extreme scorers on a test of intro-version-extraversion. Furthermore, no comparison was given of either group of no-shows with the parent population from which the samples were drawn. Leipold and James (1962) also compared the characteristics of shows and no-shows among a random sample of introductory psychology students who had been requested to serve in an experiment in order to satisfy a course requirement. Again, no sex differences were found. Interestingly enough, however, about half of Frey and Becker's no-shows notified the experimenter that they would be absent while only one of Leipold and James' 39 no-shows so demeaned himself. Finally, there is the more recent study by Wicker (1968), in which it was possible to compare the rates of pseudovolunteering by male and female subjects for a questionnaire study. These results also yielded no sex differences. Hence, three studies out of three suggest that failing to provide the investigator with data promised him probably is no more apt to be the province of males than of females.

B. Birth Order

Stemming from the work of Schachter (1959) there has been increasing interest shown in birth order as a useful independent variable in behavioral research (Altus, 1966; Warren, 1966). A number of studies have attempted to shed light on the question of whether firstborns or only-children are more likely than laterborns to volunteer for behavioral research. But for all the studies conducted there are only a few that suggest a difference in volunteering rates among first- and laterborns to be significant at even the .10 level. It is suggestive, however, that all of these studies found the firstborn to be overrepresented among the volunteering subjects. Capra and Dittes (1962) found that among their Yale University undergraduates 36 per cent of the firstborns, but only 18 per cent of the laterborns, volunteered for an experiment requiring cooperation in a small group. Varela (1964) found that among Uruguayan male and female high school students 70 per cent of the firstborns, but only 44 per cent of the laterborns, volunteered for a small group experiment similar to that of Capra and Dittes. Altus (1966) reported that firstborn males were overrepresented relative to laterborn males when subjects were asked to volunteer for testing. Altus obtained similar results when the subjects were female undergraduates, but in that case the difference in volunteering rates was not statistically significant. Suedfeld (1964) recruited subjects for an experiment in sensory deprivation and found that 79 per cent of those who appeared were firstborns while only 21 per cent were laterborns. Unfortunately we do not know for this sample of undergraduates what proportion of those who did not appear were firstborn. It seems rather unlikely, however, that the base rate for primogeniture would approach 79 per cent; Altus (1966) was unable to find a higher proportion than 66 per cent for any college population.

No differences in rates of volunteering by first- versus laterborns were found in studies by Lubin, Brady, and Levitt (1962b), Myers, Murphy, Smith, and Goffard (1966), Poor (1967), Rosnow and Rosenthal (1967, unpublished data), Schultz (1967a), Ward (1964), Wilson and Patterson (1965), and Zuckerman, Schultz, and Hopkins (1967). In these studies, in which no p reached even the .10 level, not even the trends were suggestive.

In several of the studies relating birth order to volunteering the focus was less on whether a subject would volunteer and more on the type of experiment for which he would volunteer. That was the case in a study by Brock and Becker (1965) who found no differences between first- and laterborns in their choices of individual or group experiments. Studies reported by Weiss, Wolf, and Wiltsey (1963) and by Wolf and Weiss (1965) suggest that preference for participation in group experiments by firstborn versus laterborn subjects may depend on the recruitment method. When a ranking of preferences was employed, firstborns more often volunteered for a group experiment. However, when a simple yes-no technique was employed, firstborns volunteered relatively less for group than for individual or isolation experiments.

Thus, most of the studies show no significant relationship between birth order and volunteering. However, in those few studies where there is a significant relationship, the results suggest that it is the firstborn or only child who is more likely to volunteer. This finding might be expected on the basis of work by Schachter (1959) suggesting the greater sociability of the firstborn. It is this variable of sociability to which we now turn our attention.

C. Sociability

Using as subjects male and female college freshmen, Schubert (1964) observed that volunteers ($n = 562$) for a "psychological experiment" scored higher in sociability on the Social Participation Scale of the MMPI than nonvolunteers ($n = 443$). A similar positive relationship between sociability and volunteering has been reported by others. Martin and Marcuse (1957, 1958) found that female volunteers for an experiment in hypnosis measured higher in sociability on the Bernreuter than female nonvolunteers.* London, Cooper, and Johnson (1962) found a tendency

---

* Though one would expect the factor of introversion-extraversion to be related to sociability, and so might predict greater extraversion among volunteers, Martin and

for their more serious volunteers to be somewhat more sociable than those less serious about serving science—sociability here being defined by the California Psychological Inventory, the 16 Pf, and MMPI.

Thus, it would appear that volunteers, especially females, are higher in sociability than nonvolunteers. The relationship in fact, however, is not always this simple. Although Lubin, Brady, and Levitt (1962a) observed that student nurses who volunteered for hypnosis scored higher than nonvolunteers on a Rorschach content dependency measure (a finding which is consistent with those above), it also was observed that volunteers were significantly less friendly as defined by the Guilford-Zimmerman. On intuitive grounds the latter finding would appear to be inconsistent with the simple, positive sociability-volunteering relationship. One might expect a positive relationship between sociability and dependency, but certainly not a negative relationship between sociability and friendliness. Despite the confusion, it is clear that in research on hypnosis, differences between volunteers and nonvolunteers are likely to bias results. Boucher and Hilgard (1962) have shown that subjects who are less willing to participate in hypnosis research are clearly more resistant to showing hypnotic behavior when they are conscripted for research.

A factor that is likely to complicate the sociability-volunteering relationship is the nature of the task for which volunteering is requested. When Poor (1967) solicited volunteers for a psychological experiment, he found the volunteers to be higher in sociability than nonvolunteers on the California Psychological Inventory. However, when the task was completing a questionnaire, the return rate for the less sociable subjects tended to be higher than that for the more sociable ($p < .25$).

If sociability can be defined on the basis of membership in a social fraternity, then other findings become relevant as well. Reuss (1943) obtained higher return rates among fraternity and sorority members (high sociability?) than among independents (lower sociability?). How-

---

Marcuse found no differences in introversion-extraversion between volunteers and nonvolunteers while Ora (1966) found volunteers, and especially males, to be significantly more introverted than nonvolunteers. Another surprising finding, by Frey and Becker (1958), is relevant in so far as volunteering may be related to styles of pseudovolunteering. Among those subjects who failed to keep an appointment for an experiment in which they had previously agreed to participate, those who notified the experimenter that they would be unable to attend had lower sociability scores on the Guilford than those who failed to appear without notifying the experimenter. It is difficult to explain this somewhat paradoxical finding that presumably less thoughtful pseudovolunteers are, in fact, more sociable than their more thoughtful counterparts.

ever, Abeles, Iscoe, and Brown (1954–55)—a study in which male undergraduates were invited by the president of their university to complete questionnaires concerning the Draft, the Korean War, college life, and vocational aspirations—found that fraternity men were significantly underrepresented in the initial sample of volunteers. (It can be noted that in a subsequent session, which followed a letter "ordering" the students to participate and then a personal phone call, fraternity men were significantly overrepresented in the volunteer sample.) If sociability can be defined in terms of verbosity, then another study becomes relevant. In an experiment on social participation, Hayes, Meltzer, and Lundberg (1968) noted that undergraduate volunteers were more talkative than (nonvolunteer) conscripts. The relationship is confounded by the fact that verbosity, since it was observed after the volunteer request, must be considered a dependent variable. Perhaps conscription leads to moodiness and quietude. One cannot be absolutely certain that conscripts would also have been less talkative than the volunteer subjects before the experiment began.

In some cases, characteristics of volunteers do tend to remain stable over appeals for participation in different types of tasks. Earlier we described the research of Lubin, Brady, and Levitt (1962a) in which student nurses were asked to volunteer for hypnosis research. In a related study of student nurses, Lubin, Levitt, and Zuckerman (1962) asked for the return of a mailed questionnaire. Volunteers in the hypnosis study were more dependent than nonvolunteers as defined by a Rorschach measure. In the questionnaire study, those who chose to respond were also more dependent than nonresponders despite the fact that a different definition of dependency was employed, *viz.* one based on the Edwards Personal Preference Schedule. Though there are a good many equivocal results to complicate the interpretation, and possibly even some contradictory findings, at least in the bulk of studies showing any clear difference in sociability between volunteers and nonvolunteers it would appear that volunteers tend to be the more sociable.

D. Approval Need

Crowne and Marlowe (1964) have elaborated the empirical and theoretical network of consequence that surrounds the construct of approval motivation. Using the Marlowe–Crowne (M–C) Scale as their measure of need for social approval, they have shown that high scorers are more influenceable than low scorers in a variety of situations. Directly relevant to the present chapter is their finding that high scorers report a greater willingness to serve as volunteers in an excruciatingly dull task. Consistent with this finding is the observation of Leipold and James (1962) that determined male nonvolunteers tend to score lower than volunteers on the M–C.

Similarly, Poor (1967) found that volunteers for an experiment, the nature of which was unspecified, scored higher in need for approval than nonvolunteers on the M–C Scale. Poor also found that subjects higher in need for approval were more likely than low need approvals to return mailed questionnaires to the investigator. For both of Poor's samples the significance levels were unimpressive in magnitude, but impressive in consistency; both ps were .13 (two-tail).

C. Edwards (1968) invited student nurses to volunteer for an hypnotic dream experiment and uncovered no difference between volunteers and nonvolunteers in their average M–C scores. This failure to replicate the findings above may have been due to differences in the type of subject solicited or perhaps to the nature of the experiment. Another, rather intriguing, finding was that the need for approval of the volunteers' best friends was significantly higher than the need for approval of the nonvolunteers' best friends. Also, the students' instructors rated the volunteers as significantly more defensive than the nonvolunteers. Thus, at least in their choice of best friends and in their instructors' judgment, though not necessarily in their own test scores, volunteers appear to show a greater need for social approval.

Edwards went further in his analysis of subjects' scores on the M–C Scale. He found a nonlinear trend suggesting that the volunteers were more extreme scorers on the M–C than nonvolunteers, i.e., either too high (which one might have expected) or too low (which one would not have expected). Edwards' sample size of 37 was too small to establish the statistical significance of the suggested curvilinear relationship. However, Poor (1967), in both of the samples mentioned earlier, also found a curvilinear relationship, and in both samples the direction of curvilinearity was the same as in Edwards' study. The more extreme M–C scorers were those more likely to volunteer. In Poor's smaller sample of 40 subjects who were asked to volunteer for an experiment, the curvilinear relationship was not significant. However, in Poor's larger sample of 169 subjects who were asked to return a questionnaire, the curvilinear relationship was significant at $p < .0002$ (two-tail).

So far our definition of need for approval has depended heavily on the Marlowe-Crowne Scale, but there is evidence that other paper-and-pencil measures might well give similar results. McDavid's (1965) research, using his own Social Reinforcement Scale, also indicated a positive relationship between approval-seeking and volunteering. Using still another measure of need for approval (Christie-Budnitzky), Hood and Back (1967) found their volunteers to score higher than their nonvolunteers. Their finding was significant for male subjects while for female subjects there was a tendency for the relationship between need for approval and volunteering to depend on the task for which volunteering was solicited.

With the one exception, then, of the study by C. Edwards, who recruited a different type of subject for a different type of experiment, it would appear that volunteers tend to be higher than nonvolunteers in their need for approval. However, the nonmonotonic function suggested in the results of Edwards and Poor implies that the positive relationship may only hold for the upper range of the continuum. It may be subjects showing medium need for approval who will volunteer the least.

E. Conformity

It seems almost tautological to consider the relationship between volunteering and conformity, for the act of volunteering is itself an act of conformity to some authority's request or invitation to participate. We shall see, however, that conforming to a request to volunteer is by no means identical with, and often not even related to, other definitions of conformity.

Crowne and Marlowe (1964) have summarized the evidence that subjects higher in need for approval are more likely than low need approvals to conform to the demands of an experimental task including an Asch-type situation. Since need for approval is positively related both to volunteering (at least in the upper range) and to conformity, one would expect a positive relationship between conformity in the Asch-type situation and volunteering. Foster's (1961) findings, though not statistically significant, imply such a relationship among male subjects, but just the opposite among females.

If volunteers can be characterized as conforming, then one also would expect them to be low in autonomy. Using the Edwards Personal Preference Schedule, such a finding was obtained by C. Edwards (1968) for his sample of student nurses, the volunteers also being judged by their instructors as more conforming than the nonvolunteers. However, diametrically opposite results were obtained by Newman (1956) also using the Edwards Schedule, but where the task was a perception experiment. Both male and female volunteers were significantly more autonomous than male and female nonvolunteers. When an experiment in personality was the task, no difference in autonomy was revealed between volunteers and nonvolunteers.

Lubin, Levitt, and Zuckerman (1962) also employed the Edwards Personal Preference Schedule, finding that student nurses who completed and returned a questionnaire scored lower in autonomy (and in dominance) than nonrespondents. The differences were, however, not judged statistically significant. To further confound the array of results it must be added that Martin and Marcuse (1957) found male volunteers for an hypnosis experiment to be significantly more dominant than nonvolunteers on the Bernreuter. And, Frye and Adams (1959), also using Edwards' scales, obtained no appreciable differences on any of the measures between male and female volunteers versus nonvolunteers.

There appears to be little consistency in the relationships obtained between conformity and voluntarism. In the majority of studies no significant relationship was obtained between these variables. However, considering only those studies in which a significant relationship was obtained, one might tentatively conclude that the direction of relationship is unpredictable for female subjects but that male volunteers are probably more autonomous than male nonvolunteers.

F. Authoritarianism

A number of investigators have compared volunteers with nonvolunteers on the basis of several related measures of authoritarianism. Rosen (1951), using the F Scale definition of authoritarianism, found that volunteers for personality research scored lower than nonvolunteers. Newman (1956) also found volunteers to be less authoritarian on the F Scale, but his finding was complicated by the interacting effects of type of experiment and sex of subject. Thus, only when recruitment was for an experiment in perception and only when the subjects were male was there a significant difference in authoritarianism between volunteers and nonvolunteers. When recruitment was for an experiment in personality, neither male nor female volunteers showed significantly lower authoritarianism than nonvolunteers.

Poor (1967), also employing the F scale, found that mail questionnaire respondents were less authoritarian than nonrespondents. However, in soliciting volunteers for an experiment in social psychology, Poor obtained no differences in authoritarianism between volunteers and nonvolunteers.

Martin and Marcuse (1957), in their study of volunteers for hypnosis research, employed the Ethnocentrism (E) Scale. Volunteers, especially males, were found to be significantly less ethnocentric than nonvolunteers. However, Schubert (1964), employing MMPI definitions of prejudice and tolerance, obtained no difference between volunteers and nonvolunteers for a psychological experiment.

Consistent with the general trend toward lower authoritarianism among volunteers are the results of Wallin (1949). He found that participants in survey research are politically and socially more liberal than nonparticipants. Benson, Booman, and Clark (1951) similarly found a more favorable attitude toward minority groups among people who were willing to be interviewed than among those who were not cooperative. Finally, Burchinal (1960) found that undergraduates who completed questionnaires at scheduled sessions were less authoritarian than those students who did not.

The bulk of the evidence suggests that volunteers are likely to be less authoritarian than nonvolunteers. This conclusion seems most warranted for those studies in which the subjects were asked to respond either verbally or in written form to questions of a personal nature. In all five samples where the task was to answer such personal questions, those subjects who were less authoritarian, broadly defined, were more cooperative.

G. Conventionality

There is a sense in which the more authoritarian individual is also the more conventional, so that one might expect volunteers for behavioral research to be less conventional than nonvolunteers. That seems most often, but by no means always, to be the case. Thus, Wallin (1949), who found survey respondents to be less authoritarian than nonrespondents, did not find a difference in conventionality between these types. Rosen (1951), however, found that volunteers for personality research were less conventional than nonvolunteers, while C. Edwards (1968) reported the opposite finding. In the latter study, student nurses who volunteered for an hypnotic dream experiment were judged by their instructors to be more conventional than nonvolunteers.

A number of studies have discovered that volunteers for Kinsey-type interviews tend, either in their sexual behavior or in their attitudes toward sex, to be more unconventional than nonvolunteers (Maslow, 1942; Maslow and Sakoda, 1952; Siegman, 1956). In order to determine whether this relative unconventionality of volunteers is specific to the Kinsey-type situation, one would need to know if these same volunteers were more likely than nonvolunteers to participate in other types of psychological research. It also would be helpful if one knew whether groups matched on the basis of sexual conventionality, but differing in other types of conventionality, exhibited different rates of volunteering for Kinsey-type interviews.

The Pd scale of the MMPI often is regarded clinically as reflecting dissatisfaction with societal conventions, and higher scorers may be regarded as less conventional than lower scorers. Both London *et al.* (1962) and Schubert (1964) found volunteers for different types of experiments to be less conventional by this definition, though with their army servicemen subjects, Myers, Murphy, Smith, and Goffard (1966) found volunteers for a perceptual isolation experiment to be more conventional. London *et al.* and Schubert further found volunteers to score higher on the F scale of the MMPI, which reflects a willingness to admit to unconventional experiences. The Lie scale of the MMPI taps primness and propriety, and high scorers may be regarded as more conventional than low scorers. Although Heilizer (1960) found no Lie scale differences between volunteers and nonvolunteers, Schubert (1964) found that volunteers scored lower.

These results are not unequivocal, but in general it would appear that volunteers for behavioral research tend to be more unconventional than nonvolunteers. Six studies support this conclusion. (However, two others find no difference, and two others report the opposite relationship.)

It would not be surprising if further research proved that sex differences are significant determinants of the nature of the conventionality-volunteering relationship. Recall that London *et al.* (1962) concluded, at least for hypnosis research, that females who volunteer may be significantly more interested in the novel and the unusual, whereas for males the relationship is less likely. A finding was noted earlier, under the heading of conformity, that may bear out London *et al.* That was Foster's (1961) finding which, though not statistically significant, implied that the relationship between conformity and volunteering may be in opposite directions for males versus females.

H. Arousal Seeking

On the basis of his results using over 1,000 subjects, Schubert (1964) has postulated a trait of arousal-seeking on which he found volunteers to differ from nonvolunteers. He notes that volunteers for a "psychological experiment" reported drinking more coffee, taking more caffeine pills, and (among males) smoking more cigarettes than nonvolunteers. All three types of behavior are related conceptually and empirically to arousal seeking. In partial support of Schubert's results are those obtained by Ora (1966). Though he found volunteers reporting significantly greater consumption of coffee and caffeine pills than was reported by nonvolunteers, there were no differences in cigarette smoking between volunteers and nonvolunteers. However, recent unpublished data collected by Rosnow and Rosenthal (1967), which are described in greater detail later, indicate no overall, significant relationship between volunteering for a "psychological experiment" and either smoking or coffee drinking. In fact, among males, there is a tendency for volunteers to smoke less ($p = .07$) and to drink less coffee ($p = .06$) than nonvolunteers. The relationship between smoking and coffee drinking is $+.54$. Also inconsistent with Schubert's results are the findings of Poor (1967). In both his questionnaire study and in his social psychological experiment, Poor found no significant relationship between smoking and participation by his predominantly male subjects. In fact, in both studies, Poor obtained trends opposite to those of Schubert; participants smoked less and reported drinking less alcohol than nonparticipants. In addition, Myers et al. (1966) found no relationship between smoking and volunteering for isolation experiments. On the whole, it does not appear that smokers and coffee drinkers are necessarily overrepresented among volunteers for behavioral research.

Fortunately, Schubert's construct of arousal seeking does not rely so heavily on the associated behavior of smoking and coffee drinking. He found that a variety of MMPI scales, associated with arousal seeking, discriminated significantly between volunteers and nonvolunteers. These MMPI characteristics which Schubert found associated with a greater likelihood of volunteering generally coincide with those noted by London et al. (1962). One important exception, however, is that the hypomanic (Ma) scale scores of the MMPI were found by Schubert to correlate positively with volunteering (a result of some importance to the arousal seeking hypothesis), while London et al. found a negative relationship between Ma scores and volunteering for an hypnosis experiment. This reversal weakens the generality of the arousal seeking hypothesis, which is further weakened by Rosen's (1951) finding that female volunteers scored lower on the Ma scale than female nonvolunteers.

Nevertheless, there are other data which lend support to Schubert's hypothesis that volunteers are more arousal seeking than nonvolunteers. Riggs and Kaess (1955) observed that volunteers were characterized by more cycloid emotionality on the Guilford Scale than nonvolunteers, a result that is not inconsistent with Schubert's finding of higher Ma scores among volunteers. Howe (1960) reports that volunteers willing to undergo electric shocks were characterized by less need to avoid shock than nonvolunteers, a finding that is not totally tautological and one that is consistent with the arousal seeking hypothesis. However, Riggs and Kaess also found that volunteers were characterized by more introversive thinking on the Guilford than nonvolunteers, a result which is not supportive of the arousal seeking hypothesis.

Closely related to Schubert's concept of arousal seeking is the concept of sensation-seeking discussed by Zuckerman, Schultz, and Hopkins (1967). In a number of studies Zuckerman et al. compared volunteers with nonvolunteers on a specially developed Sensation Seeking Scale

(SSS). In one study female undergraduates who volunteered for sensory deprivation were found to have scored higher than nonvolunteers on the SSS. In a second study, which also employed female undergraduates, volunteers for an hypnosis experiment scored higher in sensation seeking than nonvolunteers. In a third study, male undergraduates were invited to volunteer for sensory deprivation and/or hypnosis research. Subjects who volunteered for both experiments scored highest in sensation seeking, while those who volunteered for neither task scored lowest on the SSS and also on the Ma scale of the MMPI. The correlation between scores on the SSS and the Ma scale, though statistically significant, is low enough (+.21) that one would not expect the results obtained on the basis of the Ma scale to be attributable entirely to the results obtained with the SSS.

In another study in which Schultz (1967b) solicited volunteers for sensory deprivation, male volunteers obtained significantly higher scores on the SSS than male nonvolunteers, while among female subjects a less clearly significant difference in the same direction was revealed. Finally, Schultz (1967c) invited female undergraduates to volunteer for a sensory restriction experiment. On the basis of scores on the Cattell Scales, volunteers could be judged more adventurous than nonvolunteers.

At least when arousal seeking is defined in terms of the Sensation Seeking Scale there appears to be substantial support for Schubert's hypothesis that volunteers are more arousal seeking than nonvolunteers. When other tests or scales are used to define arousal seeking the results are less consistent, though even then the hypothesis is not completely without support.

I. Anxiety

There is no dearth of studies comparing the more or less enduring anxiety levels of volunteers and nonvolunteers. Table II summarizes the results of 11 of those studies that could be most easily categorized as to outcome. In seven of these there appeared to be no difference between volunteers and nonvolunteers, Lubin, Brady and Levitt (1962a) having employed the IPAT measure of anxiety, and the remaining studies using the Taylor Manifest Anxiety Scale or a close relative of that scale. The tasks for which volunteers were solicited included hypnosis, sensory deprivation, electric shock, Kinsey-type interviews, small groups experiments and an unspecified "psychological experiment." On the basis of these seven studies one could certainly conclude that, at least in terms of manifest anxiety, volunteers are usually no different than nonvolunteers.

However, results of the other four studies listed in Table II make

TABLE II

STUDIES OF THE ANXIETY LEVEL OF VOLUNTEERS VERSUS NONVOLUNTEERS

Volunteers more anxious	No difference	Volunteers less anxious
Rosen (1951)	Heilizer (1960)	Myers et al. (1966)
Schubert (1964)	Himelstein (1956)	Scheier (1959)
	Hood and Back (1967)	
	Howe (1960)	
	Lubin, Brady, and Levitt (1962a)	
	Siegman (1956)	
	Zuckerman, Schultz, and Hopkins (1967)	

it difficult to reach this simple conclusion, since these studies show significant differences at around the .05 level. Moreover, the fact that two find volunteers to be more anxious than nonvolunteers, while two others find just the opposite relationship, only complicates the attempt to summarize simply the collective results. One might be tempted to take the algebraic mean of the differences in anxiety level found between volunteers and nonvolunteers in these four studies, but that would be like averaging the temperature of one winter and one summer and concluding that there had been two springs. Furthermore, one cannot attribute the inconsistency in results to the instruments employed to measure anxiety. Scheier (1959) used the IPAT; Myers et al. (1966), Rosen (1951), and Schubert (1964) all employed the usual MMPI scales or derivatives (Depression Scale, Psychesthenia Scale, or Taylor Manifest Anxiety Scale).

One possibility to explain the inconsistency concerns the anxiety arousing nature of the tasks for which volunteers were solicited. The tasks for which more anxious subjects volunteered were an MMPI examination (Rosen, 1951) and participating in a "psychological experiment" (Schubert, 1964). The tasks for which less anxious subjects volunteered were a sensory deprivation study (Myers et al., 1966) and one that Scheier (1959) left unspecified but characterized as somewhat threatening. As a working hypothesis let us suggest that although most often there will be no difference in the level of chronic anxiety between volunteers and nonvolunteers, when such a difference does occur it will be the more threatening experiment that will draw the less anxious volunteer and the ordinary experiment that will draw the more anxious volunteer. Thus, the more anxious subject worries more about the consequences of his refusing to volunteer, but only so long as the task is not itself perceived as frightening. If it is frightening, then the more anxious and fearful subject may decide that he cannot tolerate the additional anxiety that his participation would engender and so chooses not to volunteer.

Some weak support for this hypothesis comes from the work of Martin and Marcuse (1958) who obtained a complicated interaction between volunteering, anxiety level and task. No differences in anxiety level were found between volunteers and nonvolunteers of either sex when recruiting for experiments in learning or attitudes toward sex. However, when volunteering was requested for a personality experiment, both male and female volunteers were found to be more anxious than nonvolunteers. When volunteering was requested for an experiment on hypnosis, male volunteers were found to be less anxious than male nonvolunteers, a difference that was not obtained among female subjects. These results seem to parallel the results of the studies listed in Table II. Most of the time no differences were found in anxiety level between volunteers and nonvolunteers. When differences were obtained, the volunteers for the more ordinary experiments were more anxious, while the (male) volunteers for the more unusual, perhaps more threatening, experiments were less anxious. The results of the Martin and Marcuse research again emphasize the importance of the variable of subject's sex as a moderating or complicating factor in the relationship between volunteering behavior and various personal characteristics.

Further support for the hypothesis that the more fearful the subject, the less he will volunteer for a frightening experiment comes from a study by Brady, Levitt, and Lubin (1961). Seventy-six student nurses were asked to indicate whether they were afraid of hypnosis. Two weeks later, volunteers for an experiment in hypnosis were solicited. Of those nurses who volunteered, 40 per cent had indicated at least some fear of hypnosis while among the nonvolunteers more than double that number (82 per cent) indicated such fear ($p < .0002$). It should be noted, however, that student nurses who volunteered did not differ in anxiety as measured by the IPAT from those who did not volunteer.

Less relevant to the question of volunteering but quite relevant to the related question of who finds their way into the role of research subject is the study by Leipold and James (1962). Male and female subjects who failed to appear for a scheduled psychological experiment were compared with subjects who kept their appointments. Among the female subjects those who appeared did not differ in anxiety on the Taylor Scale from those who did not appear. However, male subjects who failed to appear—the determined nonvolunteers—were significantly more anxious than those male subjects who appeared as scheduled. These findings not only emphasize the importance of sex differences in studies of volunteer characteristics, but also that it is not enough simply to know who volunteers; even among those subjects who volunteer there are likely to be differences between those who actually show up and those who do not.

J. Psychopathology

We now turn our attention to variables that have been related to global definitions of psychological adjustment or pathology. Some of the variables discussed earlier have also been related to global views of adjustment, but our discussion of them was intended to carry no special implications bearing on subjects' adjustment. For example, when anxiety was the variable under discussion, it was not intended that more anxious subjects be regarded as more maladjusted. Indeed, within the normal range of anxiety scores found, the converse might be equally accurate.

There is perhaps a score of studies relevant to the question of the psychological adjustment of volunteers versus nonvolunteers. Once again, however, the results are equivocal. About one-third of the studies suggest that volunteers are better adjusted; another third suggest the opposite; and the remainder reveal no difference in adjustment between volunteers and nonvolunteers. We begin by summarizing the studies that indicate that volunteers are psychologically more healthy than nonvolunteers.

Self-esteem is usually regarded as a correlate, if not a definition, of good adjustment. Maslow (1942) and Maslow and Sakoda (1952) summarized the results of six studies of volunteering for Kinsey-type interviews dealing with respondents' sexual behavior. In five cases, volunteers revealed greater self-esteem (but not greater security) than nonvolunteers as measured by Maslow's own tests. The one case that tended to show volunteers to be lower in self-esteem than nonvolunteers was a sample drawn from a class in abnormal psychology. These students were found to have an atypical distribution of self-esteem scores; both very high and very low scorers were overrepresented among the volunteers. Some time later, Siegman (1956) also solicited volunteers for a Kinsey-type interview, administering his own self-esteem scale to the subjects. He found no differences in self-esteem between volunteers and nonvolunteers.

In one of the studies by Poor (1967), subjects were requested to complete and to return a questionnaire. "Volunteers," thus, may be thought of as those subjects who returned the completed questionnaires. Poor employed a measure of self-esteem developed by Morris Rosenberg and found "volunteers," or responders, to be higher in self-esteem than "nonvolunteers" ($p < .07$). A study by Pan (1951) of residents of homes for the aged is also, at least indirectly, relevant to this discussion. Pan observed that residents who completed and returned his questionnaires were in better physical health than were nonrespondents. Only because it appears that physical and mental health are somewhat correlated do Pan's results imply that respondents may also be better adjusted psychologically than nonrespondents. There is, however, good reason to be cautious about these results, for it is possible that the superintendents of the homes may have unduly influenced the composition of the respondent group by distributing the questionnaires primarily to residents in good health.

So far we have considered nine samples in which volunteers (i.e., respondents or interviewees) were compared with nonvolunteers (nonrespondents or noninterviewees) on adjustment-related variables. In seven of those nine, volunteers appeared to be the better adjusted. In one sample, nonvolunteers were the better adjusted, and in one other, volunteers did not differ from nonvolunteers in adjustment. On the whole, then, it would seem that in questionnaire or interview studies, respondents will mainly be those subjects who tend to be psychologically well-adjusted.

When volunteering is requested for a typical psychological experiment the relationship between adjustment and volunteering becomes more equivocal. Schubert (1964), for example, found no differences in the MMPI scores on neuroticism between volunteers and nonvolunteers for a psychological experiment. He did find, however, that volunteers tended to be more irresponsible than nonvolunteers. In one of Poor's (1967) studies, subjects were solicited for a psychological experiment. Using the Rosenberg self-esteem measure, Poor found a tendency toward lower self-esteem among volunteers than among nonvolunteers ($p = .14$). It will be recalled that Poor also found just the opposite result when solicitation had been of questionnaire returns. Finally, Ora (1966), using a self-report measure of adjustment found no difference between volunteers and nonvolunteers for various psychological experiments. However, the volunteers perceived themselves in greater need of psychological assistance than did the nonvolunteers even without their feeling themselves more maladjusted. There is little basis for any conclusion to be drawn from the various findings.

We noted earlier, in discussing "shows" and "no-shows," that not all subjects who volunteer actually become part of the final data pool. There are two studies of those subjects who fail to keep research appointments that appear relevant to the adjustment variable. Silverman (1964) found that when participation was requested for a psychological experiment, it was subjects higher in self-esteem (as defined by a modified Janis and Field measure) who more often failed to keep their appointment.

This finding seems consistent with that of Poor (1967), who also found subjects lower in self-esteem more likely to end up by contributing data to the behavioral experimenter. Wrightsman (1966), however, observed that subjects who failed to keep their research appointments scored lower in social responsibility, a finding which is inconsistent with Schubert's (1964) observation that less responsible subjects are those more likely to volunteer.

The probable complexity of the relationship between psychopathology and volunteering for a fairly standard, or unspecified psychological experiment is well-illustrated in the study by Newman (1956). Male volunteers were found to be less variable in degree of self-actualization than male nonvolunteers, whereas female volunteers showed greater variability than female nonvolunteers. If one accepts self-actualization as a measure of adjustment, the implication is a U-shaped relationship between adjustment and volunteering for females when the task is a psychological experiment, but an upside down U for males. Whereas the best and the least adjusted males may be less likely to volunteer than those males who are moderately well-adjusted, the best and the least adjusted females may be more likely to volunteer than moderately well-adjusted females.

When we turn to a consideration of the somewhat less standard types of behavioral experiments, we find similar difficulties in trying to summarize the relationship between volunteering and adjustment. Schultz (1967c) reports that female undergraduate volunteers for an experiment in sensory deprivation scored higher in emotional stability on the Cattell than nonvolunteers. However, in an experiment on hypnosis, Hilgard, Weitzenhoffer, Landes, and Moore (1961) found that female undergraduate volunteers scored lower in self-control than nonvolunteers. Among male subjects they report no significant difference in self-control between volunteers and nonvolunteers. In their recruitment for volunteers for hypnosis research, Lubin, Brady, and Levitt (1962a, 1962b) found no significant difference between student nurse volunteers and nonvolunteers that could be attributed to differences in adjustment. The tendency was, however, for the volunteers to appear somewhat less well-adjusted than the nonvolunteers as defined by a variety of test scores and by obesity.

When the research for which volunteers are solicited takes on a medical appearance, the relationship between psychopathology and volunteering is a little more clear. Pollin and Perlin (1958) and Perlin, Pollin, and Butler (1958) have concluded that the more intrinsically eager a person is to volunteer for hospitalization as a normal control subject, the more likely he is to be maladjusted. Similarly, Bell (1962) reports that volunteers for studies of the effects of high temperature were more likely to be maladjusted than nonvolunteers.

Lasagna and von Felsinger (1954), recruiting subjects for drug research, noted the high incidence of psychopathology among volunteers. A similar finding has also been reported by Esecover, Malitz, and Wilkens (1961), who solicited volunteers for research on hallucinogens. They found that the better adjusted volunteers were motivated more by money, scientific curiosity, or because volunteering was a normally expected occurrence (e.g., as by medical students). Such findings are also consistent with the results of Pollin and Perlin (1958).

Thus far the results of studies of volunteers for medical research agree rather well with one another, consistently tending to show greater psychopathology among volunteers than nonvolunteers. To this impression, however, one must add the results obtained by Richards (1960), who compared volunteers and nonvolunteers for a study of mescaline on the basis of their responses to the Rorschach and TAT. Though significant differences were obtained, the nature of those differences was such that no conclusion could be drawn as to which group was the more maladjusted. It can be noted, however, that Richards' subjects were undergraduates in the medical sciences, where volunteering might well have been the expected behavior for these students who may also have been motivated by a preprofessional interest in drug research. Under such circumstances, one might not expect volunteers to reveal any excess of psychopathology over what one would obtain among nonvolunteers.

K. Intelligence

There are several studies showing a difference in intellectual performance between volunteers and nonvolunteers. Martin and Marcuse (1957) found that volunteers for an experiment in hypnosis scored higher on the ACE than nonvolunteers. In a subsequent study, Martin and Marcuse (1958) solicited volunteers for three additional experiments in personality, learning, and attitudes towards sex. For all four studies combined, volunteers were still found to score higher in intelligence than nonvolunteers. The definition of intelligence again was the score on the ACE, a test employed also by Reuss (1943) in a study of responders and nonresponders to a mail questionnaire. Reuss also found that "volunteers" (i.e., responders) scored higher in intelligence than "nonvolunteers." Myers et al. (1966), however, employing a U.S. Army technical aptitude measure of intelligence, found no significant relationship between intelligence and volunteering for isolation experiments.

In a study of high school juniors, Wicker (1968) compared the degree of participation in behavioral research of "regular" and "marginal" students. Regular students were defined as those scoring at least 105 on an IQ test and who either earned no grades below C in the preceding semester or were children of fathers engaged in managerial or professional occupations. Marginal students were defined as those having scored below 100 in IQ and either having earned two or more D or F grades in the preceding semester or who were children of fathers in "lower" occupational categories. Of the juniors in the regular group 44 per cent found their way into the research project. Of those in the marginal group less than 14 per cent made their way into the project ($p < .001$).

In requesting student nurses to volunteer for an hypnotic dream experiment, Edwards (1968) found no relationship between IQ and volunteering but, somewhat surprisingly, he observed that volunteers scored significantly lower than nonvolunteers on a test of psychiatric knowledge ($p < .01$) and that volunteers were also lower in relative class standing ($p = .07$). In addition, nonvolunteers' fathers were better educated than the fathers of volunteers ($p = .006$). These findings seem opposite in direction to those obtained by Wicker, but it can be noted that Edwards' subjects were more highly selected from the upper end of the ability distribution than were Wicker's. Edwards' findings also differ from those of Martin and Marcuse, but this inconsistency cannot be attributed to differences in the general level of intellectual performance found in the two samples.

Brower (1948) found that volunteers for a visual-motor skills experiment performed better at difficult visual-motor tasks than did coerced nonvolunteers, though there was no performance difference in a simple visual-motor task. Wolfgang (1967) solicited volunteers for a concept learning experiment, after which all subjects were administered the Shipley-Hartford test of abstract thinking ability. Male volunteers exhibited better performance than male nonvolunteers, but no difference was revealed between female volunteers and nonvolunteers. A problem common to the studies of Brower and Wolfgang is that volunteer status was established before determining the correlate of volunteering. At least in principle, it is possible that the act of volunteering or of refusing to volunteer, may affect the subject's subsequent task performance. Thus, a subject who has been coerced to participate in an experiment may be poorly motivated to perform well at tasks that have been set for him against his will. It remains problematic whether his poor performance antedated his decision not to volunteer. In an experiment in which the test to be correlated with volunteering is administered both to volunteers and nonvolunteers once the volunteers have already participated in an experiment, one must examine carefully the nature of the experimental task. If the task were similar to the test one would expect the volunteers to perform better, since the task would provide a practice session for their performance on the test.

When the definition of intelligence is in terms of a standard IQ test or even a test of visual-motor skill there are at least a half-dozen samples showing that volunteers perform better than nonvolunteers, three samples showing no difference in IQ, and no samples showing nonvolunteers to perform better than volunteers. It appears that when there are differences in intelligence between volunteers and nonvolunteers, the difference favors the volunteers.

When the definition of "intelligence" is in terms of school grades, the relationship of volunteering to intelligence becomes more equivocal. On the one hand, Edwards (1968) found that volunteers stood lower in class rankings than nonvolunteers. On the other hand, Wicker (1968), including grades in his definition of marginality of academic status, found that volunteers performed better than nonvolunteers. The relationship is further complicated by the fact that Rosen (1951) found no difference in grades between male volunteers and male nonvolunteers for behavioral research, but among female subjects the volunteers tended to earn higher grades ($p < .10$). Poor (1967) obtained no differences in grades or in intellectual interests and aspirations between respondents and nonrespondents to a mail questionnaire nor between volunteers and nonvolunteers for a psychological experiment. Though Abeles, Iscoe, and Brown (1954–55) found no overall relationship with volunteering they did find a tendency toward higher grades among early volunteers. From the few studies in which volunteering has been correlated with school grades it is difficult to draw any clear conclusions. If there is a relationship between school grades and volunteering it seems to be neither strong nor consistent.

Leipold and James (1962) found that female volunteers who showed up for the experiment as scheduled had been earning higher grades in psychology; among male subjects this relationship was not significant. Where grades are so specific to a single course they are likely to be less well-correlated with general intelligence. Perhaps grades in a psychology course are as much a measure of interest in research as they are a measure of intelligence. Such an interpretation would be consistent with the findings of Edgerton, Britt, and Norman (1947). They reported that over a period of several years winners of science talent contests responded to a mail questionnaire more than did runners-up who, in turn, responded more than "also rans." While winners of such contests may well be more intelligent than losers, the greater interest of the winners might be the more potent determinant of their cooperation.

In a recent study by Matthysse (1966) a number of volunteers for an experiment in attitude change were followed up by mail questionnaire. Somewhat surprisingly, but consistent with Edwards' (1968) findings, those who responded to the follow-up had scored lower in intellectual efficiency ($p < .10$) on the California Psychological Inventory.

Relevant to intellectual motivation, if not to intellectual performance, is a consideration of the variable of achievement motivation. In his important review of volunteer characteristics, Bell (1962) suggests that volunteers may be higher in need for achievement than nonvolunteers. The evidence for this hypothesis, however, is quite indirect. More direct data have become available from research by Lubin, Levitt, and Zuckerman (1962) and by Myers et al. (1966). In their studies of respondents and nonrespondents to a mail questionnaire, and of volunteers and nonvolunteers for an isolation experiment, respectively, a tendency, not statistically significant, was found for respondents and volunteers to score higher in need achievement on the Edwards Personal Preference Schedule than nonrespondents and nonvolunteers.

L. Education

In most of the studies described in the preceding section the subjects were students, usually in college, and the educational variance was low, a finding which is characteristic of experimental studies but not of survey research. In questionnaire or interview studies the target population is often intended to show considerable variability of educational background. Among survey researchers there has long been a suspicion that better educated people are those more apt to find their way into the final sample. The suspicion is well justified by the data. Study after

TABLE III

STUDIES SHOWING RESPONDENTS IN SURVEY RESEARCH TO BE BETTER EDUCATED

Authors	Date
Benson, Booman, and Clark	1951
Franzen and Lazarsfeld	1945
Gaudet and Wilson	1940
Pace	1939
Pan	1951
Reuss	1943
Robins	1963
Suchman and McCandless	1940
Wallin	1949
Zimmer	1956

study has shown that it is the better educated person who finds his responses constituting the final data pool. Since we could find no significant reversals to this relationship, we have simply listed in Table III the various studies in support of this conclusion.

M. Social Class

There is a high degree of correlation between amount of education and social class, the latter defined by occupational status. One would expect, therefore, that in survey research those subjects having higher occupational status roles would be more likely to answer questions and to answer them sooner than subjects lower in occupational status. Belson (1960), Franzen and Lazarsfeld (1945), and Robins (1963) have all found professional workers more likely than lower class jobholders to participate in survey research. Similarly, Pace (1939) found professionals more willing to be interviewed and to return their questionnaires more promptly than nonprofessionals. Zimmer (1956), in his study of Air Force officers and enlisted men, found that probability of responding to a questionnaire increased directly as the serviceman's rank increased. Finally, King (1967) found in his survey of Episcopal clergymen that questionnaires were more likely to be returned by (a) bishops than by rectors, (b) rectors than by curates, and (c) curates than by vestrymen. The sharp and statistically significant break came between the rectors and curates. However, there is some possibility in King's study that not all of the curates and vestrymen actually received the questionnaires.

Even discounting King's results, the trend is clear. At least for the range of occupational statuses noted here, higher status role occupants are more likely to participate in the survey research process than those lower in status.

We have been talking of the volunteer's own social class as defined by his occupational status. The picture becomes more complicated when we consider the social class of the volunteer's parents—his class of origin. Edwards (1968) reports that the fathers of volunteers for an hypnotic dream experiment had a lower educational level than the fathers of nonvolunteers. Similarly, Reuss (1943) found that the parents of respondents to a mail questionnaire had less education than the parents of nonrespondents. Rosen (1951) notes that the fathers of female volunteers for psychological research had a lower income than the fathers of nonvolunteers. Poor (1967), however, found no relationship between father's occupational status and either responding to a questionnaire or volunteering for an experiment. The trend, if any, was for the fathers of respondents to have a higher occupational status than the fathers of nonrespondents. Finally, the reader will recall the study by Wicker (1968), in which marginal students participated in research less often than nonmarginal students. For Wicker, father's occupation was part of the definition of marginality. If father's occupational status, then, made any difference at all, it was the children of higher status fathers who more often produced data for the behavioral researcher. To summarize, when father's social class makes the clearest difference it seems that children of lower class fathers are the most likely to volunteer. Since the evidence seems so clear that subjects who are themselves lower class members are less likely to volunteer, the hypothesis is suggested that those higher status persons are most likely to volunteer whose background includes vertical social mobility. In keeping with a point made earlier in this chapter, these latter persons may be those who at least in survey research would perceive themselves as having the most interesting and most acceptable answers to the investigator's questions.

N. Age

There are over a dozen studies addressed to the question of age differences between volunteers and nonvolunteers. As we already have seen with other variables, often there is no significant difference between the ages of volunteers and nonvolunteers. However, when differences are found they most often suggest that younger rather than older subjects are those who volunteer for behavioral research. Abeles, Iscoe, and Brown (1954–55) found this to be the case in their questionnaire study. Newman (1956) observed the same relationship for personality and perception experiments, although the age difference in the latter experiment was not statistically significant. In another experiment in perception, however, Marmer (1967) found volunteers to be significantly younger than nonvolunteers. Rosen (1951) found that female volunteers were significantly younger than female nonvolunteers, a difference which, however, did not hold for male subjects. For research with college students, then, even when the general trend is for volunteers to be younger, the sex of the subjects and the type of experiment for which volunteering is requested seem to complicate the relationship between age and volunteering.

From studies not employing the usual college samples there is also some evidence for the greater youthfulness of volunteers. Myers, Murphy, Smith, and Goffard (1966) requested Army personnel to volunteer for a study of perceptual isolation and found volunteers to be younger. Pan (1951), too, found his respondents among residents of homes for the aged to be younger than the nonrespondents. The same tendency was reported by Wallin (1949).

Nevertheless, opposite results also have been reported. Thus, in King's (1967) study it was the older clergymen who were most likely to reply to a brief questionnaire. In that study, however, age was very much confounded with position in the Church's status hierarchy. That situation seems to hold for the study by Zimmer (1956) as well. He found older Air Force men to respond more readily to a mail questionnaire, but the older airmen were also those of higher rank. Kruglov and Davidson (1953), in their study of male undergraduates, found the older students more willing to be interviewed than the younger students. Even allowing for the confounding effects of status in the studies by King and by Zimmer, the three studies just described weaken considerably the hypothesis that volunteers tend to be younger than nonvolunteers. That hypothesis is weakened further by several studies showing no differences in age between volunteers and nonvolunteers (Benson, Booman, and Clark, 1951; Edwards, 1968; Poor, 1967).

Further evidence for the potentially complicated nature of the relationship between age and volunteering comes from the work of Gaudet and Wilson (1940). They found that their determined nonvolunteers for a personal interview tended to be of intermediate ages with the younger and older householders more willing to participate. Similarly, curvilinearities have been reported by Newman (1956), though for his collegiate sample the curvilinearity was opposite in direction to that found by Gaudet and Wilson. Especially among Newman's female subjects, the nonvolunteers showed more extreme ages than did the volunteers. The same tendency was found among male subjects, but it was significant for males only among subjects recruited for a personality experiment, not among those recruited for a perception experiment.

O. Religion

The data are sparse that bear on the question of the relationship between volunteering and religious affiliation and attitudes. Matthysse (1966) found his respondents to a mail questionnaire to be disproportionately more often Jewish than Protestant and also to be more concerned with theological issues. The latter finding is not surprising since the questionnaire dealt with religious attitudes. Rosen (1951) also found Jews to be significantly overrepresented in his sample of volunteers for psychological research. In addition, Rosen found volunteers to be less likely to attend church services than nonvolunteers. However, Ora (1966) found no relationship between religious preference or church attendance and volunteering for various psychological experiments.

In his interview research, Wallin (1949) found Protestants somewhat more likely than Catholics to participate in a study of the prediction of marital success. The tenuousness of these findings is well illustrated in a study by Poor (1967). He, too, found no significant relationship between volunteering and either religious affiliation or church attendance. However, in his study of respondents to a mail questionnaire he reports a trend towards greater participation among Protestants than among Catholics or Jews, while in his study of volunteers for a psychological experiment, he reports a trend towards greatest participation among Catholics and least partipation among Jews. In a study of student nurses, Edwards (1968) found no association between volunteering and religious attitudes.

In summary, then, it is not possible to make any general statement concerning the relationship between volunteering and either religious affiliation, religious attitudes, or church attendance. On the basis of our earlier discussion, one might speculate that if any relationship does exist it is probably complicated by subjects' sex and the type of research for which participation is solicited.

P. Geographic Variables

In his study of respondents to a mail questionnaire, Reuss (1943) found greater participation by subjects from a rural rather than an urban background. In his study of college students, however, Rosen (1951) found no such difference between volunteers and nonvolunteers. Siegman (1956) reports that for a Kinsey-type interview, volunteering rates were higher in an Eastern than in a Midwestern university. Presumably, there were more students of rural origin in the Midwestern sample. Perhaps the nature of the volunteer request interacts with rural-urban origin to determine volunteering rates. Finally, Franzen and Lazarsfeld (1945) found that respondents to their mail questionnaire were overrepresented by residents of the East Central States but underrepresented by residents of New England and the Middle Atlantic States. In addition, residents of cities with a population of less than 100,000 were overrepresented relative to residents of cities of larger population. In view of the sparseness of the obtained data it seems best to forego any summary of the relationship between geographic variables and volunteering for behavioral research.

III. POPULATIONS INVESTIGATED

Before summarizing what is known and not known about differentiating characteristics of volunteers for behavioral research, let us consider the populations that have been discussed. All of the studies cited here sampled from populations of human subjects, situations, tasks, contexts, personal characteristics, and various measures of those characteristics (Brunswik, 1956).

A. Human Subjects

In his study of subject samples drawn for psychological research, Smart (1966) examined every article in the *Journal of Abnormal and Social Psychology* appearing in the years 1962–1964. Less than 1 per cent of the studies employed samples from the general population; 73 per cent used college students, and 32 per cent used introductory psychology students. Comparable data from the *Journal of Experimental Psychology* revealed no studies that had sampled from the general population; 86 per cent of the studies employed college students, and 42 per cent used students enrolled in introductory psychology courses. These data provide strong, current support for McNemar's 20-year-old criticism of behavioral science's being largely a science of the behavior of sophomores.

The studies discussed in this chapter provide additional support for McNemar's contention. The vast majority of the psychological experiments drew their subject samples from college populations. When the studies were in the nature of surveys, a much broader cross-section of subject populations was tapped, but even then college students were heavily represented. Such a great reliance on college populations may be undesirable from the standpoint of the representativeness of design in behavioral research generally, but it does not reflect an ecological invalidity for our present purpose. Sampling of subject populations in studies of volunteer characteristics seems to be representative of sampling of subject populations in behavioral research generally.

B. Situations, Tasks, and Contexts

A considerable variety of situations, tasks, and contexts were sampled by the studies discussed here. The tasks for which volunteering was requested included survey questionnaires, Kinsey-type interviews, psycho-pharmacological and medical control studies, and various psychological experiments focusing upon small group interaction, sensory deprivation, hypnosis, personality, perception, learning, and motor skills. Unfortunately, very few studies have employed more than one task; hence, little is known about the effects of the specific task either on the rate of volunteering to undertake it or on the nature of the relationship between volunteering and the personal characteristics of volunteers.

There is, however, some information bearing on this problem. Newman (1956), for example, employed more than one task, asking subjects to volunteer both for a personality and a perception experiment, but he found no systematic effect of these two tasks on the relationships between the variables investigated and the act of volunteering. Zuckerman, Schultz, and Hopkins (1967) similarly found no systematic effect of their two tasks (sensory deprivation and hypnosis) on the relationships between volunteering and those correlates of volunteering in which they were interested. Hood (1963), however, employed four tasks and found a significant interaction between subjects' sex and type of task. Males were more willing than females to participate in a competitive experimental task but were less willing than females to participate in studies of affiliation behavior and self-revelation, or in a relatively unspecified study. Similarly, Ora (1966) found males particularly reluctant to volunteer for a "clinical" study in which self-revelation was called for.

Martin and Marcuse (1958) employed four tasks for which volunteering was requested. They found greater personality differences between volunteers and nonvolunteers for an hypnosis experiment than were found between volunteers and nonvolunteers for experiments in learning, attitudes toward sex, and personality. Of these last three experimental situations, the personality study tended to reveal somewhat greater personality differences between volunteers and nonvolunteers than were obtained in the other two situations. Those differences that emerged from the more differentiating tasks were not specifically related conceptually to the differential nature of the tasks for which volunteering had been requested. These findings should warn us, however, that any differentiating characteristic may be a function of the particular situation for which volunteers were solicited.

Because of the obvious desirability of being able to speak about characteristics of volunteers for "generalized" behavioral research, a search was made for studies of volunteer characteristics in which the request for volunteers was nonspecific. A number of the studies previously cited met this requirement, usually by asking subjects to volunteer simply for a "psychological experiment" (e.g., Himelstein, 1956; Leipold and James, 1962; McDavid, 1965; Poor, 1967; Schubert, 1964; Silverman, 1964; Ward, 1964; Wilson and Patterson, 1965). The results of those studies revealed no tendency toward results any different from those obtained in studies in which the volunteer's task was more specifically stated.

C. Personal Characteristics

In this chapter we have tried to include every finding of a significant difference between volunteers and nonvolunteers that was available. Having once discovered a significant difference, every effort was then made to uncover studies reporting either no differences or differences in the opposite direction. For organizational and heuristic purposes, however, we have grouped the many findings together under a fairly small number of headings. Decisions to group any variables under a given heading were made on the basis of empirically established or conceptually meaningful relationships.

It should further be noted that within any category several different operational definitions may have been employed. Thus, we have discussed anxiety as defined by the Taylor Manifest Anxiety Scale as well as by the Pt scale of the MMPI. This practice was made necessary by the limited number of available studies employing identical operational definitions, except possibly for age and sex. This necessity, however, is not unmixed with virtue. If, in spite of differences of operational definition, the variables serve to predict the act of volunteering, we can feel greater confidence in the construct underlying the varying definitions and in its relevance to the predictive and conceptual task at hand.

IV. SUMMARY OF VOLUNTEER CHARACTERISTICS

For this mass of studies some attempt at summary is essential. Each of the characteristics sometimes associated with volunteering has been placed into one of three groups of statements. In the first group, statements or hypotheses are listed for which the evidence seems strongest. Though in absolute terms our confidence may not be so great, in relative terms we have most confidence in the propositions listed in this group. In the second group, statements or hypotheses are listed for which the evidence, though not unequivocal, seems clearly to lean in favor of the proposition. At least some confidence in these statements seems warranted. In the third group, statements or hypotheses are listed for which the evidence is unconvincing. Little confidence seems warranted in these propositions. Within each of the three groups of statements, the hypothesized relationships are listed in roughly descending order of warranted confidence.

A. Statements Warranting Most Confidence

1. Volunteers tend to be better educated than nonvolunteers.
2. Volunteers tend to have higher occupational status than nonvolunteers (though volunteers may more often come from a lower status background).
3. Volunteers tend to be higher in the need for approval than nonvolunteers (though the relationship may be curvilinear with least

volunteering likely among those with average leveis of need approval).

4. Volunteers, especially males, tend to score higher than nonvolunteers on tests of intelligence (though school grades seem not clearly related to volunteering).

5. Volunteers tend to be less authoritarian than nonvolunteers, especially when asked to answer personal questions.

6. Volunteers tend to be better adjusted than nonvolunteers when asked to answer personal questions, but more poorly adjusted when asked to participate in medical research. (In psychological experiments the relationship is equivocal.)

B. Statements Warranting Some Confidence

7. Volunteers tend to be more sociable than nonvolunteers.

8. Volunteers tend to be more arousal-seeking than nonvolunteers.

9. Volunteers tend to be more unconventional than nonvolunteers.

10. Volunteers tend more often than nonvolunteers to be firstborn.

11. Volunteers tend to be younger than nonvolunteers, especially when occupational status is partialled out.

12. Volunteers tend more often than nonvolunteers to be females when the task is standard and males when the task is unusual.

C. Statements Warranting Little Confidence

13. Volunteers tend to be more anxious than nonvolunteers when the task is standard and less anxious when the task is threatening.

14. Male volunteers are less conforming than male nonvolunteers.

15. Volunteers tend more often than nonvolunteers to be Jewish.

16. Volunteers more than nonvolunteers tend to be of rural origin when the task is standard and of urban origin when the task is unusual.

It is obvious that the hypothesized relationships require further investigation, especially those falling lower in the lists. There is little reason for thinking that an *experimentum crucis* would place any of these relationships on firmer footing. Many have been examined in a dozen or even a score of studies. When the summary of that many findings is equivocal, it is readily apparent that it will take more than simply a few new studies to clarify the underlying relationship.

As we have already seen, the nature of the relationship between the attributes discussed and the act of volunteering may be complicated by the interacting effects of other variables. Two of the most likely candidates for the role of moderator variable are the nature of the task for which volunteering is solicited and the sex of the subject.

V. IMPLICATIONS FOR REPRESENTATIVENESS

The results of our analysis suggest that in any given study of human behavior the chances are good that those subjects who find their way into the research will differ appreciably from those subjects who do not. Even if the direction of difference is not highly predictable, it is important to know that volunteers for behavioral research are likely to differ from nonvolunteers in a variety of characteristics. One implication of this conclusion is that limitations may be imposed on the generality of finding of research employing volunteer subjects. It is well known that the violation of the requirement of random sampling complicates the process of statistical inference. This problem is discussed in basic texts on sampling theory and has also been dealt with by some of the workers previously cited (e.g., Cochran, Mosteller, and Tukey, 1953).

Granted that volunteers are never a random sample of the population from which they were recruited, and granting further that a given sample of volunteers differs on a number of important dimensions from a sample of nonvolunteers, we still do not know whether volunteer status is a condition that actually makes any great difference with regard to our dependent variables. It is possible that in a given experiment the performance of the volunteer subjects would not differ at all from the performance of the unsampled nonvolunteers if the latter had actually been recruited for the experiment (Lasagna and von Felsinger, 1954). The point is that substantively we have little idea of the effect of using volunteer subjects. What is needed are series of investigations covering a variety of tasks and situations for which volunteers are solicited, but for which both volunteers and nonvolunteers are actually used. Thus, we could determine in what types of studies the use of volunteers actually makes a difference, as well as the kinds of differences and their magnitude. When more information is available, we can, with better conscience, enjoy the convenience of using volunteer subjects. In the meantime, the best one can do is to hypothesize what the effects of volunteer characteristics might be in any given line of inquiry.

Let us take, as an example of this procedure, the much analyzed Kinsey-type study of sexual behavior. We have already seen how volunteers for this type of study tend to have unconventional attitudes about sexuality and may in addition behave in sexually unconventional ways. This tendency, as has frequently been noted, may have had grave effects on the outcome of Kinsey-type research, possibly leading to population estimates of sexual behavior seriously biased in the unconventional direction. The extent of this type of bias could probably be partially assessed over a population of college students among whom the nonvolunteers could be converted into "volunteers" in order to estimate the effect on data outcome of initial volunteering versus nonvolunteering. Clearly, such a study would be less feasible among a population of householders who stood to gain no course credit or instructor's approval from changing their status of nonvolunteer to volunteer.

The experiment by Hood and Back (1967) has special implications for small goups research. At least among male subjects these investigators found volunteers to be more willing than nonvolunteers to disclose personal information to others. Among female subjects the relationship between volunteering and self-disclosure was complicated by the nature of the experiment for which volunteering had been requested. Especially among males, then, small groups experiments that depend upon volunteer subjects may give inflated estimates of group members' willingness to participate openly in group interaction.

In a more standard realm of experimental psychology, Greene (1937) showed that precision in discrimination tasks was related to subjects' intelligence and type of personal adjustment. To the extent that volunteers differ from nonvolunteers in adjustment and intelligence, typical performance levels in discrimination tasks may be misjudged when volunteer samples are employed. It seems reasonable to wonder, too, about the effect of the volunteer variable on the normative data required for the standardization of an intelligence test. Since, at least in the standardization of intelligence tests for adults, volunteers tend to be overrepresented, and since volunteers tend to score higher on tests of intelligence, the "mean" IQ of 100 may represent rather an inflation of the true mean that would be obtained from a more truly random sample.

It was suggested earlier that it might be useful to assess the magnitude of volunteer bias by converting nonvolunteers to volunteers. However, one problem with increasing the pressure to volunteer in a sample of nonvolunteers is that the experience of having been coerced may change the subjects' responses to the experimental task. That seems especially likely in situations where nonvolunteers are initially led to believe that they are free not to volunteer. One partial solution to this problem might be to recruit volunteers from among nonvolunteers using increasingly positive incentives, a technique that has met with some success in survey research. Even then, however, we must try to assess the effect on the subject's response of having been sent two letters rather than one, or of having been offered $2 rather than $1 as spurs to volunteering.

If volunteers differ from nonvolunteers in their response to the task set by the investigator, the employment of volunteer samples can have serious effects on estimates of such parameters as means, medians, proportions, variances, skewness, and kurtosis. In survey research, where the estimation of such parameters is the principal goal, biasing effects of volunteer samples could be disastrous. In most behavioral experiments, however, interest is not centered so much on such statistics as means and proportions but rather on such statistics as the differences between means or proportions. The investigator is ordinarily interested in relating such differences to the operation of his independent variable. The fact that volunteers differ from nonvolunteers in their scores on the dependent variable may be quite irrelevant to the behavioral experimenter. He may want more to know whether the magnitude and statistical significance of the difference between his experimental and control group means would be affected if he used volunteers. In other words, he may be interested in knowing whether volunteer status interacts with his experimental variable.

VI. IMPLICATIONS FOR EXPERIMENTAL OUTCOMES

In this section we shall describe the evidence relevant to the problem of interaction of volunteer status with various experimental variables. Compared to the evidence amassed to show inherent differences between volunteers and nonvolunteers there is little evidence available from which to decide whether volunteeer status is likely to interact with experimental variables. On logical grounds alone one might expect such interactions. If we assume for the moment that volunteers are more often firstborn than are nonvolunteers, some research by Dittes (1961) becomes highly relevant. Dittes found that lessened acceptance by peers affected the behavior of firstborns but not that of laterborns. Still assuming firstborns to be overrepresented by volunteers, a study of the experimental variable of "lessened acceptance" conducted on volunteers might show strong effects, while the same study conducted with a more nearly random sample of subjects might show only weak effects.

We can imagine, too, an experiment to test the effects of some experimental manipulation on the dependent variable of gregariousness. If a sample of highly sociable volunteers were drawn, any manipulation designed to increase gregariousness might be too harshly judged as ineffective simply because the untreated control group would already be unusually high on this factor. The same manipulation might prove effective in increasing the gregariousness of the experimental group relative to the gregariousness of the control group if the total subject sample were characterized by a less restricted range of sociability. At least in principle, then, the use of volunteer subjects could lead to an increase in Type II errors.

The opposite type of error can also be imagined. Suppose an investigator were interested in the relationship between the psychological adjustment of women and some dependent variable. If female volunteers are indeed more variable than female nonvolunteers on the dimension of adjustment, and if there were some relationship between adjustment and the dependent variable, then the magnitude of that relationship would be overestimated when calculated for a sample of volunteers relative to a sample of nonvolunteers. So far in our discussion we have dealt only with speculations about the possible effects of volunteer bias on experimental or correlational outcomes. Fortunately, we are not restricted to speculation, since there are several recent studies addressed to this problem.

A. The Hayes, Meltzer, and Lundberg Study (1968)

In this experiment the investigators were interested in learning the effects on the subject's vocal participation in dyadic task-oriented groups of (a) his possession of task-revelant information, (b) his co-discussant's possession of task-relevant information and (c) the joint possession of task-relevant information. The dyad's task was to instruct an outsider how to build a complex tinkertoy structure. The builder had no diagram, but each of the two instructors did. Amount of task-relevant information was varied by the use of good, average, and poor diagrams. One-third of the 120 undergraduates were assigned to each of the three levels of information, and within each of these three groups the co-discussants were given either good, average, or poor information. Within each of the nine conditions so generated, half the subjects were paid volunteers and half were required to serve. Results showed that there were no effects on vocal activity of a subject's own level of information but that subjects talked least when their partner had most information. In addition, paid volunteers participated significantly more than did the conscripted subjects, a finding also cited earlier in this chapter.

The results in which we are most interested are the interactions between the volunteering variable and the experimental manipulations. None of those Fs approached significance; indeed all were less than unity. From this experiment one might conclude that, while volunteers and conscriptees differ in important ways from one another, they are nevertheless similarly affected by the operation of the experimental manipulation. No serious errors of inference would have occurred had the investigators used a sample composed entirely of volunteers.

Perhaps we should be surprised to discover any difference between the volunteers and the conscriptees. Conscriptees, after all, are not nonvolunteers, but rather a mixed group, some of whom would have volunteered had they been invited and some of whom (the bona fide nonvolunteers) would have refused. A comparison between a group of volunteers and a group comprised of volunteers plus nonvolunteers (in unknown proportion) should not yield a difference so large as a comparison between volunteers and nonvolunteers. Perhaps, then, when volunteers and nonvolunteers are more clearly differentiated there may be significant interactions between the experimental variable and the volunteer variable.

Before leaving the Hayes, Meltzer, and Lundberg study one additional possibility can be noted. Since the conscriptees and the paid volunteers were contacted at different times of the school year, it is possible that the differences between the two groups were confounded by temporal academic variables, e.g., time to next examination period as well as by differences in the subject pools available at the two periods of the year.

B. The Rosnow and Rosenthal Study (1966)

The primary purpose of this experiment was to examine the differential effects of persuasive communications on volunteer and nonvolunteer samples. Approximately half of the 42 female undergraduates had volunteered for a fictitious experiment in perception, and half had not volunteered. Both the volunteer and nonvolunteer subjects then were assigned at randon to one of three groups. One group of subjects was exposed to a pro-fraternity communication; a second group was exposed to an anti-fraternity communication, and a third group received neither communication. For all subjects, prior opinions about fraternities had been unobtrusively measured one week earlier by means of fraternity opinion items embedded in a 16-item opinion survey. After exposure to pro-, anti-, or no-communication about fraternities, subjects were retested for their opinions.

Table IV shows the mean opinion change scores for each experimental condition separately for volunteers and nonvolunteers. The associated probability levels are based on t tests for correlated means, and they suggest that while opinion changes were not dramatic in their p values, they were large in magnitude and greater than might be ascribed to chance. In a set of six ps, only one would be expected to reach the .17 level by chance alone. In this study, three of the six ps reached that level despite the average of only 6 df per group. The only group to show opinion change significant at the .05 level was that comprised of volunteers exposed to the anti-fraternity communication.

Table V shows an alternative analysis in which the experimental groups' opinion changes are compared with one another separately for volunteers and nonvolunteers. The overall effect of the pro- versus anti-fraternity communications was not significantly greater among volunteers than among nonvolunteers. The magnitude of the effect, however, reached a p of .004 among volunteers compared to a p of .07 among

TABLE IV

OPINION CHANGE AMONG VOLUNTEERS AND NONVOLUNTEERS

Treatment	Volunteers		Nonvolunteers	
	Change	Two-tail $p \leq$	Change	Two-tail $p \leq$
Pro-fraternity	+1.67 (9)	.20	+2.50 (6)	.15
Control	+0.40 (5)	.90	−0.91 (11)	.15
Anti-fraternity	−3.50 (6)	.05	−1.20 (5)	.50

Note. A positive valence indicates that opinions changed in a pro-fraternity direction; a negative valence, in an anti-fraternity direction. Numbers in parentheses indicate the sample size.

TABLE V

EFFECTIVENESS OF ONE-SIDED COMMUNICATIONS
AMONG VOLUNTEERS AND NONVOLUNTEERS

Treatment difference	Volunteers	Nonvolunteers
Pro minus control	+1.27	+3.41[b]
Control minus anti	+3.90[b]	+0.29
Pro minus anti	+5.17[a]	+3.70[c]

[a] $p = .004$

[b] $p = .05$

[c] $p = .07$

nonvolunteers. An investigator employing a strict decision model of inference and adopting an alpha level of .05 or .01 would have reached different conclusions had his experiment been conducted with volunteers rather than nonvolunteers.

Table V also shows that for volunteers the anti-fraternity communication was more effective, while for nonvolunteers the pro-fraternity communication was more effective (interaction $p < .05$). It appears, then, that volunteer status can, at times, interact with experimental manipulations to affect experimental outcomes.

can only speculate on why the particular interaction occurred. Some evidence is available to suggest that faculty experimenters were seen as being moderately anti-fraternity. Perhaps volunteers, who tend to show a greater need for approval, felt they would please the experimenter more by being more responsive to his anti-fraternity communication than to his pro-fraternity communication. That does not explain, however, why nonvolunteers tended to show the opposite effect unless we assume that they also saw the experimenter as being more anti-fraternity and resisted giving in to what they saw as his unwarranted influence attempts.

Within each of the three experimental conditions the pretest-posttest reliabilities were computed separately for volunteers and nonvolunteers. The mean reliability (rho) of the volunteer subjects was .35, significantly lower than the mean reliability of the nonvolunteers (.97) at $p < .0005$. Volunteers, then, were more heterogeneous in their opinion change behavior, perhaps reflecting their greater willingness to be influenced in the direction they felt was demanded by the situation (see the chapter by Orne). The findings of this study as well as our review of volunteer characteristics suggest that volunteers may more often than nonvolunteers be motivated to confirm what they perceive to be the experimenter's hypothesis.

C. The Rosnow and Rosenthal Study (1967)

This experiment will be described in greater detail than the other studies summarized because it has not previously been published.* As in our earlier study (Rosnow and Rosenthal, 1966), the primary purpose was to examine the differential effects of communications on volunteer and nonvolunteer samples. In this study, however, two-sided as well as one-sided communications were employed.

Four introductory sociology classes at Boston University provided the 103 male and 160 female subjects. All of the students were invited by their instructors to volunteer for either or both of two fictitious psychological experiments; one of the experiments purported to deal with psycho-acoustics, the other, with social groups. Approximately one week later, all of the subjects in each class simultaneously were presented by the experimenter with one of five different booklets, representing the five treatments in this after-only design. On the cover page of every booklet were four items, which inquired as to the subject's (a) sex, (b) cigarette smoking habit, (c) coffee drinking habit, and (d) order of birth. These items were followed, beginning on the next page, by

* We thank Robert Holz, Robert Margolis, and Jeffrey Saloway for their help in recruiting volunteers and George Smiltens for his help in data processing.

a one-sided, two-sided, or control communication describing a brief epi-
sode in a day in the life of "Jim," a fictitious individual based on the
character described by Luchins (1957). The last page of every booklet
contained four 9-point graphic scales on which the subject was asked
to rate Jim in terms of how (a) friendly or unfriendly, (b) forward
or shy, (c) social or unsocial, (d) aggressive or passive he seemed,
based on the information contained in the communication.

Communications. Two one-sided communications were used. One
of the communications was a positive appeal (P), which portrayed Jim
as friendly and outgoing:

> Jim left the house to get some stationery. He walked out into
> the sun-filled street with two of his friends, basking in the sun as
> he walked. Jim entered the stationery store which was full of
> people. Jim talked with an acquaintance while he waited for the
> clerk to catch his eye. On his way out, he stopped to chat with a
> school friend who was just coming into the store. Leaving the store,
> he walked toward school. On his way out he met the girl to whom
> he had been introduced the night before. They talked for a short
> while, and then Jim left for school.

The other one-sided communication was a negative appeal (N). It portrayed Jim as shy and unfriendly:

> After school Jim left the classroom alone. Leaving the school.
> he started on his long walk home. The street was brilliantly filled
> with sunshine. Jim walked down the street on the shady side.
> Coming down the street toward him, he saw the pretty girl whom
> he had met on the previous evening. Jim crossed the street and
> entered a candy store. The store was crowded with students, and
> he noticed a few familiar faces. Jim waited quietly until the coun-
> terman caught his eye and then gave his order. Taking his drink,
> he sat down at a side table. When he had finished his drink he
> went home.

Two other descriptions, or two-sided communications, were constructed by combining the positive and negative appeals. When the
P description was immediately followed by the N description, without
a paragraph indentation between the two passages, we refer to this two-
sided communication as PN. When N immediately preceded P, we refer
to this two-sided communication an NP. All four communications were
introduced by the following passage:

> In everyday life we sometimes form impressions of people based
> on what we read or hear about them. On a given school day Jim

walks down the street, sees a girl he knows, buys some stationery, stops at the candy store. On the next page you will find a paragraph about Jim. Please read the paragraph through only once. On the basis of this information alone, answer to the best of your ability the questions on the last page of this booklet.

The control subjects received just the introductory passage above with the sentences omitted referring to the paragraph on the following page, succeeded immediately by the four rating scales.

Some of the results of this study have already been given in the relevant sections of our discussion of volunteer characteristics. Thus, females volunteered significantly more than males ($X^2 = 11.78$, $df = 2$, $p < .005$); birth order was unrelated to volunteering ($X^2 = 0.54$, $df = 2$, $p > .75$); for the total sample, and for female subjects alone, smoking and coffee drinking were unrelated to volunteering. Among male subjects, however, volunteers tended to smoke less ($p = .07$) and drink less coffee ($p = .06$) than nonvolunteers. Even among male subjects, smoking and drinking accounted for less than 4 per cent of the variance in volunteering behavior.

Because of the very unequal numbers of subjects within subgroups, all analyses of each of the four ratings made by subjects were based on unweighted means. The analyses of variance of the five treatments by volunteer status by sex of subject showed only significant effects of treatments. For each of the four ratings analyzed in turn, ps for treatment were less than .001. In these overall analyses no other ps were less than .05.

Our greatest interest, however, is in the interaction of volunteer status with treatments. This interaction was computed for each of the four dependent variables, and only two of the associated ps were less than .20. For the variable "friendly," p was .12; for the variable "social," p was .17. With so many treatment conditions, however, these Fs for unordered means are relatively insensitive, and it may be instructive to examine separately for volunteers and nonvolunteers the specific experimental effects in which we are most interested. Table VI shows separately for volunteers and nonvolunteers the difference between the control group mean and the mean of each of the four experimental groups in turn. Each of the entries in Table VI is based on the data from both male and female subjects combined without weighting.

It can be seen from Table VI that the two one-sided communications were most effective among all subjects. Although these effects were not significantly greater among volunteers than among nonvolunteers, the trend was in that direction. Of the eight tests for the significance of

TABLE VI

EFFECTIVENESS AMONG VOLUNTEERS AND NONVOLUNTEERS OF ONE-SIDED AND
TWO-SIDED COMMUNICATIONS AS COMPARED WITH A "ZERO" CONTROL

Treatment difference	Ratings	Volunteers	Nonvolunteers
Positive (P)	Friendly	+2.18[a]	+1.78[a]
minus control	Forward	+1.45[a]	+0.42
	Social	+1.92[a]	+1.30[b]
	Aggressive	+1.15[b]	+0.20
Negative (N) minus control	Friendly	−1.55[a]	−0.70
	Forward	−2.04[a]	−1.68[a]
	Social	−2.22[a]	−1.91[a]
	Aggressive	−1.36[a]	−1.56[a]
PN minus control	Friendly	−0.58	+0.64
	Forward	−0.34	−0.24
	Social	−1.08[b]	+0.24
	Aggressive	−0.34	−0.34
NP minus control	Friendly	+0.30	+0.38
	Forward	+0.04	−0.52
	Social	−0.30	+0.06
	Aggressive	−0.45	−0.52

Note. Ratings could range from +4.00, or favoring strongly the positive appeal, to
−4.00, strongly favoring the negative appeal. Entries in the table are differences
between means of treatment conditions.

[a] $p \leq .01$

[b] $p \leq .05$

the effectiveness of one-sided communications, all eight reached the
.05 level among volunteers, while only five of the eight tests reached
the .05 level among nonvolunteers. An investigator employing similar
sample sizes, and a strict decision model of inference with an alpha
of either .05 or .01, would arrive at different conclusions over one-third
of the time were he to employ volunteer rather than nonvolunteer samples. Most important, perhaps, is that whenever differences in significance
levels occurred it was the volunteers who favored the experimental hypothesis. When the communication was positive, volunteers became more
positive than nonvolunteers; when the communication was negative, volunteers became more negative than nonvolunteers.

When we consider the effects of two-sided communications there appears to be less volunteer bias. The two-sided communications were
ineffective generally regardless of whether they were compared to the
control group (as shown in Table VI) or to each other (not shown).

Of the 16 mean differences indicating the effectiveness of the two-sided communications shown in Table VI, only one was significant at the .05 level, just about what one might expect by chance. Nevertheless, that one "effect" occurred among volunteers.

D. The Marmer Study (1967)

Following a similar recruitment procedure as was used in the preceding study, Marmer administered to both volunteer and nonvolunteer subjects treatments adapted from a standard deception introduced by cognitive dissonance theorists to study the effects of decisional importance and the relative attractiveness of unchosen alternatives on post-decisional dissonance reduction. The study was carried out in three phases. In the first phase, undergraduate women at Boston University were recruited for a fictitious psychology experiment. The second phase, which began immediately thereafter, consisted of having the subjects— volunteer and nonvolunteer alike—complete an opinion survey that was represented to them as a national opinion poll of college students being conducted by the University of Wisconsin. The third phase was carried out one month later. At that time a third experimenter, who was represented as an employee of the Boston University Communication Research Center, had the subjects choose between two alternative ideas whose importance they had evaluated in Phase II. The ideas included, for example, that there should be more no-grade courses at universities, that students should unionize in order to gain a more powerful voice in running the university, that there should be courses in the use and control of hallucinatory drugs, and that there should be courses in sex education. For half the subjects a condition of high importance was created by informing them that their choices would be taken into consideration by the administration in selecting one idea to be instituted at Boston University the following year. The remaining subjects, constituting a low importance condition, were simply instructed to choose one of the two proffered alternatives, but no information was conveyed to them which would have implied that their decisions had any practical importance. Within each of these treatments, attractiveness was manipulated by having approximately half the subjects choose between alternatives that had earlier been rated either close together (high relative attractiveness of the unchosen alternative) or far apart (low attractiveness).

As predicted by cognitive dissonance theory, there was a greater spreading apart of the choice alternatives when the subjects re-evaluated their importance under conditions of high versus low manipulated importance ($p = .11$) and high versus low attractiveness ($p < .001$). This first dependent variable, however—the spreading apart of the choice alternatives after the subject had irrevocably decided to choose one of the two ideas—was not directly influenced by the volunteer variable nor by any significant interaction of volunteering and either decisional importance or attractiveness. Clearly, then, volunteering does not consistently interact with other independent variables to affect experimental outcomes. It would appear that the deception may have functioned in a similar manner as theoretically the two-sided communication did in the preceding experiment, in effect removing or disguising demand characteristics that might otherwise favor one direction of response over another.

A second dependent variable, ratings of the survey in Phase III, was employed by Marmer as a check on the success of the manipulation of perceived importance. Somewhat surprisingly, volunteers saw the Boston University survey as less important than did the nonvolunteers. In addition, volunteer status showed a tendency ($p < .08$) to interact with the experimental manipulation of the importance of the subjects' rating decisions. Nonvolunteers were more affected than volunteers by that manipulation, a finding that may weaken somewhat our hypothesis that volunteers are more sensitive and accommodating to the perceived demand characteristics of the situation.

VII. CONCLUSIONS

We began this chapter with McNemar's lament that ours is a science of sophomores. We conclude this chapter with the question of whether McNemar was too generous. Often ours seems to be a science of just those sophomores who volunteer to participate in our research and who also keep their appointment with the investigator. Our purpose in this chapter has been to summarize what has been learned about the act of volunteering and the more or less stable characteristics of those people who are likely to find their way into the role of data-contributor in behavioral research. Later in the chapter we considered the implications of volunteer bias for the respresentativeness of descriptive statistics and for the nature of the relationships found between two or more variables in behavioral research.

The act of volunteering was viewed as a nonrandom event, determined in part by more general situational variables and in part by more specific personal attributes of the person asked to participate as subject in behavioral research. More general situational variables postulated as increasing the likelihood of volunteering included the following:

1. Having only a relatively less attractive alternative to volunteering.
2. Increasing the intensity of the request to volunteer.
3. Increasing the perception that others in a similar situation would volunteer.
4. Increasing acquaintanceship with, the perceived prestige of, and liking for the experimenter.
5. Having greater intrinsic interest in the subject matter being investigated.
6. Increasing the subjective probability of subsequently being favorably evaluated or not unfavorably evaluated by the experimenter.

On the basis of studies conducted both in the laboratory and in the field, it seemed reasonable to postulate with some confidence that the following characteristics would be found more often among people who volunteer than among those who do not volunteer for behavioral research:

1. Higher educational level,
2. Higher occupational status,
3. Higher need for approval,
4. Higher intelligence,
5. Lower authoritarianism.

With less confidence we can also postulate that more often than non-volunteers, volunteers tend to be:

6. More sociable,
7. More arousal seeking,
8. More unconventional,
9. More often firstborn,
10. Younger.

Two additional and somewhat more complicated relationships may also be postulated: (a) In survey-type research volunteers tend to be better adjusted than nonvolunteers, but in medical research volunteers tend to be more maladjusted than nonvolunteers. (b) For standard tasks women tend to volunteer more than men, but for unusual tasks women tend to volunteer less than men. These more complicated relationships illustrate the likelihood that there may often be variables that complicate the nature of the relationship between the act of volunteering and various personal characteristics. Two such moderating variables appear to be the sex of the subject and the nature of the task for which volunteering is requested.

Our survey suggests that those who volunteer for behavioral research often differ in significant ways from those who do not volunteer. Most of the research that is summarized here tends to underestimate the effect of these differences on data obtained from volunteer subjects. In most of the studies, comparisons were made only between those who indicated that they would participate as research subjects versus those who indicated that they would not. However, there is considerable evidence to suggest that, of those who volunteer, a substantial proportion will never contribute their responses to the data pool. The evidence suggests that these "no-shows" are more like nonvolunteers than they are like the volunteers who keep their appointments. Therefore, comparing nonvolunteers with verbal volunteers is really comparing nonvolunteers with some other nonvolunteers mixed in unknown proportion with true volunteers. Differences found between nonvolunteers and verbal volunteers will, therefore, underestimate differences between those who do, and do not, contribute data to the behavioral researcher.

To the extent that true volunteers differ from nonvolunteers, the employment of volunteer samples can lead to seriously biased estimates of various population parameters. In addition, however, there is the possibility that volunteer status may interact with experimental variables in such a way as to increase the probability of inferential errors of the first and second kind. The direct empirical evidence at this time is rather scanty and equivocal, but there are indirect, theoretical considerations that suggest the possibility that volunteers may more often than nonvolunteers provide data that support the investigator's hypothesis.

REFERENCES

Abeles, N., Iscoe, I., and Brown, W. F. Some factors influencing the random sampling of college students. *Public Opinion Quarterly*, 1954–1955, **18**, 419–423.

Altus, W. D. Birth order and its sequelae. *Science*, 1966, **151**, 44–49.

Aronson, E., Carlsmith, J. M., and Darley, J. M. The effects of expectancy on volunteering for an unpleasant experience. *Journal of Abnormal and Social Psychology*, 1963, **66**, 220–224.

Beach, F. A. The snark was a boojum. *American Psychologist*, 1950, **5**, 115–124.

Beach, F. A. Experimental investigations of species specific behavior. *American Psychologist*, 1960, **15**, 1–18.

Bean, W. B. The ethics of experimentation on human beings. *In* S. O. Waife and A. P. Shapiro (Eds.), *The clinical evaluation of new drugs*. New York: Hoeber-Harper, 1959, 76–84.

Bell, C. R. Psychological versus sociological variables in studies of volunteer bias in surveys. *Journal of Applied Psychology*, 1961, **45**, 80–85.

Bell, C. R. Personality characteristics of volunteers for psychological studies. *British Journal of Social and Clinical Psychology*, 1962, **1**, 81–95.

Belson, W. A. Volunteer bias in test-room groups. *Public Opinion Quarterly*, 1960, **24**, 115–126.

Bennett, Edith B. Discussion, decision, commitment and consensus in "group decision". *Human Relations*, 1955, **8**, 251–273.

Benson, L. E. Mail surveys can be valuable. *Public Opinion Quarterly*, 1946, **10**, 234–241.

Benson, S., Booman, W. P., and Clark, K. E. A study of interview refusal. *Journal of Applied Psychology*, 1951, **35**, 116–119.

Blake, R. R., Berkowitz, H., Bellamy, R. Q., and Mouton, Jane S. Volunteering as an avoidance act. *Journal of Abnormal and Social Psychology*, 1956, **53**, 154–156.

Boucher, R. G., and Hilgard, E. R. Volunteer bias in hypnotic experimentation. *American Journal of Clinical Hypnosis*, 1962, **5**, 49–51.

Brady, J. P., Levitt, E. E., and Lubin, B. Expressed fear of hypnosis and volunteering behavior. *Journal of Nervous and Mental Disease*, 1961, **133**, 216–217.

Brightbill, R., and Zamansky, H. S. The conceptual space of good and poor hypnotic subjects: a preliminary exploration. *International Journal of Clinical and Experimental Hypnosis*, 1963, **11**, 112–121.

Brock, T. C., and Becker, G. Birth order and subject recruitment. *Journal of Social Psychology*, 1965, **65**, 63–66.

Brower, D. The role of incentive in psychological research. *Journal of General Psychology*, 1948, **39**, 145–147.

Brunswik, E. *Perception and the representative design of psychological experiments.* Berkeley: University of California Press, 1956.

Burchinal, L. G. Personality characteristics and sample bias. *Journal of Applied Psychology*, 1960, **44**, 172–174.

Capra, P. C., and Dittes, J. E. Birth order as a selective factor among volunteer subjects. *Journal of Abnormal and Social Psychology*, 1962, **64**, 302.

Christie, R. Experimental naïveté and experiential naïveté. *Psychological Bulletin*, 1951, **48**, 327–339.

Clark, K. E. *et al.* Privacy and behavioral research. *Science*, 1967, **155**, 535–538.

Clausen, J. A., and Ford, R. N. Controlling bias in mail questionnaires. *Journal of the American Statistical Association*, 1947, **42**, 497–511.

Cochran, W. G., Mosteller, F., and Tukey, J. W. Statistical problems of the Kinsey report. *Journal of the American Statistical Association*, 1953, **48**, 673–716.

Coffin, T. E. Some conditions of suggestion and suggestibility. *Psychological Monographs*, 1941, **53**, No. 4 (Whole No. 241).

Crowne, D. P., and Marlowe, D. *The approval motive.* New York: Wiley, 1964.

Dittes, J. E. Birth order and vulnerability to differences in acceptance. *American Psychologist*, 1961, **16**, 358. (Abstract).

Edgerton, H. A., Britt, S. H., and Norman, R. D. Objective differences among various types of respondents to a mailed questionnaire. *American Sociological Review*, 1947, **12**, 435–444.

Edwards, C. N. Characteristics of volunteers and nonvolunteers for a sleep and hypnotic experiment. *American Journal of Clinical Hypnosis*, 1968, **11**, 26–29.

Esecover, H., Malitz, S., and Wilkens, B. Clinical profiles of paid normal subjects volunteering for hallucinogenic drug studies. *American Journal of Psychiatry*, 1961, **117**, 910–915.

Foster, R. J. Acquiescent response set as a measure of acquiescence. *Journal of Abnormal and Social Psychology*, 1961, **63**, 155–160.

Franzen, R., and Lazarsfeld, P. F. Mail questionnaire as a research problem. *Journal of Psychology*, 1945, **20**, 293–320.

French, J. R. P. Personal communication. August 19, 1963.

Frey, A. H., and Becker, W. C. Some personality correlates of subjects who fail to appear for experimental appointments. *Journal of Consulting Psychology*, 1958, **22**, 164.

Frye, R. L., and Adams, H. E. Effect of the volunteer variable on leaderless group discussion experiments. *Psychological Reports*, 1959, **5**, 184.

Gaudet, H., and Wilson, E. C. Who escapes the personal investigator? *Journal of Applied Psychology*, 1940, **24**, 773–777.

Green, D. R. Volunteering and the recall of interrupted tasks. *Journal of Abnormal and Social Psychology*, 1963, **66**, 397–401.

Greene, E. B. Abnormal adjustments to experimental situations. *Psychological Bulletin*, 1937, **34**, 747–748. (Abstract).

Hayes, D. P., Meltzer, L., and Lundberg, Signe. Information distribution, interdependence, and activity levels. *Sociometry*, 1968, **31**, 162–179.

Heilizer, F. An exploration of the relationship between hypnotizability and anxiety and/or neuroticism. *Journal of Consulting Psychology*, 1960, **24**, 432–436.

Hilgard, E. R. Personal communication. February 6, 1967.

Hilgard, E. R., Weitzenhoffer, A. M., Landes, J., and Moore, Rosemarie K. The distribution of susceptibility to hypnosis in a student population: a study using the Stanford Hypnotic Susceptibility Scale. *Psychological Monographs*, 1961, **75**, 8 (Whole No. 512).

Himelstein, P. Taylor scale characteristics of volunteers and nonvolunteers for psychological experiments. *Journal of Abnormal and Social Psychology*, 1956, **52**, 138–139.

Hood, T. C. The volunteer subject: patterns of self-presentation and the decision to participate in social psychological experiments. Unpublished master's thesis, Duke University, 1963.

Hood, T. C., and Back, K. W. Patterns of self-disclosure and the volunteer: the decision to participate in small groups experiments. Paper read at Southern Sociological Society, Atlanta, April, 1967.

Howe, E. S. Quantitative motivational differences between volunteers and nonvolunteers for a psychological experiment. *Journal of Applied Psychology*, 1960, **44**, 115–120.

Hyman, H., and Sheatsley, P. B. The scientific method. *In* D. P. Geddes (Ed.), *An Analysis of the Kinsey Reports*. New York: New American Library, 1954, 93–118.

Jackson, C. W., and Pollard, J. C. Some nondeprivation variables which influence the "effects" of experimental sensory deprivation. *Journal of Abnormal Psychology*, 1966, **71**, 383–388.

Kavanau, J. L. Behavior: confinement, adaptation, and compulsory regimes in laboratory studies. *Science*, 1964, **143**, 490.

Kavanau, J. L. Behavior of captive white-footed mice. *Science*, 1967, **155**, 1623–1639.

King, A. F. Ordinal position and the Episcopal Clergy. Unpublished bachelor's thesis, Harvard University, 1967.

Kruglov, L. P., and Davidson, H. H. The willingness to be interviewed: a selective factor in sampling. *Journal of Social Psychology*, 1953, **38**, 39–47.

Larson, R. F., and Catton, W. R., Jr. Can the mail-back bias contribute to a study's validity? *American Sociological Review*, 1959, **24**, 243–245.

Lasagna, L., and von Felsinger, J. M. The volunteer subject in research. *Science,* 1954, **120**, 359–361.

Leipold, W. D., and James, R. L. Characteristics of shows and no-shows in a psychological experiment. *Psychological Reports,* 1962, **11**, 171–174.

Levitt, E. E., Lubin, B., and Brady, J. P. The effect of the pseudovolunteer on studies of volunteers for psychology experiments. *Journal of Applied Psychology,* 1962, **46**, 72–75.

Levitt, E. E., Lubin, B., and Zuckerman, M. Note on the attitude toward hypnosis of volunteers and nonvolunteers for an hypnosis experiment. *Psychological Reports,* 1959, **5**, 712.

Levitt, E. E., Lubin, B., and Zuckerman, M. The effect of incentives on volunteering for an hypnosis experiment. *International Journal of Clinical and Experimental Hypnosis,* 1962, **10**, 39–41.

Locke, H. J. Are volunteer interviewees representative? *Social Problems,* 1954, **1**, 143–146.

London, P. Subject characteristics in hypnosis research: Part I. A survey of experience, interest, and opinion. *International Journal of Clinical and Experimental Hypnosis,* 1961, **9**, 151–161.

London, P., Cooper, L. M., and Johnson, H. J. Subject characteristics in hypnosis research. II. Attitudes towards hypnosis, volunteer status, and personality measures. III. Some correlates of hypnotic susceptibility. *International Journal of Clinical and Experimental Hypnosis,* 1962, **10**, 13–21.

London, P., and Rosenhan, D. Personality dynamics. *Annual Review of Psychology,* 1964, **15**, 447–492.

Lubin, B., Brady, J. P., and Levitt, E. E. A comparison of personality characteristics of volunteers and nonvolunteers for hypnosis experiments. *Journal of Clinical Psychology,* 1962, **18**, 341–343. (a)

Lubin, B., Brady, J. P., and Levitt, E. E. Volunteers and nonvolunteers for an hypnosis experiment. *Diseases of the Nervous System,* 1962, **23**, 642–643. (b)

Lubin, B., Levitt, E. E., and Zuckerman, M. Some personality differences between responders and nonresponders to a survey questionnaire. *Journal of Consulting Psychology,* 1962, **26**, 192.

Luchins, A. S. Primacy-recency in impression formation. *In* C. I. Hovland *et al., The order of presentation in persuasion.* New Haven: Yale University Press, 1957, 33–61.

Marmer, Roberta S. The effects of volunteer status on dissonance reduction. Unpublished master's thesis, Boston University, 1967.

Martin, R. M., and Marcuse, F. L. Characteristics of volunteers and nonvolunteers for hypnosis. *Journal of Clinical and Experimental Hypnosis,* 1957, **5**, 176–180.

Martin, R. M., and Marcuse, F. L. Characteristics of volunteers and nonvolunteers in psychological experimentation. *Journal of Consulting Psychology,* 1958, **22**, 475–479.

Maslow, A. H. Self-esteem (dominance feelings) and sexuality in women. *Journal of Social Psychology,* 1942, **16**, 259–293.

Maslow, A. H., and Sakoda, J. M. Volunteer-error in the Kinsey study. *Journal of Abnormal and Social Psychology,* 1952 **47**, 259–262.

Matthysse, S. W. Differential effects of religious communications. Unpublished doctoral dissertation, Harvard University, 1966.

McDavid, J. W. Approval-seeking motivation and the volunteer subject. *Journal of Personality and Social Psychology,* 1965, **2**, 115–117.

McNemar, Q. Opinion-attitude methodology. *Psychological Bulletin*, 1946, **43**, 289–374.

Miller, S. E. Psychology experiments without subjects' consent. *Science*, 1966, **152**, 15.

Myers, T. I., Murphy, D. B., Smith, S., and Goffard, S. J. Experimental studies of sensory deprivation and social isolation. Technical Report 66–8, Contract DA 44–188–ARO–2, HumRRO, Washington, D.C.: George Washington University, 1966.

Newman, M. *Personality differences between volunteers and nonvolunteers for psychological investigations.* (Doctoral dissertation, New York University School of Education) Ann Arbor, Mich.: University Microfilms, 1956, No. 19,999.

Norman, R. D. A review of some problems related to the mail questionnaire technique. *Educational and Psychological Measurement*, 1948, **8**, 235–247.

Ora, J. P., Jr. Characteristics of the volunteer for psychological investigations. Technical Report, No. 27, November, 1965, Vanderbilt University, Contract Nonr 2149 (03).

Ora, J. P., Jr. Personality characteristics of college freshman volunteers for psychological experiments. Unpublished master's thesis, Vanderbilt University, 1966.

Orlans, H. Developments in federal policy toward university research. *Science*, 1967, **155**, 665–668.

Pace, C. R. Factors influencing questionnaire returns from former university students. *Journal of Applied Psychology*, 1939, **23**, 388–397.

Pan, Ju-Shu. Social characteristics of respondents and non-respondents in a questionnaire study of later maturity. *Journal of Applied Psychology*, 1951, **35**, 120–121.

Perlin, S., Pollin, W., and Butler, R. N. The experimental subject: 1. The psychiatric evaluation and selection of a volunteer population. *American Medical Association Archives of Neurology and Psychiatry*, 1958, **80**, 65–70.

Pollin, W., and Perlin, S. Psychiatric evaluation of "normal control" volunteers. *American Journal of Psychiatry*, 1958, **115**, 129–133.

Poor, D. The social psychology of questionnaires. Unpublished bachelor's thesis, Harvard University, 1967.

Reuss, C. F. Differences between persons responding and not responding to a mailed questionnaire. *American Sociological Review*, 1943, **8**, 433–438.

Richards, T. W. Personality of subjects who volunteer for research on a drug (mescaline). *Journal of Projective Techniques*, 1960, **24**, 424–428.

Richter, C. P. Rats, man, and the welfare state. *American Psychologist*, 1959, **14**, 18–28.

Riecken, H. W. A program for research on experiments in social psychology. *In* N. F. Washburne, (Ed.), *Decisions, values and groups.* Vol. II. New York: Pergamon, 1962, 25–41.

Riggs, Margaret M., and Kaess, W. Personality differences between volunteers and nonvolunteers. *Journal of Psychology*, 1955, **40**, 229–245.

Robins, Lee N. The reluctant respondent. *Public Opinion Quarterly*, 1963, **27**, 276–286.

Rokeach, M. Psychology experiments without subjects' consent. *Science*, 1966, **152**, 15.

Rosen, E. Differences between volunteers and non-volunteers for psychological studies. *Journal of Applied Psychology*, 1951, **35**, 185–193.

Rosenbaum, M. E. The effect of stimulus and background factors on the volunteering response. *Journal of Abnormal and Social Psychology*, 1956, **53**, 118–121.

Rosenbaum, M. E., and Blake, R. R. Volunteering as a function of field structure. *Journal of Abnormal and Social Psychology*, 1955, **50**, 193–196.

Rosenhan, D. On the social psychology of hypnosis research. *In* J. E. Gordon (Ed.), *Handbook of clinical and experimental hypnosis.* New York: Macmillan, 1967, 481–510.

Rosenthal, R. The volunteer subject. *Human Relations*, 1965, **18**, 389–406.

Rosenthal, R. *Experimenter effects in behavioral research.* New York: Appleton-Century-Crofts, 1966.

Rosnow, R. L., and Rosenthal, R. Volunteer subjects and the results of opinion change studies. *Psychological Reports*, 1966, **19**, 1183–1187.

Rosnow, R. L., and Rosenthal, R. Unpublished data (described in this chapter), 1967.

Ruebhausen, O. M., and Brim, O. G. Privacy and behavioral research. *American Psychologist*, 1966, **21**, 423–437.

Schachter, S. *The psychology of affiliation.* Stanford, Calif.: Stanford University Press, 1959.

Schachter, S., and Hall, R. Group-derived restraints and audience persuasion. *Human Relations*, 1952, **5**, 397–406.

Scheier, I. H. To be or not to be a guinea pig: preliminary data on anxiety and the volunteer for experiment. *Psychological Reports*, 1959, **5**, 239–240.

Schubert, D. S. P. Arousal seeking as a motivation for volunteering: MMPI scores and central-nervous-system-stimulant use as suggestive of a trait. *Journal of Projective Techniques and Personality Assessment*, 1964, **28**, 337–340.

Schultz, D. P. Birth order of volunteers for sensory restriction research. *Journal of Social Psychology*, 1967, **73**, 71–73. (a)

Schultz, D. P. Sensation-seeking and volunteering for sensory deprivation. Paper read at Eastern Psychological Association, Boston, April, 1967. (b)

Schultz, D. P. The volunteer subject in sensory restriction research. *Journal of Social Psychology*, 1967, **72**, 123–124. (c)

Shuttleworth, F. K. Sampling errors involved in incomplete returns to mail questionnaires. *Psychological Bulletin*, 1940, **37**, 437. (Abstract)

Siegman, A. Responses to a personality questionnaire by volunteers and nonvolunteers to a Kinsey interview. *Journal of Abnormal and Social Psychology*, 1956, **52**, 280–281.

Silverman, I. Note on the relationship of self-esteem to subject self-selection. *Perceptual and Motor Skills*, 1964, **19**, 769–770.

Smart, R. G. Subject selection bias in psychological research. *Canadian Psychologist*, 1966, **7a**, 115–121.

Stanton, F. Notes on the validity of mail questionnaire returns. *Journal of Applied Psychology*, 1939, **23**, 95–104.

Staples, F. R., and Walters, R. H. Anxiety, birth order, and susceptibility to social influence. *Journal of Abnormal and Social Psychology*, 1961, **62**, 716–719.

Suchman, E., and McCandless, B. Who answers questionnaires? *Journal of Applied Psychology*, 1940, **24**, 758–769.

Suedfeld, P. Birth order of volunteers for sensory deprivation. *Journal of Abnormal and Social Psychology*, 1964, **68**, 195–196.

Varela, J. A. A cross-cultural replication of an experiment involving birth order. *Journal of Abnormal and Social Psychology*, 1964, **69**, 456–457.

Wallin, P. Volunteer subjects as a source of sampling bias. *American Journal of Sociology*, 1949, **54**, 539–544.

Ward, C. D. A further examination of birth order as a selective factor among volunteer subjects. *Journal of Abnormal and Social Psychology*, 1964, 69, 311–313.

Warren, J. R. Birth order and social behavior. *Psychological Bulletin*, 1966, 65, 38–49.

Weiss, J. M., Wolf, A., and Wiltsey, R. G. Birth order, recruitment conditions, and preferences for participation in group versus non-group experiments. *American Psychologist*, 1963, 18, 356. (Abstract)

Wicker, A. W. Requirements for protecting privacy of human subjects: some implications for generalization of research findings. *American Psychologist*, 1968, 23, 70–72.

Wilson, P. R., and Patterson, J. Sex differences in volunteering behavior. *Psychological Reports*, 1965, 16, 976.

Wolf, A., and Weiss, J. H. Birth order, recruitment conditions, and volunteering preference. *Journal of Personality and Social Psychology*, 1965, 2, 269–273.

Wolfensberger, W. Ethical issues in research with human subjects. *Science*, 1967, 155, 47–51.

Wolfgang, A. Sex differences in abstract ability of volunteers and nonvolunteers for concept learning experiments. *Psychological Reports*, 1967, 21, 509–512.

Wolfle, D. Research with human subjects. *Science*, 1960, 132, 989.

Wrightsman, L. S. Predicting college students' participation in required psychology experiments. *American Psychologist*, 1966, 21, 812–813.

Zamansky, H. S., and Brightbill, R. F. Attitude differences of volunteers and nonvolunteers and of susceptible and nonsusceptible hypnotic subjects. *International Journal of Clinical and Experimental Hypnosis*, 1965, 13, 279–290.

Zimmer, H. Validity of extrapolating nonresponse bias from mail questionnaire follow-ups. *Journal of Applied Psychology*, 1956, 40, 117-121.

Zuckerman, M., Schultz, D. P., and Hopkins, T. R. Sensation seeking and volunteering for sensory deprivation and hypnosis experiments. *Journal of Consulting Psychology*, 1967, 31, 358–363.

Chapter 4

PRETEST SENSITIZATION*

Robert E. Lana

Temple University

When Max Planck sought an explanation for heat radiating from a black body at high temperatures, he focused not upon radiation per se but upon the radiating atom and thus became one of the men most responsible for beginning a line of thought and research which ended in the formulation of quantum theory. The development of quantum theory eventually led to major reconceptions in the field of physics, which challenged the Newtonian models that were then predominant. The wave-particle controversy was recognized as a result of the work of Schrödinger and others, and this provided a context for an interpretation of quantum theory and, within that context, for the recognition of what was called the principle of indeterminancy.

It is possible to speak of the position and the velocity of an electron as one would in Newtonian mechanics, and one can observe and measure both of these quantities. However, one cannot determine both quantities simultaneously with a limitless degree of accuracy. Relations between quantities such as these are called relations of uncertainty, or indeterminacy. Similar relations can be formulated for other experimental situations. The wave and particle theories of radiation—two complementary explanations of the same phenomenon—were interpreted in such a manner. There were limitations to the use of both the wave and the

* Many of the studies done by the author and reported in this chapter were supported by the National Institute of Mental Health, United States Public Health Service.

particle concept. These limitations are expressed by the uncertainty relations, and hence any apparent contradiction between the two interpretations disappears.

The idea of uncertainty in physics can best be illustrated by a *Gedanken* (theoretical) experiment given by Heisenberg (1958, 47). "One could argue that it should at least be possible to observe the electron in its orbit. One should simply look at the atom through a microscope of a very high resolving power, then one would see the electron moving in its orbit. Such a high resolving power could to be sure not be obtained by a microscope using ordinary light, since the inaccuracy of the measurement of the position can never be smaller than the wave length of the light. But a microscope using gamma rays with a wave length smaller than the size of the atom would do. . . . The position of the electron will be known with an accuracy given by the wave length of the gamma ray. The electron may have been practically at rest before the observation. But *in the act of observation* [italics mine] at least one light quantum of the gamma ray must have passed the microscope and must first have been deflected by the electron. Therefore, the electron has been pushed by the light quantum, it has changed its momentum and velocity, and one can show that the uncertainty of this change is just big enough to guarantee the validity of the uncertainty relations." It is evident from this *Gedanken* experiment that the very act of measurement negated the possibility of observing the phenomenon as it would have occurred had it not been observed. It is important to note, however, that we are dealing with phenomena at the limits of physical existence, namely those of sub-atomic physics. Measurement of physical activity farther from this limit (or away from the limit of infinite space and time at the other end of the continuum) is not so sensitive to the influence of the measuring instrument or technique (as, for example, when one measures the speed and position of a freely falling object at sea level). Heisenberg states, "The measuring device deserves this name only if it is in close contact with the rest of the world, if there is an interaction between the device and the observer. . . . If the measuring device would be isolated from the rest of the world, it would be neither a measuring device nor could it be described in the terms of classical physics at all."

One of the implications for life sciences of the interpretation of quantum theory through appeal to uncertainty relations has been pointed out by Neils Bohr (discussed by Heisenberg, 1958, 104–105). He noted that our knowledge of a cell's being alive may be dependent upon our complete knowledge of its molecular structure. Such a complete knowledge may be achievable only by operations which would destroy the life of the cell. It is, therefore, logically possible that life precludes the complete determination of its underlying physiochemical nature.

I. THE HAWTHORNE STUDIES

Beginning in 1927, Mayo, Roethlisberger, Whitehead and Dickson (Roethlisberger and Dickson, 1939) began a series of studies in the Hawthorne plant of the Western Electric Company. That series not only launched modern industrial psychology on its current path, but also introduced the idea that the process of measurement in social psychological situations can influence what is being measured and change its characteristics. For our purposes the most pertinent results of these studies are those which are perhaps most general. The original aim of the studies was to examine the effects on production of such work conditions as illumination, temperature, hours of work, rest periods, wage rate, etc. Six female workers were observed. The interesting result was that their production increased no matter what the manipulation. Whether hours of work or rest periods were increased or decreased, production always increased. The reason given by the authors for this effect was that the women felt honored at being chosen for the experiment. They felt that they were a team and worked together for the benefit of the group as a whole. What I wish to emphasize is that from the point of view of the experimenter the fact of measurement changed not only the magnitude of the dependent variable (rate of production), but the very nature of the social situation as well.

The principle of indeterminacy found in the physical situation is, at least analogously, operating in this social psychological situation. One finds a definite relationship between the observational process of the experimenter and the natural process of the subject. If we narrow the context of our inquiry to the effect of any specific device designed to measure some relevant characteristics of the organism, we will have arrived at the principal point of departure of this paper.

II. CURRENT METHODOLOGY

The relevant state of the organism must be determined before an experimental treatment is applied in much psychological research. This is necessary since all psychological experiments are designed to test an hypothesis of change from an initial state of the organism to some other state as a result of an experimental treatment. Therefore, some assessment of the magnitude of a given variable is necessary prior to the administration of the experimental treatment.

One may legitimately raise the question of why an experimental hypothesis of change needs to be examined by assessing the value of the dependent variable prior to treatment through the use of a pretest. It is certainly possible to substitute a randomization design for a pretest design. By randomly selecting subjects from a defined population and by randomly assigning them to the various experimental treatments in a given study, one may assume the comparability of these subjects. Any differences among the scores of the various groups are directly comparable to one another and hence a pretest is unnecessary. However, there are some reasons why the use of a pretest is preferable to a randomization design. Given a constant N, the use of a pretest will often increase the precision of measurement by controlling for individual differences within subgroups. In addition, should there be a "failure" of randomization, comparison of the subgroups' pretest means will tell us so.

Of course, it is also possible that a pretest might be administered to detect differences in initial performance, so that the effects of some experimental manipulation taking into account these differences can be examined. However, this has not been of typical interest to researchers utilizing pretest designs in attitudinal studies.

The principal point is that we are interested in demonstrating *empirically* that a given treatment either succeeds or does not succeed in changing some existing variable in the organism (such as an opinion), and the most direct way of establishing such a fact is to test that variable before and after the application of the treatment.

The ideal experiment is one in which the relevant pre-experimental state of the organism is determined without affecting that state by the very measuring process itself. Unfortunately, it is rarely possible to achieve this aim, since it is almost always necessary to manipulate the environment of the subject in some way in order to obtain the measurement. However, it is not impossible to do so, as, for example, in a situation where the subject is not aware that he is being observed and his response recorded (cf. Campbell, 1967). Several control groups, and thus various types of pretreatment manipulation of the subject, are usually necessary in most studies. The intent of this paper is to examine the nature of these pretreatment measures for sources of artifact which disrupt the legitimacy of the conclusions it is possible to draw within the context of social psychology.

Since several experimental situations found in psychological research require some preliminary manipulation involving the subject before the treatment can be applied, appropriate controls are necessary to isolate all possible sources of variation. Any manipulation of the subject or of his environment by the experimenter prior to the advent of the experimental treatment, which is to be followed by some measure of performance, allows for the possibility that the result is due either to the effect of the treatment or to the interaction of the treatment with the prior manipulation. A control group is needed to which is presented the prior manipulation followed by the measure of performance, without the treatment intervening. This control group can then be compared with the experimental group receiving prior manipulation, treatment, and the measure of performance. Should there be a significant difference between the two groups one may reach a conclusion as to the relative effectiveness of the two methods for increasing or decreasing performance. This control is diagrammed in Table I.

TABLE I

CONTROL FOR EFFECT OF PRIOR MANIPULATION

I	II
Prior Manipulation Treatment Measure of Performance	Prior Manipulation Measure of Performance

TABLE II

CONTROLS FOR EFFECT OF PRIOR MANIPULATION AND ITS
INTERACTION WITH THE TREATMENT

I	II	III
Prior Manipulation Treatment Measure of Performance	Prior Manipulation Measure of Performance	 Treatment Measure of Performance

Even though the application of this design allows one to make a direct comparison between groups and yields an evaluation of the effect on performance of the prior manipulation and the treatment, it is to be noted that there is no logical possibility of evaluating the effect of the treatment alone on the measure of performance. In order to do this, a second control group must be added. The revised design is shown in Table II.

The second control group (Group III), which presents the subject with the treatment and follows this with the measure of performance, now permits us to examine not only the effects of prior manipulation on the measure of performance, and the combined effects of prior manipulation and treatment, but also the effect of the treatment alone. Thus, three possible comparisons may now be made, Group I with Group II, Group I with Group III, and Group II with Group III. However, there is still one source of variation which remains unaccounted for in this design. Conceivably the performance of the subject alone might be quite similar in magnitude to his performance under any or all of the conditions contained in Groups I, II, and III. In order to examine this hypothesis, as indicated in Table III, a third and final control group must be added to the design.[*]

TABLE III

CONTROLS FOR EFFECTS OF PRIOR MANIPULATION, AND ITS INTERACTION
WITH THE TREATMENT AND EXISTING MAGNITUDE OF PERFORMANCE
IN THE SUBJECT

I	II	III	IV
Prior Manipulation Treatment Measure of Performance	Prior Manipulation Measure of Performance	Treatment Measure of Performance	Measure of Performance

The design is now complete and all possible effects on the dependent variable of prior manipulation and treatment have been accounted for. Obviously the design can be further complicated if the time intervals among the prior manipulation, treatment, and measure of performance are varied. However, the principle of control remains the same.

In order to apply the final design presented in Table III, certain assumptions must be made concerning the distribution of subjects in the four groups involved. Subjects must be chosen at random from the population, and randomly assigned to one of the four groups. The assumption is that subjects assigned to any one group will be similar, in all relevant characteristics, to subjects assigned to any of the other groups. A special problem arises if the prior manipulation happens to be a test tapping some already existing quality in the organism, e.g., an opinion questionnaire regarding racial prejudice or a test examining achievement in knowledge of American History, instead of being a direct manipulation such as injecting a drug where no measurement is involved. Since Groups III and IV of Table III are not exposed to prior manipula-

---

[*] Solomon (1949), in a now classic paper, was the first to discuss these groups in systematic detail.

tion (e.g., an opinion questionnaire) there is no immediate assurance that the groups are initially homogeneous with respect to the opinion being tapped. Yet, it is necessary to arrange the groups as in Table III if one wishes to control for the effects of the three elements of the design.

There are at least two possible solutions to this dilemma. One has been suggested by Solomon (1949). Since Groups I and II have pretest measures taken on them, it is possible to calculate the mean value and the standard deviation for both groups on their questionnaire scores. The mean of these means and the combined standard deviation of the two groups can then be assigned to Groups III and IV as the best estimates of the pretest scores of these groups in lieu of administering a questionnaire to them. It is then possible to examine the change from pretest mean scores to posttest (measurement of performance) mean scores for all groups, without actually having applied the pretests to Groups III and IV. The original means of Groups I and II are used in the analysis. Degrees of freedom utilized in any tests of significance should be those appropriate for each of the actual four groups. However, this method is tenuous if one has little information as to the comparability of the various groups of subjects.

An alternative or complementary solution is to examine for comparability a large number of subjects from the pool from which the final selection of experimental subjects will be chosen. Thus, should there be available 500 comparable subjects from which we wish to choose 100 for our experiment, then the following procedure would be useful. Randomly choose the 100 subjects to be used in the four groups of the experiment. Randomly assign 25 subjects to each of the four treatment groups. Randomly assign two of these four groups to the two pretest conditions, and administer the pretest. Pretest the remaining 400 people in the original pool. Finally, assign the grand mean and grand standard deviation of all 450 pretested subjects to groups III and IV, the unpretested groups. (Lana, 1959, discusses this problem and provides a related example.)

There are essentially two types of prior manipulations that are utilized in our basic design. One type (Case I) we may designate as an experimental condition of some sort, such as receiving a jolt of electricity, swallowing a pill, or pressing a button. In this type of manipulation the measure of performance (posttest) is always different from the prior manipulation; the two never require the same task from the subject. Also the prior manipulation is not a measure of performance or of previous condition of the organism as it is, e.g., when opinion questionnaires, spelling tests, etc., are used. Essentially, Case I represents the situation where some pre-treatment applied to the subject is necessary in order to examine the effects of the principal treatment. Strictly speaking, no pretest is involved, but rather a part of the experimental treatment conceptualized as a pre-condition necessary for examination of the dependent variable. In Case II the prior manipulation requires the same kind of a performance from the subjects as does the posttest and is actually a part of the dependent variable (pretest-posttest change). With the Case I type of pretreatment condition only random assignment of subjects to the initial groups can be used to assure homogeneity of subjects. When the prior manipulation is exactly the same task as the measure of performance (Case II), as, for example, when an opinion questionnaire is used for both, it is also possible to estimate pretest measures for groups which can not be pretested. These procedures, discussed above, become extremely important for this type of situation although irrelevant when the prior manipulation is non-mensurative. In most of the situations with which we shall be concerned, Case II predominates.

III. ANALYSIS OF CASE I DESIGNS

Following Solomon's article (Solomon, 1949) a good deal of work has been done in examining the effects on performance of prior manipulation in interaction with a succeeding treatment. A recent study by Ross, Krugman, Lyerly and Clyde (1962) develops the four group design for use in certain types of psychopharmacological studies and provides an example of our Case I. Although there may be instances where a psychopharmacological study might include a prior manipulation which taps an existing attribute of the subject, most pretest-treatment-interaction designs in this area are of the type where the prior manipulation is some experimental condition and is therefore not a pretest and is not repeated in the posttest. The experiment by Ross *et al.* is of this latter type and illustrates the proper statistical analysis to be used with this kind of data. The design is contained in Table IV.

TABLE IV

DESIGN OF EXPERIMENT BY ROSS, KRUGMAN, LYERLY, AND CLYDE (1962)

I	II	III	IV
Pill	Pill	No pill	No pill
Drug	No drug (Placebo)	Drug (disguised)	No drug
Task (tapping)	Task	Task	Task

It is to be noted that this design fulfills exactly the conditions summarized in Table III for permitting the assessment of prior manipulation-treatment-interactions, the effects of prior manipulation alone, and the effects of task alone. It is also to be noted that the measure of performance (a tapping task) is different from the prior manipulation which is the swallowing of a pill. Since the prior manipulation in this case is not designed to tap any existing attribute of the individual, the usual random assignment of subjects to the various groups should be utilized.

A double classification analysis of variance is the proper method of analysis in examining the various main and interaction effects. The main effects for drug and pill are examined against the mean square for error as is the interaction mean square. Degrees of freedom and appropriateness of error term are determined as in an ordinary double classification analysis of variance. A significant F-ratio for drug would suggest that the drug treatment significantly affected the performance of the task. A significant main effect for pill would suggest that the prior manipulation (actually giving a placebo in the form of a pill) significantly affected the performance of the task. A significant interaction effect would indicate that the effect of the prior manipulation and the treatment taken together affected the task and, therefore, main effects if significant would become more complex to interpret. Actually, if the main effect for drug were significant in our example, and the interaction between drug and pill were also significant, but not the main effect for pill, then depending upon the shape and magnitude of the interaction the following interpretation might be made. The drug, in itself, is powerful enough to have an effect on task performance regardless of other factors in the experiment. However, if the drug were taken in pill form this factor would also have a significant effect on the performance of the task. Obviously, any theoretical interpretation of these results would have to await further research. Should the interaction alone be significant, the interpretation would be more difficult. This situation is discussed below.

IV. ANALYSIS OF CASE II DESIGNS

Within the framework of the pretest-treatment-posttest design (i.e., prior manipulation-treatment-measure of performance) a subject's initial response to a questionnaire may provide a basis of comparison with later questionnaire responses, and thus a positive or negative correlation of some magnitude might be expected between the individual's first and second scores to the same questionnaire. This expectation of correlation between successive, similar tasks is the basis for methodological concern with repeated measurements designs.

When two treatments are performed in succession, a treatment carry-over may occur. The rotation or counterbalanced design (Cochran and Cox, 1957) is specifically intended to give information on such a treatment carryover. In the experimental situations described in this chapter, where a single pretest precedes a single treatment, the possible effects of carryover from pretest to treatment are the same as the treatment-to-treatment carryover. A rotation design is not possible when the first variable is a pretest, since by definition a pretest must precede the treatment. Consequently, any examination of the confounding effects of the pretest with the treatment must be made by experimentally manipulating the nature and application of the pretest. The major question that remains is directed at the nature of the relationship existing between these two variables. Thus the pretest-treatment-posttest research design is a special case of the general repeated measures design where there are multiple treatments or tests of the same organism over time.

Ordinarily in a pretest-posttest design, since the initial score on the pretest has a tendency to be variable over subjects, a covariance design with pretest score as the covariable is appropriate and very useful. However, as we have seen, the very nature of our interest in pretest sensitization disallows for the use of covariance, since, in order to fulfill the requirement of the four-group design, some groups will not have been pretested. Consequently, the principal design needs to be of another type.

If one can assume that there is a high probability that the unpretested groups in the four-group-control design would not be significantly different on pretest scores from the groups who were pretested, then a two-by-two factorial analysis of variance can be computed on the posttest scores of the four groups. This analysis will yield main effects for the treatment and for pretesting, and a first order interaction term between the two. Should the interaction effect not be significant, but either or both of the main effects be significant, the interpretation is straightforward. A significant main effect for treatment indicates that the treatment affected the posttest score in either a facilitative or depressive manner, depending on the direction of the mean change scores. A similar interpretation may be made for a significant pretesting main effect. Should the interactive effect of pretesting and treatment be significant, regardless of whether or not the main effects are significant, interpretation would become more complicated (see Lana and Lubin, 1961, 1963). When an interaction term is significant it can be concluded that the usual interpretations regarding the data which would ordinarily follow from the hypothesis testing model cannot be made. That is, with a significant interaction effect, the experimenter needs to exercise extreme care in the interpretation of his data and, in many instances, he may have to re-examine the manner in which he has constructed the empirical aspects of his problem. The significant interaction should lead him to reconstruct his hypotheses along somewhat different lines. Scheffe concludes, "In order to get exact tests and confidence intervals concerning the main effects it is generally necessary with the fixed-effects model (but not the random effects model or mixed model) to assume that there are no interactions." All of the studies discussed below use the fixed effects model. "It happens occasionally that the hypothesis of no interactions will be rejected by a statistical test, but the hypothesis of zero main effects for both factors will be accepted. The correct conclusion is then *not* that no differences have been demonstrated: If there are (any nonzero) interactions there must be (nonzero) differences among the cell means. The conclusion should be that there are differences, but that when the effects of the levels of one factor are averaged over the levels of the other, no difference of these averaged effects has been demonstrated" (Scheffe, 1959, 94). The point of this discussion is that since we are specifically *looking for* significant interaction terms, if we find one it should act as a warning device. The experimenter should then reformulate the problem. In the pretest-treatment-posttest design case, the use of a pretest becomes suspect for the given data of the study.

V. SENSITIZATION WHEN THE PRETEST INVOLVES LEARNING

Besides providing one of the first formal analyses of a research design capable of structuring an experiment so that a pretest treatment interaction could be isolated and measured, R. L. Solomon (1949) conducted an experiment demonstrating one source of such an interaction effect. Two grammar school classes were equated for spelling ability by teacher judgment. The three-group control design that was examined earlier was used. Each group was pretested on a list of words of equal difficulty by having the children spell the words. The groups were then given a standard spelling lesson on the general rules of spelling which served as the experimental treatment. The posttest consisted of the same list of words to spell as were used as the pretest. In the analysis which followed, there was some indication that the pretest interacted with the treatment although the usual two-way analysis of variance could not be computed. It was concluded that the taking of the pretest tended to diminish the spelling effectiveness of the subjects. In this study the errors made in the pretest somehow were resistant to the treatment and were made again during the posttest. Here then is an instance of a pretest which, at least in part, is a learning experience (or recall of already learned material) depressing the effect of the treatment, which is another related learning task.

Beginning with a re-examination of Solomon's results, Entwisle (1961a, 1961b) performed two experiments of her own and found a significant interaction effect among pretesting, IQ and sex. Pretests consisted of several multiple choice questions about state locations of large U.S. cities. Treatment consisted of showing all subjects a slide with the name of a city projected on it for .1 second. The subjects then wrote the state name, and immediately afterward the correct state name was shown

TABLE V

EXPERIMENTAL DESIGN OF LANA AND KING (1960)

Group I	Group II	Group III	Group IV
Reading	Reading	Reading	Reading
Recall	Recall		
12 days	12 days	12 days	12 days
Film		Film	
Recall	Recall	Recall	Recall

for .1 second. This procedure was repeated for all items in the pretest. Hence, the treatment consisted of a training session directly relevant to material presented as pretest. The posttest consisted of the same procedure as the pretest. There was no significant main effect of pretesting, but the triple interaction measured above was significant. Although the results are equivocal, there is a suggestion that pretesting aided recall for high IQ individuals and was "mildly hindering" for "average" IQ students. In another training study, Entwisle (1961a) found no significant interaction effect or direct effect of pretesting.

In 1960, Lana and King, using the four-group control design contained in Table V, had all groups read a short summary of the mental health film on ethnic prejudice, "The High Wall." Two of the groups were asked to recall the summary immediately after the reading as near to the original as possible by writing it out on a sheet of paper. This recall was considered the pretest. Sometime later the film was presented to one group (pretested) that had been asked to recall the summary, and to another group that had not been asked to recall the summary (unpretested). Immediately after presentation of the film all groups were posttested by asking them to recall as near to the original as possible the summary which had been read to them several days before. Accuracy of recall was measured by dividing the story into "idea units" and counting the number of units in each subject's protocol.

Even though the film used as the treatment has a definite attitudinal component to it and is clearly didactic, our interest in this study was to examine only recall components of the pretest-treatment-posttest experimental design. The results indicated a significant main effect for pretesting and no significant effects for the treatment nor for the pretest-treatment interaction. Although the content of the summary read before the first recall contained no more information than that which could be seen and heard in the film, the act of recalling the written summary was more effective than seeing the film in influencing the precision of the second recall taken after the presentation of the film. In this case, only the fact of the first recall significantly affected later recall. The combination of first recall and film viewing was not as effective in posttest recall. To the extent that a pretest serves as a device for conscious recall of meaningfully connected material, it can serve to influence posttest results. Attitude and opinion quetsionnaires used as pretests might have the same effect should part of the process of taking such a pretest involve recall of previously held attitudes or opinions.

Hicks and Spaner (1962), working with attitudes toward mental patients and hospital experience, found a pretest sensitization effect similar to that shown by Lana and King. The former investigators suggested that a learning factor might have been present in the attitude questionnaire used as the pretest.

In the studies by Solomon, Lana and King, Hicks and Spaner and the two by Entwisle, virtually all possible effects of pretesting, when pretesting was a learning or recall device, were shown. Solomon found a significant interaction between pretest and treatment which had a depressing effect on posttest score. Lana and King found a significant main effect for pretesting, indicating greater recall with pretesting than without pretesting, but no significant pretest-treatment interaction. Entwisle found a pretest-treatment interaction with a salutory effect of the pretest on posttest scores and in another study found no significant pretest-treatment interaction of any kind. Entwisle dismissed her negative results because sex was not a control variable in that study, and she later showed that when it was introduced as a variable a significant pretest-treatment-sex interaction appeared. Even though we have examined only five relevant studies we are probably safe in assuming that a pretesting procedure which, in whole or part, involves some learning process such as recall of previously learned material, may very well have an effect on the magnitude of the posttest score. Ordinarily, if the task or the recall demanded by the pretest procedure is properly understood by the subject, the effect on the posttest should be facilitative. However, as we have seen in the case of Solomon's results and some of Entwisle's, depressive effects can also occur.

There are different implications of the interpretations of pretest results, depending upon whether or not the sensitization is direct (Lana and King) or operates in concert with the treatment (Solomon, Entwisle). The former results are simpler to interpret and the experimenter need not be as concerned with the general procedure of pretesting in that experimental situation, since pretesting effects and treatment effects are independent. When the pretest-treatment interaction effect is significant there is always the danger that the interaction indicates a change in the nature of the empirical phenomenon and a distortion of that phenomenon so that it is markedly different from what it would have been had a pretest not been used. It is in this situation of measuring attitude by use of a pretest that we see an application of the principle of indeterminacy which seems to operate in a manner analogous to that found in subatomic physics.

VI. SENSITIZATION WHEN THE PRETEST INVOLVES OPINIONS AND ATTITUDES

In Solomon's 1949 article, he indicated in a footnote that some evidence was available that the pretest may reduce the variance of the posttest in attitudinal studies. The implication was that taking an attitudinal pretest may restrict the attention of the subjects so that they are not as variable in their reactions to the treatment as they would have been had they not been required to take a pretest. In 1955, E. V. Piers, at the suggestion of J. C. Stanley, used the Solomon four-group control design to measure teacher attitudes toward students. The pretest consisted of the Minnesota Teacher Attitude Inventory, and the posttest used the Adorno *et al.* F Scale, a student rating scale and a vocabulary test. No pretest effect of any kind was found. Lana (1959a) utilized the Solomon design with a questionnaire measuring opinion on vivisection as both the pretest and posttest. The treatment consisted of a taped pro-vivisection appeal. If a pretest sensitization were operating it would more likely be evident in this study, where pretest and posttest devices were identical, than in Piers' study where they were different. With the same pretest and posttest devices, a recall factor alone should produce some effect from pre-to-posttest, as was noted in the Lana and King, Solomon, and Entwisle studies. There was, however, no significant pretesting main effect nor a significant pretest treatment interaction effect. Considering the fact that the topic used, "vivisection," was probably of minor interest to the subjects, one explanation for these results is that they might have been little affected by the tasks asked of them. Lana (1959b) repeated this study using a topic (ethnic prejudice) which, it seemed reasonable to assume, was more interesting and controversial to the college student subjects than vivisection. The treatment consisted of "The High Wall," the mental health film used by Lana and King (1960). Pretest and posttest consisted of a modified version of the California Ethnocentrism Scale. There were no significant main or interactive effects involving the pretest.

DeWolfe and Governale (1964) administered to experimental and control groups of student nurses a pretest consisting of the Nurse-Patient Relationship Sort, Fear of Tuberculosis Questionnaire, and the IPAT "Trait" Anxiety Scale. The Nurse-Patient Relationship Sort was given as a posttest at the end of a specified nursing training period. Appropriate controls were utilized to allow for an examination of pretest and pretest-treatment interaction effects. The authors reported that there was no consistent sensitization or desensitization as a result of pretesting. Campbell and Stanley (1966) have indicated that studies by Anderson (1959), Duncan et al. (1957), Sobol (1959), and Zeisel (1947) also reported no sensitizing effect as a result of taking a pretest, when opinions or attitudes were involved.

In 1949, Hovland, Lumsdaine and Sheffield, in their classic work on attitudes of the American soldier during World War II, reported that something like a sensitization effect occurred as a consequence of using a pretest in attitudinal studies. They found that there was less attitude change in a group of soldiers administered pretest questionnaires on topics relevant to the war effort than in those not so pretested where all other experimental conditions were similar. By their own admission, this conclusion was extremely tenuous since the pretested group consisted of soldiers receiving infantry training at one base while the non-pretested group consisted of soldiers receiving armored vehicle training at another base. Also, the demographic characteristics of the two groups of men were not comparable. This study remains the only one involving opinions and attitudes in which even a suggestion of the occurrence of pretest sensitization is made and in which a unidirectional communication (i.e., a communication supporting only one point of view) was used.

The overwhelming lack of a pretest sensitization effect when the pretest is used to measure existing opinions or attitudes is as convincing a demonstration as one is likely to find in social psychological research. It seems reasonably safe to use a pretest without concern for its direct or interaction (with the treatment) effects on posttest results. This zero effect seems to be present over a large variety of opinions and attitudes and a large variety of treatment situations, as is evident from the diversity of techniques used in the studies cited here. The vast majority of these studies utilized a one-sided communication geared to influence opinion or attitude change in one possible direction. The Anderson study is an exception, and conceivably in the DeWolfe and Governale study the training of the nurses may have contained incidents that represented both positive and negative positions about the patient qua patient. However, by and large, the studies involved a unidirectional persuasive attempt as the treatment.

Within the context of research on order effects in persuasive communications, it was decided to check for pretest sensitization when subjects are exposed to both of two opposed arguments on the same topic. This would be much the same situation as, for example, being exposed to conflicting advertisements for similar products or to apparently contrary arguments on political issues by individuals running for the same political office. The presentation of opposed arguments seemed sufficiently different from a treatment using a unidirectional communication to warrant a renewed effort in looking for pretest sensitization.

In an experiment by Lana and Rosnow (1963), subjects were divided into various groups such that half of these groups received a questionnaire measuring opinions either on the use of nuclear weapons or on public censorship of written materials. This was accomplished by either handing the questionnaire to the subject and asking him to complete it or interspersing the questionnaire items throughout a regular Psychology I examination, thus "hiding" it from the subject. When the questionnaire is handed directly to the subject and he is asked to complete it, it is highly likely that his attention will be focused directly on the task. When the questionnaire items are interspersed throughout a regular classroom examination, the attention and expectancies of the subject are initially on a topic other than the content of the questionnaire. Conceivably, here was a way to get a measure of initial opinion on a given subject matter, and to reduce any effects of pretest sensitization. Our initial purpose in carrying out this study was to examine possible effects of pretesting on the order effects (primacy-recency) of two opposed communications. Primacy refers to the success in changing opinion of the initial argument of two opposed communications. Recency refers to a similar success of the argument presented second. Disregarding this result, a reanalysis of the data indicated that the average opinion change per group (mean absolute differences from pretest to posttest regardless of the direction of change) was significantly greater for groups where the pretest was hidden than for the groups where the pretest was exposed.

The step that next seemed most appropriate was to attempt to demonstrate this pretest sensitization when two opposed communications were used as the treatment and when some subjects received no pretest and others responded to an exposed pretest. Two experiments (Lana, 1964, 1966) were conducted for this purpose. Their results indicated that the no-pretest groups changed their opinions in either direction to a significantly greater degree than did the groups administered the exposed pretest. The mean of the unpretested groups was estimated by computing the mean of the means of the pretested groups. Consistent with our earlier discussion, it was assumed that the groups not pretested were homogeneous with those pretested since they were formed randomly from the same population.

These studies tend to support the notion that the pretest can act as a device by which the individual commits himself to maintain his opinion in the face of opposed (i.e., bidirectional) arguments presented after he has made his commitment. Campbell and Brock (1957) have shown that commitment to an attitudinal position inhibits change when commitment is elicited after an initial attempt to influence the subject, but not when response to a precommunication questionnaire constitutes the commitment. Their suggestion, however, is that there are forms of attitudinal commitment, usually made under public conditions, which inhibit opinion or attitude change as a result of materials presented later. Almost without exception, however, no pretest main or interaction effect has been found in the situation where only one opinion or attitude is measured by the pretest and where a unidirectional communication serves as the treatment. Where bidirectional arguments comprise the treatment, pretest sensitization has consistently been present (see Table VI). A possible explanation for these marked differences is the following: If the recipient initially favors the position advocated, then a unidirectional communication should yield greater opinion change, regardless of pretest conditions. This is because the communication would support the recipients' initial commitment, if no ceiling problem were encountered. If half the subjects supported the position advocated, these subjects would not need to consider their initial opinion when reacting to the posttest.* There would be no need to resolve discrepancy between

* This assumes a symmetrical distribution of pretest scores with a mean near the "indifference" point, an assumption which holds true for the great majority of the studies heretofore cited.

TABLE VI

SUMMARY OF SENSITIZATION EFFECTS INDICATED BY VARIOUS EXPERIMENTS

	No sensitization	Sensitization main effect of pretest	Sensitization interaction of pretest with treatment
Pretest A Learning Device	Entwisle (1961a)	Lana and King (1960) Hicks and Spaner (1962)	Solomon (1949) Entwisle (1961b)
Pretest An Attitudinal Device (Unidirectional)	Zeisel (1947) Duncan et al. (1957) Anderson (1959) Lana (1959a) Lana (1959b) Sobol (1959) DeWolfe and Governale (1964)	Hovland, Lumsdaine, and Sheffield (1949)	
Pretest An Attitudinal Device (Bidirectional)		Lana and Rosnow (1963) Lana (1964) Lana (1966)	

what these individuals wrote on their pretests and the point of view represented in the communication. Both would be consistent with one another. Thus there is no resistance to the communication because of prior commitment for half of the subjects. However, if two opposed arguments were presented as the communication, one of the positions would automatically be discrepant with every subject's initial commitment. Pretest commitment, challenged by one of the communications, produces resistance to change, and hence the result is a smaller change score from pretest to posttest.

VII. CAUTIONS ASSOCIATED WITH THE USE OF A PRETEST

As we have seen, when the mensurative process involves people required to respond to an experimental condition in a manner reflecting their motives, opinions, attitudes, feelings, or beliefs, the administration of a pretest to measure these characteristics which is free from influence on that process may be difficult to find. The subject's awareness of the manipulatory intent of the experimenter dealt with in detail by McGuire,

(Chapter 2), the experimenter's expectations (Rosenthal, Chapter 6), the subject's concern about being evaluated (Rosenberg, Chapter 7)—all of these can exert an influence through use of a pretest, or act as separate effects, and thereby confound the effect of the experimental treatment. Indeed all of the other chapters of this book deal with factors which, though extrinsic to the experimental situation as conceived by the experimenter, can affect the magnitude and quality of the treatment and its effect on behavior. Campbell and Stanley (1966, 20) have noted, "In the usual psychological experiment, if not in educational research, a most prominent source of unrepresentativeness is the patent artificiality of the experimental setting and the student's knowledge that he is participating in an experiment. For human experimental subjects, a higher order problem-solving task is generated, in which the procedures and experimental treatment are reacted to not only for their simple stimulus values, but also for their role as clues in divining the experimenter's intent."

Campbell and Stanley (1966) have also observed that the posttest may create an artificial "experiment participating effect" for the subject if the connections between treatment and posttest (or among pretest, treatment and posttest) are obvious. One way that this perception on the part of the subject might be changed is by using a different (e.g., equivalent form) posttest than was used as the pretest. With few exceptions (e.g., Piers, 1955) most of the studies mentioned above used identical pre- and posttests, that is, they are all examples of what was earlier referred to as Case II.

At this point the alternative to be explored is that of substituting for the pretest some other technique of observation or measurement of initial standing which lacks the obvious and telltale characteristics of the pretest (i.e., as in Case I). One alternative to administering a pretest, an alternative which allows a reasonable estimation of the strength of a subject's opinion and attitude toward some social object is the use of groups which, because of the unified stand of their members regarding the topic in question, are naturally homogeneous. For example, one might speculate that the opinions concerning birth control of members of the Catholic college organization, The Newman Club, would cluster in the negative half of the opinion continuum. In his examination of order effects when opposed communications on the same topic were presented to subjects, Lana (1964b) found that intact goups have a tendency to be more rigid in their commitment to a given opinion or attitude, although these groups are of such a nature that more information is available about their initial opinions which is useful in solving the pretest sensitization problem. It is more difficult to change their opinions via a persuasive communication than those of groups formed randomly. They are, therefore, not the most ideal subjects to use in a demonstration of the facility with which opinion or attitude change can be effected under various communicative conditions.

Recently, E. J. Webb, D. T. Campbell, R. D. Schwartz, and L. Sechrest (1966) published a book which included a summary of what may be conceived as various alternatives to the pretest questionnaire technique. It is their contention that there are "nonreactive measures" which may be used to determine relative states of the organism, measures which assure the experimenter that the organism is not affected by the process of measurement itself. In short, there are measures which eliminate the operation of the principle of indeterminacy in the opinion or attitude measurement situation. (Reactive measures are those which sensitize the subject to the fact of being measured, or of being an object of concern to the experimenter and which, therefore, serve in many instances to change the behavior of the subject as a result.) Their point is that for the researcher concerned with social and other complex conditions affecting the organism, a variety of mensurative techniques are available which do not interfere with the process being measured by virtue of the fact that the subject is totally unaware of the measurement process. They divide these "unobtrusive" measures into five categories. The first is that of physical traces. For example, it is possible to infer what displays are most popular at a museum by examining the degree of wear of the floor tiles directly in front of the exhibit. This is a nonreactive measure. In contrast, a reactive measure would be to ask a number of visitors which exhibits they spent the most time at or which they enjoyed the most. Conceivably, an individual asked this question might respond with the name of an exhibit quite at variance with the one he actually spent the most time at or most enjoyed. If the subject wished to appear "cultured," he might say that he spent more time looking at the fish fossils than he did looking at the stuffed gorilla. The second source of nonreactive data is what Webb *et al.* call the "running record," where data of a census nature have been compiled by society for purposes other than those of the experimenter, but which provide useful information for him. Examples include actuarial statistics, city budgets, and voting statistics. Episodic and private records would serve the same function as running records. Simple observation of expressive movements and casual conversation comprise another category of nonreactive measurement. The final type of measure involves the use of hidden mechanical or other devices to record behavior in situations where the subject is unaware of the ongoing measurement.

Paying all due respect to the cleverness and imagination shown by

Webb, Campbell, Schwartz and Sechrest in devising and systematizing these nonreactive, unobtrusive measures, the strongest impact on this writer after reading their book was to reinforce his belief in the necessity of looking for ways and devices to utilize reactive measures where the reaction (sensitization) on the part of the subject can either be measured or be eliminated altogether. The unobtrusive measures listed by these authors are rarely relevant to the research of a good many psychologists who use some sort of pretest measure. However, it should be noted that the authors intended these techniques to be as much "posttests" as "pretests." Since it has been shown that, at least in attitude research, pretest measures, if they have any impact at all, depress the effect being measured, any differences which can be attributed to the experimental treatment probably represent strong treatment effects. In short, when pretest measures exert any influence at all in attitude research, the effect is to produce a Type II error, which is more tolerable to most psychological researchers than is an error of the first kind.

It would seem that a researcher's decision to use a pretest or, instead, to utilize a randomization design with only posttest measures is partly based upon personal characteristics having little to do with the logic of the experiment. As we have indicated, what one gains in information by utilizing a pretest he sometimes loses in increased sensitization of the subject. What he gains in purity of experimental effect by utilizing a randomization design he loses in knowledge of pre-treatment conditions existing in the organism. In some cases the goals of the experiment set the risk one will take. However, in many situations one is caught between the Scylla of sensitization and the Charybdis of ignorance of pre-existing conditions. The choice of procedure may be arbitrary.

If, however, one does choose to utilize some form of the pretest-posttest design, disguising both pretest and posttest as much as possible may reduce sensitization of the subject. For example, as part of an as yet unfinished master's thesis, Julian Biller hid an attitudinal pretest in a questionnaire ostensibly concerned with student reaction to various university administration policies and to student life in general. It was explained to the students that the information was useful to the instructor in shaping his course toward the needs of the students. Since the pretest items were concerned with attitudes toward the American college grading system, they were not conspicuous by their content. In a similar manner, the posttest items were hidden in a different questionnaire presented to the subjects sometime after they had been exposed to a persuasive communication concerning various grading systems. Of course, the astute subject may still recognize the key items in the questionnaire as being related to the communications he listened to sometime in the past. However, recognition and therefore sensitization effects may be minimized by use of this technique.

Pretest sensitization might also be minimized by increasing the time between application of the pretest and the presentation of the persuasive communications and the posttest. However, one risks the possibility that factors external to the experimental situation may influence pretest-posttest change scores if the interval between the two is great. Conceivably an optimum time interval between pretest and treatment as well as between treatment and posttest might be found.

REFERENCES

Anderson, N. H. Test of a model for opinion change. *Journal of Abnormal and Social Psychology*, 1959, **59**, 371–381.

Campbell, D. T. Administrative experimentation, institutional records, and nonreactive measures. *In* J. C. Stanley (Ed.), *Improving experimental designs and statistical analysis.* Chicago: Rand McNally, 1967.

Campbell, D. T. and Stanley, J. C. *Experimental and quasi-experimental designs for research.* Chicago: Rand McNally, 1966.

Campbell, E. H. and Brock, T. The effects of "commitment" on opinion change following communications. *In* C. I. Hovland, *et al., The order of presentation in persuasion.* New Haven: Yale University Press, 1957.

Cochran, W. G. and Cox, Gertrude M. *Experimental design* (2nd ed.). New York: Wiley, 1957.

DeWolfe, A. S. and Governale, C. N. Fear and attitude change. *Journal of Abnormal and Social Psychology*, 1964, **69**, 119–123.

Duncan, C. P., O'Brien, R. B., Murray, D. C., Davis, L., and Gilliland, A. R. Some information about a test of psychological misconceptions. *Journal of General Psychology*, 1957, **56**, 257–260.

Entwisle, Doris R. Attensity: Factors of specific set on school learning. *Harvard Educational Review*, 1961, **31**, 84–101. (a)

Entwisle, Doris R. Interactive effects of pretesting. *Educational and Psychological Measurement*, 1961, **21**, 607–620. (b)

Heisenberg, W. *Physics and philosophy.* New York: Harper Torch Books, 1958.

Hicks, J. M. and Spaner, F. E. Attitude change and hospital experience. *Journal of Abnormal and Social Psychology*, 1962, **65**, 112–120.

Hovland, C. I., Lumsdaine, A. A. and Sheffield, F. D. *Experiments on mass communication.* Princeton: Princeton University Press, 1949.

Lana, R. E. Pretest-treatment interaction effects in attitudinal studies. *Psychological Bulletin*, 1959, **56**, 293–300. (a)

Lana, R. E. A further investigation of the pretest-treatment interaction effect. *Journal of Applied Psychology*, 1959, **43**, 421–422. (b)

Lana, R. E. and King, D. J. Learning factors as determiners of pretest sensitization. *Journal of Applied Psychology*, 1960, **44**, 189–191.

Lana, R. E. and Lubin, A. *Use of analysis of variance techniques in psychology.* Progress Report to the National Institute of Mental Health, United States Public Health Service No. M–4113(A), March, 1961.

Lana, R. E. and Lubin, A. The effect of correlation on the repeated measures design. *Educational and Psychological Measurement*, 1963, 23, 729–739.

Lana, R. E. and Rosnow, R. L. Subject awareness and order effects in persuasive communications. *Psychological Reports*, 1963, 12, 523–529.

Lana, R. E. The influence of the pretest on order effects in persuasive communications. *Journal of Abnormal and Social Psychology*, 1964, 69, 337–341. (a)

Lana, R. E. Existing familiarity and order of presentation of persuasive communications. *Psychological Reports*, 1964, 15, 607–610. (b)

Lana, R. E. Inhibitory effects of a pretest on opinion change. *Educational and Psychological Measurement*, 1966, 26, 139–150.

Piers, Ellen V. An abstract of effects of instruction on teacher attitudes: extended control group design. *Bulletin of the Maritime Psychological Association*, 1955 (Spring), 53–56.

Ross, S., Krugman, A. D., Lyerly, S. B., and Clyde, D. J. Drugs and placebos: a model design. *Psychological Reports*, 1962, 10, 383–392.

Roethlisberger, F. J. and Dickson, W. J. *Management and the worker*. Cambridge, Massachusetts: Harvard University Press, 1939.

Scheffe, H. *The analysis of variance*. New York: Wiley, 1959.

Sobol, M. G. Panel mortality and panel bias. *Journal of the American Statistical Association*, 1959, 54, 52–68.

Solomon, R. L. An extension of control group design. *Psychological Bulletin*, 1949, 46, 137–150.

Webb, E. J., Campbell, D. T., Schwartz, R. D., and Sechrest, L. *Unobtrusive measures: nonreactive research in the social sciences*. Chicago: Rand McNally, 1966.

Zeisel, H. *Say it with figures*. New York: Harper, 1947.

Chapter 5

DEMAND CHARACTERISTICS AND THE CONCEPT OF QUASI-CONTROLS*

Martin T. Orne†

*Institute of the Pennsylvania Hospital
and University of Pennsylvania*

Special methodological problems are raised when human subjects are used in psychological experiments, mainly because subjects' thoughts about an experiment may affect their behavior in carrying out the experimental task.

To counteract this problem psychologists have frequently felt it necessary to develop ingenious, sometimes even diabolical, techniques in order to deceive the subject about the true purposes of an investigation (see Stricker, 1967; Stricker, Messick, and Jackson, 1967). Deception may not be the only, nor the best, way of dealing with certain issues, yet we must ask what special characteristic of our science makes it necessary to even consider such techniques when no such need arises in, say, physics. The reason is plain: we do not study passive physical particles

* The substantive work reported in this paper was supported in part by Contract #Nonr 4731 from the Group Psychology Branch, Office of Naval Research. The research on the detection of deception was supported in part by the United States Army Medical Research and Development Command Contract #DA-49-193-MD-2647.

† I wish to thank Frederick J. Evans, Charles H. Holland, Edgar P. Nace, Ulric Neisser, Donald N. O'Connell, Emily Carota Orne, David A. Paskewitz, Campbell W. Perry, Karl Rickels, David L. Rosenhan, Robert Rosenthal, and Ralph Rosnow for their thoughtful criticisms and many helpful suggestions in the preparation of this manuscript.

143

but active, thinking human beings like ourselves. The fear that knowledge of the true purposes of an experiment might vitiate its results stems from a tacit recognition that the subject is not a passive responder to stimuli and experimental conditions. Instead, he is an active participant in a special form of socially defined interaction which we call "taking part in an experiment."

It has been pointed out by Criswell (1958), Festinger (1957), Mills (1961), Rosenberg (1965), Wishner (1965) and others, and discussed at some length by the author elsewhere (Orne, 1959b; 1962), that subjects are never neutral toward an experiment. While, from the investigator's point of view, the experiment is seen as permitting the controlled study of an individual's reaction to specific stimuli, the situation tends to be perceived quite differently by his subjects. Because subjects are active, sentient beings, they do not respond to the specific experimental stimuli with which they are confronted as isolated events but rather they perceive these in the total context of the experimental situation. Their understanding of the situation is based upon a great deal of knowledge about the kind of realities under which scientific research is conducted, its aims and purposes, and, in some vague way, the kind of findings which might emerge from their participation and their responses. The response to any specific set of stimuli, then, is a function of both the stimulus and the subject's recognition of the total context. Under some circumstances, the subject's awareness of the implicit aspects of the psychological experiment may become the principal determinant of his behavior. For example, in one study an attempt was made to devise a tedious and intentionally meaningless task. Regardless of the nature of the request and its apparently obvious triviality, subjects continued to comply, even when they were required to perform work and to destroy the product. Though it was apparently impossible for the experimenter to know how well they did, subjects continued to perform at a high rate of speed and accuracy over a long period of time. They ascribed (correctly, of course) a sensible motive to the experimenter and meaning to the procedure. While they could not fathom how this might be accomplished, they also quite correctly assumed that the experimenter could and would check their performance* (Orne, 1962). Again, in another study subjects were required to carry out such obviously dangerous activities as picking up a poisonous snake or removing a penny from fuming nitric acid with their bare hands (Orne and Evans, 1965). Subjects complied, correctly surmising that, despite appearances to the contrary, appropriate precautions for their safety had been taken.

* These pilot studies were performed by Thomas Menaker.

In less dramatic ways the subject's recognition that he is not merely responding to a set of stimuli but is doing so in order to produce data may exert an influence upon his performance. Inevitably he will wish to produce "good" data, that is, data characteristic of a "good" subject. To be a "good" subject may mean many things: to give the right responses, i.e., to give the kind of response characteristic of intelligent subjects; to give the normal response, i.e., characteristic of healthy subjects; to give a response in keeping with the individual's self-perception, etc., etc. If the experimental task is such that the subject sees himself as being evaluated he will tend to behave in such a way as to make himself look good. (The potential importance of this factor has been emphasized by Rosenberg, 1965; see Chapter 7.)

Investigators have tended to be intuitively aware of this problem and in most experimental situations tasks are constructed so as to be ambiguous to the subject regarding how any particular behavior might make him look especially good. In some studies investigators have explicitly utilized subjects' concern with the evaluation in order to maximize motivation. However, when the subject's wish to look good is not directly challenged, another set of motives, one of the common bases for volunteering, will become relevant. That is, beyond idiosyncratic reasons for participating, subjects volunteer, in part at least, to further human knowledge, to help provide a better understanding of mental processes that ultimately might be useful for treatment, to contribute to science, etc. This wish which, despite currently fashionable cynicism, is fortunately still the mode rather than the exception among college student volunteers, has important consequences for the subject's behavior. Thus, in order for the subject to see the data as useful, it is essential that he assume that the experiment be important, meaningful, and properly executed. Also, he would hope that the experiment work, which tends to mean that it prove what it attempts to prove. Reasons such as these may help to clarify why subjects are so committed to see a logical purpose in what would otherwise appear to be a trivial experiment, why they are so anxious to ascribe competence to the experimenter and, at the end of a study, are so concerned that their data prove useful. The same set of motives also helps to understand why subjects often will go to considerable trouble and tolerate great inconvenience provided they are encouraged to see the experiment as important. Typically they will tolerate even intense discomfort if it seems essential to the experiment; on the other hand, they respond badly indeed to discomfort which they recognize as due to the experimenter's ineptness, incompetence, or indifference. Regardless of the extent to which they are reimbursed, most subjects will be thoroughly alienated if it becomes apparent that, for one reason or another, their experimental performance must be discarded as data. Interestingly, they will tend to become angry if this is due to equipment failure or an error on the part of the experimenter, whereas if they feel that they themselves are responsible, they tend to be disturbed rather than angry.

The individual's concern about the extent to which the experiment helps demonstrate that which the experimenter is attempting to demonstrate will, in part, be a function of the amount of involvement with the experimental situation. The more the study demands of him, the more discomfort, the more time, the more effort he puts into it, the more he will be concerned about its outcome. The student in a class asked to fill out a questionnaire will be less involved than the volunteer who stays after class, who will in turn be less involved than the volunteer who is required to go some distance, who will in turn be less involved than the volunteer who is required to come back many times, etc., etc.*

Insofar as the subject cares about the outcome, his perception of his role and of the hypothesis being tested will become a significant determinant of his behavior. The cues which govern his perception—which communicate what is expected of him and what the experimenter hopes to find—can therefore be crucial variables. Some time ago I proposed that these cues be called the "demand characteristics of an experiment" (Orne, 1959b). They include the scuttlebutt about the experiment, its setting, implicit and explicit instructions, the person of the experimenter, subtle cues provided by him, and, of particular importance, the experimental procedure itself. All of these cues are interpreted in the light of the subject's past learning and experience. Although the explicit instructions are important, it appears that subtler cues from which the subject can draw covert or even unconscious inference may be still more powerful.

Recognizing that the subject's knowledge affects his performance, investigators have employed various means to disguise the true purpose of the research, thereby trying to alter the demand characteristics of experimental situations in order to make them orthogonal to the experimental effects. Unfortunately, the mere fact that an investigator goes to great lengths to develop a "cute" way to deceive the subject in no way guarantees that the subject is, in fact, deceived. Obviously it is

---

* Obviously, how the subject is treated will affect his motivation in this regard. If the experimenter seems casual, disinterested, or worse yet, incompetent, he will both resent it and mobilize little investment. On the other hand, if the experimenter seems both to care about the outcome and to appear competent, subjects will often want to help even at great inconvenience to themselves. Thus we have frequently seen subjects return from distant cities to complete a study.

essential to establish whether the subject or the experimenter is the one who is deceived by the experimental manipulation.

I. DEMAND CHARACTERISTICS AND EXPERIMENTER BIAS

Demand characteristics and the subject's reaction to them are, of course, not the only subtle and human factors which may affect the results of an experiment. Experimenter bias effects, which have been studied in such an elegant fashion by Rosenthal (1963; 1966), also are frequently confounding variables. Experimenter bias effects depend in large part on experimenter outcome expectations and hopes. They can become significant determinants of data by causing subtle but systematic differences in (a) the treatment of subjects, (b) the selection of cases, (c) observation of data, (d) the recording of data, and (e) systematic errors in the analysis of data.

To the extent that bias effects cause subtle changes in the way the experimenter treats different groups, they may alter the demand characteristics for those groups. In social psychological studies, demand characteristics may, therefore, be one of the important ways in which experimenter bias is mediated. Conceptually, however, the two processes are very different. Experimenter bias effects are rooted in the motives of the experimenter, but demand characteristic effects depend on the perception of the subject.

The effects of bias are by no means restricted to the treatment of subjects. They may equally well function in the recording of data and its analysis. As Rosenthal (1966) has pointed out, they can readily be demonstrated in all aspects of scientific endeavor—"N rays" being a prime example. Demand characteristics, on the other hand, are a problem only when we are studying sentient and motivated organisms. Light rays do not guess the purpose of the experiment and adapt themselves to it, but subjects may.

The repetition of an experiment by another investigator with different outcome orientation will, if the findings were due to experimenter bias, lead to different results. This procedure, however, may not be sufficient to clarify the effects of demand characteristics. Here it is the leanings of the subject, not of the experimenter, that are involved. In a real sense, for the subject an experiment is a problem-solving situation. Riecken (1962, 31) has succinctly expressed this when he says that aspects of the experimental situation lead to "a set of inferential and interpretive activities on the part of the subject in an effort to penetrate the experimenter's inscrutability. . . ." For example, if subjects are used as their own controls, they may easily recognize that differential treatment ought to produce differential results, and they may act accordingly. A similar effect may appear even when subjects are not their own controls. Those who *see themselves* as controls may on that account behave differently from those who think of themselves as the "experimentals."

It is not conscious deception by the subject which poses the problem here. That occurs only rarely. Demand characteristics usually operate subtly in interaction with other experimental variables. They change the subject's behavior in such a way that he is often not clearly aware of their effect. In fact, demand characteristics may be less effective or even have a paradoxical action if they are too obvious. With the constellation of motives that the usual subject brings to a psychological experiment, the "soft sell" works better than the "hard sell." Rosenthal (1963) has reported a similar finding in experimenter bias: the effect is weakened, or even reversed, if the experimenter is paid extra to bias his results.

It is possible to eliminate the experimenter entirely, as has been suggested by Charles Slack* some years back in a *Gedanken* experiment. He proposed that subjects be contacted by mail, be asked to report to a specific room at a specific time, and be given all instructions in a written form. The recording of all responses as well as the reinforcement of subjects would be done mechanically. This procedure would go a long way toward controlling experimenter bias. Nevertheless, it would have demand characteristics, as would any other experiment which we might conceive; subjects will always be in a position to form hypotheses about the purpose of an experiment.

Although every experiment has its own demand characteristics, these do not necessarily have an important effect on the outcome. They become important only when they interact with the effect of the independent variable being studied. Of course, the most serious situation is one where the investigator hopes to draw inferences from an experiment where one set of demand characteristics typically operates to a real life situation which lacks an analogous set of conditions.

II. PRE-INQUIRY DATA AS A BASIS FOR MANIPULATING DEMAND CHARACTERISTICS

A recent psychophysiological study (Gustafson and Orne, 1965) takes one possible approach to the clarification of demand characteristic

* Personal communication, 1959.

effects. The example is unusual only because some of its demands were deliberately manipulated and treated as experimental variables in their own right. The results of the explicit manipulation enabled us to understand an experimental result which was otherwise contrary to field findings.

In recent years there have been a number of studies on the detection of deception—more popularly known as "lie detection"—with the galvanic skin response (GSR) as the dependent variable. In one such study, Ellson, Davis, Saltzman, and Burke (1952) reported a very curious finding. Their experiment dealt with the effect which knowledge of results can have on the GSR. After the first trial, some subjects were told that their lies had been detected, while others were told the opposite. This produced striking results on the second trial: those who believed that they had been found out became *harder* to detect the second time, while those who thought they had deceived the polygraph on Trial 1 became *easier* to detect on Trial 2. This finding, if generalizable to the field, would have considerable practical implications. Traditionally, interrogators using field lie detectors go to great lengths to show the suspect that the device works by "catching" the suspect, as it were. If the results of Ellson *et al.* were generalizable to the field situation, the very procedure which the interrogators use would actually defeat the purpose for which it was intended by making subsequent lies of the suspect even harder to detect.

Because the finding of Ellson *et al.* runs counter to traditional practical experience, it seemed plausible to assume that additional variables might be involved in the experimental situation. The study by Ellson *et al.* was therefore replicated by Gustafson and Orne* with equivocal results. Postexperimental interviews with subjects revealed that many college students apparently believe that the lie detector *works with normal individuals* and that only habitual liars could deceive a polygraph. Given these beliefs, it was important for the student volunteers that they be detected. In that respect the situation of the experimental subjects differs markedly from that of the suspect being interrogated in a real life situation. Fortunately, with the information about what most experimental subjects believe, it is possible to manipulate these beliefs and thereby change the demand characteristics of the Ellson *et al.* study. Two groups of subjects were given different information about the effectiveness of the lie detector.

One group was given information congruent with this widely held belief and told: "This is a detection of deception experiment. We are trying to see how well the lie detector works. As you know, it is not

---

* Unpublished study, 1962.

possible to detect lying in the case of psychopathic personalities or habitual liars. We want you to try your very best to fool the lie detector during this experiment. Good luck." These instructions tried to maximize the kind of demand characteristics which might have been functioning in the Ellson *et al.* study, and it was assumed that the subjects would want to be detected in order to prove that they were not habitual liars. The other group was given information which prior work (Gustafson and Orne, 1963) had shown to be plausible and motivating; they were told, "This is a lie detection study and while it is extremely difficult to fool the lie detector, highly intelligent, emotionally stable, and mature individuals are able to do so." The demand characteristics in this case were designed to maximize the wish to deceive.

From that point on, the two groups were treated identically. They drew a card from an apparently randomized deck; the card had a number on it which they were to keep secret. All possible numbers were then presented by a prerecorded tape while a polygraph recorded the subjects' GSR responses. On the first such trial, the "detection ratios"— that is, the relative magnitudes of the critical GSR responses—in the two groups were not significantly different (see Table I). When the first trial was over, the experimenter gave half the subjects in each group the impression that they had been detected, by telling them what their number had been. (The experimenter had independent access to this information.) The other half were given the impression that they had fooled the polygraph, the experimenter reporting an incorrect number to them. A table of random numbers was used to determine, independent of his actual GSR, which kind of feedback each subject received.

A second detection trial with a new number was then given. The dramatic effects of the feedback in interaction with the original instructions are visible in Table II. Two kinds of subjects now gave large GSRs to the critical number: those who had wanted to be detected but yet had *not* been detected, and also those who had hoped to deceive and yet had *not* deceived. (This latter group is analogous to the field situation.) On the other hand, subjects whose hopes had been confirmed now responded less and thus became harder to detect, regardless of what those hopes had been. Those who had wanted to be detected, and indeed had been detected, behaved physiologically like those who had wanted to deceive and indeed had deceived.

This effect is an extremely powerful but also an exceedingly subtle one. The differential pretreatment of groups is not apparent on the first trial. Only on the second trial do the manipulated demand characteristics produce clear-cut differential results, in interaction with the independent variable of feedback. Furthermore, we are dealing with a dependent measure which is often erroneously assumed to be outside of volitional control, namely a physiological response—in this instance, the GSR. This study serves as a link toward resolving the discrepancy between the laboratory findings of Ellson *et al.* (1952) and the experience of interrogators using the "lie detector" in real life.

It appeared possible in this experiment to use simple variations in instructions as a means of varying demand characteristics. The success

TABLE I

NUMBER OF SUCCESSFUL AND UNSUCCESSFUL DETECTIONS ON TRIAL I
FOR THE TWO SUBGROUPS OF THE n DETECTED AND n DECEIVE GROUPS[a,b]

	Told detected (subsequently)	Told not detected (subsequently)	χ^2 between columns 1 and 2
"Need to be Detected Group"			
Detected	9	13	$\chi^2 = 1.31$
Not Detected	7	3	n.s.
"Need to Deceive Group"			
Detected	13	11	$\chi^2 = 0.17$
Not Detected	3	5	n.s.
χ^2 Between n Detected	$\chi^2 = 1.31$	$\chi^2 = 0.17$	
and n Deceive Groups	n.s.	n.s.	

Note. From: L. A. Gustafson and M. T. Orne, "Effects of perceived role and role success on the detection of deception," Journal of Applied Psychology, **49**, 1965, 412–417. Copyright (1965) by the American Psychological Association, and reproduced by permission.

[a] Note that Ss were not given information about the success of detection until *after* the trial on which these data are based.

[b] A multiple chi-square contingency analysis (Sutcliffe, 1957) was used to analyze the departures from expected frequencies in the entire table. Neither the chi-square components for each variable alone, nor the interaction between variables, were significant.

of the manipulation may be ascribed to the fact that the instructions themselves reflected views that emerged from interview data, and both sets of instructions were congruent with the experimental procedure. Only if instructions are plausible—a function of their congruence with the subjects' past knowledge as well as with the experimental procedure—will they be a reliable way of altering the demand characteristics. In this instance the instructions were not designed to manipulate the subjects' attitude directly; rather they were designed to provide differential background information relevant to the experiment. This background information was designed to provide very different contexts for the subjects' performance within the experiment. We believe this approach was effective because it altered the subjects' perception of the experimental situation, which is the basis of demand characteristics in any experiment. It is relevant that the differential instructions in no way told subjects to behave differently. Obviously subjects in an experiment will tend to do what they are told to do—that is the implicit contract of the situation—and to demonstrate this would prove little. Our effort here

TABLE II

Number of Successful and Unsuccessful Detections on Trial II
for the Two Subgroups of the *n* Detected and *n* Deceive Groups[a]

	Told detected (subsequently)	Told not detected (subsequently)	χ^2 between columns 1 and 2
"Need to be Detected Group"			
Detected	4	14	$\chi^2 = 10.28$
Not Detected	12	2	$p < .005$
"Need to Deceive Group"			
Detected	15	3	$\chi^2 = 15.36$
Not Detected	1	13	$p < .001$
χ^2 Between *n* Detected	$\chi^2 = 12.96$	$\chi^2 = 12.55$	
and *n* Deceive Groups	$p < .001$	$p < .001$	

Note. From: L. A. Gustafson and M. T. Orne, "Effects of perceived role and role success on the detection of deception," Journal of Applied Psychology, **49**, 1965, 412–417. Copyright (1965) by the American Psychological Association, and reproduced by permission.

[a] A multiple chi-square contingency analysis here shows that neither information given, nor motivation (*n* Detect *vs. n* Deceive) have significant effects by themselves. The relevant chi-square values, calculated from partitioned subtables, are $.25 (p > .95)$ and $.00$ respectively (df = 1). However, successful detection does depend significantly on the *interaction* between information and motivation ($\chi^2 = 30.94$; $p < .001$; df = 1).

was to create the kind of context which might differentiate the laboratory from the field situation and which might explain differential results in these two concepts. Plausible verbal instructions were one way of accomplishing this end. (Also see Cataldo, Silverman, and Brown, 1967; Kroger, 1967; Page and Lumia, 1968; Silverman, 1968.)

Unless verbal instructions are very carefully designed and pretested they may well fail to achieve such an end. It can be extremely difficult to predict how, if at all, demand characteristics are altered by instructions, and frequently more subtle aspects of the experimental setting and the experimental procedure may become more potent determinants of how the study is perceived.

III. DEALING WITH DEMAND CHARACTERISTICS

Studies such as the one described in which the demand characteristics are deliberately manipulated contribute little or nothing to the question of how they can be delineated. In order to design the lie detection experiment in the first place, a thorough understanding of the demand characteristics involved was essential. How can such an understanding be obtained? As was emphasized earlier, the problem arises basically because the human subject is an active organism and not a passive responder. For him, the experiment is a problem-solving situation to be actively handled in some way. To find out how he is trying to handle it, it has been found useful to take advantage of the same mental processes which would otherwise be confounding the data. Three techniques were proposed which do just that. Although apparently different, the three methods serve the same basic purpose. For reasons to be explained later, I propose to call them "quasi-controls."

A. Postexperimental Inquiry

The most obvious way of finding out something about the subject's perception of the experimental situation is the postexperimental inquiry. It never fails to amaze me that some colleagues go to the trouble of inducing human subjects to participate in their experiments and then squander the major difference between man and animal—the ability to talk and reflect upon experience.

To be sure, inquiry is not always easy. The greatest danger is the "pact of ignorance" (Orne, 1959a) which all too commonly characterizes the postexperimental discussion. The subject knows that if he has "caught on" to some apparent deception and has an excess of information about the experimental procedure he may be disqualified from participation and thus have wasted his time. The experimenter is aware that the subject who knows too much or has "caught on" to his deception will have to be disqualified; disqualification means running yet another subject, still further delaying completion of his study. Hence, neither party to the inquiry wants to dig very deeply.

The investigator, aware of these problems and genuinely more interested in learning what his subjects experienced than in the rapid collection of data, can, however, learn a great deal about the demand characteristics of a particular experimental procedure by judicious inquiry.

It is essential that he elicit what the subject perceives the experiment is about, what the subject believes the investigator hopes and expects to find, how the subject thinks others might have reacted in this situation, etc. This information will help to reveal what the subject perceives to be a good response, good both in tending to validate the hypothesis of the experiment and in showing him off to his best advantage.

To the extent that the subject perceives the experiment as a problem-solving situation where the subject's task is to ascertain the experiment's true nature, the inquiry is directed toward clarifying the subject's beliefs about its true nature. When, as is often the case, the investigator will have told the subject in the beginning something about why the experiment is being carried out, it may well be difficult for the subject to express his disbelief since to do so might put him in the position of seeming to call the experimenter a liar. For reasons such as these, the postexperimental interview must be conducted with considerable tact and skill, creating a situation where the subject is able to communicate freely what he truly believes without, however, making him unduly suspicious or, worse yet, cueing him as to what he is to say. Using another investigator to carry out the inquiry will often maximize communication, particularly if the other investigator is seen as someone who is attempting to learn more about what the subject experiences. However, it is necessary to avoid having it appear as though the inquiry is carried out by someone who is evaluating the experimenter since the student subject may identify with what he sees to be the student experimenter and try to make him look good rather than describing his real experience. The situational factors which will maximize the subject's communicating what he is experiencing are clearly exceedingly complex and conceptually similar to those which need to be taken into account in clinical situations or in the study of taboo topics. Examples of the factors are merely touched upon here.

It would be unreasonable to expect a one-to-one relationship between the kind of data obtained by inquiry and the demand characteristics which were actually perceived by the subject in the situation. Not only do many factors mitigate against fully honest communication, but the subject cannot necessarily verbalize adequately what he may have dimly perceived during the experiment, and it is the dimly perceived factors which may exert the greatest effect on the subject's experimental behaviors. More important than any of these considerations, however, is the fact that an inquiry may be carried out at the end of a complex experiment and that the subject's perception of the experiment's demand characteristics may have changed considerably during the experiment. For example, a subject might "catch on" to a verbal conditioning experiment only at the very end or even in retrospect during the inquiry itself, and he may then verbalize during the inquiry an awareness that will have had little or no effect on his performance during the experiment. For this reason, one may wish to carry out inquiry procedures at significant junctures in a long experiment.* This technique is quite expensive and time-consuming. It requires running different sets of subjects to different points in the experiment, stopping at these points as if the experiment were over (for these subjects it, in fact, is), and carrying out inquiries. While it would be tempting to use the same group of subjects and to continue to run them after the inquiry procedure, such a technique would in many instances be undesirable because exhaustive inquiries into the demand characteristics, as the subject perceives them at a given point in time, make him unduly aware of such factors subsequently.

While inquiry procedures may appear time-consuming, in actual practice they are relatively straightforward and efficient. Certainly they are vastly preferable to finding at the conclusion of a large study that the data depend more on the demand characteristics than on the independent variables one had hoped to investigate. It is perhaps worth remembering that, investigators being human, it is far easier to do exhaustive inquiry during pilot studies when one is still motivated to find out what is really happening than in the late stages of a major investigation. Indeed this is one of the reasons why pilot investigations are an essential prelude to any substantive study.

B. Non-experiment

Another technique—and a very powerful one—for uncovering the demand characteristics of a given experimental design is the "pre-inquiry" (Orne, 1959a) or the "non-experiment."† This procedure was independently proposed by Riecken (1962). A group of persons representing the same population from which the actual experimental subjects will eventually be selected are asked to imagine that they are subjects themselves. They are shown the equipment that is to be used and the room in which the experiment is to be conducted. The procedures are explained in such a way as to provide them with information equivalent to that which would be available to an experimental subject. However, they do not actually go through the experimental procedure; it is only explained. In a non-experiment on a certain drug, for example, the partici-. pant would be told that subjects are given a pill. He would be shown the pill. The instructions destined for the experimental subjects would

---

* These results may also be conceptualized in terms of learning theory.

† Ulric Neisser suggested this persuasive term.

be read to him. The participant would then be asked to produce data as if he actually had been subjected to the experimental treatment. He could be given posttests or asked to fill out rating scales or requested to carry out any behavior that might be relevant for the actual experimental group.

The non-experiment yields data similar in quality to inquiry material but obtained in the same form as actual subjects' data. Direct comparison of non-experimental data and actual experimental data is therefore possible. But caution is needed. If these two kinds of data are identical, it shows only that the subject population in the actual experiment could have guessed what was expected of them. It does not tell us whether such guesses were the actual determinants of their behavior.

Kelman (1965) has recently suggested that such a technique might appropriately be used as a social psychological tool to obviate the need for deception studies. While the economy of this procedure is appealing, and working in a situation where subjects become quasi-collaborators instead of objects to be manipulated is more satisfying to many of us, it would seem dangerous to draw inferences to the actual situation in real life from results obtained in this fashion. In fact, when subjects in pre-inquiry experiments perform exactly as subjects do in actual experimental situations, it becomes impossible to know the extent to which their performance is due to the independent variables or to the experimental situation.

In most psychological studies, when one is investigating the effect of the subject's best possible performance in response to different physical or psychological stimuli, there is relatively little concern for the kind of problems introduced by demand characteristics. The need to concern oneself with these issues becomes far more pronounced when investigating the effect of various interventions such as drugs, psychotherapy, hypnosis, sensory deprivation, conditioning of physiological responses, etc., on performance or experiential parameters. Here the possibility that the subject's response may inadvertently be determined by altered demand characteristics rather than the process itself must be considered. Equally subject to these problems are studies where attitude changes rather than performance changes are explored. The investigator's intuitive recognition that subjects' perceptions of an experiment and its meaning are very likely to affect the nature of his responses may have been one of the main reasons why deception studies have been so popular in the investigation of attitude change.

Festinger's cognitive dissonance theory (1957) has been particularly attractive to psychologists probably because it makes predictions which appear to be counterexpectational; that is, the predictions made on the basis of intuitive "common sense" appear to be wrong whereas those made on the basis of dissonance are both different and borne out by data. Bem (1967) has shown in an elegant application of pre-inquiry techniques that the findings are not truly counterexpectational in the sense that subjects to whom the situation is described in detail but who are not really placed in the situation are able to produce data closely resembling those observed in typical cognitive dissonance studies. On the basis of these findings, Bem (1967) appropriately questions the assertion that the dissonance theory allows counterexpectational predictions. His use of the pre-inquiry effectively makes the cognitive dissonance studies it replicates far less compelling by showing that subjects could figure out the way others might respond. It would be unfortunate to assume that Bem's incisive critique of the empirical studies with the pre-inquiry technique makes further such studies unnecessary. On the contrary, his findings merely show that the avowed claims of these studies were not, in fact, achieved and provide a more stringent test for future experiments that aim to demonstrate counterexpectational findings.

It would appear that we are in the process of completing a cycle. At one time it was assumed that subjects could predict their own behavior, that in order to know what an individual would do in a given situation it would suffice merely to ask him. It became clear, however, that individuals could not always predict their behavior; in fact, serious questions about the extent to which they could make any such predictions were raised when studies showing differences between what individuals thought they do and what they, in fact, do became fashionable. With a sophisticated use of the pre-inquiry technique Bem (1967) has shown that individuals have more knowledge about what they might do than has been ascribed to them by psychologists. Although it is possible to account for a good deal of variance in behavior in this way, it is clear that it will not account for all of the variance. We are confronted now with a peculiar paradox. When pre-inquiry data correctly predict the performance of the subject in the actual experiment—the situation that is most commonly encountered—the experimental findings strike us as relatively trivial, in part because at best we have validated our intuitive common sense but also because we cannot exclude the nagging doubt that the subject may have merely been responsive to the demand characteristics in the actual experiment. Only when we succeed in setting up an experiment where the results are counterexpectational in the sense that a pre-inquiry would yield different findings from those obtained from the subjects in the actual situation can we be relatively comfortable that these findings represent the real effects of the experimental treatment rather than being subject to alternative explanations.

For the reasons discussed above, pre-inquiry can never supplant the actual investigation of what subjects do in concrete situations although, adroitly executed, it becomes an essential tool to clarify these findings.

C. Simulators

This principle can be carried one step further to provide yet another method for uncovering demand characteristics: the use of simulators (Orne, 1959a). Subjects are asked to pretend that they have been affected by an experimental treatment which they did not actually receive or to which they are immune. For subjects to be able to do this, it is crucial that they be run by another experimenter who they are told is unaware of their actual status, and who in fact really is unaware of their status. It is essential that the subjects be aware that the experimenter is blind as well as that the experimenter actually be blind for this technique to be effective. Further, the fact that the experimenter is "blind" has the added advantage of forcing him to treat simulators and actual subjects alike. This technique has been used extensively in the study of hypnosis (e.g., Damaser, Shor, and Orne, 1963; Orne, 1959a; Orne and Evans, 1965; Orne, Sheehan, and Evans, 1968). For an extended discussion, see Orne (1968). It is possible for unhypnotized subjects to deceive an experimenter by acting as though they had been hypnotized. Obviously, it is essential that the simulators be given no special training relevant to the variables being studied, so that they have no more information than what is available to actually hypnotized subjects. The simulating subjects must try to guess what real subjects might do in a given experimental situation in response to instructions administered by a particular experimenter.

This design permits us to separate experimenter bias effects from demand characteristic effects. In addition to his other functions, the experimenter may be asked to judge whether each subject is a "real" or a simulator. This judgment tends to be random and unrelated to the true status of the subjects. Nevertheless, we have often found differences between the behaviors of subjects contingent on whether or not the experimenter judges that they are hypnotized or just simulating. Such differences may be ascribed to differential treatment and bias, whereas differences between actually hypnotized subjects and actual simulators are likely to be due to hypnosis itself.

Again, results obtained with this technique need careful evaluation. It is important not to jump to a negative conclusion if no difference is found between deeply hypnotized subjects and simulators. Such data are not evidence that hypnosis consists only of a reaction to demand characteristics. It may well have special properties. But so long as a given form of behavior is displayed as readily by simulators as by "reals," our procedure has failed to demonstrate those properties. The problem here is the same as that discussed earlier in the pre-inquiry. Most likely there will be many real effects due to hypnosis which can be mimicked successfully by simulators. However, only when we are able to demonstrate differences in behavior between real and simulating subjects do we feel that an experiment is persuasive in demonstrating that a given effect is likely to be due to the presence of hypnosis.

IV. QUASI-CONTROLS: TECHNIQUES FOR THE EVALUATION OF EXPERIMENTAL ROLE DEMANDS

The three techniques discussed above are not like the usual control groups in psychological research. They ask the subject to participate actively in uncovering explicit information about possible demand characteristic effects. The quasi-control subject steps out of his traditional role, because the experimenter redefines the interaction between them to make him a co-investigator instead of a manipulated object. Because the quasi-control is outside of the usual experimenter-subject relationship, he can reveal the effects of this relationship in a new perspective. An inquiry, for example, takes place only after the experiment has been defined as "finished," and the subject joins the experimenter in reflecting on his own earlier performance as a subject. In the non-experiment, the quasi-control cooperates with the experimenter in second-guessing what real subjects might do. Most dramatically, the simulating subject reverses the usual relationship and deceives the experimenter.

It is difficult to find an appropriate term for these procedures. They are not, of course, classical control groups since, rather than merely omitting the independent variable, the groups are treated differently. Thus we are dealing with treatment groups that facilitate inference about the behavior of both experimental and control groups. Because these treatment groups are used to assess the effect that the subject's perception of being under study might have upon his behavior in the experimental situation, they may be conceptualized as role demand controls in that they clarify the demand characteristic variables in the experimental situation for the particular subject population used. As quasi-controls, the subjects are required to participate and utilize their cognitive processes to evaluate the possible effect that thinking about the total situation might have on their performance. They could, in this sense, be considered active, as opposed to passive, controls.

A unique aspect of quasi-controls is that they do not permit inference to be drawn about the effect of the independent variable. They can never prove that a given finding in the experimental group is due to the demand characteristics of the situation. Rather, they serve to suggest alternative explanations not excluded by the experimental design employed. The inference from quasi-control data, therefore, primarily concerns the adequacy of the experimental procedure. In this sense, the term design control or evaluative control would be justified.

Since each of these various terms focuses upon different but equally important aspects of these comparison groups, it would seem best to refer to them simply as quasi-controls. This explicitly recognizes that we are not dealing with control groups in the true sense of the word and are using the term analogously to the way in which Campbell and Stanley (1963) have used the term quasi-experiments. However, while they think of quasi-experiments as doing the best one can in situations where "true experiments" cannot be carried out, the concept of quasi-controls is intended to refer specifically to techniques for the assessment of demand characteristic variables in order to evaluate how such factors might effect the experimental outcome. The term "quasi-" in this context says that these techniques are similar to—but not really—control groups. It does not mean that these groups are any less important in helping to evaluate the data obtained from human subjects. In bridging the gap from the laboratory experiments to situations where the individual does not perceive himself to be a subject under investigation, techniques of this kind are of vital importance.

It is frequently pointed out that investigators often discuss the experimental procedures with colleagues in order to clarify their meaning. Certainly many problems in experimental design will be obvious only to expert colleagues. These types of issues have typically been discussed in the context of quantitative methods and have led to some more elaborate techniques of experimental design. There is no question that expert colleagues are sensitive to order effects, baseline phenomena, practice effects, sampling procedures, individual differences, and so on, but how a given subject population would, in fact, perceive an experimental procedure is by no means easily accessible to the usual tools of the psychologists. Whether in a deception experiment the subject may be partially or fully aware of what is really going on is a function of a great many cues in the situation not easily explicated, and the prior experience of the subject population which might in some way be relevant to the experiment is also not easily ascertained or abstracted by any amount of expert discussion. The use of quasi-controls, however, allows the investigator to estimate these factors and how they might affect the experimental results.

The kind of factors which we are discussing here relate to the manner in which subjects are solicited (for example, the wording of an announcement in an ad), the manner in which the secretary or research assistant answers questions about the proposed experiment when subjects call in to volunteer, the location of the experiment (i.e., psychiatric hospital versus aviation training school), and, finally, a great many details of the experimental procedure itself which of necessity are simplified in the description, not to speak of the subtle cues made available by the investigator himself. Quasi-controls are designed to evaluate the total impact of these various cues upon the particular kind of population which is to be used. It will be obvious, of course, that a verbal conditioning experiment carried out with psychology students who have been exposed to the original paper is by no means the same as the identical experiment carried out with students who have not been exposed to this information. Again, quasi-controls allow one to estimate what the demand characteristics might be for the particular subject population being used.

Quasi-controls serve to clarify the demand characteristics but they can never yield substantive data. They cannot even prove that a given result is a function of demand characteristics. They provide information about the adequacy of an investigative procedure and thereby permit the design of a better one. No data are free of demand characteristics but quasi-controls make it possible to estimate their effect on the data which we do obtain.

V. THE USE OF QUASI-CONTROLS TO MAKE POSSIBLE A STUDY MANIPULATING DEMAND CHARACTERISTICS

When extreme variations of experimental procedures are still able to elicit surprisingly similar results or identical experimental procedures carried out in different laboratories yield radically different results, the likelihood of demand characteristic effects must be seriously considered. An area of investigation characterized in this way were the early studies on "sensory deprivation." The initial findings attracted wide attention because they not only had great theoretical significance for psychology but seemed to have practical implications for the space program as well. A review of the literature indicated that dramatic hallucinatory effects and other perceptual changes were typically observed after the subject had been in the experiment approximately two-thirds of the total time; however, it seemed to matter relatively little whether the total time was three weeks, two weeks, three days, two days, twenty-four hours, or eight hours. Clearly, factors other than physical conditions would have to account for such discrepancies. As a first quasi-control we interviewed subjects who had participated in such studies.* It became clear that they had been aware of the kind of behavior that was expected of them. Next, a pre-inquiry was carried out, and, from participants who were guessing how they might respond if they were in a sensory deprivation situation, we obtained data remarkably like that observed in actual studies.† We were then in a position to design an actual experiment in which the demand characteristics of sensory deprivation were the independent variables (Orne and Scheibe, 1964). Our results showed that these characteristics, by themselves, could produce many of the findings attributed to the condition of sensory deprivation. In brief, one group of the subjects were run in a "meaning deprivation" study which included the accoutrements of sensory deprivation research but omitted the condition itself. They were required to undergo a physical examination, provide a short medical history, sign a release form, were "assured" of the safety of the procedure by the presence of an emergency tray containing various syringes and emergency drugs, and were taken to a well-lighted cubicle, provided food and water, and given an optional task. After taking a number of pretests, the subjects were told that if they heard, saw, smelled, or experienced anything strange they were to report it through the microphone in the room. They were again reassured and told that if they could not stand the situation any longer or became discomforted they merely had to press the red "panic button" in order to obtain immediate release.

They were then subjected to four hours of isolation in the experimental cubicle and given posttests. The control subjects were told that they were controls for a sensory deprivation study and put in the same objective conditions as the experimental subjects. Table III summarizes the findings which indicate that manipulation of the demand characteristics by themselves could produce many findings that had previously been ascribed to the sensory deprivation condition. Of course, neither the quasi-controls nor the experimental manipulation of the demand characteristics sheds light on the actual effects of the condition of sensory deprivation. They do show that demand characteristics may produce similar effects to those ascribed to sensory deprivation.

* Unpublished study.

† Stare, F., Brown, J., and Orne, M. T. Demand characteristics in sensory deprivation studies. Unpublished seminar paper, Massachusetts Mental Health Center and Harvard University, 1959.

TABLE III

SUMMARY AND ANALYSIS OF TEN TESTS FOR CONTROL AND EXPERIMENTAL GROUPS

Test and group	Pretest M	Posttest M	Difference statistic
Mirror Tracing (errors)			
Experimental	28.1	19.7	
Control	35.8	15.2	$F = 1.67^a$
Spatial Orientation			
Angular deviation			
Experimental	45.7	53.9	
Control	52.5	59.1	$F = .25^a$
Linear deviation			
Experimental	5.3	5.4	
Control	6.4	5.7	$F = 3.34^b$
Word Recognition (N correct)			
Experimental	17.3	15.6	
Control	15.2	12.3	$t = .50$
Reversible Figure (rate per minute)			
Experimental	29.0	35.0	
Control	20.1	25.0	$F = 1.54^a$
Digit Symbol (N correct)			
Experimental	98.2	109.9	
Control	99.2	111.9	$F = .05^a$
Mechanical Ability			
Tapping speed (N completed)			
Experimental	33.9	32.2	
Control	32.9	35.0	$F = 2.26$
Tracing speed (N completed)			
Experimental	55.6	52.3	
Control	53.1	58.4	$F = 4.57^b$
Visual pursuit (N completed)			
Experimental	5.7	8.9	
Control	5.7	9.2	$F = .22^a$
Simple Forms (N increment distortions)			
Experimental	—	3.1	
Control	—	0.8	$U = 19^c$
Size Constancy (change in steps)			
Experimental	—	0.6	
Control	—	0.0	$t = 1.03^a$
Spiral Aftereffect			
Duration, seconds			
Experimental	24.4	27.1	
Control	15.6	16.1	$F = .99^a$
Absolute Change			
Experimental	—	7.0	
Control	—	2.7	$t = 3.38^d$
Logical Deduction (N correct)			
Experimental	—	20.3	
Control	—	22.1	$t = 1.64$

Note. F = adjusted postexperimental scores, analysis of covariance; $t = t$ tests; U = Mann-Whitney U test, where plot of data appeared grossly abnormal. (From: M. T. Orne and K. E. Scheibe, "The contribution of nondeprivation factors in the production of sensory deprivation effects: The psychology of the 'panic button,'" Journal of Abnormal and Social Psychology, **68**, 1964, 3–12. Copyright [1964] by the American Psychological Association, and reproduced by permission.)

[a] Indicates differences between groups were in predicted direction.

[b] $p < .05$, one-tailed.

[c] $p = .01$, one-tailed.

[d] $p < .001$, nondirectional measure.

VI. THE PROBLEM OF INFERENCE

Great care must be taken in drawing conclusions from experiments of this kind. In the case of the sensory deprivation study, the demand characteristics of the laboratory and those which might be encountered by individuals outside of the laboratory differ radically. In other situations, however, such as in the case of hypnosis, the expectations of subjects about the kind of behavior hypnosis ought to elicit in the laboratory are similar to the kind of expectations which patients might have about being hypnotized for therapeutic purposes. To the extent that the hypnotized individual's behavior is determined by these expectations we might find similar findings in certain laboratory contexts and certain therapeutic situations. When demand characteristics become a significant determinant of behavior, valid accurate predictions can only be made about another situation where the same kind of demand characteristics prevails. In the case of sensory deprivation studies, accurate predictions would therefore not be possible but, even in the studies with hypnosis, we might still be observing an epiphenomenon which is present only as long as consistent and stable expectations and beliefs are present. In order to get beyond such an epiphenomenon and find intrinsic characteristics, it is essential that we evaluate the effect that demand characteristics may have. To do this we must seek techniques specifically designed to estimate the likely extent of such effects.

VII. PSYCHOPHARMACOLOGICAL RESEARCH AS A MODEL FOR THE PSYCHOLOGICAL EXPERIMENT

What are here termed the demand characteristics of the experimental situation are closely related to what the psychopharmacologist considers a placebo effect, broadly defined. The difficulty in determining what aspects of a subject's performance may legitimately be ascribed to the independent variable as opposed to those which might be due to the demand characteristics of the situation is similar to the problem of determining what aspects of a drug's action are due to pharmacological effect and what aspects are due to the subject's awareness that he has been given a drug. Perhaps because the conceptual distinction between a drug effect and the effect of psychological factors is readily made, perhaps because of the relative ease with which placebo controls may be included, or most likely because of the very significant consequences of psychopharmacological research, considerable effort has gone into differentiating pharmacological action from placebo effects. A brief review of relevant observations from this field may help clarify the problem of demand characteristics.

In evaluating the effect of a drug it has long been recognized that a patient's expectations and beliefs may have profound effects on his experiences subsequent to the taking of the drug. It is for this reason that the use of placebos has been widespread. The extent of the placebo effect is remarkable. Beecher (1959), for example, has shown that in battlefield situations saline solution by injection has 90 per cent of the effectiveness of morphine in alleviating the pain associated with acute injury. In civilian hospitals, postoperatively, the placebo effect drops to 70 per cent of the effectiveness of morphine, and with subsequent administrations drops still lower. These studies show not only that the placebo effect may be extremely powerful, but that it will interact with the experimental situation in which it is being investigated.

It soon became clear that it was not sufficient to use placebos so long as the investigator knew to which group a given individual belonged. Typically, when a new, presumably powerful, perhaps even dangerous medication is administered, the physician takes additional care in watching over the patient. He tends to be not only particularly hopeful but also particularly concerned. Special precautions are instituted, nursing care and supervision are increased, and other changes in the regime inevitably accompany the drug's administration. When a patient is on placebo, even if an attempt is made to keep the conditions the same, there is a tendency to be perfunctory with special precautions, to be more cavalier with the patient's complaints, and in general to be less concerned and interested in the placebo group. For these reasons, the doctor, as well as the patient, is required to be blind as to the true nature of a drug; otherwise differential treatment could well account for some of the observed differences between drug and placebo (Modell and Houde, 1958). The problems discussed here would be conceptualized in social psychological terms as E-bias effects or differential E-outcome expectations.

What would appear at first sight to be a simple problem—to determine the pharmacological action of a drug as opposed to those effects which may be attributed to the patient's awareness that he is being treated by presumably effective medication—turns out to be extremely difficult. Indeed, as Ross, Krugman, Lyerly, and Clyde (1962) have pointed out, and as discussed by Lana (Chapter 4), the usual clinical techniques can never evaluate the true pharmacological action of a drug. In practice, patients are given a drug and realize that they are being treated; therefore one always observes the pharmacological action of the drug confounded with the placebo effect. The typical study with placebo controls compares the effect of placebo and drug versus the effect of placebo alone. Such a procedure does not get at the psychopharmacological action of the drug without the placebo effect, i.e., the patient's awareness that he is receiving a drug. Ross *et al.* elegantly demonstrate this point by studying the effect of chloral hydrate and amphetamine in a 3×3 design. Amphetamine, chloral hydrate, and placebo were used as three agents with three different instructions: (a) administering each capsule with a brief description of the amphetamine effect, (b) administering each capsule with a brief description of the chloral hydrate effect, and (c) administration without the individual's awareness that a drug was being administered. Their data clearly demonstrate that drug effects interact with the individual's knowledge that a drug is being administered.

For clinical psychopharmacology, the issues raised by Ross *et al.* are somewhat academic since in medical practice one is almost always dealing with combinations of placebo components and drug effects. Studies evaluating the effect of drugs are intended to draw inference about how drugs work in the context of medical practice. To the extent that one would be interested in the psychopharmacological effect as such— that is, totally removed from the medical context—the type of design Ross *et al.* utilized would be essential.

In psychology, experiments are carried out in order to determine the effect of an independent variable so that it will be possible to draw inference to non-experimental situations. Unfortunately the independent variables tend to be studied in situations that are explicitly defined as experimental. As a result, one observes the effect of an experimental context in interaction with a particular independent variable versus the effect of the experimental context without this variable.

The problem of the experimental context in which an investigation is carried out is perhaps best illustrated in psychopharmacology by research on the effects of meprobamate (known under the trade names of Equanil and Miltown). Meprobamate had been established as effective in a number of clinical studies but, when carefully controlled investigations were carried out, it did not appear to be more efficacious than placebo. The findings from carefully controlled studies appeared to contradict a large body of clinical observations which one might have a tendency to discount as simply due to placebo effect. It remained for Fisher, Cole, Rickels, and Uhlenhuth (1964) to design a systematic investigation to clarify this paradox, using physicians displaying either a "scientific," skeptical attitude toward medication or enthusiasm about the possible help which the drug would yield. The study was run double-blind. The patients treated by physicians with a "scientific" attitude toward medication showed no difference between drug and placebo; however, those treated by enthusiastic physicians clearly demonstrated an increased effectiveness of meprobamate! It would appear that there is a "real" drug effect of meprobamate which may, however, be totally obscured by the manner in which the drug is administered. The effect of the drug emerges only when medication is administered with conviction and enthusiasm. The striking interaction between the drug effects and situation-specific factors not only points to limitations in conclusions drawn from double-blind studies in psychopharmacology but also has broad methodological implications for the experimental study of psychological processes. An example of these implications from an entirely different area is the psychotherapy study by Paul (1966) which showed differences in improvement between individuals expecting to be helped at some time in the future and a matched control group who were not aware that they were included in the research.

VIII. DEALING WITH THE PLACEBO EFFECT: AN ANALOGY TO DEALING WITH DEMAND CHARACTERISTICS

Drug effects that are independent of the patient's expectations, beliefs, and attitudes can of course be studied with impunity without concern about the psychological effects that may be attributed to the taking of medication. For example, the antipyretic fever-reducing effect of aspirin is less likely to be influenced by the patient's beliefs and expectations than is the analgesic effect, though even here an empirical approach is considerably safer than *a priori* assumptions.

Of greatest relevance are the psychological effects of drugs. The problems encountered in studying these effects, while analogous to those inherent in other kinds of psychological research, seem more evident here. Since the drug constitutes a tangible independent variable (subject to study by pharmacological techniques), it is conceptually easily distinguished from another set of independent variables, psychological in nature, that also may play a crucial part in determining the patient's response.

The totality of these non-drug effects which are a function of the patient's expectations and beliefs in interaction with the medical procedures that are carried out, the doctor's expectations, and the manner in which he is treated have been conceptualized as placebo effect. This is, of course, analogous to the demand characteristic components in psychological studies; the major difference is that the concept of placebo component directly derives from methodological control procedures used to evaluate it.

The placebo is intended to produce the same attitudes, expectations, and beliefs of the patient as would the actual drug. The double-blind technique is designed to equate the environmental cues which would interact with these attitudes. For this model to work, it is essential that the placebo provide subjective side effects analogous to the actual drug lest the investigator and physician be blind but the patient fully cognizant that he is receiving a placebo. For these reasons an active placebo should be employed which mimics the side effects of the drug without exerting a central pharmacological action.

With the use of active placebos administered by physicians having appropriate clinical attitudes in a double-blind study a technically difficult but conceptually straightforward technique is available for the evaluation of the placebo effect. This approach satisfies the assumptions of the classical experimental model. One group of patients responds to the placebo effect and the drug, the other group to the placebo effect alone, which permits the investigator to determine the additive effect that may be attributed to the pharmacological action of the drug. Unfortunately such an ideal type of control is not generally available in the study of other kinds of independent variables. This is particularly true regarding the context of such studies. Thus, the placebo technique can be applied in clinical settings where the patient is not aware that he is the object of such study whereas psychological studies most frequently are recognized as such by our subjects who typically are asked to volunteer. Because a true analog to the placebo is not readily available, quasi-control techniques are being proposed to bridge the inferential gap between experimental findings and the influence of the experimental situation upon the subject who is aware that he is participating in an experiment.

The function of quasi-controls to determine the possible contextual effects of an experimental situation is perhaps clarified best when we contrast them with the use of placebos in evaluating possible placebo effect. Assume that we wish to evaluate an unknown drug purporting to be a powerful sedative and that neither pharmacological data nor placebo controls are available as methodological tools. All that we are able to do is to administer the drug under a variety of conditions and observe its effects. This is in many ways analogous to the kind of independent variable that we normally study in psychology. In fact, in this example the unknown drug will be sodium amytal, a powerful hypnotic with indisputable pharmacological action.

On giving the drug the first time, with considerable trepidation of course, we might well observe relatively little effect. Then as we get used to the drug a bit we might see it causes relaxation, a lessening of control, perhaps even some slurring of speech; in fact, some of the kind of changes typically associated with alcohol.

At this point, working with relatively small dosages of the drug, we would find that there were wide individual differences in response, some individuals actually becoming hyperalert, and one might wonder to what extent the effects could be related to subjects' beliefs and expectations. Under these circumstances the inquiry procedures discussed earlier could be carried out after the drug had been given. One would focus the inquiry on what the subject feels the drug might do, the kind of side effects he might expect, what he anticipated he would experience subsequent to taking the drug, what he thought we would have expected to happen, what he believed others might have experienced after taking the drug, etc. Data of this kind might help shed light on the patient's behavior.

Putting aside the difficulty of interpreting inquiry material, and assuming we are capable of obtaining a good approximation of what the subject really perceived, we are still not in position to determine the extent to which his expectations actually contributed to the effects that had been observed. Consider if a really large dose of amytal had been given: essentially all subjects would have gone to sleep and would most likely have correctly concluded they had been given a sleeping pill—the inquiry data in this instance being the result of the observed effect rather than the cause of it. Inquiry data would become suggestive only if (in dealing with relatively small dosages) it were found that subjects who expected or perceived that we expected certain kinds of effects did in fact show these effects whereas subjects who had no such expectations failed to show the effects. Even if we obtained such data, however, it would still be unclear whether the subject's perceptions were *post hoc* or *propter hoc*. The most significant use of inquiry material would be in facilitating the recognition of those cues in the situation which might communicate what is expected to the subject so that these cues could be altered systematically. Neither subject nor investigator is really in a position to evaluate how much of the total effect may legitimately be ascribed to the placebo response and how much to drug effect. Evaluation becomes possible only after subsequent changes in procedure can be shown to eliminate certain effects even though the same drug is being administered, or, conversely, subjects' perceptions upon inquiry are changed without changing the observed effect. The approach then would be to compare the effect of the drug in interaction with different sets of demand characteristics in order to estimate how much of the total effect can reasonably be ascribed to demand characteristic components. (The paper previously mentioned by Ross *et al.* [1962] reports precisely such a study with amytal and showed clear-cut differences.)

It is clear that the quasi-control of inquiry can only serve to estimate the adequacy of the various design modifications. Inference about these changes must be based on effects which the modifications are shown to produce in actual studies of subjects' behavior.

The non-experiment can be used in precisely the same manner. It has the advantage and disadvantage of eliminating cues from the drug experience. Here one would explain to a group of subjects drawn from the usual subject pool precisely what is to be done, show them the drug that is to be taken, give them the identical information provided to those individuals who actually take the drug, and, finally, ask them to perform on the tests to be used as if they had received the drug. This procedure has the advantage that the experimenter need no longer infer what the subject could have deduced about what was expected and how these perceptions could then have affected his performance. Instead of requiring the experimenter to interpret inquiry data and make many assumptions about how presumed attitudes and beliefs could manifest themselves on the particular behavioral indices used, the subject provides the experimenter with data in a form identical to that provided by those individuals who actually take the drug.

The fact that the non-experimental subject yields data in the form identical to that yielded by the actual experimental subject must not, however, seduce the investigator into believing that the data are in other ways equivalent. Inference from such a procedure about the actual demand characteristic components of the drug effect would need to be guarded indeed.

Such findings merely indicate that sufficient cues are present in the situation to allow a subject to know what is expected and these could, but need not, be responsible for the data. To illustrate with our example, if in doing the non-experiment one tells the subject he will be receiving three sleeping capsules and then asks him to do a test requiring prolonged concentration, the subject is very likely to realize that he ought to perform as though he were quite drowsy and yield a significantly subnormal performance. The fact that these subjects do behave like actual subjects receiving three sleeping capsules of sodium amytal would not negate the possible real drug effects which, in our example, are known to be powerful. The only thing it indicates is that the experimental procedure allows for an alternative explanation and needs to be refined. Again, the non-experiment would facilitate such refinement: if subjects instead of being told that they would receive sleeping capsules were told we are investigating a drug designed to increase peripheral blood flow and were given a description of an experimental procedure congruent with such a drug study, they would not be likely to show a decrement in performance data. However, subjects who were run with the drug and such instructions would presumably yield the standard subnormal performance. In other words, the quasi-control of the non-experiment has allowed us to economically assess the possible effects of instructional sets rather than allowing drug inference. It is an efficient way of clarifying the adequacy of experimental procedures as a prelude to the definitive study.*

A somewhat more elaborate procedure would be to instruct subjects to simulate.† It would be relatively easy to use simulators in a fashion analogous to that suggested in hypnosis research. Two investigators would be employed, one who would administer the medication and one who would carry out all other aspects of the study. The simulators would, instead of receiving the drug, be shown the medication, would read exactly the information given to the drug subjects, but would be told they would not be given the drug. Instead, their task would be to deceive the other experimenter and to make him think they had actually received the drug. They would further be told the other experimenter was blind and would not know they were simulating; if he really caught on to their identity, he would disqualify them; therefore, they should not be afraid they would give themselves away since, as long as they were not disqualified, they were doing well. The subject would then be turned over to the other experimenter who would, in fact, be blind as to the true status of the subject. The simulating subject, under these circumstances, would get no more and no less information than the subject receiving the actual drug (except cues of subjective side effects from the drug). He would be treated by the experimenter in essentially the same fashion. This procedure avoids some of the possible difficulties of differential treatment inherent in the non-experiment. Even under these circumstances, however, if both groups produce, let's say, identical striking alterations of subjective experience, it would still be

---

* Obviously, extreme caution is needed in interpreting differences in performance of the individuals actually receiving the drug and that of the non-experimental control. The subjects in a non-experiment cannot really be given the identical cues and role support provided the subject who is actually taking the drug. While the identical instructions may be read to him, it is essentially impossible to treat such subjects in the same fashion. Obviously the investigator is not concerned about side effects, possible dangers, etc. A great many cues which contribute to the demand characteristics, including drug side effects, are thus different for the subject receiving the actual drug, and differences in performance could be due to many aspects of this differential treatment.

† The use of simulators as an alternative to placebo in psychopharmacological studies was suggested by Frederick J. Evans.

erroneous to conclude that there is no drug effect. Rather one would have to conclude that the experimental procedure is inadequate, that the experience of the subjects receiving the drug could (but need not) be due to placebo effects. Whether this is in fact the case cannot be established with this design. The only conclusion which can be drawn is that the experimental procedure is not adequate and needs to be modified. Presumably an appropriate modification of the demand characteristics would, if there is a real drug effect, eventually allow a clear difference to emerge between subjects who are receiving drugs and subjects who are simulating.

The interpretation of findings where the group of subjects receiving drugs performs differently from those who are simulating also requires caution. While such findings suggest that drug effect could not be due simply to the demand characteristics because it differs from the expectations of the simulators who are not exposed to the real treatment, the fact that the simulating group is a different treatment group must be kept in mind. Thus, some behavior may be due to the request to simulate. Greater evasiveness on the part of simulating subjects, for example, could most likely be ascribed to the act of simulation. Greater suspiciousness on the part of a simulator could equally be a function of the peculiar situation into which the subject is placed. These observations underline the fact that the simulator, who is a quasi-control, is effective primarily in clarifying the adequacy of the research procedure. The characteristic of this treatment group is that it requires the subjects actively to participate in the experiment in contrast to the usual control group which receives the identical treatment omitting only the drug, as would be the case when placebos are used properly.

The problem of inference from data obtained through the use of quasi-controls is seen relatively easily when one attempts to evaluate the contributions which demand characteristics might make to subjects' total behavior after receiving a drug. Clearly the placebo design properly used is the most adequate approach. This will tell us how much of the behavior of those individuals receiving the drug can be accounted for on the basis of their receiving a substance which is inert as to the specific effect but which mimics the side effects when the total experimental situation and treatment of the subject are identical. The placebo effect is the behavioral consequence which results from the demand characteristics which are (1) perceived and (2) responded to.* In other

---

* For a discussion of the placebo response, see Beecher (1959) and Honigfeld (1964). Undoubtedly it has a large number of components and is influenced by both situational and personality factors; particularly its relationship to suggestibility (Evans, 1967) is of considerable interest and is by no means clear. These issues, however, go beyond the scope of this paper.

words, in any given context there are a large number of demand characteristics inherent in the situation and the subject responds only to those aspects of the demand characteristics which he perceives (there will be many cues which are not recognized by a particular subject) and, of those aspects of the demand characteristics which are perceived at some level by the subject, only some will have a behavioral consequence.

One might consider any given experiment as having demand characteristics which fall into two groups: (a) those which will be perceived and responded to and are, therefore, active in creating experimental effects (that is, they will operate differentially between groups) and (b) those which are present in the situation but either are not readily perceived by most subjects or, for one reason or another, do not lead to a behavioral response by most of the subjects. Quasi-control procedures tend to maximally elicit the subject's responses to demand characteristics. As a result, the behavior seen with quasi-control subjects may include responses to aspects of the demand characteristics which for the real subjects are essentially inert. All that possibly can be determined with quasi-controls is what could be salient demand characteristics in the situation; whether the subjects actually respond to those same demand characteristics cannot be confirmed. Placebo controls or other passive control groups such as those for whom demand characteristics are varied as independent variables are necessary to permit firmer inference.

IX. A FINAL EXAMPLE

The problem of inference from quasi-controls is illustrated in a study (Evans, 1966; Orne and Evans, 1966) carried out to investigate what happens if the hypnotist disappears after deep hypnosis has been induced. This question is by no means easy to examine. The hypnotist's disappearance must be managed in such a way as to seem plausible and truly accidental in order to avoid doing violence to the implicit agreement between subject and hypnotist that the latter is responsible for the welfare of the former during the course of the experiment. Such a situation was finally created in a study requiring two sessions with subjects previously trained to enter hypnosis readily. It was explained to them that in order to standardize the procedure all instructions, including the induction and termination of hypnosis, would be carried out by tape recording.

The experimenter's task was essentially that of a technician—turning on the tape recorder, applying electrodes, presenting experimental materials, etc. He did not say anything throughout the study since every item of instruction was given by means of the tape recorder. Each subject came for two such sessions. During the second session, while the subject was deeply hypnotized and tapping his foot in rhythm with hallucinated music, the tape recorder came to a grinding halt, the light went out on the desk, and the experimenter tried in vain to reactivate the machine by flicking the switch. He then muttered under his breath that the fuse must be blown and dashed from the room.

The subject's behavior was observed through a one-way screen throughout the experiment in order to determine what would happen once the experimenter had left the room. Would hypnosis be terminated immediately once the subject was alone as some theories would predict, or would it take a period of time for the subject to pull himself out of hypnosis as one would expect if the condition were some special altered state?

Despite the "cuteness" of the deception procedure of the simulated power failure there was no certainty whether the subject would accept it as such. For this reason quasi-controls were run. In this particular paradigm simulating subjects were the most appropriate kind of quasi-control and these were included without the hypnotist being aware which subjects were in fact deeply hypnotizable and which were un-hypnotizable individuals instructed to simulate. The findings were clear-cut: five out of the six deeply hypnotized subjects did not arouse immediately when the hypnotist left. They required varying periods of time to apparently pull themselves out of the state. When they did, they appeared somewhat disoriented and confused. In contrast, five out of the six simulating subjects continued to simulate hypnosis for the whole half-hour period until the technician returned, presumably having fixed the fuse. During the subsequent postexperimental inquiry it became clear that the simulators caught on to the fact that the power failure was contrived and that they behaved as they thought a hypnotized subject would if there were a true power failure. The simulating subjects quite cogently pointed out that having been instructed to fool the experimenter put them on their guard lest they themselves be fooled. In contrast, only one of the hypnotized subjects suspected that the power failure was contrived.

Because the quasi-control subjects are a special treatment group their purpose is not primarily as a comparison with actual subject populations; rather, it is to clarify the adequacy of the experimental procedure. Since the simulators caught on to the fact that the power failure was contrived it was plausible that at some level the hypnotized subjects could have responded to the same cues though they did not verbalize such awareness. Therefore despite statistically significant differences between these two groups these results do not permit any conclusions to be drawn about the nature of the hypnotic phenomenon. The behavior of the quasi-controls demonstrates an inadequacy of the deception procedure and indicates that the behavior of the hypnotized subjects could not be interpreted at face value.

Having found the deception manipulation wanting we re-examined in detail the cues which might allow the subject to become aware that the power failure was a planned part of the experiment and that his behavior would actually be observed subsequent to it. The kind of nitty-gritty details which most investigators fail to publish and which, even if they wished to, most editors will delete for the sake of brevity, are crucial in this regard: to wit, in the study just described, to facilitate observation after the "power failure," the overhead lights remained on and only the bright desk lamp went out as the tape recorder stopped; an obvious one-way mirror had always been in the room to which we had hoped (in vain) the subject would have adapted; further, a small polygraph continued to run in the experimental room after the "power failure," etc. We now redesigned the study with considerable attention to such details. The one-way screen was eliminated and replaced by another less well-known and carefully hidden means of observation. When the power failure occurred all lights in the room were extinguished. Just enough light was filtered into the room through the window curtains from daylight—or from a strategically placed parking light outside at night—to make observation possible. Furthermore, physiological recordings were made by means of a large Ampex instrumentation tape recorder and a small polygraph. Both of these machines stopped, along with the lights and the tape recorder, with the power failure. (Actually, the wires from the subject were run through to another room at some distance in order to permit continuous recording of relevant data.) When the experimenter left the room the hall lights were out. Every effort was made by scrupulous attention to such details to make the power failure plausible.

With these revised conditions simulating and hypnotized subjects were run in another experiment by a blind experimenter. Here five out of six simulating subjects stopped simulating the moment the technician left the room, indulging in exploratory and other private behavior clearly indicating that they felt themselves to be unobserved. On the other hand, the hypnotized group behaved much as they had in the earlier experiment, pulling themselves out of this state only after a considerable period of time had elapsed. This behavior was in line with the data provided during an inquiry, indicating that both real and simulating subjects accepted the power failure as genuine.

Significant differences were again obtained but, in contrast to the findings of the first study, those from the second study allow meaningful inference. The behavior of the quasi-controls clearly indicates that the power failure was accepted as genuine and therefore it is plausible to accept the behavior of the hypnotized individuals at face value.

It will be clear that the purpose served by the quasi-controls was simply to determine whether or not there were sufficient cues in the experimental situation to allow the subjects to surmise that the power failure was staged rather than spontaneous. However, this issue is crucial if we hope to draw inference to a situation which is perceived by the subject as extra-experimental. Though it entailed a great deal of trouble to test the adequacy of the deception manipulation, without quasi-controls we would have had no empirical test of the procedure's adequacy. It is not possible, without techniques such as this, to evaluate the kind of cues presented to the subject in an experimental situation, and yet the extent to which such cues are present will determine the kind of inference which legitimately can be drawn from experimental findings.

X. CONCLUSION

Research with human subjects introduces a new set of difficulties because the subjects are sentient beings who are affected by the act of observation and, particularly in experimental contexts, are by no means neutral to the outcome of the study. The kinds of variables which affect subjects' perceptions about the experiment, its purposes, what one hopes to find, how they may perform as good subjects, and so forth—especially those not specifically communicated but rather inherent in what the subject learns about the experiment and the procedure itself—have been termed the demand characteristics of the experimental situation. The nature of the effects of demand characteristics is such that certain findings may be observed—and may even be replicated in laboratory situations—but be specific to the experimental situation. In order to make inference beyond the experimental context to phenomena occurring outside the laboratory the possible effects introduced by demand characteristics must be considered. These difficulties have led some to suggest that psychologists must leave the laboratory and conduct research exclusively in naturalistic settings. Certainly it is desirable to obtain data of this kind, but the experimental paradigm remains the most powerful tool of analysis we have available. Although we must recognize the problem of inference from one context to another,

other sciences have had to do likewise. Thus, aerodynamics has had to develop conversion factors before data obtained in the wind tunnel could be safely applied to a place in flight. Similarly, inference from the action of an antibiotic in the test tube to its medical effects on the organism depends on recognition that effects *in vitro* may differ from those *in vivo*. We cannot afford to give up either laboratory research or observation in a naturalistic setting. Both kinds of data are an integral part of behavioral science.

In addition to the usual control procedures which are recognized as necessary in isolating the action of an independent variable in any experiment, studies with human subjects require a set of controls designed to look at the effect of the experimental technique itself. These controls do not permit a direct inference about the independent variable. Rather, they are designed to allow the investigator to estimate the effects which are due to the situation under which a study is being carried out. The term quasi-control has been suggested to differentiate these techniques from the more typical control measures. The kinds of quasi-controls outlined here all share the feature that they utilize the ability of subjects to reflect upon the context in which they are being investigated, as a means of understanding the way in which this context might affect their own and other subjects' behavior. Undoubtedly other quasi-controls will need to be developed in order to facilitate inference about human behavior from one context to another.

While the difficulty of inference from one context to another is recognized by all scientists, psychology and the other behavioral sciences are in a peculiar position. The object of our study is man. The implications of our research relate to man's behavior. It is not surprising that our findings are of considerable interest to individuals outside of scientific disciplines. Studies in the behavioral sciences tend increasingly to affect policy decisions. Even the scientist in pure research may find his data quoted as the basis of a decision where he himself would feel there is little relevance. Whether we welcome this tendency or view it with alarm, it seems likely to continue.

With the increasing interest in and dissemination of knowledge about behavioral research, it becomes important to see what is needed before meaningful generalization is possible. This problem is particularly acute in experimental work, although the Hawthorne studies (Roethlisberger and Dickson, 1939) demonstrate that it also exists in research outside of the laboratory. Perhaps our responsibility extends beyond our subjects and our disciplines, to include a concern with the kinds of generalizations which may be drawn from our work. The leap is one which others are so eager to make that we can hardly avoid considering it ourselves.

REFERENCES

Beecher, H. K. *Measurement of subjective responses: Quantitative effects of drugs.* New York: Oxford University Press, 1959.

Bem, D. J. Self-perception: An alternative interpretation of cognitive dissonance phenomena. *Psychological Review,* 1967, **74,** 183–200.

Campbell, D. T., and Stanley, J. C. Experimental and quasi-experimental designs for research. *In* N. L. Gage (Ed.), *Handbook of research on teaching.* Chicago: Rand McNally, 1963.

Cataldo, J. F., Silverman, I., and Brown, J. M. Demand characteristics associated with semantic differential ratings of nouns and verbs. *Educational and Psychological Measurement,* 1967, **27,** 83–87.

Criswell, Joan H. The psychologist as perceiver. *In* R. Tagiuri and L. Petrullo (Eds.), *Person perception and interpersonal behavior.* Stanford: Stanford University Press, 1958, 95–109.

Damaser, Esther C., Shor, R. E., and Orne, M. T. Physiological effects during hypnotically requested emotions. *Psychosomatic Medicine,* 1963, **25,** 334–343.

Ellson, D. G., Davis, R. C., Saltzman, I. J., and Burke, C. J. A report on research on detection of deception. (Contract N6onr–18011 with Office of Naval Research) Bloomington, Indiana: Department of Psychology, Indiana University, 1952.

Evans, F. J. The case of the disappearing hypnotist. Paper read at American Psychological Association, New York, September, 1966.

Evans, F. J. Suggestibility in the normal waking state. *Psychological Bulletin,* 1967, **67,** 114–129.

Festinger, L. *A theory of cognitive dissonance.* New York: Row and Peterson, 1957.

Fisher, S., Cole, J. O., Rickels, K., and Uhlenhuth, E. H. Drug-set interaction: The effect of expectations on drug response in outpatients. *In* P. B. Bradley, F. Flügel, and P. Hoch (Eds.), *Neuropsychopharmacology.* Vol. 3. New York: Elsevier, 1964, 149–156.

Gustafson, L. A., and Orne, M. T. Effects of heightened motivation on the detection of deception. *Journal of Applied Psychology,* 1963, **47,** 408–411.

Gustafson, L. A., and Orne, M. T. Effects of perceived role and role success on the detection of deception. *Journal of Applied Psychology,* 1965, **49,** 412–417.

Honigfeld, G. Non-specific factors in treatment. I: Review of placebo reactions and placebo reactors. *Diseases of the Nervous System,* 1964, **25,** 145–156.

Kelman, H. C. The human use of human subjects: The problem of deception in social-psychological experiments. Paper read at American Psychological Association, Chicago, September, 1965.

Kroger, R. O. The effects of role demands and test-cue properties upon personality-test performance. *Journal of Consulting Psychology,* 1967, **31,** 304–312.

Mills, T. M. A sleeper variable in small group research: The experimenter. Paper read at American Sociological Association, St. Louis, September, 1961.

Modell, W., and Houde, R. W. Factors influencing the clinical evaluation of drugs: With special reference to the double-blind technique. *Journal of the American Medical Association,* 1958, **167,** 2190–2199.

Orne, M. T. The nature of hypnosis: Artifact and essence. *Journal of Abnormal and Social Psychology,* 1959, **58,** 277–299. (a)

Orne, M. T. The demand characteristics of an experimental design and their implications. Paper read at American Psychological Association, Cincinnati, September, 1959. (b)

Orne, M. T. On the social psychology of the psychological experiment: With particular reference to demand characteristics and their implications. *American Psychologist*, 1962, 17, 776–783.

Orne, M. T. The simulation of hypnosis: Method, rationale, and implications. Paper presented at the meeting of the Society for Clinical and Experimental Hypnosis, Chicago, November, 1968.

Orne, M. T., and Evans, F. J. Social control in the psychological experiment: Antisocial behavior and hypnosis. *Journal of Personality and Social Psychology*, 1965, 1, 189–200.

Orne, M. T., and Evans, F. J. Inadvertent termination of hypnosis on hypnotized and simulating subjects. *International Journal of Clinical and Experimental Hypnosis*, 1966, 14, 61–78.

Orne, M. T., and Scheibe, K. E. The contribution of nondeprivation factors in the production of sensory deprivation effects: The psychology of the "panic button." *Journal of Abnormal and Social Psychology*, 1964, 68, 3–12.

Orne, M. T., Sheehan, P. W., and Evans, F. J. Occurrence of posthypnotic behavior outside the experimental setting. *Journal of Personality and Social Psychology*, 1968, 9, 189–196.

Page, M. M., and Lumia, A. R. Cooperation with demand characteristics and the bimodal distribution of verbal conditioning data. *Psychonomic Science*, 1968, 12, 243–244.

Paul, G. L. *Insight vs. desensitization in psychotherapy: An experiment in anxiety reduction*. Stanford, Calif.: Stanford University Press, 1966.

Riecken, H. W. A program for research on experiments in social psychology. Paper read at Behavioral Sciences Conference, Albuquerque, 1958. *In* N. F. Washburne (Ed.), *Decisions, values and groups* Vol. 2. New York: Pergamon Press, 1962, 25–41.

Roethlisberger, F. J., and Dickson, W. J. *Management and the worker*. Cambridge, Mass.: Harvard University Press, 1939.

Rosenberg, M. J. When dissonance fails: On eliminating evaluation apprehension from attitude measurement. *Journal of Personality and Social Psychology*, 1965, 1, 28–42.

Rosenthal, R. On the social psychology of the psychological experiment: The experimenter's hypothesis as unintended determinant of experimental results. *American Scientist*, 1963, 51, 268–283.

Rosenthal, R. *Experimenter effects in behavioral research*. New York: Appleton-Century-Crofts, 1966.

Ross, S., Krugman, A. D., Lyerly, S. B., and Clyde, D. J. Drugs and placebos: A model design. *Psychological Reports*, 1962, 10, 383–392.

Silverman, I. Role-related behavior of subjects in laboratory studies of attitude change. *Journal of Personality and Social Psychology*, 1968, 8, 343–348.

Stricker, L. J. The true deceiver. *Psychological Bulletin*, 1967, 68, 13–20.

Stricker, L. J., Messick, S., and Jackson, D. N. Suspicion of deception: Implications for conformity research. *Journal of Personality and Social Psychology*, 1967, 5, 379–389.

Sutcliffe, J. P. A general method of analysis of frequency data for multiple classification designs. *Psychological Bulletin*, 1957, 54, 134–137.

Wishner, J. Efficiency: Concept and measurement. *In* O. Milton (Ed.), *Behavior disorders: Perspectives and trends*. Philadelphia: Lippincott, 1965, 133–154.

Chapter 6

INTERPERSONAL EXPECTATIONS:
Effects of the Experimenter's Hypothesis*

Robert Rosenthal

Harvard University

The social situation which comes into being when a behavioral scientist encounters his research subject is a situation of both general and unique importance to the behavioral sciences. Its general importance derives from the fact that the interaction of experimenter and subject, like other two-person interactions, may be investigated empirically with a view to teaching us more about dyadic interaction in general. Its unique importance derives from the fact that the interaction of experimenter and subject, *un*like other dyadic interactions, is a major source of our knowledge in the behavioral sciences.

To the extent that we hope for dependable knowledge in the behavioral sciences, we must have dependable knowledge about the experimenter-subject interaction specifically. Without an understanding of the data collection situation we can no more hope to acquire accurate information for our disciplines than astronomers and zoologists could hope to acquire accurate information without their understanding the operation of their telescopes and microscopes. It is for these reasons that increasing interest has been shown in the investigation of the experimenter-subject interaction system. And the outlook is anything but bleak.

* Preparation of this chapter and much of the research summarized here was supported by research grants (G–17685, G–24826, GS–177, GS–714; and GS–1741) from the Division of Social Sciences of the National Science Foundation.

It does seem that we can profitably learn about those effects which the behavioral scientist unwittingly may have on the results of his research.

I. UNINTENDED EFFECTS OF THE EXPERIMENTER

It is useful to think of two major types of effects, which the behavioral scientist can have upon the results of his research. The first type operates, so to speak, in the mind, in the eye, or in the hand of the investigator. It operates without affecting the actual response of the human or animal subjects of the research; it is not interactional. The second type of experimenter effect is interactional; it operates by affecting the actual response of the subject of the experiment. It is a sub-type of this latter effect, the effects of the investigator's expectancy or hypothesis on the results of his research, that will occupy most of the discussion. First, however, some examples of other effects of the investigator on his research will be mentioned.

A. Observer Effects

In any science, the experimenter must make provision for the careful observation and recording of the events under study. It is not always so easy to be sure that one has, in fact, made an accurate observation. That lesson was learned by the psychologists, who were grateful to learn it, but it was not the psychologists who focused attention on it originally. It was the astronomers.

Just near the end of the 18th century, the royal astronomer at the Greenwich Observatory, Maskelyne, discovered that his assistant, Kinnebrook, was consistently "too slow" in his observations of the movement of stars across the sky. Maskelyne cautioned Kinnebrook about his "errors" but the errors continued for months. Kinnebrook was discharged.

The man who might have saved that job was Bessel, the astronomer at Königsberg, but he was 20 years too late. It was not until then that he arrived at the conclusion that Kinnebrook's "error" was probably not willful. Bessel studied the observations of stellar transits made by a number of senior astronomers. Differences in observation, he discovered, were the rule, not the exception (Boring, 1950).

This early observation of the effects of the scientist on the observations of science made Bessel perhaps the first student of the psychology of scientists. More contemporary research on the psychology of scientists has shown that, while observer errors are not necessarily serious, they do tend to occur in a biased manner. By that we mean that, more often than we would expect by chance, when errors of observation occur they tend to give results more in the direction of the observer's hypothesis (Rosenthal, 1966).

1. Recording Errors. As data collectors observe the behavior of their subjects, their observations must in some way be recorded. It is no revelation to point out that errors of recording do occur, but it may be of interest to try to obtain some estimates of the incidence of such errors. Table I shows four such estimates based on an older study of

TABLE I

RECORDING ERRORS IN FOUR EXPERIMENTS

Study	Observers	Recordings	Errors	Error %	Bias %
1. [a]	28	11,125	126	1.13%	68%
2. [b]	30	3,000	20	.67%	75%
3. [c]	11	828	6	.72%	67%
4. [d]	34	1,770	30	1.69%	85%
Combined	103	16,723	182	1.09%	71%

[a] Kennedy and Uphoff, 1939

[b] Rosenthal, Friedman, Johnson, *et al.*, 1964

[c] Persinger, Knutson, and Rosenthal, 1968.

[d] Weiss, 1967

errors in recording responses to a telepathy task, two more recent studies of errors in recording responses to a person perception task, and one recent study of errors in recording responses to a numerosity estimation task. The next to last column shows the range of misrecording rates to be in the neighborhood of one per cent and the last column shows that perhaps over two-thirds of the errors that do occur are biased in the direction of the observer's hypothesis.

A more preliminary assessment of computational errors is summarized in Table II. About two-thirds of the experimenters err computationally, though it seems safe to suggest that, given enough computations to perform, all experimenters will make computational errors. More interesting is the combined finding that nearly three out of four experimenters, when they do err computationally, err in the direction of their hypothesis.

In general, the magnitudes of errors, both biased and unbiased, tend to be small, and the overall effects of recording and computational errors on grand means of different treatment conditions tend to be trivial.

TABLE II

BIASED COMPUTATIONAL ERRORS IN THREE STUDIES

	Experimenters			
Study	Total N	Erring N	Erring %	Bias %
Laszlo and Rosenthal, 1967	3	3	100%	100%
Rosenthal, Friedman, Johnson, et al., 1964	30	18	60%	67%
Rosenthal and Hall, 1968[a]	1	1	100%	100%
Combined	34	22	65%	73%

[a] For a sample of five research assistants performing 5,012 calculations and transcriptions there were 41 errors detected on recheck for an .82 per cent error rate.

A few of the experimenters studied, however, made errors sufficiently large and sufficiently non-canceling to have affected the conclusions of an experiment in which they were the only data recorders and data processors.

Successive independent checking and rechecking of a set of observations can give us whatever degree of accuracy is needed, though an absolute zero level of error seems an unlikely goal to achieve. A more historical and theoretical discussion of observer effects and their control is available elsewhere (Rosenthal, 1966).

B. Interpreter Effects

The interpretation of the data collected is part of the research process, and a glance at any of the technical journals of contemporary behavioral science will suggest strongly that, while we only rarely debate one another's observations, we often debate the interpretation of those observations. It is as difficult to state the rules for accurate interpretation of data as it is to state the rules for accurate observation of data but the variety of interpretations offered in explanation of the same data imply that many of us must turn out often to be wrong. The history of science generally, and the history of psychology more specifically, suggest that more of us are wrong longer than we need to be because we hold our theories not quite lightly enough. The common practice of theory monogamy has its advantages, however. It does keep us motivated to make more crucial observations. In any case, interpreter effects seem less serious than observer effects. The reason is that the former are public while the latter are private. Given a set of observations, their interpretations become generally available to the scientific community. We are free to agree or disagree with any specific interpretation. Not so with the case of the observations themselves. Often these are made by a single investigator so that we are not free to agree or disagree. We can only hope that no observer errors occurred, and we can, and should, try to repeat the observations.

Examples of interpreter effects in the physical, biological, and behavioral sciences are not hard to come by, and to an earlier theoretical discussion and inventory of examples (Rosenthal, 1966) we need only add some recent instances. In the physical sciences, Polanyi (1967) refers to the possible interpretations of those data which appeared to support Velikovsky's controversial theory dealing with the history of our planet and the origin of the planet Venus. In the same paper, Polanyi gives us other examples of interpreter effects and places them all into a broad conceptual framework in which the antecedent plausibility plays a prominent role.

In a disarming retraction of an earlier interpretation, Bradley (1968, 437) told how the microscopic particles he found, turned out not to be the unmineralized fossil bacteria he had originally believed them to be. The minute spheres, it turned out, were artifactually formed fluorite. "I was as completely taken in as Don Quixote . . .".

Carlson and Armelagos (1965) discuss a considerably more macroscopic "find" reported in the literature of paleopathology. They argue convincingly that the prehistoric curved bark bands earlier interpreted as orthopedic corsets were actually hoods for Indian cradleboards. Additional recent discussions of interpreter effects in the behavioral sciences can be found in Honorton (1967) and Shaver (1966).

C. Intentional Effects

It happens sometimes in undergraduate laboratory science courses that students "collect" and report data too perfect to be true. (That probably happens most often when students are taught to be scientists by being told what results they must get to do well in the course, rather than being taught the logic of scientific inquiry and the value of being quite open-eyed and open-minded.) Unfortunately, the history of science tells us that not only undergraduates have been dishonest in science.

Intentional effects, though rare, must be regarded as part of the inventory of the effects of the investigator himself, and some historically important cases from the physical, biological, and behavioral sciences have been described in detail elsewhere (Rosenthal, 1966). Additional anecdotal evidence is presented for the case of behavioral research by Roth (1965) and Gardner (1966). Martin Gardner, professional magician and editor of the "Mathematical Games" section of the *Scientific American,* provides an excellent summary of how behavioral scientists can be deceived by their over-eager subjects of research in dermo-optical perception, and also how they can prevent such deception.

Intentional effects, interpreter effects, and observer effects all operate without the investigator's influencing his subject's response to the experimental task. In those effects of the experimenter himself to which we now turn, we shall see that the subject's response to the experimental task is influenced.

D. Biosocial Effects

The sex, age, and race of the investigator have all been found to affect the results of his research (Rosenthal, 1966). What we do not know and what we need to learn is whether subjects respond differently simply to the presence of experimenters varying in these biosocial attributes or whether experimenters varying in those attributes behave differently toward their subjects and, therefore, obtain different responses from them because they have, in effect, altered the experimental situation for their subjects. So far the evidence suggests that male and female experimenters conduct the "same" person perception experiment quite differently so that the different results they obtain may be attributable to those unintentionally different manipulations. Male experimenters, for example, were found in two experiments to be more friendly to their subjects than female experimenters (Rosenthal, 1967).

Biosocial attributes of the subject can also affect the experimenter's behavior, which, in turn, may affect the subject's responses. In one study, for example, the interactions between experimenters and their subjects were recorded on sound films. It was found that only 12 per cent of the experimenters ever smiled at their male subjects, while 70 per cent of the experimenters smiled at their female subjects. Smiling by the experimenters, it was discovered, affected the subjects' responses. From this evidence and from some more detailed analyses which suggest that female subjects may be more protectively treated by their experimenters (Rosenthal, 1966, 1967), it might be suggested that in the psychological experiment, chivalry is not dead. This news may be heartening socially, and it is interesting psychologically, but it is very disconcerting methodologically. Sex differences are well established for many kinds of behavior. But a question must now be raised as to whether sex differences which emerge from psychological experiments are due to the subject's genes, morphology, enculturation, or simply to the fact that the experimenter treated his male and female subjects differently so that, in a sense, they were not really in the same experiment at all.

So far we have seen that both the sex of the experimenter and the sex of the subject can serve as significant determinants of the way in which the investigator conducts his research. In addition, however, we find that when the sex of the experimenter and the sex of the subject are considered simultaneously, certain interaction effects emerge. Thus, male experimenters contacting female subjects, and female experimenters contacting male subjects, tend to require more time to collect portions of their data than do male or female experimenters contacting subjects of the same sex (Rosenthal, 1967). This tendency for opposite-sex dyads to prolong their data-collection interactions has also been found in a verbal conditioning experiment by Shapiro (1966).

Other interesting interaction effects occur when we examine closely the sound motion pictures of male and female experimenters contacting male and female subjects. Observations of experimenters' friendliness were made by two different groups of observers. One group watched the films but did not hear the sound track. The other group listened to the sound track but did not view the films. From the resulting ratings, a measure of motor or visual friendliness and an independent measure of verbal or auditory friendliness were available. (The correlation between ratings of friendliness obtained from these independent channels was only .29.) Among male experimenters, there was a tendency (not statistically significant) for their movements to show greater friendliness than their tone of voice, and to be somewhat unfriendly toward their male subjects in the auditory channel of communication. It was among the female experimenters that the more striking effects occurred. The females were quite friendly toward their female subjects in the visual channel but not in the auditory channel. With male subjects, the situation was reversed significantly. Though not friendly in the visual mode, female experimenters showed remarkable friendliness in the auditory channel when contacting male subjects.

The quantitative analysis of sound motion pictures is not yet far enough developed that we can say whether such channel discrepancy in the communication of friendliness is generally characteristic of women in our culture, or only of advanced female students in psychology, or only of female investigators conducting experiments in person perception. Perhaps it would not be farfetched to attribute the obtained channel discrepancy to an ambivalence over how friendly they ought to be. Quite apart from considerations of unintended effects of the experimenter, such findings may have some relevance for a better understanding of communication processes in general.

Though the sex of the experimenter does not always affect the performance of the subject, in a great many cases it does. Gall and Mendelsohn (1966) found, for example, that male experimenters elicited more creative problem solutions than did female experimenters and that, in general, female subjects were more affected in their performance than male subjects by the sex of the experimenter. Cieutat (1965), on the other hand, found that female experimenters elicited intellectual performance from children superior to that obtained by male experimenters. In addition, children tended to perform better for examiners of the opposite sex. Follow-up research by Cieutat and Flick (1967), however, found these effects to be appreciably diminished. Glixman (1967) presents partial support for the proposition that the sex of the experimenter may interact with the type of task required to determine, in part, the subject's response, and Kintz, Delprato, Mettee, Persons, and Schappe (1965) have data suggesting that sex of experimenter may be a variable affecting the maze behavior of albino rats.

The race or ethnic grouping of the experimenter also often affects the subject's response. Vaughn (1963) found that Maori and pakeha experimenters differentially affected the responses of Maori and pakeha school-children such that the Maori children preferred figures of their own race considerably more when the experimenter was also Maori. Wenk (1966) found that Negro subjects scored appreciably higher on nonlanguage tests of intellectual functioning when the examiner was Negro rather than white. Summers and Hammonds (1966) found that the presence of a Negro investigator considerably decreased self-reports of anti-Negro prejudice. But in a more clinical context, Womack and Wagner (1967) found only personal characteristics other than race to affect the patients' responses to professionally identified interviewers.

E. Psychosocial Effects

Experimenters who differ along such personal and social dimensions as anxiety, need for approval, status, and warmth tend to obtain different responses from their research subjects, and a summary of the effects of these and other variables is available (Rosenthal, 1966). But what, for example, does the more anxious experimenter do in the experiment that leads his subjects to respond differently? We might expect more anxious experimenters to be more fidgety, and that is just what they are. Experimenters scoring higher on the Taylor Manifest Anxiety scale have been observed from sound-motion pictures (Rosenthal, 1967) to show a greater degree of general body activity and to have a less dominant tone of voice. What effects just such behavior on the part of the experimenter will have on the subjects' responses depends no doubt on the particular experiment being conducted and, very likely, on various characteristics of the subject as well. In any case, we must assume that a more anxious experimenter cannot conduct just the same experiment as a less anxious experimenter. It appears that in experiments which have been conducted by just one experimenter, the probability of successful replication by another investigator is likely to depend on the similarity of his personality to that of the original investigator.

Anxiety of the experimenter is just one of the experimenter variables affecting the subjects' responses in an unintended manner. Crowne and Marlowe (1964) have shown that subjects who score high on their scale of need for approval tend to behave in such a way as to gain the approval of the experimenter. Now there is evidence that suggests that experimenters who score high on this measure also behave in such a way as to gain approval from their subjects. Analysis of filmed interactions showed that experimenters scoring higher on the Marlowe–Crowne scale spoke to their subjects in a more enthusiastic and a more friendly tone of voice. In addition, they smiled more often at their subjects and slanted their bodies more toward their subjects than did experimenters lower in the need for approval.

Earlier research by Towbin (1959) has shown that the examiner's power to control his patient's fate can be a partial determinant of the patient's Rorschach responses, though the status of the examiner, independent of his power to control the patient's destinies, had little effect. We might suppose that a Roman Catholic priest would obtain different responses to personal questions asked of Roman Catholic subjects than would a Roman Catholic layman. That was the question addressed in an experiment by Walker, Davis, and Firetto (1968). They had a layman and a priest, each garbed sometimes as layman and sometimes as priest, administer a series of personal questions to male and female subjects. The results were complex but interesting, male and female subjects responding differentially not so much to priest versus layman but rather to whether the priest and layman were playing their true roles or simulating those roles. While this study showed no simple effect of being contacted by a priest as opposed to a layman, an earlier study did show such differences (Walker and Firetto, 1965).

"Warmer" experimenters have also been found often to obtain quite different responses from their subjects than "cooler" experimenters. Some of the more recent support for this proposition comes from the work of Engram (1966) with children and of Goldblatt and Schackner (1968) with college students. These latter workers found that their subjects' judgments of affect in photographs were dramatically influenced by the degree of friendliness shown by the data collectors. A pioneering study by Malmo, Boag, and Smith (1957) showed that within-experimenter variation could also serve as a powerful unintended determinant of subjects' responses. A particular data-collector's variations in feeling state were found to be related to his subjects' physiological responses. When the experimenter had a "bad day," his subjects' heart rate showed significantly greater acceleration than when he had a "good day." Surprisingly, the data collector's feeling state was not particularly related to his own physiological responses.

F. Situational Effects

The degree of acquaintanceship between experimenter and subject, the experimenter's level of experience, and the things that happen to him before and during his interaction with his subject have all been shown to affect the subject's responses (Rosenthal, 1966). Most recently, for example, Jourard (1968) has shown that experimenters better acquainted with their subjects and more open to them obtain not only the more open responses we might expect on the basis of reciprocity, but also obtain superior performance in a paired associate learning task.

1. Experimenter Experience. The kind of person the experimenter is *before* he enters his laboratory can in part determine the responses he obtains from his subjects. From the observation of experimenters' behavior during their interaction with their subjects there are some clues as to how this may come about. There is also evidence that the kind of person the experimenter becomes *after* he enters his laboratory may alter his behavior toward his subjects and lead him, therefore, to obtain different responses from his subjects.

In the folklore of psychologists who conduct experiments, there is the notion that sometimes, perhaps more often than we would expect, subjects contacted early in an experiment behave differently from subjects contacted later. There may be something to this bit of lore even if we make sure that subjects seen earlier and later in an experiment come from the same population. The difference may be due to changes over the course of the experiment in the behavior of the experimenter. From what we know of performance curves, we might predict both a practice effect and a fatigue effect on the part of the experimenter. There is evidence for both. In experiments which were filmed (Rosenthal, 1966), experimenters became more accurate and faster in the reading of their instructions to their later-contacted subjects. That seems simply to be a practice effect. In addition, experimenters became more bored or less interested over the course of the experiment as observed from their behavior in the experimental interaction. As we might also predict, experimenters became less tense with more experience. The changes which occur in the experimenters' behavior during the course of their experiment affect their subjects' responses. In the experiments which were filmed, for example, subjects contacted by experimenters whose behavior changed as described rated stimulus persons as less successful (Rosenthal, 1966).

2. Subject Behavior. The experimenter-subject communication system is a complex of intertwining feedback loops. The experimenter's behavior, we have seen, can affect the subject's response. But the subject's behavior can also affect the experimenter's behavior, which in turn affects the subject's behavior. In this way, the subject plays a part in the indirect determination of his own response. The experimental details are given elsewhere (Rosenthal, 1966; Rosenthal, Kohn, Greenfield, and Carota, 1965). Briefly, in one experiment, half the experimenters had their experimental hypotheses confirmed by their first few subjects, who were actually accomplices. The remaining experimenters had their experimental hypotheses disconfirmed. This confirmation or disconfirmation of their hypotheses affected the experimenters' behavior sufficiently so that from their next subjects, who were bona fide and not accomplices, they obtained significantly different responses not only to the experimental task, but on standard tests of personality as well. These responses were predictable from a knowledge of the responses the experimenters had obtained from their earlier-contacted subjects.

There is an interesting footnote on the psychology of the accomplice which comes from the experiment alluded to. The accomplices had been trained to confirm or to disconfirm the experimenter's hypothesis by the nature of the responses they gave the experimenter. These accomplices did not, of course, know when they were confirming an experimenter's hypothesis or, indeed, that there were expectancies to be confirmed at all. In spite of the accomplices' training, they were significantly affected in the adequacy of their performance as accomplices by the expectancy the experimenter had of their performance, and by whether the experimenter's hypothesis was being confirmed or disconfirmed by the accomplices' responses. We can think of the accomplices as experimenters, and the experimenters as the accomplices' targets or "victims." It is interesting to know that experimental targets are not simply affected by experimental accomplices. The targets of our accomplices, like the subjects of our experimenters, are not simply passive responders. They "act back."

3. Experimental Scene. One of the things that happens to the experimenter which may affect his behavior toward his subject, and thus the subject's response, is that he falls heir to a specific scene in which to conduct his experiment. Riecken (1962) has pointed out how much there is that we do not know about the effects of the physical scene in which an experimental transaction takes place. We know little enough about how the scene affects the subject's behavior; we know even less about how the scene affects the experimenter's behavior.

The scene in which the experiment takes place may affect the subject's response in two ways. The effect may be direct, as when a subject judges others to be less happy when his judgments are made in an "ugly" laboratory (Mintz, 1957). Or, the effect may be indirect, as when the scene influences the experimenter to behave differently and this change in the experimenter's behavior leads to a change in the subject's response. Evidence that the physical scene may affect the experimenter's behavior comes from some data collected with Suzanne Woolsey. We had available eight laboratory rooms which were varied as to the "professionalness," the "orderliness," and the "comfortableness" of their appearance. The 14 experimenters of this study were randomly assigned to the eight laboratories. Experimenters took the experiment significantly more seriously if they had been assigned to a laboratory which was both more disordered and less comfortable. These experimenters were graduate students in the natural sciences or in law school. Perhaps they felt that scientifically serious business is carried on best in the cluttered and severely furnished laboratory which fits the stereotype of the scientist's ascetic pursuit of truth.

In this same experiment, subjects described the behavior of their experimenter during the course of the experiment. Experimenters who had been assigned to more professional appearing laboratories were described by their subjects as significantly more expressive-voiced, more expressive-faced, and as more given to the use of hand gestures. There were no films made of these experimenters interacting with their subjects, so we cannot be sure that their subjects' descriptions were accurate. There is a chance that the experimenters did not really behave as described but that subjects in different appearing laboratories perceived their experimenters differently because of the operation of context effects. The direct observation of experimenters' behavior in different physical contexts should clear up the matter to some extent.

4. The Principal Investigator.   More and more research is carried out in teams and groups so that the chances are increasing that any one experimenter will be collecting data not for himself alone. More and more there is a chance that the data are being collected for a principal investigator to whom the experimenter is responsible. The basic data are presented elsewhere (Rosenthal, 1966), but here it can be said that the response a subject gives his experimenter may be determined in part by the kind of person the principal investigator is and by the nature of his interaction with the experimenter.

More specifically, personality differences among principal investigators, and whether the principal investigator has praised or reproved the experimenter for his performance of his data-collecting duties, affect the subjects' subsequent perception of the success of other people and also affect subjects' scores on standardized tests of personality (e.g., Taylor Manifest Anxiety scale).

In one experiment, there were 13 principal investigators and 26 experimenters. The principal investigators first collected their own data and it was found that their anxiety level correlated positively with the ratings of the success of others (pictured in photographs) they obtained from their subjects ($r = .66$, $p = .03$). Each principal investigator was then to employ two research assistants. On the assumption that principal investigators select research assistants who are significantly like or significantly unlike themselves, the two research assistants were assigned to principal investigators at random. That was done so that research assistants' scores on the anxiety scale would not be correlated with their principal investigator's anxiety scores. The randomization was successful in that the principal investigators' anxiety correlated only .02 with the anxiety of their research assistants.

The research assistants then replicated the principal investigators' experiments. Remarkably, the principal investigators' level of anxiety also predicted the responses obtained by their research assistants from their new samples of subjects ($r = .40$, $p = .07$). The research assistants' own level of anxiety, while also positively correlated with their subjects' responses ($r = .24$), was not as good a predictor of their subjects' responses as was the anxiety level of the principal investigators. Something in the covert communication between the principal investigator and his research assistant altered the assistant's behavior when he subsequently contacted his subjects. We know that the effect of the principal investigator was mediated in this indirect way to his assistant's subjects, because the principal investigator had no contact of his own with those subjects.

Other experiments show that the data obtained by the experimenter depend in part on whether the principal invesigator is male or female, whether the principal investigator makes the experimenter self-conscious about the experimental procedure, and whether the principal investigator leads the experimenter to believe he has himself performed well or poorly at the same task the experimenter is to administer to his own subjects. The evidence comes from studies in person perception, verbal conditioning, and motor skills (Rosenthal, 1966).

As we would expect, these effects of the principal investigator on his assistant's subjects are mediated by the effects on the assistant's behavior toward his subjects. Thus, experimenters who have been made more self-conscious by their principal investigator behave less courteously toward their subjects, as observed from films of their interactions with their subjects. In a different experiment, involving this time a verbal conditioning task, experimenters who had been given more favorable evaluations by their principal investigator were described by their subsequently contacted subjects to be more casual and more courteous. These same experimenters, probably by virtue of their altered behavior toward their subjects, obtained significantly more conditioning responses from their subjects. All ten of the experimenters who had been more favorably evaluated by their principal investigator showed conditioning effects among their subjects, but only five of the nine experimenters who felt unfavorably evaluated obtained any conditioning.

G. Modeling Effects

From the fields of survey research, child development, clinical psychology and from laboratory experiments, there is a reasonable amount of evidence to suggest that the nature of the data collector's own task performance may be a nontrivial determinant of his subject's subsequent task performance (Rosenthal, 1966). Though most of the evidence for such modeling effects comes from studies in which the experimenter-subject contact is very brief, there are some studies, usually of the "field study" variety that are based on more prolonged contact. One of these, the classic study of Escalona (1945), shows that modeling effects do not depend on verbal communication. The subjects were 50 babies, most of them less than one year old. On alternate days they were given orange juice and tomato juice and many of the babies drank more heartily of one juice than of the other. It turned out that the ladies who fed the babies also had marked preferences for one juice over the other and that babies fed by orange juice preferrers, preferred orange juice while babies fed by tomato juice preferrers, preferred tomato juice. When babies were reassigned to new feeders with a different preference, the babies tended to change their preference to coincide with that of the new feeder. In another long term experiment, Yando and Kagan (1966) found that first-graders taught by teachers whose decision-making was "reflective" became significantly more reflective during the course of the school year relative to the children taught by teachers whose decision-making was "impulsive."

In a recent report of a more short-term interpersonal contact, Barnard (1968) found that the experimenter's degree of disturbance on hostile phrases of a phrase-association test was significantly predictive of subjects' subsequent degree of disturbance on hostile phrases. Similarly, in a Rorschach study, Marwit (1968) found that experimenters whose vocal behavior was more hostile, elicited significantly more hostile behavior from their subjects. Finally, Klinger (1967) has shown that even when based entirely on nonverbal cues, an experimenter who appeared more achievement-motivated, elicited significantly more achievement-motivated responses from his subjects.

II. THE EXPERIMENTER'S EXPECTANCY

In the discussion just concluded we have considered briefly some sources of artifact deriving from the experimenter himself. We have seen that a variety of personal and situational variables associated with the experimenter may unintentionally affect the subject's responses. Our discussion was not exhaustive but only illustrative and a number of sources are available for obtaining a more complete picture (Krasner and Ullman, 1965; Masling, 1960, 1966; McGuigan, 1963; Rosenthal, 1966; Sarason, 1965; Sattler and Theye, 1967; Stevenson, 1965; Zax, Stricker, and Weiss, 1960). We turn our attention now to a somewhat more detailed consideration of another potential source of artifact associated with the experimenter—his research hypothesis.

The particular expectation a scientist has of how his experiment will turn out is variable, depending on the experiment being conducted, but the presence of some expectation is virtually a constant in science. The independent and dependent variables selected for study by the scientist are not chosen by means of a table of random numbers. They are selected because the scientist expects a certain relationship to emerge among them. Even in those less carefully planned examinations of relationships called "fishing expeditions" or, more formally, "exploratory analyses," the expectation of the scientist is reflected in the selection of the entire set of variables chosen for examination. Exploratory analyses of data, like real fishing expeditions, do not take place in randomly selected pools.

These expectations of the scientist are likely to affect the choice of the experimental design and procedure in such a way as to increase the likelihood that his expectation or hypothesis will be supported. That is as it should be. No scientist would select intentionally a procedure likely to show his hypothesis in error. If he could too easily think of procedures that would show this, he would be likely to revise his hypothesis. If the seelction of a research design or procedure is regarded by another scientist as too "biased" to be a fair test of the hypothesis, he can test the hypothesis employing oppositely biased procedures or less biased procedures by which to demonstrate the greater value of his hypothesis. The designs and procedures employed are, to a great extent, public knowledge, and it is this public character that permits relevant replications to serve the required corrective function.

The major concern of this chapter is with the effects of the experimenter's expectation on the responses he obtains from his subjects. The consequences of such an expectancy bias can be quite serious. Expectancy effects on subjects' responses are not public matters. It is not only that other scientists cannot know whether such effects occurred in the experimenter's interaction with his subjects; the investigator himself may not know whether these effects have occurred. Moreover, there is the likelihood that the experimenter has not even considered the possibility of such unintended effects on his subjects' responses. This is not so different from the situations already discussed wherein the subject's response is affected by any attribute of the experimenter. Later, the problem will be discussed in more detail. For now it is enough to note that while the other attributes of the experimenter affect the subject's response, they do not necessarily affect these responses differentially as a function of the subject's treatment condition. Expectancy effects, on the other hand, always do. The sex of the experimenter does not change as a function of the subject's treatment condition in an experiment. The experimenter's expectancy of how the subject will respond does change as a function of the subject's treatment condition.

Although the focus of this chapter is primarily on the effects of a particular person—the experimenter—on the behavior of a specific other—the subject—it should be emphasized that many of the effects of the experimenter, including the effects of his expectancy, may have considerable generality for other social relationships.

That one person's expectation about another person's behavior may contribute to a determination of what that behavior will actually be has been suggested by various theorists. Merton (1948) developed the very appropriate concept of "self-fulfilling prophecy." One prophesies an event and the expectation of the event then changes the behavior of the prophet in such a way as to make the prophesied event more likely. Gordon Allport (1950) applied the concept of interpersonal expectancies to an analysis of the causes of war. Nations expecting to go to war affect the behavior of their opponents-to-be by the behavior which reflects their expectations of armed conflict. Nations that expect to remain out of wars at least sometimes manage to avoid entering into them.

Drawn from the general literature, and the literatures of the healing professions, survey research, and laboratory psychology, there is consid-

erable evidence for the operation of interpersonal self-fulfilling prophecies. This evidence, while ranging from the anecdotal to the experimental, with emphasis on the former, permits us to begin consideration
of more recent research on expectancy effects with possibly more than
very gentle priors (Mosteller and Tukey, 1965). The literatures referred
to have been reviewed elsewhere (Rosenthal, 1964a,b, 1965, 1966; Rosenthal and Jacobson, 1968), but it may be of interest here to give one
illustration from experimental psychology. The example is one known
generally to psychologists as a case study of an artifact in animal research. It is less well known, however, as a case study of the effect
of experimenter expectancy. While the subject sample was small, the
experimenter sample was very large indeed. The case, of course, is that
of Clever Hans (Pfungst, 1911). Hans, it will be remembered, was the
horse of Mr. von Osten, a German mathematics teacher. By means of
tapping his foot, Hans was able to add, subtract, multiply, and divide.
Hans could spell, read, and solve problems of musical harmony. To
be sure, there were other clever animals at the time, and Pfungst tells
about them. There was "Rosa," the mare of Berlin, who performed similar feats in vaudeville, and there was the dog of Utrecht, and the reading
pig of Virginia. All these other clever animals were highly trained performers who were, of course, intentionally cued by their trainers.

Von Osten, however, did not profit from his animal's talent, nor did
it seem at all likely that he was attempting to perpetrate a fraud. He
swore he did not cue the animal, and he permitted other people to
question and to test the horse even without his being present. Pfungst
and his famous colleague, Stumpf, undertook a program of systematic
research to discover the secret of Hans' talents. Among the first discoveries made was that if Hans could not see the questioner, then the
horse was not clever at all. Similarly, if the questioner did not himself
know the answer to the question. Hans could not answer it either. Still,
Hans was able to answer Pfungst's questions as long as the investigator
was present and visible. Pfungst reasoned that the questioner might
in some way be signaling to Hans when to begin and when to stop
tapping his foot. A forward inclination of the head of the questioner
would start Hans tapping, Pfungst observed. He tried then to incline
his head forward without asking a question and discovered that this
was sufficient to start Hans tapping. As the experimenter straightened
up, Hans would stop tapping. Pfungst then tried to get Hans to stop
tapping by using very slight upward motions of the head. He found
that even the raising of his eyebrows was sufficient. In fact, even the
dilation of the questioner's nostrils was a cue for Hans to stop tapping.
When the questioner bent forward more, the horse would tap faster.

This added to the reputation of Hans as brilliant. That is, when a large number of taps was the correct response, Hans would tap rapidly until he approached the region of correctness, and then he would begin to slow down. It was found that questioners typically bent forward more when the answer was a long one, gradually straightening up as Hans got closer to the correct number.

For some experiments, Pfungst discovered that auditory cues functioned additively with visual cues. When the experimenter was silent, Hans was able to respond correctly 31 per cent of the time in picking one of many placards with different words written on it, or cloths of different colors. When auditory cues were added, Hans responded correctly 56 per cent of the time.

Pfungst himself then played the part of Hans, tapping out responses to questions with his hand. Of 25 questioners, 23 unwittingly cued Pfungst as to when to stop tapping in order to give a correct response. None of the questioners (men and women of all ages and occupations) knew the intent of the experiment. When errors occurred, they were usually only a single tap from being correct. The subjects of this study, including an experienced psychologist, were unable to discover that they were unintentionally emitting cues.

Hans' amazing talents, talents rapidly acquired too by Pfungst, serve to illustrate the power of the self-fulfilling prophecy. Hans' questioners, even skeptical ones, expected Hans to give the correct answers to their queries. Their expectation was reflected in their unwitting signal to Hans that the time had come for him to end his tapping. The signal cued Hans to stop, and the questioner's expectation became the reason for Hans' being, once again, correct.

Not all of Hans' questioners were equally good at fulfilling their prophecies. Even when the subject is a horse, apparently, the attributes of the experimenter make a considerable difference in determining the subject's response. On the basis of his studies, Pfungst was able to summarize the characteristics of those of Hans' questioners who were more successful in their covert and unwitting communication with the horse. Among the characteristics of the more successful unintentional influencers were those of tact, an air of dominance, attention to the business at hand, and a facility for motor discharge. Pfungst's observations of 60 years ago seem not to have suffered excessively for the lack of more modern methods of scaling observations. To anticipate some of the research findings to be presented later, it must be said that Pfungst's description seems also to fit those experimenters who are more likely to affect their human subject's response by virtue of their experimental hypothesis.

In summarizing his difficulties in learning the nature of Clever Hans' talents, Pfungst felt that he had been too long off the track by "looking for, in the horse, what should have been sought in the man." Perhaps, too, when we conduct research in the behavioral sciences we are sometimes caught looking at our subjects when we ought to be looking at ourselves. It was to this possibility that much of the research to be reviewed here was addressed.

A. Animal Learning

A good beginning might have been to replicate Pfungst's research, but with horses hard to come by, rats were made to do (Rosenthal and Fode, 1963a).

A class in experimental psychology had been performing experiments with human subjects for most of a semester. Now they were asked to perform one more experiment, the last in the course, and the first employing animal subjects. The experimenters were told of studies that had shown that maze-brightness and maze-dullness could be developed in strains of rats by successive inbreeding of the well- and the poorly-performing maze-runners. Sixty laboratory rats were equitably divided among the 12 experimenters. Half the experimenters were told that their rats were maze-bright while the other half were told that their rats were maze-dull. The animal's task was to learn to run to the darker of two arms of an elevated T-maze. The two arms of the maze, one white and one gray, were interchangeable; and the "correct" or rewarded arm was equally often on the right as on the left. Whenever an animal ran to the correct side he obtained a food reward. Each rat was given 10 trials each day for five days to learn that the darker side of the maze was the one which led to the food.

Beginning with the first day and continuing on through the experiment, animals *believed* to be better performers *became* better performers. Animals believed to be brighter showed a daily improvement in their performance, while those believed to be dull improved only to the third day and then showed a worsening of performance. Sometimes an animal refused to budge from his starting position. This happened 11% of the time among the allegedly bright rats; but among allegedly dull rats it happened 29% of the time. When animals did respond correctly, those believed to be brighter ran faster to the rewarded side of the maze than did even the correctly responding rats believed to be dull ($z = +2.05$).

When the experiment was over, all experimenters made ratings of their rats and of their own attitudes and behavior vis-à-vis their animals. Those experimenters who had been led to expect better performance viewed their animals as brighter, more pleasant, and more likeable. These same experimenters felt more relaxed in their contacts with the animals and described their behavior toward them as more pleasant, friendly, enthusiastic, and less talkative. They also stated that they handled their rats more often and also more gently than did the experimenters expecting poor performance.

The next experiment to be described also employed rat subjects, using this time not mazes but Skinner boxes (Rosenthal and Lawson, 1964). Because the experimenters (39) outnumbered the subjects (14), experimenters worked in teams of two or three. Once again about half the experimenters were led to believe that their subjects had been specially bred for excellence of performance. The experimenters who had been assigned the remaining rats were led to believe that their animals were genetically inferior.

The learning required of the animals in this experiment was more complex than that required in the maze learning study. This time the rats had to learn in sequence and over a period of a full academic quarter the following behaviors: to run to the food dispenser whenever a clicking sound occurred, to press a bar for a food reward, to learn that the feeder could be turned off and that sometimes it did not pay to press the bar, to learn new responses with only the clicking sound as a reinforcer, (rather than the food), to bar-press only in the presence of a light and not in the absence of the light, and, finally, to pull on a loop which was followed by a light which informed the animal that a bar-press would be followed by a bit of food.

At the end of the experiment the performance of the animals alleged to be superior was, in fact, superior to that of the allegedly inferior animals ($z = +2.17$) and the difference in learning favored the allegedly brighter rats in all five of the laboratory sections in which the experiment was conducted.

Just as in the maze learning experiment, the experimenters of the present study were asked to rate their animals and their own attitudes and behaviors toward them. Once again those experimenters who had expected excellence of performance judged their animals to be brighter, more pleasant, and more likeable. They also described their own behavior as more pleasant, friendly, enthusiastic, and less talkative, and they felt that they tended to watch their animals more closely, to handle them more, and to talk to them *less*. One wonders what was said to the animals by those experimenters who believed their rats to be inferior.

The absolute amount of handling of animals in this Skinner box experiment was considerably less than the handling of animals in the maze learning experiment. Nonetheless, those experimenters who believed their animals to be Skinner box bright handled them relatively more, or said they did, than did experimenters believing their animals to be dull. The extra handling of animals believed to be brighter may have contributed in both experiments to the superior learning shown by these animals.

In addition to the differences in handling reported by the experimenters of the Skinner box study as a function of their beliefs about their subjects, there were differences in the reported intentness of their observation of their animals. Animals believed to be brighter were watched more carefully, and more careful observation of the rat's Skinner box behavior may very well have led to more rapid and appropriate reinforcement of the desired response. Thus, closer observation, perhaps due to the belief that there would be more promising responses to be seen, may have made more effective teachers of the experimenters expecting good performance.

Cordaro and Ison (1963) employed 17 experimenters to conduct conditioning experiments with 34 planaria. Five of the experimenters were led to expect that their worms (two apiece) had already been taught to make many turning and contracting responses. Five of the experimenters were led to expect that their worms (also two apiece) had not yet been taught to make many responses and that in "only 100 trials" little turning and contracting could be expected. The seven experimenters of the third group were each given both these opposite expectancies, one for each of the their two worms. Behavior of the worms was observed by the experimenters looking down into a narrow ($\frac{1}{2}''$) and shallow ($\frac{1}{4}''$) v-shaped trough into which each worm was placed.

The results of the Cordaro and Ison experiment are easily summarized. Regardless of whether the experimenter prophesied the same results for both his worms or prophesied opposite results for his two worms, when the experimenter expected more turning and contracting he obtained more turning and contracting ($z > +3.25$). Similar results in studies of planaria have been obtained in two studies reported by Hartry (1966) and in studies of rats by Ingraham and Harrington (1966), and Burnham (1966) to whose study we shall later return. From the results of these studies we cannot be sure that the behavior of the animal was actually affected by the expectation of the experimenter, though that possibility cannot be ruled out. It is also possible, however, that only the experimenter's perception of the animal's behavior was affected by his hypothesis. That view of the results as examples of observer effects is quite plausible in the case of the planaria studies. Those worms, after all, are hard to see. That same view, however, is far less plausible in the case of the rat studies. It is difficult, for example, to confuse a rat's going out on the right arm of the maze with his going out on the left arm. Everything we know about the effects of handling on performance, the effects of set on reaction time (which would make an experimenter expecting bright Skinner box performance a faster and better "shaper"), and the base rate for recording errors, suggest that it is more plausible to think that the rat's behavior was affected than that the experimenters saw so badly or lied so much.

But what about those worms? Surely an experimenter cannot affect a worm in a trough to behave differently as a function of his expectation? Perhaps not, but perhaps so. Ray Mulry (1966) has pointed out in a personal communication how when the control of an unconditioned stimulus to the worm is not automatic, the experimenter may unwittingly teach worms differentially by his application of the unconditioned stimulus. Even in fully automated set-ups, however, we cannot yet rule out the possibility that worms can be affected differentially by a closely observing experimenter. Stanley Ratner (1966) has suggested in a personal communication that changes in the respiration or even temperature of the experimenter might (or might not) affect the worm's response. Relative to the small worm, in a small amount of water, the closely watching experimenter presents a potentially large source of various physical stimuli. The hypothesis of worm sensitivity to experimenter respiration changes is especially interesting in view of earlier research on dogs suggesting that they were substantially influenced by changes in their trainers' respiration (Rosenthal, 1965).

We have now described a number of experiments in which the effects of experimenter expectancy were investigated in studies of animal learning. We have given only enough details of a few of these studies to show the type of research conducted, but it would be desirable to have some systematic way to summarize the results of all the experiments conducted, including those only briefly mentioned. Our need to develop some systematic way to summarize runs of studies is greater when shortly we turn to a consideration of human subjects, for there we shall have over 80 studies to consider.

III. APPRAISAL OF A RESEARCH DOMAIN

We all join in the clarion calls for "more research" and echo the sentiment that this or that research is in (1. some, 2. much, 3. sore, 4. dire) need of replication. But sometimes we seem not quite sure of what to do with the replication when we have it. Behavioral scientist X finds A > B at $p < .05$. What shall be his conclusion after replication as a function of his second result? If replication yields B > A at $p < .05$ he can conclude that A is not always larger than B, that A is too often too different from B or, and only in this case is he likely to err, that on the average, A = B. For the moment putting aside considerations of statistical power differences between replications, it would seem that considerable information could be conveyed by just the direction of difference in the two studies and the associated p values. These p values can be handily traded in for standard normal deviates (z) and they, in turn, can be added, subtracted, multiplied, and divided. An algebraically signed normal deviate gives the direction and likelihood of a difference, while an unsigned normal deviate gives the nondirectional likelihood. If we have 10 experiments showing A > B at p = .05 and 10 experiments showing B > A at $p = .05$, then the average directional z is zero but the average nondirectional z is large enough so that we would be rash to conclude that A = B. Instead we would probably want to conclude that A and B differ too often, but unpredictably, and the research task might then be to reduce this unpredictability.

There is another important advantage to translating the results of runs of experiments to the standard normal deviate equivalents of the p values obtained. That advantage accrues from the fact that the sum of a set of standard normal deviates when divided by the square root of the number of zs, yields an overall z that tells the overall likelihood of the obtained results considered as a set (Mosteller and Bush, 1954).

In the summary of what is now known about the effects on research results of the experimenter's expectancy, we shall want to make use of these helpful characteristics of the standard normal deviate. But our purpose will not be solely to summarize the results of what we know about expectancy effects. An additional purpose is to employ these data as an illustration of how we may deal in a more global, overall way with the results of runs of experiments which, despite their differences in sampling, in procedure, and in outcome, are all addressed essentially to the same hypothesis or proposition. There may be sufficient usefulness to the method to warrant its more widespread adoption by those undertaking a comprehensive review of a given segment of the literature of the behavioral sciences.

With the increased interest in the effect of the experimenter's expectancy there have been increasing numbers of literature summaries (Rosenthal, 1963, 1964a, 1966, 1968a; Barber and Silver, 1968). These summaries have been generally cumulative, but none have been sufficiently systematic. Even the most recent ones have considered less than half the available experimental evidence.

Altogether, well over a hundred studies are known to have been conducted, all based on independent samples and all addressed to the central proposition that interpersonal expectancies in the research situation may be a significant source of artifact in behavioral research. For over 80 of these, more or less formal reports are available. These reports include published papers, papers presented at professional meetings, doctoral dissertations, master's theses, honors theses, and some unpublished manuscripts. The remaining studies, in various stages of completion or availability posed a problem; should they be included or not? It was decided that any research, even if lacking a formal report, would be included if (a) at least an informal description of the procedures were available and (b) the raw data were available for analysis. An additional dozen studies met this criterion and are listed in the references as "unpublished data." Of the remaining studies several will shortly become available to the writer and two reports have been seen but not yet used. Both of these reports presented data insufficient for the computation or even reasonable estimation of a z value. One of these reports claimed effects of experimenter expectancy and one claimed the absence of such effects.

For most of the studies summarized, no exact p was given, only that p was less than or greater than some arbitrary value. In those cases, exact ps were computed for our present purpose. Sometimes there was more than a single overall test of the same hypothesis of expectancy effect and in those cases median ps are presented. In a few studies, orthogonal overall tests were made of the effects of two different types of expectancies and in those cases only the more extreme z was retained after a correction was made for having made two tests. The correction involved doubling the p before finding the corrected associated z value. The same correction was employed in those cases where a specific p was computed and it was stated that another test yielded a larger p but without that p being given.

The basic paradigm in the experiments to be summarized has been to establish two groups of experimenters and to generate for each group a different expectation for their subjects' responses. For the studies following this paradigm it was a straightforward procedure to compute the overall exact p along with its corresponding directional z value. For the purpose of overall assessment, it was convenient to divide the obtained zs into three groups: those of $+1.28$ or greater, those falling between ± 1.28, and those of -1.28 or smaller. We expect 10 per cent of the results to fall in the first group, 80 per cent of the results to fall in the second group, and 10 per cent of the results to fall in the third group under the hypothesis of no expectancy effect. For the sake of simplicity, exact zs were recorded only for zs greater than $+1.28$

or less than —1.28 with zs falling between those values entered simply as .00. The net effect of this procedure, as we shall see, was to make our overall assessments somewhat too conservative or Type II Error-prone, but advantages of simplicity and clarity seemed to outweigh this disadvantage. The sign of the z value, of course, was positive when the difference between groups was in the predicted direction and negative when the difference was in the unpredicted direction.

A special problem occurred, however, for those studies in which the basic paradigm was extended to include additional experimental or control group conditions. Thus, there were some studies in which a control group was included whose experimenters had been given no expectations for their subjects' responses. In those cases the z value associated with the overall test of expectancy effects has a meaning somewhat different from the situation in which there are only two experimental groups. A large nondirectional z means that the experimenter's expectancy made some difference in subjects' responses but it is not so easy to prefix the algebraic sign of the z. It often happened that the control group differed more from the two experimental groups than the experimental groups differed from each other. Essentially, then, considering all available studies there were two hypotheses being tested rather than just one. The first hypothesis is that experimenters' expectations significantly affect their subjects' responses in some way and it is tested by considering the absolute magnitude of the zs obtained. The second hypothesis is that experimenters' expectations affected their subjects' responses in such a way as to lead to too many responses in the direction of the experimenter's expectation. This hypothesis is tested by considering the algebraic magnitude of the zs obtained. For those studies in which the overall z was only a test of the first hypothesis, an additional directional z was also computed addressed to the question of the degree to which the experimental manipulation of expectations led to hypothesis-confirming responses.

One more difficult decision was to be made. That had to do with determining the number of studies to be counted for each paper. Many papers described more than one experiment but sometimes investigators regarded these as several studies with no overall test of significance and sometimes investigators pooled the data from several studies and tested the overall significance. The guiding principle employed in an earlier summary (Rosenthal, 1968a) was to count as more than one experiment only those within a given paper that employed *both* a different sample of subjects *and* a substantial difference in procedure. For this more comprehensive review it was felt to be more informative to count as a separate experiment those that employed *either* a different sample of subjects *or* a substantial difference in procedure for some of their subjects. It was often difficult to decide when some procedural difference was substantial and quite unavoidably this had to remain a matter of the writer's judgment. There is no doubt that other workers might have classified some procedures as substantially different that were here regarded as essentially similar, and that some studies treated separately here would have been regarded by others as essentially the same. The major protection against serious errors of inference due to this matter of judgment comes from subsequent analyses that consider all research done by a given principal investigator or at a given laboratory as a single result.

Judgment and, therefore, possible error also entered into the calculation of each of the many z values. Methods of dealing with multiple p values have been referred to, but sometimes (e.g., when no overall p had been computed) it was necessary to decide on the most appropriate overall test. Here, too, it seems certain that, for any given study, different workers might have chosen different tests as most appropriate. Because of the large amounts of raw data analyzed by the writer, and because of the many secondary analyses performed when the original was felt to be inappropriate, a rule of thumb aimed primarily at the goal of convenience was developed. Given a choice of several more-or-less equally defensible procedures (e.g. multiple regression, analysis of covariance, treatments by levels analysis of variance) the most simple procedure was selected (e.g. treatments by levels) with the criterion of simplicity geared to the use of a desk calculator. This rule of thumb probably had the effect of decreasing more zs than it increased, since, in general, the more elegant procedures use more of the information in the data and generally lead to a reduction of Type II errors. This is likely to be especially true when the distribution of obtained z values is as radically skewed as the one obtained.

Despite these sources of errors of conservatism, the possibility of biased judgment and sheer error on the part of the writer cannot and should not be ruled out. As protection against the possibility of these biases we shall later want to make some very stringent corrections.

Since we have already summarized partially the results of studies of expectancy effect employing animal subjects, that seems a good subdomain with which to illustrate our systematic summarization procedure. Table III lists nine studies testing the hypothesis of expectancy effects. Burnham conducted a single study by our criterion, but the next three sets of authors conducted two apiece. For Cordaro and Ison and for Ingraham and Harrington one experiment was defined as that in which

TABLE III

EXPECTANCY EFFECTS IN STUDIES OF ANIMAL LEARNING

Code number	Study Authors			Standard normal deviate	
				Nondirectional	Directional
1.	Burnham	1966	I	1.50	+ 1.95
2.	Cordaro and Ison,	1963	I	3.96	+ 3.96
3.	Cordaro and Ison,	1963	II	3.25	+ 3.25
4.	Hartry,	1966	I	5.38	+ 5.38
5.	Hartry,	1966	II	3.29	+ 3.29[b]
6. [a]	Ingraham and Harrington,	1966	I	1.48	+ 1.48
7. [a]	Ingraham and Harrington,	1966	II	2.10	+ 2.10
8.	Rosenthal and Fode,	1963a	I	2.33	+ 2.33
9.	Rosenthal and Lawson,	1964	I	2.17	+ 2.17
			Sum	25.46	+25.91
			$\sqrt{9}$	3	3
			z	8.49	+ 8.64
			$p <$	1/(million)^2	1/(million)^2

[a] See also Rosenthal, 1967b, 1967c.

[b] Not based on exact p; exact z probably exceeds 5 or 6.

one group of experimenters was given one expectation while the other group of experimenters was given the opposite expectation. In both these papers, the second experiment was defined as that in which another group of experimenters held positive expectations for one group of their subjects and negative expectations for another group of their subjects. To put it another way, when experimenter expectancy was a between-experimenter source of variation that was regarded as an experiment different from that in which experimenter expectancy was a within-experimenter source of variation. Finally, the experiments reported by Hartry were simply two independent experiments conducted at different times by different experimenters and with differences in procedures. Interestingly, it was the second study with its tighter controls for inexperience of the experimenters, for observer errors, and for intentional errors, that showed the greater magnitude of expectancy effect with planaria subjects.

For each of the studies in Table III, two z values are given. The first is the z associated with an overall test of the hypothesis that the groups of experimenters employed showed some difference. The second is the z associated with the specific test that experimenters given one expectation obtained data in the direction of that expectation more than when experimenters were given some other expectation. For each column of zs the sum of the zs is indicated, as is the square root of the number of zs and the new z obtained when the former is divided by the latter. Finally, the p associated with the overall z is given. As it turned out for studies involving animal subjects, the nondirectional zs are identical in absolute value to the directional zs in every case except one. That was because in only that study was there a comparison among more groups than simply those reflecting each of two different expectations. The combined probability of obtaining the overall z based either on the nondirectional or the directional zs is infinitesimally low. In order to bring the combined p value for the directional test to .05, another 239 experiments with an average directional z value of exactly .00 would have to be conducted.

TABLE IV

EXPECTANCY EFFECTS IN STUDIES OF ANIMAL LEARNING
BY PRINCIPAL INVESTIGATORS

Principal investigator		Standard normal deviate	
Code number	Name	Nondirectional	Directional
I	Burnham	1.50	+ 1.95
II	Ison	5.11	+ 5.11
III	Hartry	6.15	+ 6.15
IV	Harrington	2.54	+ 2.54
V	Rosenthal	3.19	+ 3.19
	Sum	18.49	+18.94
	$\sqrt{5}$	2.24	2.24
	z	8.25	+ 8.46
	$p <$	$1/(\text{million})^2$	$1/(\text{million})^2$

In addition to a "per experiment" appraisal it was mentioned earlier that a "per principal investigator" appraisal might protect us from some erroneous inferences. Table IV gives the "per principal investigator" results and they are found to be very similar to those based on experiments. It would take over 127 new principal investigators obtaining an average directional z value of exactly .00 to bring the combined p value to the .05 level. The zs given for each principal investigator are usually based on the method of combining ps described earlier in detail. In a few cases, however, an overall test of the expectancy effect for the several studies was already available and then that overall value was employed.

IV. HUMAN SUBJECTS

So far we have given only the results of studies of expectancy effect in which the subjects were rats or worms. Most of the research available, however, is based on human subjects and it is those results that we now consider. In this set of experiments at least 20 different specific tasks have been employed, but some of these tasks seemed sufficiently related to one another that they could reasonably be regarded as a family of tasks or a research area. These areas include human learning and ability, psychophysical judgments, reaction time, inkblot tests, structured laboratory interviews, and person perception. We consider each in turn.

A. Learning and Ability

Table V summarizes the results of the per experiment and the per principal investigator analysis. There appeared to be no appreciable

TABLE V

Expectancy Effects in Studies of Learning and Ability

Study				Standard normal deviate	
Code number	Authors			Nondirectional	Directional
1.	Getter, M, H, W,	1967	I	.00	.00
2.	Hurwitz and Jenkins,	1966	I	1.28	+1.28
3.	Johnson,	1967	I	3.89	+3.89[a]
4.	Kennedy, E, W,	1968	I	.00	.00
5.	Kennedy, C, B,	1968	I	2.27	+2.27[a]
6.	Larrabee and Kleinsasser,	1967	I	1.60	+1.60
7.	Timaeus and Lück,	1968b	I	.00	.00
8.	Wartenberg–Ekren,	1962	I	.00	.00
9.	Wessler,	1968b	I	.00	.00
SUMMARY		Sum		9.04	+9.04
		$\sqrt{9}$		3	3
By Study		z		3.01	+3.01
		$p <$		.0015	.0015
		Sum		8.38	+8.38
By Principal		$\sqrt{8}$		2.83	2.83
Investigator		z		2.96	+2.96
		$p =$		.0015	.0015

[a] Indicates that experimenter expectancy interacted with another variable at $z \geq /1.28/$.

effects of the experimenter's expectancy on subjects' performance of (a) the Wechsler Adult Intelligence Scale (Getter et al.,), (b) the Block Design subtest of the same Scale (Wartenberg–Ekren) (c) a color-recognition-task (Timaeus and Lück), and (d) a dot-tapping task (Wessler). Two of the experiments (Kennedy et al.) employed a verbal conditioning task and in the second of these studies those experimenters expecting greater "conditioning" obtained greater conditioning than did the experimenters expecting less conditioning. In this experiment, as indicated by the asterisk of Table V, as in many others, there was also an interaction effect (defined as $z \geq +1.28$ or $z \leq -1.28$) between experimenter expectancy and some other variable. In this study the interaction took the form that those experimenters of a more "humanistic" or optimistic disposition obtained greater biasing effects of expectations than did experimenters of a more "deterministic" or pessimistic disposition.

The earlier experiment by Kennedy et al. also varied expectations about subjects' conditioning scores but half the time the experimenters had visual contact with their subjects (i.e., sat across from them) and half the time they had no visual contact with subjects (i.e., sat behind them). Because the same experimenters were employed in both conditions we count this as only one experiment and the overall test of significance showed the directional $z < +1.28$ and no interaction at $z = /1.28/$ between expectancy and visual contact. It was nevertheless of interest to note that in the face-to-face condition, experimenters expecting greater conditioning obtained greater conditioning ($z = +1.95$) than did the experimenters expecting less conditioning. In the condition of no visual contact the analogous z was very close to zero. These results, though summarized as a "failure to replicate," do suggest that visual cues may be important to the communication of experimenter expectations to the subjects of a verbal conditioning experiment as they were important to the communication of expectations to Clever Hans. The second experiment in the Kennedy series was conducted with experimenter and subject in face-to-face contact.

Especially instructive for its unusual within-subject experimental manipulation was the study by Larrabee and Kleinsasser. They employed five experimenters to administer the Wechsler Intelligence Scale for Children (WISC) to 12 sixth-graders of average intelligence. Each subject was tested by two different experimenters—one administering the even-numbered items and the other administering the odd-numbered items. For each subject, one of the experimenters was told that the child was of above average intelligence while the other experimenter was told that the child was of below average intelligence. When the child's experimenter expected superior performance the total IQ earned was 7.5 points higher on the average than when the child's experimenter expected inferior performance. When only the performance subtests of the WISC were considered, the advantage to the children of having been expected to do well was less than three IQ points and could easily have occurred by chance. When only the verbal subtests of the WISC were considered, the advantage of having been expected to do well, however, exceeded 10 IQ points. The particular subtest most affected by experimenters' expectancies was Information. The results of this study are especially striking in view of the very small sample size (12) of subjects employed.

In the experiment by Hurwitz and Jenkins the tasks were not standardized tests of intelligence, but rather two standard laboratory tests of learning. Three male experimenters administered a rote verbal learning task and a mathematical reasoning task to a total of 20 female subjects. From half their subjects the experimenters were led to expect superior performance; from half they were led to expect inferior performance.

In the rote learning task, subjects were shown a list of pairs of nonsense syllables and were asked to remember one of the pair members from a presentation of the other pair member. Subjects were given six trials to learn the syllable pairs. Somewhat greater learning occurred on the part of the subjects contacted by the experimenters believing subjects to be brighter although the difference was not large numerically and $z < +1.28$; subjects alleged to be brighter learned 11 per cent more syllables. The curves of learning of the paired nonsense syllables, however, did show a difference between subjects alleged to be brighter and those alleged to be duller. Among "brighter" subjects, learning increased more monotonically over the course of the six trials than was the case for "duller" subjects. (The coefficient of determination between accurate recall and trial number was .50 for the "bright" subjects and .25 for the "dull" subjects; $z > 2.00$ but not used in assessing overall significance.)

In the mathematical reasoning task, subjects had to learn to use three sizes of water jars in order to obtain exactly some specified amount of water. On the critical trials the correct solution could be obtained by a longer and more routine procedure which was scored for partial credit or by a shorter but more novel procedure which was given full credit. Those subjects whose experimenters expected superior performance earned higher scores than did those subjects whose experimenters expected inferior performance. Among the latter subjects, only 40 per cent ever achieved a novel solution, while among the allegedly superior subjects 88 per cent achieved one or more novel solutions.

Subjects expected to be dull made 57 per cent again as many errors as did subjects expected to be bright. In this experiment, with two tasks performed by each subject, the overall z was based on subjects' performance on both tasks.

The final experiment to be mentioned in this section is of special importance because of the elimination of plausible alternatives to the hypothesis that it is the subject's response that is affected by the experimenter's expectancy. In his experiment, Johnson employed the Stevenson marble-dropping task. Each of the 20 experimenters was led to believe that marble-dropping rate was related to intelligence. More intelligent subjects were alleged to show a greater increase in rate of marble-dropping over the course of six trials. Each experimenter then contacted eight subjects, half of whom were alleged to be brighter than the remaining subjects.

The recording of the subject's response was by means of an electric counter, and the counter was read by the investigator who was blind to the subject's expectancy condition. As can be seen from Table V, the results of this study, one of the best controlled in this area, were the most dramatic. Experimenters expecting a greater increase in marble-dropping rate obtained a greater increase than they did when expecting a lesser increase. In this study, too, there was an interaction effect between the expectation of the experimenter, the sex of the experimenter, and the sex of the subject. Same-sex dyads showed a greater effect of experimenter expectation ($z = 1.80$).

Considering the studies of human learning and ability as a set, it appears that the effects of experimenter expectancy may well operate as unintended determinants of subjects' performance. The magnitudes of the effects obtained, however, are considerably smaller than those obtained with animal subjects. It would take only another 21 experiments with an average directional z of .00 to bring the overall p to the .05 level compared to the 239 experiments required in the area of animal learning. Another 18 principal investigators averaging zero z results would bring the combined p to .05 in the area of human learning and abilities.

Because there are few experiments in this set employing exactly the same task it is difficult to be sure of any pattern in the magnitudes of zs obtained in individual studies or by individual investigators. Perhaps it does appear, however, that standardized intelligence tests employed with adults are relatively not so susceptible to the effects of the experimenter's expectancy. The Hurwitz and Jenkins results, however, weaken that conclusion somewhat. With only one study each for color recognition and dot-tapping perhaps any conclusion would be premature.

B. Psychophysical Judgments

Table VI shows the results of nine studies employing tasks we may refer to loosely as requiring psychophysical judgments, and Table VII shows the per investigator summary. Five of the six studies yielding directional $zs < +1.28$ employed a number estimation task (Adair; Müller & Timaeus; Shames and Adair, I, II; Weiss).

Adair, though he found no main effect of experimenter expectancy, did find that the magnitude of expectancy effect could be predicted from a knowledge of the sex of experimenter and sex of subject. Greater expectancy effects were found when experimenter and subject were of the opposite rather than the same sex ($z = 2.33$). Müller and Timaeus found that the effect of experimenter expectation was to decrease the variability of obtained responses relative to a control group, while Weiss found that relative to the control subjects, subjects whose experimenters had been given any expectation underestimated the number of dots presented. Shames and Adair (I) found that those experimenters who were judged by their subjects as more courteous, more pleasant, and more given to the use of head gestures showed a tendency (all $zs > 1.96$) to obtain data opposite to that which they had been led to expect.

The experiments by Horst and by Wessler both employed a line length

TABLE VI

Expectancy Effects in Studies of Psychophysical Judgments

Study			Standard normal deviate	
Code number	Authors		Nondirectional	Directional
1.	Adair,	1968 I	.00	.00[a]
2.	Horst,	1966 I	1.74	+1.94
3.	Müller and Timaeus,	1967 I	1.88	.00[a]
4.	Shames and Adair,	1967 I	.00	.00[a]
5.	Shames and Adair,	1967 II	.00	.00
6.	Weiss,	1967 I	1.39	.00[a]
7.	Wessler,	1968b I	.00	.00
8.	Zoble,	1968 I	3.29	+3.70
9.	Zoble,	1968 II	2.02	+2.02
		Sum	10.32	+7.66
		$\sqrt{9}$	3	3
		z	3.44	+2.55
		$p \le$	.0003	.006

[a] Indicates that experimenter expectancy interacted with another variable at $z \ge /1.28/$.

TABLE VII

EXPECTANCY EFFECTS IN STUDIES OF PSYCHOPHYSICAL JUDGMENTS
BY PRINCIPAL INVESTIGATORS

Principal investigator		Standard normal deviate	
Code number	Name	Nondirectional	Directional
I	Adair	.00	.00
II	Horst	1.74	+1.94
III	Timaeus	1.88	.00
IV	Weiss	1.39	.00
V	Wessler	.00	.00
VI	Zoble	3.77	+4.06
	Sum	8.78	+6.00
	$\sqrt{6}$	2.45	2.45
	z	3.58	+2.45
	$p \leq$	.0002	.007

estimation task. Data presented by Wessler suggest that the z associated with the effect of experimenter expectancy might well be $> +1.28$ but because it could not be determined exactly from the data available, and because no effect appeared in two other tasks administered to the same subjects, we count the z as .00. Horst, however, found line length estimation to be affected by the experimenter's expectancy and more so by those experimenters rated by their subjects as more pleasant, bolder, and less awkward. In addition, Horst found (just as Weiss did) that, relative to the control subjects, subjects whose experimenters had been given any expectation showed a greater tendency to underestimate.

The largest effects of interpersonal expectancies were found in the studies of tone length discrimination by Zoble. In both his studies, which differed from each other in the mental sets induced in the subjects, he found that the experimenter's expectancy was a significant determinant of subjects' discriminations. In addition, while he found that either the visual or the auditory channel was probably sufficient to serve as mediator of expectancy effects, the data suggested that the visual channel was more effective than the auditory channel ($z = +1.44$).

On the whole, the area of psychophysical judgment, particularly when the judgment is of numerosity, seems less susceptible to the effects of experimenter expectancy than the other areas considered so far. The number of additional experiments with a mean directional z of .00 required to bring the overall p to the .05 level for the area of psychophysical judgments is only a dozen. On a per investigator basis, only seven additional investigators with mean .00 findings would bring the cumulative p to .05.

C. Reaction Time

Table VIII shows the results of three studies by three different investigators in which the dependent variable was one form or another of reaction time. Employing visual stimuli, McFall found no effects of experimenter expectancy, but Wessler did. Wessler also found that the effects of experimenter expectancy were greater on earlier trials and that, over time, there was a monotonic decrease of expectancy effect ($z = 1.65$). The remaining experiment, by Silverman, employed verbal rather than visual stimuli.

TABLE VIII

EXPECTANCY EFFECTS IN STUDIES OF REACTION TIME

Study				Standard normal deviate	
Code number	Authors			Nondirectional	Directional
1.	McFall,	1965	I	.00	.00
2.	Silverman,	1968	I	1.88	+1.88[a]
3.	Wessler,	1966, 1968a	I	1.46	+1.46[a]
			Sum	3.34	+3.34
			$\sqrt{3}$	1.73	1.73
			z	1.93	+1.93
			$p <$	.03	.03

[a] Indicates that experimenter expectancy interacted with another variable at $z \geq /1.28/$.

Silverman employed 20 students of advanced psychology as experimenters to administer a word association test to 333 students of introductory psychology. Half the experimenters were led to expect that some of their subjects would show longer latencies to certain words than would their control group subjects. The remaining experimenters were given no expectations and served as an additional control condition. Results showed that latencies did not differ between the two baseline conditions but that when experimenters expected longer latencies from their subjects, they obtained longer latencies.

For some of the experimenters, Silverman found a significant tendency to commit scoring errors in the direction of their expectations, but there was some evidence to suggest that such scoring errors could not very well account for the effects obtained. Silverman had found an interaction of experimenter expectation by sex of experimenter and sex of subject ($z = 1.95$). The nature of this interaction was the same as that found by Adair. When experimenters and subjects were of the opposite sex they showed greater expectancy effects than when they were of the same sex. Silverman's plausible reasoning was that scoring errors on the part of the experimenters ought not to be differentially related to their subjects' sex as a function of their own sex.

Because of the small number of experiments conducted in this area it would take only one additional study (or principal investigator) with an associated z of zero to bring the combined p level to .05. Thus though two of the three studies obtained zs of $+1.28$ or greater we can not have the confidence in the expectancy hypothesis that seems warranted for other research.

D. Inkblot Tests

Table IX summarizes by study and by principal investigator the results of research on expectancy effects employing as the dependent variable subjects' perceptions of inkblot test materials. In the first of these studies, Masling employed 14 graduate student experimenters to administer the Rorschach to a total of 28 subjects. Half the experimenters were led to believe that it would reflect more favorably upon themselves if they

TABLE IX

EXPECTANCY EFFECTS IN STUDIES OF INKBLOT TESTS

Study			Standard normal deviate	
Code number	Authors		Nondirectional	Directional
1.	Marwit,	1968 I	1.80	+1.80
2.	Marwit and Marcia,	1967 I	3.25	+3.25
3.	Masling,	1965, 1966 I	2.05	+2.05
4.	Strauss,	1968 I	2.32	.00[a]
SUMMARY		Sum	9.42	+7.10
		$\sqrt{4}$	2	2
By Study		z	4.71	+3.55
		$p \leq$	.0000015	.0002
By Principal		Sum	7.95	+5.63
Investigator		$\sqrt{3}$	1.73	1.73
		z	4.60	+3.25
		$p =$	.0000025	.0006

[a] Indicates that experimenter expectancy interacted with another variable at $z \geq /1.28/$.

obtained more human than animal responses. The remaining experimenters were given the opposite value, belief, or expectation. All experimenters were forcefully warned not to coach their two subjects and all administrations of the Rorschach were tape-recorded. Results showed that experimenters led to prize animal responses obtained one-third again as high an animal to human response ratio as did the experimenters led to prize human responses. Analysis of the tape recordings revealed no evidence favoring the hypothesis that differential verbal reinforcement of subjects' responses might have accounted for the differences obtained. In addition, none of the subjects reported that their experimenter seemed to show any special interest in any particular type of response. The cues by which an experimenter unintentionally informs his subject of the desired response appear likely to be subtle ones.

In the experiment by Marwit and Marcia 36 advanced undergraduate experimenters administered five of the Holtzman inkblots to a total of 53 students of elementary psychology. Some of the experimenters expected many responses from their subjects either on the basis of their own hypotheses or because that was what they had been led to expect. The remaining experimenters expected few responses from their subjects. The overall results showed that experimenters expecting more responses obtained more responses than did experimenters expecting fewer responses. Among the experimenters who had developed their own hypotheses, those who expected more responses obtained 59 per cent more responses than did the experimenters who expected fewer responses. Among the experimenters who were given "ready-made" expectancies, those who expected more obtained 61 per cent more responses than those who expected fewer responses.

In this experiment almost one-third of the experimenters admitted to being aware that their own expectancy effects were under investigation. Interestingly enough, this admitted awareness bore no relationship to magnitude of expectancy effect exerted. In addition, there was no overall relationship between the number of verbal inquiries made by experimenters and the number of responses obtained from their subjects ($r = .07$). However, an interesting reversal of what we might expect occurred when it was shown that the subgroup of experimenters who asked the most questions were the experimenters who had been led to expect few responses ($z = 2.40$). Finally, there was an interesting tendency, not found in earlier studies, for those inkblots shown later to manifest greater expectancy effects than those inkblots shown earlier. If some form of unintended reinforcement were employed by the experimenters, it is at least unlikely to have been anything so obvious as differential questioning.

In his experiment, Strauss employed five female experimenters each of whom was to administer the Rorschach to six female undergraduates. For two of the subjects each experimenter was led to expect an "intro-versive" experience balance; for another two of the subjects each experi-menter was led to expect an "extratensive" experience balance; and for the remaining two subjects, experimenters were given no expectations. Subjects' actual experience balance, measured by the difference between relative standings in human movement (M) and color $(Sum\ C)$ produc-tion, was found overall to be unrelated to the experimenter's expectancy. There was an interesting difference, however, in the variability of ob-tained responses across the three treatment groups (F max = 19.22, $p < .05$), with the control group of subjects for whom experimenters had been given no expectation showing least individual differences among experimenters. Relative to the control group subjects, subjects contacted by the different experimenters in both conditions of expectancy obtained experience balance scores that were both too high and too low.

As a check on the success of the induction of the expectations, Strauss asked his experimenters to predict the experience balance that would be obtained from each subject. The analysis showed very clearly that, on the average, experimenters predicted experience balance scores very much in line with those they had been led to expect. In addition, how-ever, an interaction effect was obtained ($z > 2.58$) which showed that one of the five experimenters predicted results opposite to those he had been led to expect, while another predicted an unusually great difference between his introversive and extratensive subjects, but in the right direction. These two extreme predictors, it turned out, both showed a tendency to obtain responses opposite to those they had been led to expect (mean expectancy effect in standard score units = −1.74). The remaining three experimenters all obtained more positive effects (mean expectancy effect in standard score units = +1.45). With so small a sample of experimenters ($df = 3$) such a comparison ($z = 1.44$) can be at best suggestive, but it may serve to alert other investigators to the interesting possibility that experimenters, when given a prophecy for a subject's behavior, may be more likely to fulfill that prophecy if they believe neither too much nor too little that the prophecy will be fulfilled.

In the most recent of the inkblot experiments, Marwit employed 20 graduate students in clinical psychology as his experimenters and 40 undergraduate students of introductory psychology as his subjects. Half the experimenters were led to expect some of their subjects to give many Rorschach responses and especially a lot of animal responses.

Half the experimenters were led to expect some of their subjects to give few Rorschach responses but proportionately a lot of human responses. Results showed that subjects who were expected to give more responses gave more responses ($z = +1.55$) and that subjects who were expected to give a greater number of animal relative to human responses did so ($z = +2.04$). Marwit also found trends for the first few responses to have been already affected by the experimenter's expectancy and for later-contacted subjects to show greater effects of experimenter expectancy than earlier-contacted subjects.

In summarizing the four inkblot experiments we can say that three investigations obtained substantial effects of experimenters' expectancies while one investigation did not. Perhaps we can account for the differences in results in terms of differences in procedure. In the three experiments showing expectancy effects, the expectancy induced was for a more simple Rorschach response—animal or human content in one study, number of responses in another, and both in the third. In the study showing no significant expectancy effect, the expectancy induced was for a more complex response, one involving a relationship of two response categories to one another, human movement and color.

In the three experiments showing expectancy effects, each experimenter entertained the same hypothesis for each of his experimental group subjects. In the experiment not showing the expectancy effect, each experimenter contacted subjects under opposite conditions of expectation. There have been many experiments with human and animal subjects showing that expectancy effects may occur even when the different expectations are held in the mind of the same experimenters. There are, however, a number of studies showing that under these conditions, from 12 to 20 per cent of the experimenters show *significant* reversals of expectancy effect. The word significant is italicized to emphasize that we speak not of failures to obtain data in the predicted direction, but of obtaining data opposite to that expected with non-Gaussian gusto (Rosenthal, 1967c, 520). In the study by Strauss not showing expectancy effects on the obtained Rorschach experience balance, such extreme reversals were not obtained but the sample of experimenters was small (five).

Finally, in the study not showing expectancy effects, the experimenters were more experienced than those of the studies that did show expectancy effects. There is, however, some other evidence to suggest that more experienced, more competent, and more professional experimenters may be the ones to show greater rather than smaller expectancy effects (Rosenthal, 1966).

Pending the results of additional research, perhaps all we can now say is that some inkblot responses may, under some conditions, be fairly susceptible to the effects of the experimenter's expectancy. For the set of experiments described here, the overall p level can be brought to the .05 level by the addition of 15 new results of an average directional z value of .00. For the set of principal investigators, the overall p level can be brought to the .05 level by the additional results of nine principal investigators obtaining an average directional z value of .00.

Later we shall have occasion to discuss more systematically the results of studies of experimenter expectancy as a function of the laboratory in which they were conducted. For now it should only be mentioned that the one study of inkblot responses showing no overall directional effect of experimenter expectancy was the one conducted in the writer's laboratory.

E. Structured Laboratory Interviews

Table X shows the per investigation and per investigator results of the research in what must be the most miscellaneous of our research areas. In one of the earliest of these studies, Pflugrath investigated the effects of the experimenter's expectancy on scores earned on a standardized paper-and-pencil test of anxiety. He employed nine graduate student counselors, each of whom was to administer the Taylor Manifest Anxiety Scale to two groups of students of introductory psychology. In each group there was an average of about eight subjects. Three

TABLE X

EXPECTANCY EFFECTS IN STUDIES OF STRUCTURED LABORATORY INTERVIEWS

Study				Standard normal deviate	
Code number	Authors			Nondirectional	Directional
1.	Cooper, E, R, D,	1967	I	3.37	+ 3.37
2.	Jenkins,	1966	I	1.34	+ 1.34[a]
3.	Pflugrath,	1962	I	1.75	.00
4.	Raffetto,	1967, 1968	I	5.24	+ 5.24[a]
5.	Rosenthal, P, V, F,	1963b	I	1.48	+ 1.48
6.	Timaeus and Lück,	1968a	I	1.55	+ 1.55
	Sum			14.73	+12.98
	$\sqrt{6}$			2.45	2.45
	z			6.01	+ 5.30
	p			1/500 million	1/10 million

[a] Indicates that experimenter expectancy interacted with another variable at $z \geq /1.28/$.

of the experimenters were led to believe that their groups of subjects were very anxious, three were led to believe that their groups of subjects were not at all anxious, and three were given no expectations about their subjects' anxiety level.

Pflugrath found no difference among the three treatment conditions in his analysis of variance but his X^2 was large. The bulk of the obtained X^2 was due to the fact that, among experimenters led to expect high anxiety scores, more subjects actually scored lower in anxiety. This finding, while certainly not predicted, was at least interpretable in the light of the experimenters' status as counselors-in-training. Told that they would be testing very anxious subjects who had required help at the counseling center, these experimenters may well have brought their developing therapeutic skills to bear upon the challenge of reducing these subjects' anxiety. If the subject's performance on even well-standardized paper-and-pencil tests, administered in a group situation, may be affected by the experimenter's perception of the subject, then it is not unreasonable to suppose that such effects may occur with some frequency in the more intense and more personal relationship that characterizes the more typical clinical assessment situation.

As a check on the success of his experimental induction of expectancies, Pflugrath asked his experimenters to predict the level of anxiety they would actually find in each of their groups of subjects. Although there was a tendency for examiners to predict the anxiety level that they had been led to expect, this tendency did not reach an associated z of $+1.28$. The experimentally manipulated expectations, then, were not very effectively induced. It is of interest to note, however, that all three of the experimenters who specifically predicted higher anxiety obtained higher anxiety scores than did any of the experimenters who specifically predicted lower anxiety ($z > +1.65$). Because the results of the Pflugrath experiment showed some effects in the predicted direction and some effects in the opposite direction the directional z is entered as .00 in Table X. The nondirectional z, however, retains the information that some differences were associated with the effects of experimenter expectancy.

The experiment by Raffetto was addressed to the question of whether the experimenter's expectation for greater reports of hallucinatory behavior might be a significant determinant of such reports.

Raffetto employed 96 paid, female volunteer students from a variety of less advanced undergraduate courses to participate in an experiment on sensory restriction. Subjects were asked to spend one hour in a small room that was relatively free from light and sound. Eight more advanced students of psychology served as the experimenters, with each one interviewing 12 of the subjects before and after the sensory restriction experience. The preexperimental interview consisted of factual questions such as age, college major, and college grades. The postexperimental interview was relatively well-structured including questions to be answered by "yes" or "no" as well as more open-ended questions—e.g., "Did you notice any particular sensations or feelings?" Postexperimental interviews were tape-recorded.

Half the experimenters were led to expect high reports of hallucinatory experiences, and half were led to expect low reports of hallucinatory experiences. Obtained scores of hallucinatory experiences ranged from zero to 32 with a grand mean of 5.4. Of the subjects contacted by experimenters expecting more hallucinatory experiences, 48 per cent were scored above the mean on these experiences. Of the subjects contacted by experimenters expecting fewer hallucinatory experiences, only 6 per cent were scored above the mean.

Since in this experiment the experimenters scored their own interviews for degree of hallucinatory experience, it is possible that scoring errors accounted for part of the massive effects obtained. It seems unlikely, however, in the light of what we now know of such errors that effects as dramatic as these could have been due entirely to scoring errors even if such errors were very great. Fortunately this question can be answered in the future since Raffetto did tape record the interviews conducted so that they can be rated by "blind" observers. When Raffetto himself checked the experimenters' scoring he found no significant scoring errors, but we must note, as did Raffetto, that he was not blind to the interviewers' condition of expectancy. The work of Beez (1968), however, amply documents the fact that such dramatic effects of expectancy may occur even in the absence of scoring errors.

In the experiment conducted by Rosenthal et al., 18 graduate students served as experimenters in a study of verbal conditioning conducted with 65 undergraduate subjects. Half the experimenters were led to expect from their subjects high rates of awareness of having been conditioned, while the remaining experimenters were led to expect low rates of awareness of having been conditioned. Questionnaires assessing subjects' degree of awareness were scored blindly by two psychologists. Of the subjects expected to show a low degree of awareness, 43 per cent were subsequently judged as "aware." Of the subjects expected to show a high degree of awareness, 68 per cent were subsequently judged as "aware."

In the experiment by Timaeus and Lück of the University of Cologne, subjects were asked to estimate the level of aggression to be found in a Milgram type experiment. When experimenters had been led to expect high levels of aggression, they obtained higher levels of aggression than when experimenters had been led to expect lower levels of aggression. Jenkins found in her experiment that factual information about a stimulus person could be communicated unintentionally from experimenter to subject. Subjects contacted by experimenters believing one set of factual statements to be true of a stimulus person more often also believed those factual statements to be true of the stimulus person than did subjects contacted by experimenters believing the opposite factual statements to be true of the stimulus person. The experiment by Cooper *et al.* is one we shall consider later in more detail. Their research showed that the degree of certainty of having to take a test as a function of the degree of preparatory effort was successfully predicted from a knowledge of the experimenters' expectations.

Considering the results of these experiments (or principal investigators) as a set, it would require 56 additional studies (or investigators) finding a mean directional z of .00 to bring the overall p level to .05.

F. Person Perception

Table XI shows the results of 57 studies of expectancy effect in which a standardized task of person perception was employed. Table XII shows the analogous results based not on studies but on principal investigators. The basic paradigm of these investigations has been sufficiently uniform that we need only an illustration (Rosenthal and Fode, 1963b I).

Ten advanced undergraduate and graduate students of psychology served as the experimenters. All were enrolled in an advanced course in experimental psychology and were already involved in conducting research. Each student-experimenter was assigned as his subjects a group of about 20 students of introductory psychology. The experimental procedure was for the experimenter to show a series of ten photographs of people's faces to each of his subjects individually. The subject was to rate the degree of success or failure shown in the face of each person pictured in the photos. Each face could be rated as any value from −10 to +10, with −10 meaning extreme failure and +10 meaning extreme success. The 10 photos had been selected so that, on the average, they were rated as neither successful nor unsuccessful, but rather as neutral with an average numerical score of zero.

All ten experimenters were given identical instructions on how to administer the task to their subjects and were given identical instructions to read to their subjects. They were cautioned not to deviate from these instructions. The purpose of their participation, it was explained to all experimenters, was to see how well they could duplicate experimental

TABLE XI

EXPECTANCY EFFECTS IN STUDIES OF PERSON PERCEPTION

Code number	Authors			Standard normal deviate	
				Nondirectional	Directional
1.	Adair and Epstein,	1967	I	1.65	+ 1.65
2.	Adair and Epstein,	1967	II	1.64	+ 1.64
3.	Adler,	1968	I	4.42	+ 4.42
4.	Adler,	1968	II	2.33	− 2.33
5.	Adler,	1968	III	1.50	− 1.50
6.	Barber, C, F, M, C, B,	1967	I	.00	.00[a]
7.	Barber, C, F, M, C, B,	1967	II	.00	.00
8.	Barber, C, F, M, C, B,	1967	III	.00	.00
9.	Barber, C, F, M, C, B,	1967	IV	.00	.00
10.	Barber, C, F, M, C, B,	1967	V	1.58	.00
11.	Bootzin,	1968	I	2.14	+ 2.14[b]
12.	Bootzin,	1968	II	1.64	− 1.64[b]
13.	Bootzin,	1968	III	1.44	+ 1.44[b]
14.	Carlson and Hergenhahn,	1968	I	.00	.00[b]
15.	Carlson and Hergenhahn,	1968	II	.00	.00[b]
16.	Connors,	1968	I	.00	.00[b]
17.	Connors and Horst,	1966	I	.00	.00[b]
18.	Fode,	1967	I	2.81	+ 2.81[b]
19.	Horn,	1968	I	2.01	+ 2.01
20.	Jenkins	1966	I	1.61	+ 1.61[b]
21.	Laszlo and Rosenthal	1967	I	1.80	+ 1.80[b]
22.	Marcia,	1961	I	.00	.00[b]
23.	Marcia,	1961	II	.00	.00[b]
24.	McFall,	1965	I	.00	.00[b]
25.	Moffatt,	1966	I	.00	.00
26.	Nichols,	1967	I	.00	.00[b]
27.	Persinger,	1962	I	.00	.00[b]
28.	Persinger, K, R,	1966	I	1.88	+ 1.88[b]
29.	Persinger, K, R,	1968	I	1.64	+ 1.64[b]
30.	Rosenthal and Fode,	1963b	I	2.46	+ 2.46
31.	Rosenthal and Fode,	1963b	II	3.94	+ 3.44
32.	Rosenthal and Fode,	1963b	III	1.64	+ 1.64[b]
33.	Rosenthal, F, J, F, S, W, V,	1964	I	1.52	− 1.52[b]
34.	Rosenthal, K, G, C,	1965	I	1.69	+ 1.69[b]
35.	Rosenthal, K, G, C,	1965	II	.00	.00[b]
36.	Rosenthal and Persinger,	1968	I	1.29	+ 1.29[b]
37.	Rosenthal and Persinger,	1968	II	.00	.00[b]
38.	Rosenthal, P, M, V, G,	1964a	I	1.44	+ 1.44[b]
39.	Rosenthal, P, M, V, G,	1964a	II	.00	.00[b]
40.	Rosenthal, P, M, V, G,	1964b	I	2.33	.00[b]
41.	Rosenthal, P, M, V, G,	1964b	II	2.58	.00

TABLE XI (*continued*)

Code number	Study		Standard normal deviate	
	Authors		Nondirectional	Directional
42.	Rosenthal, P, V, F,	1963a I	2.17	+ 2.33[b]
43.	Rosenthal, P, V, M,	1963 I	.00	.00
44.	Rosenthal, P, V, M,	1963 II	1.96	+ 1.96[b]
45.	Shames and Adair,	1967 I	1.70	+ 1.70
46.	Smiltens,	1966 I	1.28	− 1.28[b]
47.	Trattner,	1966, 1968 I	.00	.00[b]
48.	Uno, F, R,	1968 I	1.99	− 1.99[b]
49.	Uno, F, R,	1968 II	.00	.00[b]
50.	Uno, F, R,	1968 III	.00	.00
51.	Uno, F, R,	1968 IV	2.17	− 2.17[b]
52.	Uno, F, R,	1968 V	.00	.00
53.	Weick,	1966 I	2.33	+ 2.33[b]
54.	Wessler,	1968b I	.00	.00
55.	Wessler and Strauss,	1968 I	1.65	.00
56.	White,	1962 I	2.81	− 1.51[b]
57.	Woolsey and Rosenthal,	1966 I	1.34	+ 1.34[b]
		Sum	68.38	+30.72
		$\sqrt{57}$	7.55	7.55
		z	9.06	+ 4.07
		$p \leq$	1/(million)^2	.000025

[a] See also Rosenthal, 1967d, 1968b.

[b] Indicates that experimenter expectancy interacted with another variable at $z \geq /1.28/$.

results which were already well-established. Half the experimenters were told that the "well-established" finding was such that their subjects should rate the photos as being of successful people (ratings of +5) and half the experimenters were told that their subjects should rate the photos as being of unsuccessful people (ratings of −5). Results showed that experimenters expecting higher photo ratings obtained higher photo ratings than did experimenters expecting lower photo ratings. Although all of the other experiments shown in Table XI were also intended as replications of the basic finding, most of the work summarized was designed particularly to learn something of the conditions which increase, decrease, or otherwise modify the effects of experimenter expectancy. That intent has characterized the work of 18 of the 20 principal investigators listed in Table XII. It was the role of auditory cues, for example, that engaged the interest of Adair and Epstein.

TABLE XII

EXPECTANCY EFFECTS IN STUDIES OF PERSON PERCEPTION
BY PRINCIPAL INVESTIGATORS

Principal investigator		Standard normal deviate	
Code number	Name	Nondirectional	Directional
I	Adair	2.88	+ 2.88
II	Adler	4.77	.00
III	Barber	1.40	.00
IV	Bootzin	3.02	.00
V	Carlson	.00	.00
VI	Connors	.00	.00
VII	Fode	2.81	+ 2.81
VIII	Horn	2.01	+ 2.01
IX	Jenkins	1.61	+ 1.61
X	Marcia	.00	.00
XI	McFall	.00	.00
XII	Moffat	.00	.00
XIII	Nichols	.00	.00
XIV	Persinger	.00	.00
XV	Rosenthal	6.91	+ 3.52
XVI	Smiltens	1.28	− 1.28
XVII	Trattner	.00	.00
XVIII	Weick	2.33	+ 2.33
XIX	Wessler	.00	.00
XX	White	2.81	− 1.51
	Sum	31.83	+12.37
	$\sqrt{20}$	4.47	4.47
	z	7.12	+ 2.77
	$p \leq$	$1/(4 \text{ million})(10^5)$	.003

They first conducted a study which was essentially a replication of the basic experiment on the self-fulfilling effects of experimenters' hypotheses. Results showed that, just as in the original studies, experimenters who expected the perception of success from their subjects fulfilled their expectations as did the experimenters who had prophesied the perception of failure by their subjects.

During the conduct of this replication experiment, Adair and Epstein tape-recorded the experimenters' instructions to their subjects. The second experiment was then conducted not by "live" experimenters, but by tape-recordings of experimenters' voices reading standard instructions to their subjects. When the tape-recorded instructions had originally been read by experimenters expecting success perception by their subjects, the tape-recordings evoked greater success perceptions from their subjects. When the tape-recorded instructions had originally been read by experimenters expecting failure perception by their subjects, the tape-recordings evoked greater failure perceptions from their subjects. Self-fulfilling prophecies, it seems, can come about as a result of a prophet's voice alone. Since, in the experiment described, all experimenters read standard instructions, self-fulfillment of prophecies may be brought about by the tone in which the prophet prophesies.

Adler, in her recent research, investigated the effects on experimenter expectancy of several experimenter sets or orientations toward outcomes. When experimenters were made to feel that it was important to obtain certain results, experimenters obtained the expected results. When experimenters were made to feel that it was very important to follow certain scientific procedures, they obtained results significantly opposite to those that they had been led to expect. In the control condition, in which no special orientations toward outcome were specially generated, experimenters also showed the reversal tendency. For the particular sample of experimenters and subjects employed, it seems possible that a general process-consciousness was operating that contributed to the reversal effect among the experimenters of the control group.

Many of the experiments listed in Table XI with an associated directional $z < +1.28$ showed one or more interaction effects of experimenter expectancy and some other variable. These interactions and those found between experimenter expectancy and other variables in the earlier described research areas will not be described here but will be drawn upon in a later discussion of factors complicating the effects of experimenter expectancy.

For many of the experiments listed with $z < +1.28$ there is no ready explanation for the low z but sometimes the design of the experiment was intentionally such as to minimize the effects of experimenter expectancy. Thus Carlson and Hergenhahn (II) interposed a screen between experimenters and subjects and used a tape recorder to administer instructions to subjects (I, II), both of these procedures having been suggested as techniques for the reduction of expectancy effects (Rosenthal, 1966). Similarly, Moffat's experimenters were made to remain mute.

It has been suggested that higher status experimenters may show greater expectancy effects (Rosenthal, 1966). In only nine of the studies listed in Table XI was no attempt made to have the experimenters exceed their undergraduate subjects in class standing, age, or training in psychology (Bootzin I, II, Carlson and Hergenhahn, I, II, Barber et al., I, II, III, IV, V). Only one of these nine studies, or 11 per cent, showed a directional z of $+1.28$ or greater, about what we might expect

by chance. Of the remaining 45 studies employing college samples
(Persinger, Knutson, and Rosenthal, 1966, 1968, and Trattner, 1966, 1968,
employed neuropsychiatric patients), 19, or 42 per cent, showed an
associated z of $+1.28$ or greater. Apparently, for college samples, when
the experimenter's status exceeds that of his subject in the person perception task, the chances are almost quadrupled that expectancy effects
will be obtained compared to the situation in which experimenter and
subject are of the same status. This latter situation, of course, is relatively
rare not only in our sample of studies but also in the real world of
laboratory experiments.

On the whole, the person perception task seems less susceptible to
the effects of experimenter expectancy than most of the other areas
investigated though the large number of studies conducted makes the
overall combined p a fairly stable one. It would take the addition of
278 studies (or 36 principal investigators) with a mean directional z
of .00 to bring the overall p to the .05 level. Compared to all other
research areas combined, however, the person perception task shows
fewer directional z results of $+1.28$ or greater $(X^2 = 6.51, p \cong .01)$.

V. AN OVERVIEW OF EXPECTANCY EFECTS

Now that we have considered the results of studies of expectancy
effects for seven areas of research, it will be convenient to have a summary. Table XIII presents such a summary based on experiments, and
Table XIV presents a summary based on principal investigators. For
each research area the combined zs, both nondirectional and directional,
are given as well as the per cent of the studies (or investigators) that
reached the specified value of z. The next to last row of Tables XIII
and XIV give the grand overall zs based on all studies and all investigators. The experiment by Wessler (1968) was represented in each of
three research areas and that by Jenkins in each of two research areas.
For each of these studies the mean z was used as the entry in the
next to last row of Tables XIII and XIV in order to have each entry
based on independent samples. Based either on these overall zs of all
studies (or all investigators), or on the results of the binomial tests
shown in the last row of Tables XIII and XIV, the overall p associated
with expectancy effects is infinitesimally small. In both tables it can
be seen that though the combined nondirectional zs are larger than
the combined directional zs in the next to last row, the directional zs
are larger when based on the binomial test. The reason, of course,
is that we expect twice as many of the nondirectional zs to reach a
given magnitude and the binomial test knows that fact.

TABLE XIII

EXPECTANCY EFFECTS IN SEVEN RESEARCH AREAS

Research area	Studies	Nondirectional z		Directional z	
		z	$\% \geq /1.28/$	z	$\% \geq + 1.28$
Animal Learning	9	8.49	100%	+ 8.64	100%
Learning and Ability	9[a]	3.01	44%	+ 3.01	44%
Psychophysical Judgments	9[a]	3.44	56%	+ 2.55	33%
Reaction Time	3	1.93	67%	+ 1.93	67%
Inkblot Tests	4	4.71	100%	+ 3.55	75%
Laboratory Interviews	6[b]	6.01	100%	+ 5.30	83%
Person Perception	57[a,b]	9.06	60%	+ 4.07	39%
All Studies	94[c]	14.35	67%	+ 9.82	50%
Binomial test z (N = 94)		11.39		+12.92	

[a] Indicates a single experiment represented in each of three areas.

[b] Indicates a different experiment represented in each of two areas.

[c] Three entries were nonindependent and the mean z across areas was used for the independent entry.

TABLE XIV

EXPECTANCY EFFECTS IN SEVEN RESEARCH AREAS BY PRINCIPAL INVESTIGATORS

Research area	Investigators	Nondirectional z		Directional z	
		z	$\% \geq /1.28/$	z	$\% \geq + 1.28$
Animal Learning	5	8.25	100%	+8.46	100%
Learning and Ability	8[a]	2.96	50%	+2.96	50%
Psychophysical Judgments	6[a]	3.58	67%	+2.45	33%
Reaction Time	3	1.93	67%	+1.93	67%
Inkblot Tests	3	4.60	100%	+3.25	67%
Laboratory Interviews	6[b]	6.01	100%	+5.30	83%
Person Perception	20[a,b]	7.12	55%	+2.77	30%
All Investigators	48[c]	13.28	71%	+9.55	52%
Binomial test z (N = 48)		8.81		+9.71	

[a] Indicates a single investigator represented in each of three areas by the same subject sample.

[b] Indicates another investigator represented in two areas by the same subject sample.

[c] Three entries were non-independent and the mean z across areas was used for the independent entry.

In comparing the likelihoods of expectancy effects in the various research areas, the use of the zs may be somewhat misleading. A large number of investigations with only a moderately large number of zs reaching a specified level will make for a very large z, while a small number of investigations with a relatively large number of zs reaching a specified level will make for a smaller z. For this reason, the percentage of zs reaching a specified level may be a better basis on which to compare the likelihood of expectancy effects in the various research areas.

By chance, we expect 10 per cent of the directional zs to reach or exceed $+1.28$ but half of all directional zs reach that value. Effects of the experimenter's expectancy are found most often in studies of animal learning, laboratory interviews, inkblot tests, and reaction time. They are found least often in studies of psychophysical judgments and person perception, and about half the time in studies of human learning and ability.

There is one sense in which some of the entries of Table XIV are not independent. Some of the principal investigators conducted experiments in more than one area of research. In addition, we have so far considered as principal investigators anyone reporting an experiment regardless of the laboratory of origin. For these reasons it was felt to be instructive to summarize the results of all experiments conducted in different laboratories with each laboratory given equal weight with every other. Table XV lists 29 laboratories and the principal investigator associated with each. Again the overall probabilities are very low and the median laboratory had about two-thirds of their experimental results reach a directional z value of $+1.28$ compared to the 10 per cent we would expect by chance. While we expect one of the 29 laboratories to show a directional z of $+1.82$ or greater by chance, Table XV shows that 15 of the laboratories obtained zs of that value or greater. Though with so many laboratories we would expect one directional z of -1.82 to occur by chance, it is of interest to note that the one negative z of that size was obtained in the laboratory of a different culture—Japan.

Because so much of the business of the behavioral sciences is transacted at certain specified p levels, the percentage of experiments and of laboratories reaching each of a set of standard p levels is shown in Table XVI.* In addition, the last row shows the number of future replicates obtaining a directional mean z of exactly .00 required to bring the overall p to the .05 level.

---

* Since the preparation of this chapter another nine experiments, by four principal investigators, became available (Becker, 1968; Minor, 1967, 1967a; Peel, 1967; Zegers, 1968). The combined p for the nine experiments was .03, ($\Sigma\ z = +5.59$) for the four investigators $p < .04$ ($\Sigma\ z = +3.58$).

TABLE XV

EXPECTANCY EFFECTS OBTAINED IN DIFFERENT LABORATORIES

Investigator	Location	Studies	Nondirectional z		Directional z	
			z	$\% \geq /1.28/$	z	$\% \geq +1.28$
1. Adair	Manitoba	6	2.04	50%	+ 2.04[b]	50%
2. Adler	Wellesley	3	4.77	100%	.00	33%
3. Barber	Medfield[a]	5	1.40	20%	.00[b]	0%
4. Bootzin	Purdue	3	3.02	100%	.00[b]	67%
5. Burnham	Earlham	1	1.50	100%	+ 1.95	100%
6. Carlson	Hamline	2	.00	0%	.00[b]	0%
7. Cooper	CC, CUNY	1	3.37	100%	+ 3.37	100%
8. Getter	Connecticut	1	.00	0%	.00	0%
9. Harrington	Iowa State	2	2.54	100%	+ 2.54	100%
10. Hartry	Occidental	2	6.15	100%	+ 6.15	100%
11. Horn	Geo. Washington	1	2.01	100%	+ 2.01	100%
12. Ison	Rochester	2	5.11	100%	+ 5.11	100%
13. Johnson	New Brunswick	1	3.89	100%	+ 3.89[b]	100%
14. Kennedy	Tennessee	2	1.61	50%	+ 1.61[b]	50%
15. Larrabee	South Dakota	1	1.60	100%	+ 1.60	100%
16. Marcia	SUNY, Buffalo	2	3.58	100%	+ 3.58	100%
17. Masling	SUNY, Buffalo	2	2.44	100%	+ 1.45[b]	50%
18. McFall	Ohio State	2	.00	0%	.00[b]	0%
19. Moffat	British Columbia	1	.00	0%	.00	0%
20. Persinger	Fergus Falls[a]	2	2.50	100%	+ 2.50[b]	100%
21. Raffetto	San Francisco State	1	5.24	100%	+ 5.24[b]	100%
22. Rosenthal	Harvard	35	8.04	69%	+ 4.83[b]	49%
23. Silverman	SUNY, Buffalo	1	1.88	100%	+ 1.88[b]	100%
24. Timaeus	Cologne	3	1.98	67%	.00[b]	33%
25. Uno	Keio (Tokyo)	5	1.86	40%	− 1.86[b]	0%
26. Wartenberg– Ekren	Marquette	1	.00	0%	.00	0%
27. Weick	Purdue	1	2.33	100%	+ 2.33	100%
28. Wessler	St. Louis	3	1.80	67%	.00[b]	33%
29. Zoble	Franklin and Marshall	2	3.77	100%	+ 4.06	100%
	Sum		74.43		+54.28	
	$\Sigma/\sqrt{29}$		13.81		+10.07	
	Means		2.57	71%	+ 1.87	61%
	Medians		2.04	100%	+ 1.88	67%
	Binomial test z (N = 29)		8.47		9.32	

[a] State Hospitals.

[b] Indicates that experimenter expectancy interacted with other variables at $z \geq /1.28/$.

TABLE XVI

PERCENTAGE OF EXPERIMENTS AND LABORATORIES
OBTAINING RESULTS AT SPECIFIED p LEVELS

p	Experiments	Laboratories
	N = 94	N = 29
.10	50%	62%
.05	35%	52%
.01	17%	38%
.001	12%	28%
.0001	5%	21%
.00001	3%	14%
.000001	2%	14%
Grand Sum z	95.27	54.28
Tolerance for Future Negative Results[a]	3,260	1,060

[a] Replicates required to bring overall p to .05, assuming all replicates to yield a mean z of .00 exactly.

Earlier, the possibility was raised that certain judgments and computations made by the present writer might be in error so that a correction factor for these errors would be desirable. In addition, there is the possibility that studies showing no effects of experimenter expectancy might be less likely to be reported or called to the attention of the writer. This latter possibility cannot be ruled out in any way, though, at the time of this writing, interest in publication of "negative findings" seems as great as interest in publication of "positive findings" of expectancy effects.

As a fairly stringent correction for the possibility of the writer's errors and for the possibility of a biased availability of studies, we assume that the total number of experiments and of laboratories is ten times greater than that reported here. The factor of ten was selected on the basis of the widespread, intentionally exaggerated, and perhaps cynical fear among behavioral scientists that any given critical value of p gives the proportion of experiments conducted that come to public knowledge (Rosenthal, 1966). Since the directional z defined as worth listing in this review was that associated with a p of .10, the factor of ten was selected. If we assume that instead of 94 experiments conducted as tests of the hypothesis of expectancy effects there were actually 940 conducted, what becomes of the overall combined z? It goes to $+3.10$, $p < .001$, assuming that the additional 846 experiments found a mean directional z of zero exactly. Similarly, if we assume that instead of 29 investigating laboratories there were 290, the overall combined z

for laboratories goes to $+3.18$, $p < .0008$, assuming that the additional 261 laboratories found a mean directional z of zero exactly.

Additional protection against any errors leading us to entertain with insufficient basis the possibility of expectancy effects comes from considering any $z < /1.28/$ to be a z of zero. As Table XVI shows, the distribution of zs is highly skewed such that too many are very much greater than zero. It seems most likely, therefore, though the check would have been an onerous task, that the bulk of the zs considered as equal to .00 was actually also skewed such as to give too many zs of positive value.

A. Principal Investigators

With so many experiments in a series it becomes possible to examine the relationship between outcome and various characteristics of the principal investigator. Of the 94 experiments, 18 were conducted primarily by female principal investigators. Of these studies 44 per cent yielded directional zs of $+1.28$ or greater compared to the 51 per cent of studies conducted by male principal investigators, a difference which is quite trivial ($X^2 = .07$).

In 37 of the 94 experiments, the principal investigator was a student, and in 43 per cent of these studies the directional z reached or exceeded $+1.28$. In those studies in which the senior investigator was not a student (e.g. a faculty member), 54 per cent of the results reached or exceeded that value of z. The difference, however, was very small in the sense of X^2 (.71).

For reasons described in greater detail elsewhere (Rosenthal, 1966) it was felt to be desirable to compare the outcomes of experiments conducted in the present writer's laboratory with those conducted elsewhere. Of the 35 experiments conducted in the writer's laboratory, 49 per cent showed a directional z of $+1.28$ or greater. Of the 59 experiments conducted elsewhere, 51 per cent showed zs of that magnitude. The difference between these percentages was trivial ($X^2 = .00$).

Of the 35 experiments conducted in the writer's laboratory, 15 were conducted by students, and of these 15 investigations, only four, or 27 per cent, showed a directional z of $+1.28$ or greater. That proportion was just half the proportion of 54 per cent found in the remaining 79 studies ($X^2 = 2.86$, $p < .10$). Since the sample sizes of the experiments conducted by the writer's students were not systematically lower than those of the remaining investigations, the differences in outcomes were probably not due to differences in statistical power, though such differences might account for the failure of individual studies to reach a directional z of $+1.28$. There seems to be no ready explanation for the differences in outcome, but one hypothesis, suggested by the work of Adler (1968), may be considered. Adler's results suggested that experimenters made particularly sensitive to the importance of "following scientific procedures" tended to obtain data that not only did not confirm their expectations but actually tended significantly to disconfirm their expectations. Perhaps a similar phenomenon may occur among principal investigators. Emphasis on the investigator's remaining blind to experimenters' treatment conditions may generate a sensitivity to procedures among student investigators that tends to reverse the directionality of expectancy effects. Consistent with such an hypothesis would be the finding that among these students, a greater proportion obtain zs of -1.28 or less. Although the total number of such negative zs is too small to permit strong inference, it is of interest to note that 13 per cent of the students' experiments found zs that low compared to 8 per cent of the remaining investigations.

B. Magnitude of Expectancy Effects

So far we have discussed the results of studies of expectancy effect only in terms of the zs obtained. By itself such information does not tell us how large the effects of expectancy tend to be. Given a very large sample size, even effects of trivial magnitude can reach any specified level of z. We want, therefore, to have some estimates of the magnitude of expectancy effects quite apart from the question of the "reality" of the phenomenon.

One such estimate can be obtained by computing the proportion of experimenters whose obtained responses have been brought into line with their expectations. For this computation we need the mean of the responses obtained by each experimenter in each of two different conditions of expectation. For those experiments in which each experimenter was given one expectation for some of his subjects and a different expectation for other subjects, the mean difference between responses of the two groups of subjects is all that is needed. If an experimenter obtained more of the expected responses from the subjects of whom he expected them than from the other subjects, that experimenter is counted as showing expectancy effects.

For those experiments in which experimenters were given the same expectancy for all their subjects, a preliminary computation was required. For all the experimenters given one of the expectations, the grand mean response obtained was computed separately for all experimenters given one expectation and again for all experimenters given the opposite expectation. An experimenter in the condition of expecting more X type responses was counted as showing expectancy effect if his mean obtained responses showed more X than did the grand mean of the experimenters in the condition led to expect fewer X responses. An experimenter in the condition of expecting fewer X type responses was counted as showing expectancy effect if his mean obtained responses showed fewer X than did the grand mean of the experimenters in the condition led to expect more X responses. The analogous procedure was also employed for estimating the proportion of subjects whose responses were in the direction of their experimenter's expectancy.

Table XVII shows the results of the analyses performed. There were

TABLE XVII

PROPORTIONS OF SUBJECTS AND EXPERIMENTERS SHOWING EXPECTANCY EFFECTS

	Subjects	Experimenters
Number of Studies	27	57
Median z of studies	+1.28	.00
Number of Ss or Es (N)	1370	523
Mean N per Study	51	9
Weighted Percent of Biased Ss or Es	59%	69%
Median Percent of Biased Ss or Es	62%	75%

27 studies for which the counts for subjects could be made with moderate effort. The selection was based not on a random sampling basis but rather on the basis of the availability of the data required. Data were also available from two other studies but because both were associated with such unusually large directional z values, they were not included in the analysis. The mean directional z of the subsample of studies employed was identical to that of all the experiments we have considered. Approximately 60 per cent of subjects gave responses consistent with the expectation of their experimenter.

For the analysis based on experimenters, more of the studies provided the necessary information so that we have the data based on 57 experiments. The median directional z of these experiments, however, was less than +1.28 so that the sample is biased slightly in the direction of overrepresenting studies scored as .00 z values. Approximately 70 per cent of experimenters obtained data in the direction of their hypotheses.

How are we to account for the difference in proportion of subjects versus proportion of experimenters affected by expectancy effects? It was possible, of course, that the difference was in some way only an artifact of the difference in samples of experiments yielding the appropriate information. If the difference were not an artifact, however, it would suggest that expectancy effects are relatively more widespread among experimenters but that the effects per experimenter are relatively smaller. This interpretation is made more plausible by the results of an analysis comparing the proportion of experimenters showing expectancy effects with the proportion of subjects affected for just those experiments for which both types of information were available. There were 26 such samples, and for 24 of them the proportions of affected subjects and experimenters were either both above the grand median or both below it ($z = 3.94$). The median percentage of affected subjects was 66 per cent, and the median percentage of affected experimenters was 75 per cent. The latter value is identical to the percentage based on all 57 studies so that it seems likely that the studies for which subject data were available were not unrepresentative of the larger number of studies for which experimenter data were available. Because neither in the case of the analysis based on subjects nor in that based on experimenters was the analysis sufficiently exhaustive, nor even necessarily representative, we should not take these estimates as very precise. Perhaps as a crude guide to the estimation of expectancy effects and to the planning of the sample sizes required in future research, we can give as a reasonable index that about two-thirds of subjects and of experimenters will give or obtain responses in the direction of the experimenter's expectancy.

Though we have been able to arrive at some estimate, however crude, of the magnitude of expectancy effects, we will not know quite how to assess this magnitude until we have comparative estimates from other areas of behavioral research. Such estimates are not easy to come by ready-made, but it seems worthwhile for us to try to obtain such estimates in the future. Although in individual studies, investigators occasionally give the proportion of variance accounted for by their experimental variable, it is more rare that systematic reviews of bodies of research literature give estimates of the overall magnitude of effects of the variable under consideration. It does not seem an unreasonable guess, however, to suggest that in the bulk of the experimental literature of the behavioral sciences, the effects of the experimental variable are not impressively "larger," either in the sense of magnitude of obtained zs or in the sense of proportion of subjects affected than the effects of experimenter expectancy. The best support for such an assertion would come from experiments in which the effects of experimenter expectancy are compared directly in the same experiment, with the effects of some other experimental variable believed to be a significant determinant of behavior. Fortunately, there are two such experiments to shed light on the question.

The first of these was conducted by Burnham (1966). He had 23 experimenters each run one rat in a T-maze discrimination problem. About half the rats had been lesioned by removal of portions of the brain, and the remaining animals had received only sham surgery which involved cutting through the skull but no damage to brain tissue. The purpose of the study was explained to the experimenters as an attempt to learn the effects of lesions on discrimination learning. Expectancies were manipulated by labeling each rat as lesioned or nonlesioned. Some of the really lesioned rats were labeled accurately as lesioned but some were falsely labeled as unlesioned. Some of the really unlesioned rats were labeled accurately as unlesioned but some were falsely labeled as lesioned. Table XVIII shows the standard scores of the ranks of

TABLE XVIII

Discrimination Learning as a Function of Brain Lesions and Experimenter Expectancy

| Brain state | Expectancy | | Σ | z of difference |
	Lesioned	Unlesioned		
Lesioned	46.5	49.0	95.5	
Unlesioned	48.2	58.3	106.5	$+1.40^a$
Σ	94.7	107.3		
z of Difference	$+1.60^b$			

[a] By unweighted means F test; $z = +1.47$ by U test.
[b] By unweighted means F test; $z = +1.95$ by U test.

performance in each of the four conditions. A higher score indicates superior performance. Animals that had been lesioned did not perform as well as those that had not been lesioned and animals that were believed to be lesioned did not perform as well as those that were believed to be unlesioned. What makes this experiment of special interest is that the effects of experimenter expectancy were at least as great as those of actual removal of brain tissue (the z associated with the interaction was only about 1.0).

A number of techniques for the control of experimenter expectancy effects have been described elsewhere in detail (Rosenthal, 1966). One of these techniques, the employment of expectancy control groups, is well illustrated by Burnham's design. The experimenter expectancy variable is permitted to operate orthogonally to the experimental variable in which the investigator is ordinarily most interested. Ten major types of outcomes of expectancy-controlled experiments have been outlined and Burnham's result fits most closely that outcome labeled as Case 3 (Rosenthal, 1966, 382). If an investigator interested in the effects of brain lesions on discrimination learning had employed only the two most commonly employed conditions, he could have been seriously misled by his results. Had he employed experimenters who believed the rats to be lesioned to run his lesioned rats and compared their results to those obtained by experimenters running unlesioned rats and believing them to be unlesioned, he would have greatly overestimated the effects on discrimination learning of brain lesions. For the investigator interested in assessing for his own area of research the likelihood and magnitude of expectancy effects, there appears to be no substitute for the employment of expectancy control groups. For the investigator interested only in the reduction of expectancy effects, other techniques such as blind or minimized experimenter-subject contact or automated experimentation (Kleinmuntz and McLean, 1968; McGuigan, 1963; Miller, Bregman, and Norman, 1965) are among the techniques that may prove to be useful.

The first of the experiments to compare directly the effects of experimenter expectancy with some other experimental variable employed animal subjects. The next such experiment to be described employed human subjects. Cooper, Eisenberg, Robert, and Dohrenwend (1967) wanted to compare the effects of experimenter expectancy with the effects of effortful preparation for an examination on the degree of belief that the examination would actually take place.

Each of ten experimenters contacted ten subjects; half of the subjects were required to memorize a list of 16 symbols and definitions that were claimed to be essential to the taking of a test that had a 50-50 chance of being given, while the remaining subjects, the "low effort" group, were asked only to look over the list of symbols. Half of the experimenters were led to expect that "high effort" subjects would be more certain of actually having to take the test, while half of the experimenters were led to expect that "low effort" subjects would be more certain of actually having to take the test.

Table XIX gives the subjects' ratings of their degree of certainty of having to take the test. There was a very slight tendency for subjects who had exerted greater effort to believe more strongly that they would be taking the test. Surprising in its magnitude was the finding that experimenters expecting to obtain responses of greater certainty obtained such responses to a much greater degree than did experimenters expecting responses of lesser certainty. The ratio of expectancy effect to effort

TABLE XIX

Certainty of Having to Take a Test as a Function of
Preparatory Effort and Experimenter Expectancy

	Expectancy			
Effort level	High	Low	Σ	z of difference
High	+ .64	− .40	+ .24	
Low	+ .56	− .52	+ .04	+0.33[a]
Σ	+1.20	− .92		
z of Difference		+3.37[a]		

[a] By F test.

effect mean squares exceeds 112. In the terms of the discussion of expectancy control groups referred to earlier, these results fit well the so-called case 7 (Rosenthal, 1966, 384). Had this experiment been conducted employing only the two most commonly encountered conditions, the investigators would have been even more seriously misled than would have been the case in the earlier mentioned study of the effects of brain lesions on discrimination learning. If experimenters, while contacting high effort subjects expected them to show greater certainty, and if experimenters, while contacting low effort subjects, expected them to show less certainty, the experimental hypothesis might quite artifactually have appeared to have earned strong support. The difference between these groups might have been ascribed to effort effects while actually the difference seems due almost entirely to the effects of the experimenter's expectancy.

VI. MODERATING VARIABLES

Except for the very first few experiments in each of the research domains described, the bulk of the 94 studies summarized were not designed primarily to test the hypothesis of expectancy effects. Rather, these studies were designed to learn something of the conditions which increase, decrease, or otherwise modify the effects of experimenter expectancy. Approximately half of the experiments (49 per cent) and half of the laboratories (52 per cent) obtained one or more interactions of experimenter expectancy with some other variable with an associated $z > /1.28/$. Many of the specific interactions were investigated in more than one experiment.

A. Sex of Participants

In a great many of the experiments summarized, it would have been possible to examine the interaction of expectancy effects with sex of experimenter, sex of subject, and sex of dyad. This was done, however, or reported in only a fraction of the studies so that it was not possible to have an exhaustive inventory of such interactions. Therefore, we can not sensibly employ the technique of combining zs to obtain an overall estimate of the interaction of experimenter expectancy with the sex of the participants. What was possible was to find those experiments in which a relationship was found or reported in which z reached an absolute value of 1.28. Summaries based on such results, then, will have little to offer in the way of estimating the frequency of a relationship. Instead they will be limited to estimating the proportion of results in a specific direction for just that subsample of studies in which results reached the specified value of $|z|$.

Table XX shows the directional zs associated with interactions of expectancy effects with sex of participants for studies of person perception. In the first column, a positive z means that male experimenters showed greater expectancy effects than did female experimenters. When more than a single study is associated with a single z it means that the interaction was based on the combined samples. The finding of all four zs as positive suggests that when differences in expectancy effects are found between male and female experimenters, male experimenters tend to show the greater expectancy effect. It is interesting to note that all six of the studies listed in this first column were tabulated

TABLE XX

Expectancy Effects as a Function of Sex
of Participants in Studies of Person Perception

I		II		III	
Sex of experimenter		Sex of subject		Sex of dyad	
Study	z	Study	z	Study	z
14[a], 15	+1.44	14, 15	−1.44	6–10	+1.51
22, 23	+1.41	18	−2.85	38	+1.64
39	+1.96	39	+2.58	39	+1.51
43[b]	+2.07	40, 41	+1.96		
		42	+1.64		

[a] Numbers refer to those of Table XI.

[b] Refers to expectancy effects transmitted via research assistants, see Rosenthal, 1966, 232.

as showing directional zs $< +1.28$. Though it would be difficult to attach an exact p value to this result, the fact that such consistent results of tests of interactions were obtained from studies showing no main effects of experimenter expectancy, puts an additional strain on the credibility of the null hypothesis that expectancy effects do not occur.

All the interactions shown in Table XX were based on the person perception task. The reason for this was that for no other task was there more than a single study available to shed light on the nature of the interaction of expectancy effects and sex of experimenter and/or subject. Another experiment testing the difference between male and female experimenters in magnitude of expectancy effect was available. That was the study by Raffetto (1967, 1968) of reports of hallucinatory experiences. At $z = -1.65$ he found that for this task it was female experimenters who showed the greater expectancy effects. It seems possible that whether male or female experimenters show the greater expectancy effects may depend upon the specific nature of the experiment conducted.

In the second column of Table XX a positive z means that female subjects were more susceptible to the effects of experimenter expectancy. There is no consistency to these results and perhaps all that can be said is that sometimes male subjects and sometimes female subjects show greater susceptibility to expectancy effects. Of the seven studies represented in Column II, five were tabulated earlier as showing directional zs $< +1.28$. In his experiment employing a marble-dropping task, Johnson (1967) had found female subjects to be more susceptible than male subjects to expectancy effects ($z = +1.72$) at least under some conditions.

In the third column of Table XX we find the results of a highly specific three way interaction between sex of subject, sex of experimenter, and experimenter expectancy. The first of these studies (38) found net positive expectancy effects among male experimenters contacting either male or female subjects and among female experimenters contacting female subjects. However, when female experimenters contacted male subjects, the expectancy effect was reversed, with subjects responding in the direction opposite to that which experimenters had been led to expect. Just that same pattern was obtained in two other analyses. Of the seven studies represented in column III, all but one was tabulated earlier as showing diectional zs $< + 1.28$.

Three other studies have reported interactions involving simultaneously the sex of experimenter and subject and magnitude of expectancy effect. Johnson (1967), in his marble-dropping experiment, found that when experimenter and subject were of the same sex there were greater expectancy effects than when experimenter and subject were of the opposite sex ($z = +1.80$). Just the opposite results, however, were obtained by Adair (1968) employing a numerosity estimation task ($z = -2.33$) and by Silverman (1968) employing a reaction time measure ($z = -1.61$). Both these investigators found greater expectancy effects when experimenters and subjects were of the opposite sex. The joint effects of experimenter and subject sex may sometimes be significant determinants of the direction and magnitude of expectancy effects, but it seems likely that the type of task employed may be a further complicating variable.

B. Experimenter Dominance

On the basis of a variety of evidence presented elsewhere (Rosenthal, 1966), it was suggested that experimenters showing greater dominance or a greater degree of professionalness in their behavior were likely to show greater effects of their experimental hypotheses. This interaction of a specific experimenter characteristic with magnitude of expectancy effect has recently received some fairly strong support in three experiments conducted by Bootzin, 1968. In all three studies, Bootzin found more dominant experimenters to show greater effects of their induced expectations. The three obtained zs were $+2.05$, $+3.30$, and $+2.17$; the combined z was $+4.35$, $p < .000008$.

This result may well be related to the finding that where there are differences between male and female experimenters in magnitude of expectancy effects, it is the male experimenters who are likely to show the greater effects. It seems reasonable to suppose that, in general, male experimenters are likely to be classed as more dominant than are female experimenters.

C. Other Variables

There are a good many other variables that have been shown to interact significantly with the effects of experimenter expectancy. Later, we shall have occasion to refer to some, but because so many of these interactions have been described elsewhere in some detail (Rosenthal, 1966) we need give here only some illustrations.

Through the employment of accomplices serving as the first few subjects is was learned that when the responses of the first few subjects confirmed the experimenter's hypothesis, his behavior toward his subsequent subjects was affected in such a way that these subjects tended to confirm further the experimenter's hypothesis. When accomplices serving as the first few subjects intentionally disconfirmed the expectation of the experimenter, the real subjects subsequently contacted were affected by a change in the experimenter's behavior also to disconfirm his experimental hypothesis. It seems possible, then, that the results of behavioral research can, by virtue of the early data returns, be determined partially by the performance of just the first few subjects (Rosenthal, 1966).

In some of the experiments conducted, it was found that when experimenters were offered a too-large and a too-obvious incentive to affect the results of their research, the effects of expectancy tended to diminish. It speaks well for the integrity of student-experimenters that when they felt bribed to obtain the data they had been led to expect, they seemed actively to oppose the principal investigators. There was a tendency for those experimenters to "bend over backward" to avoid the biasing effects of their expectation, but sometimes with their bending so far backward that the results of their experiments tended to be significantly opposite to the results they had been led to expect (Rosenthal, 1966).

In several experiments in which each experimenter was given two different expectancies for two allegedly different subsamples of subjects, the distribution of expectancy effects showed a significant and interesting skew. In each of three such studies, which were not at all homogeneous in the overall magnitude of expectancy effects obtained, a significant minority of experimenters obtained results more negative in direction than could reasonably be expected by chance. These three studies are summarized in Table XXI in which the first listed study employed animal subjects and the others employed human subjects performing the photo rating task.

Since each experimenter had contacted some subjects under different conditions of expectation, magnitude of expectancy effect was defined simply as the mean response obtained under one condition of expectation minus the mean response obtained under the opposite condition of expectation. In order to make the units of measurement of the different studies more comparable, each distribution of difference scores was divided into ten equal intervals, five above an absolute difference score of .00 and five below. All three studies show a substantial minority (14 to 20 per cent) of experimenters to obtain data significantly opposite to what they had been led to expect. This type of finding suggests the possibility that there are some experimenters who react to being given an expectancy either by bending over backward to avoid biasing their data, or perhaps because of resentment at being told what to expect, by in some way showing the expectancy inducer that he was wrong to make the prediction he made. If these minority reactions to induced expectancies were widespread, it might be of interest to try to learn

TABLE XXI

PROPORTIONS OF EXPERIMENTERS SHOWING VARIOUS
MAGNITUDES OF EXPECTANCY EFFECTS IN THREE STUDIES

	Study			
Effect	I & H, 1966, II	R,P,M,V,G, 1964b I	R,P,M,V,G, 1964b II	Combined
	(N = 15)	(N = 13)	(N = 7)	(N = 35)
+5	.00	.00	.00	.00
+4	.00	.00	.00	.00
+3	.13	.08	.00	.09
+2	.40	.31	.00	.29
+1	.27	.23	.43	.29
-1^a	.00	.23	.43	.17
−2	.00	.00	.00	.00
−3	.00	.00	.00	.00
−4	.13	.08	.00	.09
−5	.07	.08	.14	.09
z^b	+2.58	+2.33	+2.58	+4.33

[a] Includes .00 effect.

[b] For Asymmetry.

the personal correlates of membership in this subset of experimenters who react to induced expectations with such negative and non-Gaussian gusto.

On the basis of an earlier analysis suggested by Fred Mosteller (Rosenthal, 1966, 312–313), it was proposed that one effect of experimenter expectancies might be not on measures of central tendency but on measures of variance. In an experiment employing three groups of experimenters, two experimental groups and one control, it was found that experimenters of the control group obtained data that were more variable than the data obtained by experimenters of the two experimental groups. Two more recent studies showed similar effects.

In an experiment on verbal conditioning, Kennedy, Edwards, and Winstead (1968) found that those experimenters who had been given no expectation obtained more variable responses than did experimenters expecting either high or low rates of conditioning ($z = +2.22$). Similarly, in an experiment on judging the frequency of light flashes, Müller and Timaeus (1967) found that control group experimenters obtained more variable responses than did experimenters expecting either overestimation or under-estimation ($z = +1.88$). In both of these experiments, as was often the case in studies showing interaction effects, the directional zs associated with the main effects of experimenter expectancy were less than $+1.28$ and, therefore, were recorded as zs of .00.

Earlier, reference was made to the experiment by Adler (1968) in which the set given the experimenters was an important determinant of the direction of the subsequent expectancy effects. Other such results have also been reported (Rosenthal, 1966; Rosenthal and Persinger, 1968) as have results showing the effects of subject set on the direction and magnitude of expectancy effects (Rosenthal, 1966; White, 1962).

In a number of studies where there was a conflict between what an experimenter had been led to expect and what he himself actually expected, these two sources of hypothesis were found to interact significantly (Bootzin, 1968; Nichols, 1967; Strauss, 1968); but sometimes they did not (Marcia, 1961; Marwit & Marcia, 1967).

For two samples of male experimenters, it has been reported that those who exchanged fewer glances with their subjects during the instruction-reading phase of the person perception experiment, subsequently showed greater expectancy effects (Rosenthal, 1966, 268). The more recent work of Connors (1968) bears out this finding ($z = +2.12$).

Other studies of variables complicating the effects of experimenter expectancy have investigated the effects of experimenter and subject need for approval, experimenter and subject anxiety, degree of acquaintanceship between experimenter and subject, experimenter status, and characteristics of the laboratory in which the interaction occurs. In general, the results of these studies have been complex, with far too many results of large zs, but with the signs sometimes in one direction and sometimes in the other. For many of these moderating variables there appear to be meta-moderating variables (Rosenthal, 1966).

VII. THE MEDIATION OF EXPECTANCY EFFECTS

How are we to account for the results of the experiments described? How does an experimenter unintentionally inform his subjects just what response is expected of him? Our purpose in this section is to review the evidence that may shed light on this question. First, however, we must take up the proposition that there is nothing to be explained, that our talk about an artifact is based on nothing but other artifacts.

A. Expectancy Effects as Artifacts

Cheating and recording errors have been suggested as prime candidates for consideration as the artifacts leading to the false conclusion that experimenters' expectancies may serve as significant partial determinants of subjects' responses (Barber and Silver, 1968; Rosenthal, 1964a). There is no way to rule out with any certainty the operation of either intentional "errors" or errors of observation in most of the individual experiments investigating the effects of experimenter expectancy—but there is no way to rule out the operation of these errors in the vast majority of the research in the behavioral sciences. What we can do is to rule out the operation of cheating and observer errors as necessary factors operating in studies of expectancy effects. There are a number of experiments which do permit us to rule out the operation of such errors.

Earlier, the experiment by Adair and Epstein (1967, II) was described. It will be recalled that in this study there were no experimenters, only tape recordings of the voices of experimenters, and tape recordings cannot err either intentionally or unintentionally. In this experiment, in which subjects recorded their own responses, the directional z associated with expectancy effects was $+1.64$.

The experiment by Johnson (1967) similarly ruled out the operation of intentional or observer errors. The recording of subjects' responses was accomplished by an electrical system which did the bookkeeping. The tallies were then transcribed by the principal investigator who was blind to the experimental condition of experimenter expectancy in which each subject had been contacted. Despite the tightness of the controls for cheating and for observer errors, Johnson's results showed a very large effect of experimenter expectancy with a directional z of $+3.89$.

The experiment by Weick (described in Rosenthal, 1966) was another in which cheating and observer errors were unlikely to occur. That experiment was conducted in a classroom under the watchful eyes of students in a class in experimental social psychology. Despite the restraint such an audience might be presumed to impose on the intentional errors or the careless errors of an experimenter, the obtained directional z was $+2.33$.

Because of the small size of the animals involved, experiments employing planaria would seem to be especially prone to quasi-intentional errors or to errors of recording. Since it is often difficult to judge the behavior of planaria, experimenters might too often judge or claim a response to have occurred when that response was expected. Hartry (1966) conducted two experiments on the effects of experimenter expectancy on the results of studies of planaria performance. In one of these studies, special pains were taken to reduce the likelihood of observer or intentional errors. Experimenters were given more intensive training, an instructor was present during the conduct of the experiment, and three observers were present to record the worm's response. Quite surprisingly, the effects of experimenter expectancy were greater in the study with better controls for observer errors and cheating. In the less well-controlled study, experimenters expecting more responses obtained an average of 73 per cent more responses than did the experimenters expecting fewer responses. In the better-controlled study, however, experimenters expecting more responses obtained an average of 211 per cent more responses than did the experimenters expecting fewer responses.

The experiment by Persinger, Knutson, and Rosenthal (1968) was filmed and tape-recorded without the knowledge of experimenters or subjects. Independent observers then recorded subjects' responses directly from the tape recordings and these recordings were compared to those of the original experimenters. It was found that .72 per cent of the experimenters' transcriptions were in error and that .48 per cent of the transcriptions erred in the direction of the experimenters' hypothesis while .24 per cent of the transcriptions erred in the direction opposite to that of the experimenters' hypothesis. These latter errors, however, tended to be larger than the errors favoring the hypothesis, so that the mean net error per experimenter was $-.0003$ in the direction opposite to the experimenters' expectancies and so trivial in magnitude that analyses based on either the corrected or uncorrected transcriptions gave the same results (directional z of $+1.64$).

Analysis of the films of this and of other experiments (Rosenthal, 1966) in which experimenters did not know they were being filmed, gave no evidence to suggest any attempts to cheat on the part of the experimenters. Similarly, other analyses of the incidence of recording errors show their rates to be too low to account for the results of studies of experimenter expectancy or most other studies for that matter. It is, of course, possible that in any single experiment in the behavioral sciences, cheating or recording errors may occur to a sufficient extent to account for the obtained results. It seems unlikely, however, that any replicated findings of the behavioral sciences, especially if replicated in different laboratories, could reasonably be ascribed either to intentional errors or to recording errors.

Our discussion has been of cheating and of observer errors serving as artifacts in the production of an effect which can itself be regarded as an artifact in behavioral research, the expectancy of the experimenter. Our discussion would be incomplete, however, without a systematic consideration of what it would mean if we had found effects of experimenter expectancy to be associated with artifacts of cheating and of observer errors. Earlier discussions of this problem have, unfortunately, been incomplete in this regard (Barber and Silver, 1968; Rosenthal, 1964a). Barber and Silver, for example, suggest that if it could be established that such meta-artifacts as cheating and observer errors accounted for the results of studies showing expectancy effects at some specified level of z, then this would be sufficient to rule out the effects of experimenter expectancy as a source of artifact in other research. Unfortunately, the situation is a good deal more complex than that simple inference would suggest.

Table XXII presents a schema for the consideration of a variety of experimental outcomes in relation to the artifact of expectancy effects and the meta-artifacts of intentional and recording errors. We let the "primary variable" stand for whatever a given behavioral researcher

TABLE XXII

Schema for the Consideration of Experimental Results As a Function of Artifacts and Meta-Artifacts

Experimental results	Effects of meta-artifact		
	Decrease z	Trivial effect	Increase z
PRIMARY VARIABLE			
Positive z	Case 1	Case 2	Case 3
Trivial z	Case 4	Case 5	Case 6
Negative z	Case 7	Case 8	Case 9
EXPECTANCY EFFECT			
Positive z	Case 10[a]	Case 11	Case 12
Trivial z	Case 13	Case 14	Case 15
Negative z	Case 16	Case 17	Case 18

[a] The best documented case of cheating among experimenters to come to our attention occurred in research involving animal subjects in which allegedly dull animals were helped to perform better, thus decreasing the effects of experimenter expectancy.

is currently investigating, other than expectancy effects. The three columns of Table XXII represent the three broad classes of effects of cheating or recording errors: (a) effects decreasing the obtained z, (b) effects of arbitrarily trivial magnitude, and (c) effects increasing the obtained z. The suggestion by Barber and Silver was essentially to look only at the cell labeled Case 12. If, in an experiment on expectancy effects, there were errors to inflate the z, then we need not concern ourselves any longer with the role of expectancy effects an an artifact in behavioral research. The conclusion, of course, does not follow. We want to consider the rest of the possible outcomes.

In Case 15, for example, we have a trivial z for expectancy effect which may have been made trivial by the meta-artifact which increased the z from a negative to a near zero level. We want to know about

Case 16 to be sure that a negative z for expectancy effects was not due to the meta-artifact, or about Case 13 to be sure that a near zero z was not depressed from a positive z by cheating or recording errors. Although our empirical evidence suggests most errors due to cheating or misrecording to be trivial, it must be kept in mind that these errors can cut two ways. They can artifactually deflate the obtained effects as much as they can artifactually inflate the obtained effects.

What makes our schema still more complicated is the necessity for considering simultaneously the effect of our meta-artifact on expectancy effects relative to its effect on the primary variable. There is no basis in data to think so, but if we assume for the moment that Case 12 effects were found, we would want to compare their magnitude and frequency with those of the Case 3 effects. If it were found that Case 12 occurs often but Case 3 occurs seldom, *then* we would legitimately begin to wonder whether expectancy effect research might not be particularly prone to meta-artifact. But our inquiry would be far from over since it must first be seen whether Cases 10, 13, and 16 are not also over-represented relative to Cases 1, 4, and 7. What we want, in short, is something like a $3 \times 3 \times 2$ contingency table that would permit us to say something of the effect of our meta-artifact on experimenter expectancy and of the relative effects of the meta-artifact and of experimenter expectancy on the primary variable.

B. Operant Conditioning

If intentional errors and recording errors will not do as explanations of the results of studies of expectancy effect, what will? The most obvious hypothesis was that experimenters might quite unwittingly reinforce those responses of their subject that were consistent with their hypothesis. Any small reinforcer might serve—a smile, a glance, a nod. Under an hypothesis of operant conditioning, we would expect to find that the very first response of a given subject is not affected by the experimenter's expectancy and that, in general, later responses are more affected than earlier responses.

Elsewhere, there is a summary of four experiments showing that, on the average, expectancy effects are greater for the subject's very first response than for his later responses (Rosenthal, 1966, 289–293). A more recent experiment by Wessler (1966) also showed a decrease in expectancy effect from the subjects' earlier to later responses ($z = +1.65$).

The experiment by Adair and Epstein (1967), in which tape recordings served as experimenters, also served to rule out the operation of operant conditioning as a necessary mediator of expectancy effects. Additional, though "softer," evidence that operant conditioning was not a factor in the mediation of expectancy effects has been presented by Marwit (1968) and Masling (1965, 1966), though Marwit and Marcia's (1967) data suggested that sometimes operant conditioning might be a factor.

Just as was the case in our consideration of cheating and recording errors as explanations of expectancy effect, we cannot conclude that operant conditioning never operates as a mechanism mediating expectancy effects. What we can conclude, just as in the case of cheating and recording errors, is that expectancy effects do occur in the absence of operant conditioning. Operant conditioning, like cheating and observer errors, cannot explain the results of studies of expectancy effect.

C. Communication Channels

The fact that the very first response of an experimental subject can be affected by the expectancy of the experimenter suggests that the mediation of expectancy effects must occur, at least sometimes, during that phase of the data-collection situation in which the experimenter greets, seats, and instructs his subject. Some beginnings have been made to learn what the experimenter does unintentionally during this phase of the experiment to inform his subject of the expected response. These beginnings are not characterized by spectacular success (Rosenthal, 1966). Data of a more modest sort, however, are beginning to sketch some picture of the classes of cues likely to be involved in the mediation of expectancy effects.

There are two experiments to show that auditory cues alone may be sufficient to mediate expectancy effects. One of these is the study by Adair and Epstein (1967) in which subjects heard only the instructions tape-recorded earlier by experimenters given different expectancies. The z for expectancy effect based upon voice alone was $+1.64$. The other experiment was by Troffer and Tart (1964) in which the experimenters were all experienced hypnotists. They were to read standard passages to subjects in each of two conditions which may have affected the expectation of the experimenters. When experimenters had reason to expect lower suggestibility scores, their voices were found to be significantly less convincing in their reading of the instructions to their subjects ($z = +2.81$). This result was obtained despite the fact that experimenters (a) were cautioned to treat their subjects identically, (b) were told that their performances would be tape-recorded and (c) were all aware of the problem of experimenter effects. This experiment tells us of the importance of the auditory cues, but because there was a plausible rival hypothesis to the hypothesis of expectancy effects the study was not included in our earlier summary of studies of expectancy effects. That an hypnotist-experimenter's expectancy may affect his treatment of a research subject has been documented earlier, though the sample sizes involved only a single hypnotist-experimenter and a single subject (Shor and Schatz, 1960).

The two experiments described suggest that auditory cues may be sufficient to serve as mediators of expectancy effects. There are two additional experiments in support of this proposition, both of which have the additional merit of permitting estimates of the effects on the magnitude of expectancy effects of subjects' having available only auditory cues as compared to having access to both auditory and visual cues. The possibility of obtaining such estimates depends on having available at least three groups of experimenters. For two of these groups, subjects must have access to both visual and auditory cues from their experimenters, but each group of experimenters must have a different expectation for their subjects' responses. The difference between the mean response obtained by experimenters of these two groups is considered the base line of magnitude of expectancy effect when both channels of information are available. The third group of experimenters is given one of the two possible expectations, but subjects' access to visual cues from these experimenters is cut off. The difference between the mean response obtained by experimenters in this condition and the mean response obtained by experimenters expecting the opposite response is considered the magnitude of expectancy effect when only auditory cues are available. This magnitude can be divided by the base line magnitude for an estimate of the proportion of expectancy effect obtained when only auditory cues were available.

The two experiments meeting these requirements have been tabulated earlier as Rosenthal and Fode, 1963b, II and as Zoble, 1968 (the former study was a master's thesis by Fode). Fode's study employed the person perception task and his data showed that 47 per cent of the total expectancy effect was obtained when subjects had access only to auditory cues from their experimenter. Zoble's study employed a task requiring subjects to make tone-length discriminations but his results were remarkably similar to Fode's. Zoble's data showed that 53 per cent of the total expectancy effect was obtained when subjects were restricted to purely auditory cues. The combined z associated with finding expectancy effects with only auditory cues available to subjects was $+4.01$.

Additional evidence for the importance of the auditory channel to the mediation of expectancy effects comes from an analysis by Duncan and Rosenthal (1968). Sound motion pictures were available of three male experimenters administering the person perception task to 10 different subjects. An analysis of the experimenters' vocal emphases showed that no subject was exposed to identical differential emphases of those portions of the instructions that listed the subject's response alternatives. All five subjects who heard relatively greater vocal emphasis on the response alternatives associated with high photo ratings subsequently assigned higher photo ratings than did any of the five subjects who heard relatively greater vocal emphasis on the response alternatives associated with low photo ratings ($z = +2.65$).

The three experimenters on whose differential vocal emphases these paralinguistic analyses were made had been selected because they were known to have shown expectancy effects. We expect, therefore, by definition, to find a large correlation between the various expectancies given each experimenter and the mean photo rating given by the subject contacted under each different expectation. That correlation was $+.60$ ($z = +1.75$) a finding obviously not reported in support of the hypothesis of expectancy effect, but rather to establish a base line for comparison. The correlation between an experimenter's differential vocal emphasis on the various response alternatives in the instructions read to subjects and the subjects' subsequent response was $+.72$ ($z = +2.33$). That was a promising chain of correlations. The experimenter's expectancy predicted his subjects' responses and the differential vocal emphasis of the experimenter also predicted his subjects' responses. It remained only to show that the experimenter's expectancy was a good predictor of how he read his instructions to his subjects. Then everything would fall nicely into place. Unfortunately, that is not what we found. The correlation between an experimenter's expectancy and his instruction-reading behavior was only $+.24$, a correlation that is difficult to defend as being really different from zero with a maximum of eight degrees of freedom. The correlation between experimenters' differential vocal emphases and their subjects' subsequent photo ratings with the effects of experimenter expectancy partialed out showed no shrinkage; it was $+.74$. Therefore, though this analysis gave further evidence of the importance of the auditory channel of communication, it did not turn out to provide the key to the specific signal employed by subjects to learn what it was that their experimenter expected. Evidence for such a signal would have been provided only if the correlation between an experimenter's expectation and his differential vocal emphasis during instruction-reading had been substantial.[*]

[*] Rosenberg, in collaboration with Duncan, has recently replicated the effects on subjects' responses of differential emphasis in the instruction-reader's listing of response alternatives. That research was based, of course, on a different sample of experimenters. For a more detailed discussion of the interaction between differential vocal emphasis and subjects' evaluation apprehension, see the chapter by Rosenberg in this volume.

With all the data available to suggest the importance of the auditory channel in the mediation of expectancy effect, it should not surprise us that those studies of expectancy effect permitting the subject little or no auditory access to the experimenter generally failed to obtain expectancy effects. That was the case in the two studies listed for Carlson and Hergenhahn (1968) and in that listed for Moffatt (1966), all three of these studies having been tabulated as showing directional zs of less than $+1.28$. The same result occurred in one group of experimenters in the study conducted by Fode (Rosenthal and Fode, 1963b, II) though in that study the overall effects of experimenter expectancy were still associated with a $z > 3.00$.

So far we have focused on the auditory channel of communication but there are also data available to show the importance of the visual channel. One important finding comes from the research by Zoble (1968) described earlier. As one of his many experimental groups, Zoble had one group of subjects who had access only to visual cues from their experimenter. Despite the fact that Zoble's results helped to support the importance of auditory cues, his data nevertheless showed that visual cues were more effective than auditory cues in the mediation of expectancy effects ($z = +1.44$). Whereas those subjects who had access only to auditory cues were affected by their experimenter's expectancy only 53 per cent as much as those subjects who had access to both visual and auditory cues, those subjects who had access only to visual cues were affected by their experimenter's expectancy 75 per cent as much as those subjects who had access to both information channels. Zoble's results suggest a possible nonadditivity of the information carried in the visual and auditory channel. It may be that, when subjects are deprived of either visual or auditory information, they focus more attention on the channel that is available to them. This greater attention and perhaps greater effort may enable subjects to extract more information from the single channel than they could, or would, from that same channel if it were only one part of a two-channel information input system.

Much earlier we tabulated the results of two studies of verbal conditioning by Kennedy's group. In one of those studies, Kennedy, Edwards, and Winstead (1968) found the overall directional z associated with expectancy effects to be less than $+1.28$. That experiment we count as a directional z of .00 in our bookkeeping system but for our present purpose we can afford a closer look at that study. Part of the time experimenters were face-to-face with their subjects, and part of the time subjects had no visual access to their experimenter. The failure of the overall directional z to reach $+1.28$ seems due entirely to the condition in which subjects were deprived of visual cues from their experimenter.

When the analysis was based only on the condition in which visual cues were available, the directional z for expectancy effect was $+1.95$.

Both the studies described suggest that visual cues may also be important for the mediation of expectancy effects, though the experiment by Fode (Rosenthal and Fode, 1963b, II) found mute but visible experimenters to exert no expectancy effects. Further indirect evidence for the importance of visual cues comes from the experiment by Woolsey and Rosenthal (1966). In the first stage of that experiment, subjects had no visual access to their experimenters, but in the second stage they did. When the screens were removed from between experimenters and subjects, expectancy effects became significantly greater ($z = +2.04$). This evidence must be held very lightly, however, since experimenters contacting subjects with visual contact differed in several other ways from experimenters contacting subjects without visual contact. One difference was that experimenters with visual contact had gained greater experience, and more experienced experimenters appear to show greater expectancy effects, a topic to which we now turn.

D. Expectancy Effects as Interpersonal Learning

For a number of experiments on expectancy effects, sound motion pictures were available that had been obtained without the experimenters' or subjects' prior knowledge. The analyses of some of these films have been reported elsewhere (Friedman, 1967; Friedman, Kurland and Rosenthal, 1965; Rosenthal, 1966; Rosenthal, 1967; Rosenthal, Friedman, and Kurland, 1966). For all the hundreds of hours of careful observation, and for all the valuable things learned about experimenter-subject interaction, no well-specified system of unintentional cueing has been uncovered. But if the students of experimenter behavior do not know how experimenters unintentionally cue their subjects to give the expected response, then how do experimenters themselves know how? Perhaps they do not know, but perhaps within the context of the given experiment they can come to know. Expectancy effects may be a learned phenomenon and learned in interaction with a series of research subjects. Each experimenter may have some types of unintended signaling in common with other experimenters, but beyond that each experimenter may have some unique unintended signals that work only for him. Whether this is so is a problem for the psycholinguist, the paralinguist, the kinesicist, and the sociolinguist. But if there were this unique component to the unintentional cueing behavior of the experimenter, it might account for our difficulty in trying to isolate very specific but very widespread cueing systems.

The experimenter, who very likely knows no more than we about his cueing behavior, may begin his experiment with little ability to exert expectancy effects. But all the time, in his interaction with his first subject, he is emitting a myriad of unprogrammed and unintended cues in the visual and auditory channels. If whatever pattern of cues he is emitting happens to affect the subject's response, so that the experimenter obtains the response he expects to obtain, that pattern of cues may be more likely to recur with the next subject. In short, obtaining an expected response may be the reinforcement required to shape the experimenter's pattern of unintentional cueing. Subjects, then, may teach experimenters how to behave kinesically and paralinguistically so as to increase the likelihood that the next subject's response will be more in the direction of the experimenter's expectancy. Our old friend Pfungst, the student of Clever Hans, found that as experimenter-questioners gained experience in questioning Hans, they became better unintentional signalers to Hans.

If we are seriously to entertain the proposition that expectancy effects are learned in an interpersonal context, then we must be able to show that, in fact, experimenters are more successful in their unintentional influencing of subjects later, rather than earlier, in the sequence of subjects contacted. Elsewhere there is a report of six analyses investigating this question. In three of the samples studied, subjects contacted later in the series showed greater effects ($z \gtrsim +1.28$) of experimenter expectancy, while three of the samples showed no order effect (Rosenthal, 1966). The overall directional z in support of the learning hypothesis was $+2.73$ ($\Sigma z = +6.70$, $N = 6$). Since that earlier summary a number of other relevant findings have become available.

Connors and Horst (1966), in whose research the overall magnitude of expectancy effect did not reach a directional z of $+1.28$, nevertheless found that later contacted subjects showed significantly ($z = +1.81$) greater exepctancy effects than did earlier contacted subjects. That same result was obtained by Uno, Frager, and Rosenthal (1968 II), a study in which the overall magnitude of expectancy effect was tabulated as a z of .00 although later contacted subjects showed significantly greater expectancy effects ($z = +1.70$). In the two other studies by this group showing no overall expectancy effect ($z = .00$) there were no order effects reaching a z of /1.28/. In the two studies by this same group showing negative expectancy effects ($zs = -1.99$, -2.17), the first showed an increase of the negative expectancy effect over time ($z = +1.85$) but the second showed a decrease ($z = -1.46$).

Altogether, then, there are 12 studies investigating the tendency for expectancy effects to increase as more subjects are seen. Six of the results support the hypothesis at $z \gtrsim -1.28$, one of the results runs counter to the hypothesis at $z \lessgtr -1.28$, and five of the results neither support nor run counter to the hypothesis. The overall directional z in support of the hypothesis is $+3.06$, $p = .0011$. The five studies by Uno's group were conducted in Japan, and for just that set of studies the combined z is less than $+1.28$. The remaining seven studies were conducted in the United States and for them the combined z was $+3.21$. Whether this difference may be due to differences in communication patterns between the two cultures is currently under investigation. For the time being, at least, it seems reasonable to believe that when there is a difference in magnitude of expectancy effect from earlier to later contacted subjects, it is among the later seen subjects that expectancy effects are likely to be larger. The hypothesis that the mediation of expectancy effects is learned by experimenters in the interpersonal context of the experiment, seems worthy of further investigation.

VIII. RESEARCH ON UNINTENDED INFLUENCE

Quite apart from the methodological implications of research on experimenter expectancy effects there are substantive implications for the study of interpersonal relationships. Perhaps the most general implication is that people can engage in effective unprogrammed and unintended communication with one another and that this process of unintentional influence can be investigated experimentally.

A great deal of effort within the behavioral sciences has gone into the study of such intentional influence processes as education, persuasion, coercion, propaganda, and psychotherapy. In each of these cases the influencer intends to influence the recipient of his message and the message is usually encoded linguistically. Without diminishing efforts to understand these processes better, greater effort should perhaps be expended to understand the processes of unintentional influence in which the message is often encoded nonlinguistically. The question, in short, is how people "talk" to one another holding constant what it is they say.

At the present time not only do we not know the specific signals by which people unintentionally influence one another, we do not even know all the channels of communication involved. There is reason, though, to be optimistic. There appears to be a great current increase of interest in nonlinguistic behavior as it may have relevance for human communication (e.g., Sebeok, Hayes, and Bateson, 1964). Most interest seems to have been centered in the auditory and visual channels of communication and those are the channels investigated in the research described in this chapter. Other sense modalities will also bear investigation, however.

For example, Geldard (1960) has brought into focus the role of the skin senses in human communication and has presented evidence that the skin may be sensitive to human speech. Even when the sense modality involved is the auditory, it need not be only speech and speech-related stimuli to which the ear is sensitive. Kellogg (1962), and Rice and Feinstein (1965) have shown that, at least among blind humans, audition can provide a surprising amount of information about the environment. Employing a technique of echo ranging, Kellogg's subjects were able to assess accurately the distance, size, and composition of various external objects. The implications for interpersonal communication of these senses and of olfaction, or of even less commonly discussed modalities (e.g., Ravitz, 1950, 1952), are not yet clear but are worthy of more intensive investigation.

Since expectancies of another person's behavior seem often to be communicated to that person unintentionally, the basic experimental paradigm employed in our research program might be employed even if the interest were not in expectancy effects per se. Thus if we were interested in unintentional communication among different groups of psychiatric patients, some could be given expectancies for others' behavior. Effectiveness of unintentional influence could then be measured by the degree to which other patients were influenced by expectancies held of their behavior. There might be therapeutic as well as theoretical significance to knowing what kind of psychiatric patients were most successful in the unintentional influence of other psychiatric patients. The experiment by Persinger, Knutson, and Rosenthal (1966, described in Rosenthal, 1966) employed such a pradigm.

Twelve experimenters administered a standard photo rating task to 94 neuropsychiatric patients who could be classified as either relatively more anxious than hostile (schizophrenic or neurotic) or as relatively more hostile than anxious (paranoid or character disorder). Each experimenter was led to expect half his subjects to judge the stimulus photos as being of more successful people while the remaining subjects were expected to judge the photos as being of less unsuccessful people. What made this experiment unusual was that the experimenters were themselves patients in a mental hospital who had been classified into the same categories as their subjects.

Just as was the case with graduate student and advanced undergraduate student experimenters, mental patient experimenters obtained responses from their mental patient subjects consistent with their expectations ($z = +1.88$). Our primary interest in this study, however, was to examine the magnitude of unintended influence or communication as a joint function of the experimenters' and subjects' nosologies. Results showed that when both experimenters and subjects could be characterized as more anxious than hostile, experimenters showed the greatest positive unintended influence. However, when both experimenters and subjects were characterized more by hostility than anxiety, the predicted unintended communication was least effective.

Findings of this kind may have implications for the treatment of psychiatric disorders. The belief is increasing that an important source of informal treatment is the association with other patients. If, as seems likely, such treatment is more unintentional than intentional, then the grouping of patients might be arranged so that patients are put into contact with those other patients with whom they can "talk" best, even if this "talk" be nonlinguistic.

Perhaps success as an unintentional influencer of another's behavior also has relevance for the selection of psychotherapists to work with certain types of patients. The general strategy of trying to "fit the therapist to the patient" has been considered and has aroused considerable interest (e.g., Betz, 1962). That such selection may be made on the basis of unintentional communication patterns may also be suggested. In one recent study, it was found that the degree of hostility in the doctor's speech was unrelated to his success in getting alcoholic patients to accept treatment. However, when the content of the doctor's speech was filtered out, the degree of hostility found in the tone of his voice alone was significantly and negatively related to his success in influencing alcoholics to seek treatment (Milmoe, Rosenthal, Blane, Chafetz, and Wolf, 1965; see also Milmoe, Novey, Kagan, and Rosenthal, 1968).

One variable in particular, the "AB" variable, has been employed in a promising series of studies relevant to patient-therapist pairing (Betz, 1962; Berzins and Seidman, 1968; Carson, 1967). There are indications that so-called "A" type therapists (as defined by a paper and pencil test) are more effective with more disturbed patients while "B" type therapists are more effective with less disturbed patients. With these indications in mind we conducted a series of studies in which A and B type experimenters administered the standard photo rating task to subjects under different conditions of expectation. The general prediction was that the differential effectiveness of unintended communication by A and B type experimenters vis-à-vis their subjects would parallel the differential therapeutic effectiveness of A and B type therapists vis-à-vis their patients. Three such studies were conducted (Jenkins, 1966; Persinger, Knutson, and Rosenthal, 1968; Trattner, 1966, 1968).

For her sample of college student experimenters and subjects, Jenkins found that B type experimenters showed greater effects of their expectations than did A type experimenters ($z = +2.72$). Although the literature of the AB variable is addressed more to mental patients than to college students, we need only assume that college students are not so disturbed as schizophrenic patients to have Jenkins' finding lend some support to the proposition that B type influencers are more effective with less disturbed influencers.

In his experiment, Trattner employed psychiatric aides as experimenters and hospitalized schizophrenics as his subjects. Following the standard procedure, some subjects were represented to their experimenters as success perceivers, others as failure perceivers. When A type experimenters contacted more chronically disturbed (process-type) patients, experimenters showed greater effects of their expectations than when they contacted less chronically disturbed (reactive-type) patients. Similarly consistent with what we might expect on the basis of the AB literature, the B type experimenters were more successful unintentional influencers when they contacted the less chronically disturbed patients than when they contacted the more chronically disturbed patients (interaction $z = +1.81$).

In the study by Persinger, et al., a variety of mental patients served as subjects while male and female ward personnel served as experimenters. Once again effectiveness of unintended communication was defined by the degree to which experimenters obtained the responses they had been led to expect. In this experiment patients were not selected on the basis of severity of disturbance but rather on the basis of primary categorization as relatively more anxious than hostile (schizophrenic and neurotic) or as relatively more hostile than anxious (paranoid and character disorder). Results showed that greater expectancy effects were exerted by A type male experimenters and by B type female experimenters when patients were categorized as relatively more anxious. When patients were categorized as relatively more hostile, it was the B type male experimenters and the A type female experimenters who showed the greater unintended effects of their expectations (interaction $z = 2.06$).

The results of these studies lend support to the idea that the AB varible may be important in the prediction of interpersonal influence, but that is not the reason for their having been reported here. Rather the major purpose has been to illustrate the potential utility to studies of unintended interpersonal influence of the interpersonal expectancy paradigm.

It seems to be an uncomplicated procedure to induce in one member of a dyad (A) an expectancy for the behavior of the other member

(B). On the basis of the experiments summarized in this chapter, the odds are not unfavorable that the expectancy will be communicated to the other member of the dyad. With that a likely occurrence, the student of processes of covert communication has a focus for his attention. He will be looking for what A does differently in the interaction as a function of what is expected from B.

Depending on the tastes and questions of the investigator, either an experimental or an observational approach can be employed. If the investigator were interested, for example, in finding out the proportion of information carried in various channels of communication, the openness of these channels could be systematically varied. If the investigator were more interested in a global description of communication processes, he might permit all channels to remain fully open while trying to give as complete a description as possible of the type and amount of information carried in each channel. This can be partially accomplished by having different observers focus on channels that have been artificially isolated from one another. In the case of sound motion pictures, for example, some observers can be given access only to the silent film while others are given access only to the sound track. Potentially as instructive as the analysis of individual channels of communication may be the analysis of differences between the signals sent through different channels.

IX. BEYOND THE LABORATORY

The vast majority of the experiments summarized in this chapter were conducted in psychological laboratories. Even when the subjects were not sophomores but psychiatric patients, the interaction between experimenter and subject took place in a setting that unquestionably spelled "laboratory." For reasons quite apparent to any reader of this volume on artifacts in behavioral research, there are considerable advantages to testing laboratory-derived relationships in nonlaboratory settings. The laboratory gives us convenience, the control of variance-increasing variables, and perhaps a sense of security. The world beyond the laboratory gives us inconvenience, frequent increases in error variance, and a feeling of insecurity when mostly we do our work in the basement of the Psychology Building. But if a relationship obtained in the laboratory is to be viewed as uncontaminated by the procedures, subjects, and setting of the laboratory itself, it must be taken out of the artificial light of the lab and examined in the harsher light of the world beyond.

In the case of the variable of interpersonal expectancy, if we should want to regard it as a phenomenon of general interest and one not restricted in its implications to the data-collecting work of the behavioral scientist, we must see whether interpersonal expectancies can also be made to show themselves in other interpersonal contexts. The context selected was that of ongoing educational systems (Rosenthal and Jacobson, 1968).

All of the children in an elementary school serving a lower socio-economic status neighborhood were administered a non-verbal test of intelligence. The test was disguised as one that would predict intellectual "blooming." There were 18 classrooms in the school, three at each of the six grade levels. Within each grade level the three classrooms were composed of children with above average ability, average ability, and below average ability, respectively. Within each of the 18 classrooms approximately 20 per cent of the children were chosen at random to form the experimental group. Each teacher was given the names of the children from her class who were in the experimental condition. The teacher was told that these children had scored on the "test for intellectual blooming" such that they would show remarkable gains in intellectual competence during the next eight months of school. The difference between the experimental group and the control group children, then, was in the minds of the teachers.

Eight months later, at the end of the school year, all of the children were retested with the same IQ test. This intelligence test, while relatively nonverbal in the sense of requiring no speaking, reading, or writing was not entirely nonverbal. Actually there were two subtests: one requiring a greater comprehension of English—a kind of picture vocabulary test; the other requiring less ability to understand any spoken language, but more ability to reason abstractly. For shorthand purposes we refer to the former as a "verbal" subtest and to the latter as a "reasoning" subtest. The pretest correlation between these subtests was $+.42$.

For the school as a whole, the children of the experimental groups showed only a slightly greater gain in verbal IQ (2 points) than did the control group children. However, in total IQ (4 points), and especially in reasoning IQ (7 points), the experimental group children gained appreciably more than did the control group children.

When educational theorists have discussed the possible effects of teachers' expectations, they have usually referred to the children at lower levels of scholastic achievement. It was interesting, therefore, to find that in the present study, children of the highest level of achievement showed as great a benefit as did the children of the lowest level of achievement of having their teachers expect intellectual gains.

At the end of the school year of this study, all teachers were asked to describe the classroom behavior of their pupils. Those children from whom intellectual growth was expected were described as having a significantly better chance of becoming successful in the future, as significantly more interesting, curious, and happy. There was a tendency, too, for these children to be seen as more appealing, adjusted, and affectionate and as lower in the need for social approval. In short, the children from whom intellectual growth was expected become more intellectually alive and autonomous, or at least they were so perceived by their teachers.

We have already seen that the children of the experimental group gained more intellectually so that perhaps it was the fact of such gaining that accounted for the more favorable ratings of these children's behavior and aptitude. But a great many of the control group children also gained in IQ during the course of the year. We might expect that those who gained more intellectually among these undesignated children would also be rated more favorably by their teachers. Such was not the case. The more the control group children gained in IQ the more they were regarded as less well-adjusted, as less interesting, and as less affectionate. From these results it would seem that when children who are expected to grow intellectually do so, they are considerably benefited in other ways as well. When children who are not especially expected to develop intellectually do so, they seem either to show accompanying undesirable behavior or at least are perceived by their teachers as showing such undesirable behavior. If a child is to show intellectual gain it seems to be better for his real or perceived intellectual vitality and for his real or perceived mental health if his teacher has been expecting him to grow intellectually. It appears worthwhile to investigate further the proposition that there may be hazards to unpredicted intellectual growth.

A closer analysis of these data, broken down by whether the children were in the high, medium, or low ability tracks or groups, showed that these effects of unpredicted intellectual growth were due primarily to the children of the low ability group. When these slow track children were in the control group so that no intellectual gains were expected of them, they were rated more unfavorably by their teachers if they did show gains in IQ. The greater their IQ gains, the more unfavorably were they rated, both as to mental health and as to intellectual vitality. Even when the slow track children were in the experimental group (so that IQ gains were expected of them) they were not rated as favorably relative to their control group peers as were the children of the high or medium track despite the fact that they gained as much in IQ relative to the control group children as did the experimental group children of the high group. It may be difficult for a slow track child, even one whose IQ is rising, to be seen by his teacher as a well-adjusted child and as a potentially successful child, intellectually.

The effects of teacher expectations had been most dramatic when measured in terms of pupils' gains in reasoning IQ. These effects on reasoning IQ, however, were not uniform for boys and girls. Although all the children of this lower socio-economic status school gained dramatically in IQ, it was only among the girls that greater gains were shown by those who were expected to bloom compared to the children of the control group. Among the boys, those who were expected to bloom gained less than did the children of the control group (interaction $F = 9.27$, $p = .003$).

In part to check this finding, the experiment originally conducted on the West Coast was repeated in a small Midwestern town (Rosenthal and Evans, 1968). This time the children were from substantial middle-class backgrounds, and this time the results were completely and significantly reversed. Now it was the boys who showed the benefits of favorable teacher expectations. Among the girls, those who were expected to bloom intellectually gained less in reasoning IQ than did the girls of the control group (interaction $F = 9.10$, $p = .003$). Just as in the West Coast experiment, however, all the children showed substantial gains in IQ. These results, while they suggest the potentially powerful effects of teacher expectations also indicate the probable complexity of these effects as a function of pupils' sex, social class, and, as time will no doubt show, other variables as well.

In both the experiments described, IQ gains were assessed after a full academic year had elapsed. However, the results of another experiment suggest that teacher expectations can significantly affect students' intellectual performance in a period as short as two months (Anderson and Rosenthal, 1968). In this small experiment, the 25 children were mentally retarded boys with an average pretest IQ of 46. Expectancy effects were significant only for reasoning IQ and only in interaction with membership in a group receiving special remedial reading instruction in addition to participating in the school's summer day camp program ($p < .03$). Among these specially tutored boys those who were expected to bloom showed an expectancy disadvantage of nearly 12 IQ points; among the untutored boys who were participating only in the school's summer day camp program, those who were expected to bloom showed an expectancy advantage of just over three IQ points. (For verbal IQ, in contrast, the expectancy disadvantage of the tutored boys was less than one IQ point, while the expectancy advantage for the untutored boys was over two points).

The results described were based on posttesting only two months after the initiation of the experiment. Follow-up testing was undertaken seven months after the end of the basic experiment. In reasoning IQ, the boys who had been both tutored and expected to bloom intellectually made up the expectancy disadvantage they had shown after just two months. Now, their performance change was just like that of the control group children, both groups showing an IQ loss of four points over the nine month period. Compared to these boys who had been given both or neither of the two experimental treatments, the boys who had been given either tutoring or the benefit of favorable expectations showed significantly greater gains in reasoning IQ scores ($p < .025$). Relative to the control group children, those who were tutored showed a 10 point advantage while those who were expected to bloom showed a 12 point advantage. While both tutoring and a favorable teacher expectation were effective in raising relative IQ scores, it appeared that when these two treatments were applied simultaneously, they were ineffective in producing IQ gains over the period from the beginning of the experiment to the nine month follow-up. One possible explanation of this finding is that the simultaneous presence of both treatments led the boys to perceive too much pressure. The same pattern of results reported for reasoning IQ was also obtained when verbal IQ and total IQ were considered, though the interaction was significant only in the case of total IQ ($p < .03$).

In the experiment under discussion, a number of other measures of the boys' behavior were available as were observations of the day-camp counselors' behavior toward the boys. Preliminary analysis suggests that boys who had been expected to bloom intellectually were given less attention ($p = .09$) by the counselors and developed a greater degree of independence ($p < .02$) compared to the boys of the control group.

Another study, this time conducted in an East Coast school with upper middle class pupils, again showed the largest effect of teachers' expectancies to occur when the measure was of reasoning IQ (Conn, Edwards, Rosenthal, and Crowne, 1968). In this study, both the boys and the girls who were expected to bloom intellectually showed greater gains in reasoning IQ than did the boys and girls of the control group, and the magnitude of the expectancy effect favored the girls very slightly. Also in this study, we had available a measure of the children's accuracy in judging the vocal expressions of emotion of adult speakers. It was of considerable theoretical interest to find that greater benefits of favorable teacher expectations accrued to those children who were more accurate in judging the emotional tone expressed in an adult female's voice. These findings, taken together with the research of Adair and Epstein (1967) described earlier, give a strong suggestion that vocal cues may be important in the covert communication of interpersonal expectations.

In all the experiments described so far, the same IQ measure was employed, the Flanagan (1960) Tests of General Ability. Also employing the same instrument with his sample of first graders, Claiborn (1968) found a tendency ($z = -1.45$) for children he designated as potential bloomers to gain less in IQ than the children of the control group.

With fifth grade boys as his subjects and males as teachers, Pitt (1956) found no effect on achievement scores of arbitrarily adding or subtracting ten IQ points to the children's records. In her study, Heiserman (1967) found no effect of teacher expectations on her 7th graders' stated levels of occupational aspiration.

There have been two studies in which teachers' expectations were varied not for specific children within a classroom but rather for classrooms as a whole (Biegen, 1968; Flowers, 1966). In both cases the performance gains were greater for those classrooms expected by their teachers to show the better performance.

A radically different type of performance measure was employed in the research by Burnham (1968); not intelligence or scholastic achievement this time, but swimming ability. His subjects were boys and girls aged 7–14 attending a summer camp for the disadvantaged. None of the children could swim at the beginning of the two week experimental period. Half the children were alleged by the camp staff to have shown unusual potential for learning to swim as judged from a battery of psychological tests. Children were, of course, assigned to the "high potential" group at random. At the end of the two week period of the experiment all the children were retested on the standard Red Cross Beginner Swimmer Test. Those children who had been expected to show greater improvement in swimming ability showed greater improvement than did the children of the control group.

We may conclude now with the brief description of just one more experiment, this one conducted by Beez (1968), who kindly made his data available for the analyses to follow. This time the pupils were 60 pre-schoolers from a summer Headstart program. Each child was taught the meaning of a series of symbols by one teacher. Half the 60 teachers had been led to expect good symbol-learning and half had been led to expect poor symbol-learning. Most (77 percent) of the children alleged to have better intellectual prospects learned five or more symbols, but only 13 per cent of the children alleged to have poorer intellectual prospects learned five or more symbols ($p < 2$ in one million). In this study the children's actual performance was assessed by an experimenter who did not know what the child's teacher had been told about the child's intellectual prospects. Teachers who had been given favorable expectations about their pupil tried to teach more symbols to their pupil than did the teachers given unfavorable expectations about their pupil. The difference in teaching effort was dramatic. Eight or more symbols were taught by 87 per cent of the teachers expecting better performance, but only 13 per cent of the teachers expecting poorer performance tried to teach that many symbols to their pupil ($p < 1$ in 10 million).

These results suggest that a teacher's expectation about a pupil's performance may sometimes be translated not into subtle vocal nuances but rather into overt and even dramatic alterations in teaching style. The magnitude of the effect of teacher expectations found by Beez is also worthy of comment. In all the earlier studies described, one group of children had been singled out for favorable expectations while nothing was said of the remaining children of the control group. In Beez' short-term experiment it seemed more justified to give negative as well as positive expectations about some of the children. Perhaps the very large effects of teacher expectancy obtained by Beez were due to the creation of strong equal but opposite expectations in the minds of the different teachers. Since strong negative expectations doubtless exist in the real world of classrooms, Beez' procedure may give the better estimate of the effects of teacher expectations as they occur in everyday life.

In the experiment by Beez it seems clear that the dramatic differences in teaching style accounted at least in part for the dramatic differences in pupil learning. However, not all of the obtained differences in learners' learning was due to the differences in teachers' teaching. Within each condition of teacher expectation, for example, there was no relationship between number of symbols taught and number of symbols learned. In addition, it was also possible to compare the performances of just those children of the two conditions who had been given an exactly equal amount of teaching benefit. Even holding teaching benefits constant, the difference favored the children believed to be superior ($t = 2.89$, $p < .005$, one-tail) though the magnitude of the effect was now diminished by nearly half.

We have now seen at least a brief description of 11 studies of the effects of interpersonal expectancies in natural learning situations. That is too many to hold easily in mind and Table XXIII provides a convenient summary. For each experiment the directional standard normal deviate is given as well as a brief identification of the dependent variables employed. As has been the custom in this chapter, a standard normal deviate greater than -1.28 and smaller than $+1.28$ has been recorded as zero. Of the five experiments tabulated as showing no main

TABLE XXIII

EXPECTANCY EFFECTS IN EDUCATIONAL SETTINGS

Study		Directional standard normal deviate	Dependent variable
1. Anderson and Rosenthal	1968	.00[a]	Total IQ
2. Beez	1968	+ 4.67	Symbol learning
3. Biegen	1968	+ 1.83	Achievement
4. Burnham[b]	1968	+ 2.61[a]	Swimming skill
5. Claiborn	1968	− 1.45[a]	Total IQ
6. Conn, et al.	1968	.00[a]	Total IQ
7. Flowers	1966	+ 1.60	Achievement + IQ
8. Heiserman	1967	.00	Aspiration
9. Pitt	1956	.00	Achievement
10. Rosenthal and Evans	1968	.00[a]	Total IQ
11. Rosenthal and Jacobson	1968	+ 2.11[a]	Total IQ
	Sum	+11.37	
	$\sqrt{11}$	3.32	
	z	+ 3.42	
	p	.00033	

[a] Indicates that teacher expectancy interacted with another variable at $z \geq /1.28/$.

[b] See also Burnham and Hartsough (1968).

effect of teacher expectation, it should be noted that three of them showed significant interactions of teacher expectation with some other primary variable such as special tutoring (study 1), accuracy of emotion perception (6), and sex of pupil (10). The combined one-tail p of the main effects of teacher expectancy in the studies shown in Table XXIII is less than 1 in 3,000. It would take an additional 37 studies of a mean associated z value of .00 to bring the overall combined p to above .05.*

Shall we view this set of experiments in natural learning situations in isolation or would it be wiser to see them simply as more of the same type of experiment that has been discussed throughout this chap-

* Combining the ps of the 105 studies of Tables XXIV together with the results of the nine studies of footnote 2 gives a grand sum z of +112.23. The overall z associated with this set of results is +10.51 and 4,540 new experiments with a mean z of .00 are required to bring the overall p level to .05. (As this chapter went to press, the results of another study of teacher expectation effects became available. Meichenbaum, Bowers, and Ross, at the University of Waterloo, found that favorable teacher expectations led to a significant increase in the appropriateness of classroom behavior of a sample of adolescent female offenders ($df = 12$, $z = +2.02$.)

ter? Since the type of experimental manipulation involved in the laboratory studies is essentially the same as that employed in the studies beyond the laboratory, it seems more parsimonious to view all the studies as members of the same set. If, in addition to the communality of experimental procedures, we find it plausible to conclude a communality of outcome patterns between the laboratory and field experiments, perhaps we can have the greater convenience and power of speaking of just one type of effect of interpersonal expectancy. Table XXIV allows each reader to make his own test for goodness of fit. At each level of p we find the proportion of laboratory and educational studies reaching that or a lower level of p. The agreement between the two types of studies appears to be remarkably close. In addition, the mean z value obtained from the 94 laboratory experiments is nearly identical to that obtained from the 11 studies of educational settings.

If there were a systematic difference in sample size between studies conducted in laboratories and those involving teachers, then we might expect to find that for similar zs the average effects would be smaller in magnitude for the set comprised of larger sample sizes. For this reason it seems necessary also to compare magnitudes of expectancy effect for studies involving experimenters and teachers. Table XXV shows this comparison. For 57 studies of experimenters and for six studies of teachers it was possible to calculate the proportion of each that was affected in the predicted direction by their expectancy. Again the agreement is very good. Depending upon the particular method of computation selected, about 7 out of 10 experimenters or 7 out of 10 teachers

TABLE XXIV

PERCENTAGE OF STUDIES OF EXPECTANCY EFFECTS IN
LABORATORIES AND EDUCATIONAL SETTINGS
OBTAINING RESULTS AT SPECIFIED p LEVELS

p	Laboratories N = 94	Educational settings N = 11
.10	50%	45%
.05	35%	36%
.01	17%	18%
.001	12%	9%
.0001	5%	9%
.00001	3%	9%
.000001	2%	0%
Grand Sum z	+95.27	+11.37
Mean z	+ 1.01	+ 1.03

TABLE XXV

Proportions of Experimenters and Teachers
Showing Expectancy Effects

	Experimenters	Teachers
Number of Studies	57	6
Median z	.00	.00
Number of Es or Ts	523	115
Mean N per Study	9	19
Weighted Percent of Biased Es or Ts	69%	75%
Median Percent of Biased Es or Ts	75%	66%

can be expected to show the effects of their expectation on the performance of their subjects or pupils.

This chapter began its discussion of interpersonal expectancy effects by suggesting that the expectancy of the behavioral researcher might function as a self-fulfilling prophecy. This unintended effect of the investigator's research hypothesis must be regarded as a potentially damaging artifact. But interpersonal self-fulfilling prophecies do not operate only in laboratories and while, when there, they may act as artifacts, they are more than that. Interpersonal expectancy effects occur also among teachers and, there seems no reason to doubt it, among others as well. What started life as an artifact continues as an interpersonal variable of theoretical and practical interest. Today's artifact, as Bill McGuire so wisely said, is tomorrow's main effect; and tomorrow is today.

REFERENCES

Adair, J. G. Demand characteristics or comformity? Suspiciousness of deception and experimenter bias in conformity research. Unpublished manuscript, University of Manitoba, 1968.

Adair, J. G., and Epstein J. Verbal cues in the mediation of experimenter bias. Paper presented at the meeting of the Midwestern Psychological Association, Chicago, May, 1967.

Adler, N. E. The influence of experimenter set and subject set on the experimenter expectancy effect. Unpublished AB thesis, Wellesley College, 1968.

Allport, G. W. The role of expectancy. In H. Cantril (Ed.), Tensions that cause wars. Urbana, Illinois: University of Illinois Press, 1950, 43–78.

Anderson, D. F., and Rosenthal, R. Some effects of interpersonal expectancy and social interaction on institutionalized retarded children. Proceedings of the 76th Annual Convention of the American Psychological Association, 1968, 479–480.

Barber, T. X., Calverley, D. S., Forgione, A., McPeake, J. D., Chaves, J. F., and Bowen, B. Five attempts to replicate the experimenter bias effect. Unpublished manuscript, Harding, Mass.: Medfield Foundation, 1967.

Barber, T. X., and Silver, M. J. Fact, fiction, and the experimenter bias effect. *Psychological Bulletin Monograph Supplement,* 1968, **70,** 1–29.

Barnard, P. G. Interaction effects among certain experimenter and subject characteristics on a projective test. *Journal of Consulting and Clinical Psychology,* 1968, **32,** 514–521.

Becker, H. G. Experimenter expectancy, experience, and status as factors in observational data. Unpublished master's thesis, University of Saskatchewan, 1968.

Beez, W. V. Influence of biased psychological reports on teacher behavior and pupil performance. *Proceedings of the 76th Annual Convention of the American Psychological Association,* 1968, 605–606.

Berzins, J. I., and Seidman, E. Differential therapeutic responding of A and B quasi-therapists to schizoid and neurotic communications. Unpublished manuscript, University of Kentucky, 1968.

Betz, J. Experiences in research in psychotherapy with schizophrenic patients. In H. H. Strupp and L. Luborsky (Eds.), *Research in psychotherapy.* Washington, D.C.: American Psychological Association, 1962, 41–60.

Biegen, D. A. Unpublished data. University of Cincinnati, 1968.

Bootzin, R. R. The experimenter: a credibility gap in psychology. Unpublished manuscript, Purdue University, 1968.

Boring, E. G. *A history of experimental psychology,* (2nd ed.). New York: Appleton-Century-Crofts, 1950.

Bradley, W. H. Unmineralized fossil bacteria: A retraction. *Science,* 1968, **160,** 437.

Burnham, J. R. Experimenter bias and lesion labeling. Unpublished manuscript, Purdue University, 1966.

Burnham, J. R. Effects of experimenter's expectancies on children's ability to learn to swim. Unpublished master's thesis, Purdue University, 1968.

Burnham, J. R., and Hartsough, D. M. Effect of experimenter's expectancies ("the Rosenthal effect") on children's ability to learn to swim. Paper presented at the meeting of the Midwestern Psychological Association, Chicago, May, 1968.

Carlson, J. A., and Hergenhahn, B. R. Use of tape-recorded instructions and a visual screen to reduce experimenter bias. Unpublished manuscript, Hamline University, 1968.

Carlson, R. L., and Armelagos, G. J. Cradleboard hoods, not corsets. *Science,* 1965, **149,** 204–205.

Carson, R. C. A and B therapist "types": A possible critical variable in psychotherapy. *Journal of Nervous and Mental Diseases,* 1967, **144,** 47–54.

Cieutat, V. J. Examiner differences with the Stanford-Binet IQ. *Perceptual and Motor Skills,* 1965, **20,** 317–318.

Cieutat, V. J., and Flick, G. L. Examiner differences among Stanford-Binet items. *Psychological Reports,* 1967, **21,** 613–622.

Claiborn, W. L. An investigation of the relationship between teacher expectancy, teacher behavior and pupil performance. Unpublished doctoral dissertation, Syracuse University, 1968.

Conn, L. K., Edwards, C. N., Rosenthal, R., and Crowne, D. Perception of emotion and response to teachers' expectancy by elementary school children. *Psychological Reports,* 1968, **22,** 27–34.

Connors, A. M. Two experimenter behaviors as mediators of experimenter expectancy. Unpublished AB thesis, Harvard University, 1968.

Connors, A. M., and Horst, L. The relationship between subjects' unbiased response tendencies and subsequent responses under two conditions of experimenter expectancy. Unpublished manuscript, Harvard University, 1966.

Cooper, J., Eisenberg, L., Robert, J., and Dohrenwend, B. S. The effect of experimenter expectancy and preparatory effort on belief in the probable occurrence of future events. *Journal of Social Psychology*, 1967, **71**, 221–226.

Cordaro, L., and Ison, J. R. Observer bias in classical conditioning of the planarian. *Psychological Reports*, 1963, **13**, 787–789.

Crowne, D. P., and Marlowe, D. *The approval Motive*. New York: Wiley, 1964.

Duncan, S., and Rosenthal, R. Vocal emphasis in experimenters' instruction reading as unintended determinant of subjects' responses. *Language and speech*, 1968, **11**, Part 1, 20–26.

Escalona, S. K. Feeding disturbances in very young children. *American Journal of Orthopsychiatry*, 1945, **15**, 76–80.

Flanagan, J. C. *Test of general ability: technical report*. Chicago: Science Research Associates, 1960.

Flowers, C. E. Effects of an arbitrary accelerated group placement on the tested academic achievement of educationally disadvantaged students. Unpublished doctoral dissertation, Teachers College, Columbia University, 1966.

Fode, K. L. The effects of experimenters' anxiety, and subjects' anxiety, social desirability and sex, on experimenter outcome-bias. Unpublished doctoral dissertation, University of North Dakota, 1967.

Friedman, N. *The social nature of psychological research*. New York: Basic Books, 1967.

Friedman, N., Kurland, D., and Rosenthal, R. Experimenter behavior as an unintended determinant of experimental results. *Journal of Projective Techniques and Personality Assessment*, 1965, **29**, 479–490.

Gall, M., and Mendelsohn, G. A. Effects of facilitating techniques and subject-experimenter interaction on creative problem solving. Unpublished manuscript, University of California, Berkeley, 1966.

Gardner, M. Dermo-optical perception: A peek down the nose. *Science*, 1966, **151**, 654–657.

Geldard, F. A. Some neglected possibilities of communication. *Science*, 1960, **131**, 1583–1588.

Getter, H., Mulry, R. C., Holland, C., and Walker, P. Experimenter bias and the WAIS. Unpublished data, University of Connecticut, 1967.

Glixman, A. F. Psychology of the scientist: XXII. Effects of examiner, examiner-sex, and subject-sex upon categorizing behavior. *Perceptual and Motor Skills*, 1967, **24**, 107–117.

Goldblatt, R. A., and Schackner, R. A. Categorizing emotion depicted in facial expressions and reaction to the experimental situation as a function of experimenter "friendliness." Paper presented at the meeting of the Eastern Psychological Association, Washington, D.C., April, 1968.

Hartry, A. Experimenter bias in planaria conditioning. Paper presented at the meeting ing of the Western Psychological Association, Long Beach, April, 1966.

Heiserman, M. S. The relationship between teacher expectations and pupil occupational aspirations. Unpublished master's thesis, Iowa State University, Ames, 1967.

Honorton, C. Review of C. E. M. Hansel's *ESP: A scientific evaluation*. New York: Scribner's, 1966. *Journal of Parapsychology*, 1967, **31**, 76–82.

Horn, C. H. The field dependent and field independent person's response to experimenter bias. Unpublished manuscript, George Washington University, 1968.

Horst, L. Research in the effect of the experimenter's expectancies—a laboratory model of social influence. Unpublished manuscript, Harvard University, 1966.

Hurwitz, S., and Jenkins, V. The effects of experimenter expectancy on performance of simple learning tasks. Unpublished manuscript, Harvard University, 1966.

Ingraham, L. H., and Harrington, G. M. Experience of E as a variable in reducing experimenter bias. Psychological Reports, 1966, 19, 455–461.

Jenkins, V. The unspoken word: A study in non-verbal communication. Unpublished AB thesis, Harvard University, 1966.

Johnson, R. W. Subject performance as affected by experimenter expectancy, sex of experimenter, and verbal reinforcement. Unpublished master's thesis, University of New Brunswick, 1967.

Jourard, S. M. Project replication: Experimenter-subject acquaintance and outcome in psychological research. Unpublished manuscript, University of Florida, 1968.

Kellogg, W. N. Sonar system of the blind. Science, 1962, 137, 399–404.

Kennedy, J. J., Cook, P. A., and Brewer, R. R. An examination of the effects of three selected experimenter variables in verbal conditioning research. Unpublished manuscript, University of Tennessee, 1968.

Kennedy, J. J., Edwards, B. C., and Winstead, J. C. The effects of experimenter outcome expectancy in a verbal conditioning situation: A failure to detect the "Rosenthal Effect." Unpublished manuscript, University of Tennessee, 1968.

Kennedy, J. L., and Uphoff, H. F. Experiments on the nature of extrasensory perception: III. The recording error criticism of extrachance scores. Journal of Parapsychology, 1939, 3, 226–245.

Kintz, B. L., Delprato, D. J., Mettee, D. R., Parsons, C. E. and Schappe, R. H. The experimenter as a discriminative stimulus in a T-maze, Psychological Record, 1965, 15, 449–454.

Kleinmuntz, B., and McLean, R. S. Computers in behavioral science: Diagnostic interviewing by digital computer. Behavioral Science, 1968, 13, 75–80.

Klinger, E. Modeling effects on achievement imagery. Journal of Personality and Social Psychology, 1967, 7, 49–62.

Krasner, L., and Ullman, L. P. (Eds.) Research in behavior modification: New developments and implications. New York: Holt, Rinehart and Winston, 1965.

Larrabee, L. L., and Kleinsasser, L. D. The effect of experimenter bias on WISC performance. Unpublished paper. Psychological Associates, St. Louis, 1967.

Laszlo, J. P., and Rosenthal, R. Subject dogmatism, experimenter status, and experimenter expectancy effects. Unpublished manuscript, Harvard University, 1967.

Malmo, R. B., Boag, T. J., and Smith, A. A. Physiological study of personal interaction. Psychosomatic Medicine, 1957, 19, 105–119.

Marcia, J. E. Hypothesis-making, need for social approval, and their effects on unconscious experimenter bias. Unpublished master's thesis, Ohio State University, 1961.

Marwit, S. J. An investigation of the communication of tester-bias by means of modeling. Unpublished doctoral dissertation, State University of New York at Buffalo, 1968.

Marwit, S. J., and Marcia, J. E. Tester bias and response to projective instruments. Journal of Consulting Psychology, 1967, 31, 253–258.

Masling, J. The influence of situational and interpersonal variables in projective testing. Psychological Bulletin, 1960, 57, 65–85.

Masling, J. Differential indoctrination of examiners and Rorschach responses. Journal of Consulting Psychology, 1965, 29, 198–201.

Masling, J. Role-related behavior of the subject and psychologist and its effects upon psychological data. In D. L. Levine (Ed.), Nebraska Symposium on Motivation, Lincoln, Nebraska: University of Nebraska Press, 1966. 67–103.

McFall, R. M. "Unintentional communication": The effect of congruence and incongruence between subject and experimenter constructions. Unpublished doctoral dissertation, Ohio State University, 1965.

McGuigan, F. J. The experimenter: A neglected stimulus object. Psychological Bulletin, 1963, 60, 421–428.

Merton, R. K. The self-fulfilling prophecy. Antioch Review, 1948, 8, 193–210.

Miller, G. A., Bregman, A. S., and Norman, D. A. The computer as a general purpose device for the control of psychological experiments. In R. W. Stacy and B. D. Waxman (Eds.), Computers in biomedical research. Vol. I. New York: Academic Press, 1965. 467–490.

Milmoe, S., Novey, M. S., Kagan, J., and Rosenthal, R. The mother's voice: Postdictor of aspects of her baby's behavior. Proceedings of the 76th Annual Convention of the American Psychological Association, 1968, 463–464.

Milmoe, S., Rosenthal, R., Blane, H. T., Chafetz, M. E., and Wolf, I. The doctor's voice: postdictor of successful referral of alcoholic patients. Journal of Abnormal Psychology, 1967, 72, 78–84.

Minor, M. W. Experimenter expectancy effect as a function of evaluation apprehension. Unpublished doctoral dissertation, University of Chicago, 1967.

Minor, M. W. Unpublished data, University of Chicago, 1967. (a)

Mintz, N. On the psychology of aesthetics and architecture. Unpublished manuscript, Brandeis University, 1957.

Moffat, M. C. Unpublished data. University of British Columbia, 1966.

Mosteller, F., and Bush, R. R. Selected quantitative techniques. In G. Lindzey (Ed.) Handbook of social psychology, Vol. I. Cambridge, Mass.: Addison-Wesley, 1954. 289–334.

Mosteller, F., and Tukey, J. W. Data analysis, including statistics. Unpublished manuscript, Harvard University, 1965.

Müller, W. and Timaeus, E. Conformity behavior and experimenter bias. Unpublished manuscript, University of Cologne, 1967.

Nichols, M. Data desirability and experimenter expectancy as unintended determinants of experimental results. Unpublished data, Harvard University, 1967.

Peel, W. C. Jr. The influence of the examiner's expectancy and level of anxiety on the subject's responses to the Holtzman Inkblots. Unpublished master's thesis, Memphis State University, 1967.

Persinger, G. W. The effect of acquaintanceship on the mediation of experimenter bias. Unpublished master's thesis, University of North Dakota, 1962.

Persinger, G. W., Knutson, C., and Rosenthal, R. Communication of interpersonal expectations among neuropsychiatric patients. Unpublished data, Harvard University, 1966.

Persinger, G. W., Knutson, C., and Rosenthal, R. Communication of interpersonal expectations of ward personnel to neuropsychiatric patients. Unpublished data, Harvard University, 1968.

Pflugrath, J. Examiner influence in a group testing situation with particular reference to examiner bias. Unpublished master's thesis, University of North Dakota, 1962.

Pfungst, O. Clever Hans (the horse of Mr. von Osten): a contribution to experimental, animal, and human psychology. (Translated by C. L. Rahn) New York: Holt, 1911. Republished by Holt, Rinehart and Winston, 1965.

Pitt, C. C. V. An experimental study of the effects of teachers' knowledge or incorrect knowledge of pupil IQ's on teachers' attitudes and practices and pupils' attitudes and achievement. Unpublished doctoral dissertation, Columbia University, 1956.

Polanyi, M. The society of explorers. *Encounter*, 1967.

Raffetto, A. M. Experimenter effects on subjects' reported hallucinatory experiences under visual and auditory deprivation. Unpublished master's thesis, San Francisco State College, 1967.

Raffetto, A. M. Experimenter effects on subjects' reported hallucinatory experiences under visual and auditory deprivation. Paper presented at the meeting of the Midwestern Psychological Association, Chicago, May, 1968.

Ravitz, L. J. Electrometric correlates of the hypnotic state. *Science*, 1950, **112**, 341–342.

Ravitz, L. J. Electrocyclic phenomena and emotional states. *Journal of Clinical and Experimental Psychopathology*, 1952, **13**, 69–106.

Rice, C. E. and Feinstein, S. H. Sonar system of the blind: size discrimination. *Science*, 1965, **148**, 1107–1108.

Riecken, H. W. A program for research on experiments in social psychology. In N. F. Washburne (Ed.), *Decisions, values, and groups*, Vol. 2. New York: Pergamon Press, 1962. 25–41.

Rosenthal, R. On the social psychology of the psychological experiment: The experimenter's hypothesis as unintended determinant of experimental results. *American Scientist*, 1963, **51**, 268–283.

Rosenthal, R. The effect of the experimenter on the results of psychological research. In B. A. Maher (Ed.) *Progress in experimental personality research*. Vol. 1. New York: Academic Press, 1964. 79–114. (a)

Rosenthal, R. Experimenter outcome-orientation and the results of the psychological experiment. *Psychological Bulletin*, 1964, **61**, 405–412. (b)

Rosenthal R. Clever Hans: a case study of scientific method. Introduction to Pfungst, O. *Clever Hans: (the horse of Mr. von Osten)*. New York: Holt, Rinehart and Winston, 1965. ix–xlii.

Rosenthal, R. *Experimenter effects in behavioral research*. New York: Appleton-Century-Crofts, 1966.

Rosenthal, R. Covert communication in the psychological experiment. *Psychological Bulletin*, 1967, **67**, 356–367. (a)

Rosenthal, R. Experimenter expectancy, experimenter experience, and Pascal's Wager. *Psychological Reports*, 1967, **20**, 619–622. (b)

Rosenthal, R. Experimenter expectancy, one tale of Pascal, and the distribution of three tails. *Psychological Reports*, 1967, **21**, 517–520. (c)

Rosenthal, R. The eternal triangle: Investigators, data, and the hypotheses called null. Unpublished manuscript, Harvard University, 1967. (d)

Rosenthal, R. Experimenter expectancy and the reassuring nature of the null hypothesis decision procedure. *Psychological Bulletin Monograph Supplement*, 1968, **70**, 30–47. (a)

Rosenthal, R. On not so replicated experiments and not so null results. *Journal of Consulting and Clinical Psychology*, 1968, in press. (b)

Rosenthal, R., and Evans, J. Unpublished data, Harvard University, 1968.

Rosenthal, R. and Fode, K. L. The effect of experimenter bias on the performance of the albino rat. *Behavioral Science*, 1963, **8**, 183–189. (a)

Rosenthal, R., and Fode, K. L. Three experiments in experimenter bias. *Psychological Reports*, 1963, **12**, 491–511. (b)

Rosenthal, R., Friedman, C. J., Johnson, C. A., Fode, K. L., Schill, T. R., White, C. R., and Vikan-Kline, L. L. Variables affecting experimenter bias in a group situation. *Genetic Psychology Monographs*, 1964, **70**, 271–296.

Rosenthal, R., Friedman, N., and Kurland, D. Instruction-reading behavior of the experimenter as an unintended determinant of experimental results. *Journal of Experimental Research in Personality*, 1966, **1**, 221–226.

Rosenthal, R., and Hall, C. M. Computational errors in behavioral research. Unpublished data, Harvard University, 1968.

Rosenthal, R., and Jacobson, L. *Pygmalion in the classroom: Teacher expectation and pupils' intellectual development*. New York: Holt, Rinehart and Winston, 1968.

Rosenthal, R., Kohn, P., Greenfield, P. M., and Carota, N. Experimenters' hypothesis-confirmation and mood as determinants of experimental results. *Perceptual and Motor Skills*, 1965, **20**, 1237–1252.

Rosenthal, R., and Lawson, R. A longitudinal study of the effects of experimenter bias on the operant learning of laboratory rats. *Journal of Psychiatric Research*, 1964, **2**, 61–72.

Rosenthal, R, and Persinger, G. W. Subjects' prior experimental experience and experimenters' outcome consciousness as modifiers of experimenter expectancy effects. Unpublished manuscript, Harvard University, 1968.

Rosenthal, R. Persinger, G. W., Mulry, R. C., Vikan-Kline, L. L., and Grothe, M. Changes in experimental hypotheses as determinants of experimental results. *Journal of Projective Techniques and Personality Assessment*, 1964, **28**, 465–469. (a)

Rosenthal, R., Persinger, G. W., Mulry, R. C., Vikan-Kline, L. L., and Grothe, M. Emphasis on experimental procedure, sex of subjects, and the biasing effects of experimental hypotheses. *Journal of Projective Techniques and Personality Assessment*, 1964, **28**, 470–473. (b)

Rosenthal, R., Persinger, G. W., Vikan-Kline, L. L., and Fode, K. L. The effect of early data returns on data subsequently obtained by outcome-biased experimenters. *Sociometry*, 1963, **26**, 487–498. (a)

Rosenthal, R., Persinger, G. W., Vikan-Kline, L. L., and Fode, K. L. The effect of experimenter outcome-bias and subject set on awareness in verbal conditioning experiments. *Journal of Verbal Learning and Verbal Behavior*, 1963, **2**, 275–283. (b)

Rosenthal, R., Persinger, G. W., Vikan-Kline, L. L., and Mulry, R. C. The role of the research assistant in the mediation of experimenter bias. *Journal of Personality*, 1963, **31**, 313–335.

Roth, J. A. Hired hand research. *American Sociologist*, 1965, **1**, 190–196.

Sarason, I. G. The human reinforcer in verbal behavior research. *In* L. Krasner and L. P. Ullman (Eds.), *Research in behavior modifications: New developments and implications*. New York: Holt, Rinehart and Winston, 1965. 231–243.

Sattler, J. M. and Theye, F. Procedural, situational, and interpersonal variables in individual intelligence testing. *Psychological Bulletin*, 1967, **68**, 347–360.

Sebeok, T. A., Hayes, A. S., and Bateson, M. C. (Eds.) *Approaches to semiotics*. The Hague: Mouton, 1964.

Shames, M. L., and Adair, J. G. Experimenter bias as a function of the type and structure of the task. Paper presented at the meeting of the Canadian Psychological Association, Ottawa, May, 1967.

Shapiro, J. L. The effects of sex, instructional set, and the problem of awareness in a verbal conditioning paradigm. Unpublished master's thesis, Northwestern University, 1966.

Shaver, J. P. Experimenter bias and the training of observers. *Proceedings of the Utah Academy of Sciences, Arts, and Letters,* 1966, Part I, **43**, 143–152.

Shor, R. E., and Schatz, J. A critical note on Barber's case-study on "Subject J". *Journal of Psychology,* 1960, **50**, 253–256.

Silverman, I. The effects of experimenter outcome expectancy on latency of word association. *Journal of Clinical Psychology,* 1968, **24**, 60–63.

Smiltens, G. J. A study of experimenter expectancy effects with two expectancies being manipulated. Unpublished AB thesis, Harvard University, 1966.

Stevenson, H. W. Social reinforcement of children's behavior. *In* L. P. Lipsitt and C. C. Spiker (Eds.), *Advances in child development and behavior.* Vol. 2. New York: Academic Press, 1965. 97–126.

Strauss, M. E. Examiner expectancy: effects on Rorschach Experience Balance. *Journal of Consulting and Clinical Psychology,* 1968, **32**, 125–129.

Summers, G. F., and Hammonds, A. D. Effect of racial characteristics of investigator on self-enumerated responses to a Negro prejudice scale. *Social Forces,* 1966, **44**, 515–518.

Timaeus, E., and Lück, H. E. Experimenter expectancy and social facilitation I: Aggression under the condition of coaction. Unpublished manuscript, University of Cologne, 1968. (a)

Timaeus, E., and Lück, H. E. Experimenter expectancy and social facilitation II: Stroop-test performance under the condition of audience. Unpublished manuscript, University of Cologne, 1968. (b)

Towbin, A. P. Hostility in Rorschach content and overt aggressive behavior. *Journal of Abnormal and Social Psychology,* 1959, **58**, 312–316.

Trattner, J. H. The Whitehorn-Betz "AB" Scale and the communication of expectancies to "process" and "reactive" schizophrenics. Unpublished manuscript, Harvard University, 1966.

Trattner, J. H. The Whitehorn-Betz AB Scale and the communication of expectancies to high and low social competence schizophrenics. Unpublished master's thesis, Northwestern University, 1968.

Troffer, S. A., and Tart, C. T. Experimenter bias in hypnotist performance. *Science,* 1964, **145**, 1330–1331.

Uno, Y., Frager, R. D., and Rosenthal, R. Interpersonal expectancy effects among Japanese experimenters. Unpublished data, Harvard University, 1968.

Vaughan, G. M. The effect of the ethnic grouping of the experimenter upon children's responses to tests of an ethnic nature. *British Journal of Social and Clinical Psychology,* 1963, **2**, 66–70.

Walker, R. E., Davis, W. E., and Firetto, A. An experimenter variable: The psychologist-clergyman. *Psychological Reports,* 1968, **22**, 709–714.

Walker, R. E., and Firetto, A. The clergyman as a variable in psychological testing. *Journal for the Scientific Study of Religion,* 1965, **4**, 234–236.

Wartenberg-Ekren, U. The effect of experimenter knowledge of a subject's scholastic standing on the performance of a reasoning task. Unpublished master's thesis, Marquette University, 1962.

Weick, K. E. Unpublished data, University of Minnesota, 1966.

Weiss, L. R. Experimenter bias as a function of stimulus ambiguity. Unpublished manuscript, State University of New York at Buffalo, 1967.

Wenk, E. A. Notes on some motivational aspects of test performance of white and Negro CYA inmates. Unpublished manuscript, Deuel Vocational Institution, Tracy, California, 1966.

Wessler, R. L. The experimenter effect in a task-ability problem experiment. Unpublished doctoral dissertation, Washington University, 1966.

Wessler, R. L. Experimenter expectancy effects in psychomotor performance. *Perceptual and Motor Skills*, 1968, **26**, 911–917. (a)

Wessler, R. L. Experimenter expectancy effects in three dissimilar tasks. Unpublished manuscript, St. Louis University, 1968. (b)

Wessler, R. L., and Strauss, M. E. Experimenter expectancy: a failure to replicate. *Psychological Reports*, 1968, **22**, 687–688.

White, C. R. The effect of induced subject expectations on the experimenter bias situation. Unpublished doctoral dissertation, University of North Dakota, 1962.

Womack, W. M., and Wagner, N. N. Negro interviewers and white patients. *Archives of General Psychiatry*, 1967, **16**, 685–692.

Woolsey, S. H., and Rosenthal, R. Unpublished data, Harvard University, 1966.

Yando, R. M., and Kagan, J. The effect of teacher tempo on the child. Unpublished manuscript, Harvard University, 1966.

Zax, M., Stricker, G., and Weiss, J. H. Some effects of nonpersonality factors on Rorschach performance. *Journal of Projective Techniques*, 1960, **24**, 83–93.

Zegers, R. A. Expectancy and the effects of confirmation and disconfirmation. *Journal of Personality and Social Psychology*, 1968, **9**, 67–71.

Zoble, E. J. Interaction of subject and experimenter expectancy effects in a tone length discrimination task. Unpublished AB thesis, Franklin and Marshall College, 1968.

Chapter 7

THE CONDITIONS AND CONSEQUENCES
OF EVALUATION APPREHENSION

Milton J. Rosenberg

University of Chicago

Just as it keeps rats pressing levers, intermittent reinforcement keeps psychologists theorizing and neologizing. The best reinforcer I know is not the student's imitation of his professor's crotchets, nor is it a "successful replication" of one's experiment by another: instead it is to have some theoretical term that one has coined be often quoted and then to watch the quotation marks fade away as the term begins to enjoy some common usage. To put a phrase into the language (even if that language is spoken by only a few dozen others) confirms the sometimes faltering sense that one has really said something.

This seems to have begun to happen with the term "evaluation apprehension" which I first used in some unpublished documents in 1960–61 and in an obscure article in 1963, and which I then explicated in a more visible one in 1965. Yet the diffusion of the term is not at all due to its being the key to some arcane and profound insight. Most experimental psychologists had long since come to the unhappy awareness that their subjects were prone to "faking it" and, particularly, to faking it "good." But as a sort of contrast to Mark Twain's aphorism about people and the weather, the problem of self presentation in experiments seemed to be something that virtually nobody was talking about* though a great deal could be done about it.

* One clear voice that helped break the silence was that of Henry Riecken. In a valuable article published in 1962 he proffered a general view of the psychologi-

That the term "evaluation apprehension" has recently gained some currency must, then, be due to its helping to fill a need—the need, I should say, for experimental psychologists, social and otherwise, to come to terms with an obvious and fascinating source of trouble in their experimental procedures and rituals. In recent years my own sense of that need has led me beyond the initial conceptualization and into this possibly paradoxical commitment: to try to do systematic experimentation on evaluation apprehension as a source of systematic bias in psychological experiments.

This chapter is intended as a rather loose, narrative account of the main directions taken and the major findings gleaned in that research program. All but the first of the studies to be described are previously unpublished, though they have been presented in various colloquia over the last two years. Some of these studies will be described in full detail in forthcoming articles; and it is my ambition to bring all this work, and related studies, into tight but expansive focus in an as yet unwritten book.

I. EVALUATION APPREHENSION AS CONCEPT AND PROCESS

To begin, I had better not assume that the partial diffusion of the term "evaluation apprehension" has also spread abroad its full intended conceptual meaning. Thus what is called for, first, is a statement of definition. Then I shall need to outline my conception of how evaluation apprehension gets aroused and, after arousal, sometimes interacts with features of the experimental situation in ways that produce systematic biasing of experimental response data. Following these necessary preliminaries I shall turn, in the last portion of this introductory section, to some of the reasoning that lies behind the basic conceptualization and then we can begin to look at its research implications.

---

cal experiment as a sort of ritualized exchange between subject and experimenter. An important aspect of the exchange dynamic, as he saw it, was the subject's desire to "put his best foot forward." However, in Riecken's view, this was basically a source of "unintended variance" in data and the possibility that it could exert systematic influence making for false confirmation or disconfirmation of hypotheses was not directly examined.

Also focussed upon the self-presentation process were the inquiries by Edwards (1957) and Crowne and Marlowe (1964) concerning the "social desirability" variable. In distinction to the work described in this chapter, their basic interest has been with the contaminating influence of positive self-presentation upon psychological testing and its results rather than upon psychological experiments.

What, then, is the working conception of evaluation apprehension around which my recent research and this chapter are organized? The summary given in an earlier article (Rosenberg, 1965) is, I think, worth repeating here:

"It is proposed that the typical human subject approaches the typical psychological experiment with a preliminary expectation that the psychologist may undertake to evaluate his (the subject's) emotional adequacy, his mental health or lack of it. Members of the general public, including students in introductory psychology courses, have usually learned (despite our occasional efforts to persuade them otherwise) to attribute special abilities along these lines to those whose work is perceived as involving psychological interests and skills. Even when the subject is convinced that his adjustment is not being directly studied he is likely to think that the experimenter is nevertheless bound to be sensitive to any behavior that bespeaks poor adjustment or immaturity.

"In experiments the subject's initial suspicion that he may be exposing himself to evaluation will usually be confirmed or disconfirmed (as he perceives it) in the early stages of his encounter with the experimenter. Whenever it *is* confirmed, or to the extent that it is, the typical subject will be likely to experience *evaluation apprehension;* that is, an active, anxiety-toned concern that he win a positive evaluation from the experimenter, or at least that he provide no grounds for a negative one. Personality variables will have some bearing upon the extent to which this pattern of apprehension develops. But equally important are various aspects of the experimental design such as the experimenter's explanatory 'pitch,' the types of measures used, and the experimental manipulations themselves.

"Such factors may operate with equal potency across all cells of an experiment; but we shall focus upon the more troublesome situation in which treatment differences between experimental groups make for differential arousal and confirmation of evaluation apprehension. The particular difficulty with this state of affairs is that subjects in groups experiencing comparatively high levels of evaluation apprehension will be more prone than subjects in other groups to interpret the experimenter's instructions, explanations, and measures for what they may convey about the kinds of responses that will be considered healthy or unhealthy, mature or immature. In other words, they will develop *hypotheses* about how to win positive evaluation or to avoid negative evaluation. And usually the subjects in such an experimental group are enough alike in their perceptual reactions to the situation so that there will be considerable similarity in the hypotheses at which they separately arrive. This similarity may, in turn, operate to systematically influence experimental responding in ways that foster false confirmation of the experimenter's predictions."

What suggests this view of the secret side of the structured transaction between experimenter and subject? What, if anything, confirms the view?

One answer to the first of these questions concerns the modal theme that is usually encountered when one engages subjects in extended post-experimental discussion. Experienced experimenters who bother to talk to their subjects have all heard questions like these: "How did I do—were my responses (answers) normal?" "What were you really trying to find out, whether I'm some kind of neurotic?" "Did I react the same as most people do?" If one goes further in postexperimental inquiry, as I have regularly tried to do in recent years in my experimental work on attitude change (see Abelson, et al., 1968; Rosenberg et al., 1960), and asks subjects to attempt a reconstruction of their private experience of the experimental transaction, one often picks up another theme that I take to be quite significant. Subjects will report—sometimes with uncertainty and sometimes with great clarity—that they were burdened or preoccupied with the question "What is the real purpose of this experiment?"; and that when some striking aspect of the experimental situation was revealed to them (whether through further instructions from the experimenter or, often, through first encounter with the instrument designed to elicit dependent variable measures) this generated a flash of "insight" about what the experimenter was "really trying to find out about me." Though such "insights" are almost always incorrect they are of the sort that is capable of affecting the subject's further behavior in the experimental situation. The fact that such influence upon experimental responding has occurred is often the precise burden of the subject's remarks.

Thus, conversations with subjects, (and also with graduate students and colleagues as they muse upon their memories from undergraduate years when they were the recruited subjects rather than the recruiters) have helped to shape the basic conception of the evaluation apprehension process. Yet another contributing influence has been the fact that experienced experimental social psychologists seem to share a certain basic style when engaged in professional "yesbutism." What I mean is that when they suspect that someone else's data "are too neat—and the hypothesis can't be *that* true" their first line of reinterpretation is usually to suggest that something about the experimental instructions or manipulations probably "aroused" the subjects in some unintended way or direction. Who has not heard reinterpretations similar to these illustrative ones? "The instructions probably made the subjects in the experimental group quite anxious about how they would be accepted and that, rather than the attributions of expertise as such, would be enough to make them conform to the views of the other group members." Or: "By telling the subjects that prejudiced people are people who have repressed their hostility toward parents you are really making it necessary for them to show that the tolerance message influences them; it isn't 'insight' that accounts for the change, it's their need to get the psychologist's approval."

The penchant for this sort of reinterpretation in terms of self-presentation dilemmas is widespread. Is this simply because it is a normative style in our profession; or has it become so because it reflects a persisting social psychological reality in the conduct of psychological research? Obviously, I would suggest that the latter is the case.

But if observations and speculations of the sort that I have indicated have helped to suggest the evaluation apprehension view, they do not, of course, in any way serve to confirm it. Confirmation can only be accomplished through further research. Thus, one of the basic aims of the experimental program that I and my various colleagues have been conducting has been to demonstrate that evaluation apprehension, once aroused, can significantly influence dependent variable data. We have intended also to show that this influence often works not merely to increase "random error variance" but rather that it exerts *systematic* bias upon experimental responding; i.e., it "tilts" data distributions toward one or the other end of the response continuum and thus generates "significant" findings that happen also to be illusory ones.

We have had other purposes in mind as well—particularly to investigate the conditions under which evaluation apprehension is more or less likely to be aroused and, if aroused, more or less likely to induce systematic bias in dependent variable data.

I shall return to these matters later. Our first task is to review and discuss some "demonstration" studies. What they are intended to demonstrate is, simply, that when evaluation apprehension is aroused (and when it is coupled with the provision of cues that hint how the normal or "healthy" person would be likely to respond) this can induce systematic bias. Of course, it must be clearly understood that any demonstration that this can happen does not establish that it always or usually will happen. But there is no point in worrying about evaluation apprehension at all or in spending effort on trying to control and reduce it, unless we have first satisfied ourselves that it can actually be shown to exert biasing influence upon experimental responding.

II. DEMONSTRATION THROUGH ALTERED REPLICATION

There are at least two ways in which our basic point can be demonstrated. The one that will occupy us now is, in essence, a classic strategy. It is the one that is commonly employed when one suspects that the findings obtained in some reported "successful" experiment are in reality not due to the validity of the experimenter's hypothesis but to some unintended influence let loose by his poorly designed operations of manipulation or measurement. In this strategy one redesigns the suspected operations and repeats the experiment. If, despite the operational changes, the original findings are replicated one now has presumptive evidence that one's objections and doubts were ill taken; if meaningfully different, nonreplicative data are obtained, one has some claim (though it should not be over-indulged) to emit the prideful chortle: "I told you so" or "Thus do I refute Professor Berkeley."

How does this bear upon our intention to confirm, by empirical demonstration, that unsuspected arousal of evaluation apprehension does sometimes generate false confirmations of hypotheses? Obviously, when we suspect that this has happened, and where we have a speculative interpretation of how it happened, we may undertake an altered replication of the original study. The object would be to change those operations which we believe to have aroused evaluation apprehension and to have fostered the expectation that a certain way of responding would bring positive evaluation from the experimenter. If such an altered replication were to yield data that, as predicted, were quite different from the findings of the original study this could be taken as evidence that our original concern over evaluation apprehension was neither excessive nor misplaced. In effect, such an outcome would be a demonstration, through the construct validation method, that evaluation apprehension can generate systematic bias in experimental data—though, of course, a single successful instance would hardly stand as an incontrovertibly definitive demonstration.

The strategy that I have just described was the first one employed in the demonstration phase of our inquiry into the evaluation apprehension phenomenon. The substantive area of concern was research in support of a basic hypothesis derived from cognitive dissonance theory. Some early experiments—most notably those by Festinger and Carlsmith (1959) and Cohen (in Brehm and Cohen, 1962) had supposedly confirmed the hypothesized relationship: when counterattitudinal advocacy (i.e., arguing in support of an attitude position opposite to one's own true conviction) is undertaken with little justification (e.g. for a small monetary reward) this will induce more attitude change in the advocate than when counterattitudinal advocacy is undertaken with strong justification (e.g. for a comparatively large monetary reward).

However, as many observers (among them Chapanis and Chapanis, 1964; Brown, 1962) have pointed out, dissonance studies of this type confront the subjects (particularly those in "low dissonance" experimental groups) with startling and ambiguous experiences and conditions. Agreeing with Chapanis and Chapanis that a likely consequence will be the arousal of "suspicion," I thought it possible to be even more specific about the intervening, response-affecting, patterns of arousal that may occur with subjects in such studies. The particular case in point upon which we focussed was the well-known study by Cohen. In this experiment Yale undergraduates had been recruited to write essays in support of a position opposite to the one they actually held on a currently salient campus issue. The issue concerned "the actions of the New Haven police" in a recent campus riot. The undergraduates uniformly felt that the police had behaved badly. The essay they were requested to write was on the topic: "Why the actions of the New Haven police were justified."

Having appeared at randomly chosen dormitory rooms the experimenter requested the potential subject to write such an essay and as an inducement offered a financial reward of either $.50, $1.00, $5.00 or $10.00. After the essay had been completed the experimenter asked the subject to fill out an attitude measure indicating how much he approved or disapproved of "the actions of the New Haven police." As this measure was handed to him the subject was invited to take into account, if he so chose, the pro-police arguments he had just improvised in writing the counterattitudinal essay.

The prediction derived from dissonance theory was that the lesser magnitude of reward would generate a greater magnitude of dissonance and thus greater attitude change: i.e., an inverse monotonic relationship was expected between the amount of money offered to elicit the counterattitudinal advocacy and the degree of attitude change toward the pro-police position. This prediction was apparently confirmed; the $.50 reward group showed greatest attitude change in the pro-police direction, the $1.00 group next greatest change and the $5.00 and $10.00 reward groups did not differ from a control group which, without any prior counterattitudinal advocacy, had merely filled out an attitude scale concerning the question of whether "the actions of the New Haven police" were justified.

On the basis of attitude theory considerations that need not be reviewed here I thought that the opposite prediction made more sense: that the degree of attitude change would be a positive, rather than an inverse, function of the amount of monetary payment that was offered to elicit the counterattitudinal advocacy. Also it seemed likely to me that Cohen's results could be due to an unsuspected arousal of evaluation apprehension and a strong, but implicit, cueing which would have led most low dissonance (i.e. high reward) subjects to withhold evidence that they had influenced themselves in the pro-police direction.

Exactly what leads us toward this sort of interpretation of what really happened in this and similar early dissonance experiments on attitude change? The answer can best be conveyed by some extended quotations from the original article (Rosenberg, 1965) which posed the evaluation apprehension reinterpretation of the Cohen study and then went on to report the altered replication by which that reinterpretation was tested.

"It seems quite conceivable that in certain dissonance experiments the use of surprisingly large monetary rewards for eliciting counterattitudinal arguments may seem quite strange to the subject, may suggest that he is being treated disingenuously. This in turn is likely to confirm initial expectations that evaluation is somehow being undertaken. As a result the typical subject, once exposed to this manipulation, may be aroused to a comparatively high level of evaluation apprehension; and, guided by the figural fact that an excessive reward has been offered, he may be led to hypothesize that the experimental situation is one in which his autonomy, his honesty, his resoluteness in resisting a special kind of bribe, are being tested. Thus, given the patterning of their initial expectations and the routinized cultural meanings of some of the main features of the experimental situation, most low-dissonance subjects may come to reason somewhat as follows: 'they probably want to see whether getting paid so much will affect my own attitude, whether it will influence me, whether I am the kind of person whose views can be changed by buying him off.'

"The subject who has formulated such a subjective hypothesis about the real purpose of the experimental situation will be prone to resist giving evidence of attitude change: for to do so would, as he perceives it, convey something unattractive about himself, would lead to his being negatively evaluated by the experimenter. On the other hand, a similar hypothesis would be less likely to occur to the subject who is offered a smaller monetary reward and thus he would be less likely to resist giving evidence of attitude change."

On the basis of these speculative considerations I suggested, regarding Cohen's experiment, that

". . . in this study, as in others of similar design, the low-dissonance (high-reward) subjects would be more likely to suspect that the experimenter had some unrevealed purpose. The gross discrepancy between spending a few minutes writing an essay and the large sum offered, the fact that this large sum had not yet been delivered by the time the subject was handed the attitude questionnaire, the fact that he was virtually invited to show that he had become more positive toward the New Haven police: all these could have served to engender suspicion and thus to arouse evaluation apprehension and negative affect toward the experimenter. Either or both of these motivating states could probably be most efficiently reduced by the subject refusing to show anything but fairly strong disapproval of the New Haven police; for the subject who had come to believe that his autonomy in the face of a monetary lure was being assessed, remaining 'anti-police' would demonstrate that he *had* autonomy; for the subject who perceived an indirect and disingenuous attempt to change his attitude and felt some reactive anger, holding fast to his original attitude could appear to be a relevant way of frustrating the experimenter. Furthermore, with each *step* of increase in reward we could expect an increase in the proportion of subjects who had been brought to a motivating level of evaluation apprehension or affect arousal."

But such a reinterpretation is merely another instance of applied "wise-guyism" unless one attempts to put it to a close and demanding further experimental test. To properly employ the altered replication strategy that I have already described, it was necessary to remove the posited evaluation apprehension dynamic, or at least to subdue it, and otherwise to hew as closely as possible to the design and operations of the original study.

How might the first of these desiderata best be implemented? The reinterpretation in terms of evaluation apprehension had an obvious methodological implication. If the posited data biasing dynamic had actually occurred this had been made possible by the fact that the experimenter conducted both the dissonance arousal and subsequent attitude measurement. For evaluation apprehension and negative affect, if they had been aroused in the high reward subjects, would have been focused upon the experimenter; and it would have been either to avoid his negative evaluation or to frustrate him, or both, that the high reward subject would hold back (from the experimenter and possibly even from himself) any evidence that he had been influenced by the pro-police arguments that he had elaborated in the essay he had just completed.

Thus, quoting again from the original article (Rosenberg, 1965), these considerations led us toward the basic alteration employed in our replication:

"The most effective way then to eliminate the influence of the biasing factors would be to separate the dissonance arousal phase of the experiment from the attitude measurement phase. The experiment should be organized so that it appears to the subject to be two separate, unrelated studies, conducted by investigators who have little or no relationship with each other and who are pursuing different research interests. In such a situation the evaluation apprehension and negative affect that are focused upon the dissonance-arousing experimenter would probably be lessened and, more important, they would not govern the subject's responses to the attitude-measuring experimenter and to the information that he seeks from the subject."

We need not tarry here over the details of the staging of the two-experiment disguise. It will suffice to say that the disguise (judged by what the subjects said in quite probing postexperimental interviews) worked well, and that adaptations of it have since been used successfully both by others (e.g., Carlsmith, Collins, and Helmreich, 1966) and in my own continuing research program on attitude change (Rosenberg, 1968).

Nor do we have to linger over precise descriptions of the instructions and measurement procedures used with the subjects. Except for changes required by our use of the two-experiment disguise all but two aspects of the procedure were identical with those used by Cohen in the original experiment. The two deviations from the original experiment were necessitated by the fact that it was conducted at Yale University and the altered replication at Ohio State University. Thus in the second study Yale undergraduates did not serve as subjects and the issue for counter-attitudinal advocacy could not be the same one employed at Yale.

The issue that was used concerned the subjects' attitudes toward a proposed ban upon any further participation by the O.S.U. football team in the Rose Bowl contest. Such a ban had been enacted, and later rescinded, by the faculty senate during the previous year and extreme student opposition had been expressed through demonstrations and some riot-like group activity.

The experimental subjects wrote essays favoring the restoration of the Rose Bowl ban. The three experimental groups wrote the essays for promised rewards (delivered after completion of the essay) of $.50, $1.00 and $5.00 respectively. A control group merely took the dependent variable measure—a questionnaire on seven different campus issues, one of which was the Rose Bowl ban, while another dealt with the desirability of O.S.U. abandoning its policy of giving athletic scholarships.

On the Rose Bowl issue the Kruskal–Wallis one-way analysis of variance disclosed a significant relationship ($p < .001$) and inspection shows this to be of the positive, monotonic type: the larger the financial reward for counterattitudinal advocacy the greater the degree of attitude change (as estimated by comparison to the baseline attitude data provided by the control group). The \$.50 and \$1.00 groups showed greater favorability toward the Rose Bowl ban than did the control group ($p < .01$) and less favorability than the \$5.00 group ($p < .02$).*

A similar overall finding ($p < .005$) was obtained on the athletic scholarship issue, though the differences between the groups were of lesser (but still significant) magnitude. This finding was also predicted, and is interpreted as evidence of some generalization of the main attitude change effect to a related, antiathletic issue.

Avoiding the lure of another theoretical area I have so far said nothing about the substantive issues in this experiment. And I shall resist the temptation to do so now—except to note that the positive relationship obtained between degree of reward for counterattitudinal advocacy and degree of resultant attitude change confirms the prediction drawn from my own affective-cognitive consistency theory and disconfirms the prediction derived from dissonance theory. But these issues of attitude theory need not be examined here. They are fully treated in some of my earlier publications (Rosenberg 1956; 1960a; 1960b; 1968) and in a published debate between myself and Aronson, the latter writing as an advocate of a sophisticated, modified version of dissonance theory (Aronson, 1966; Rosenberg, 1966).

Before I turn away completely from the whirlpool of attitude theory around which I have been skirting, I should like to make clear that the controversy concerning counterattitudinal advocacy effects was not, by any means, fully resolved on the basis of this one study. Indeed, new issues have since been discovered in this by now middle-aged area of theoretical debate, experiment and counter-experiment. But the two-experiment disguise is now fairly standard in this particular research area. Also, the fact that under some conditions, at least, the "incentive" rather than the "dissonance" relationship does obtain is now credited

---

* The probabilities reported here as confirming the differences between the groups in this study are all based upon the one-tailed test. Throughout this chapter the same convention has been employed whenever the direction of a difference was predicted—though, as will be seen, most of the findings would easily retain their statistical significance even if the more stringent, but less appropriate, two-tailed standard were applied. Within the tables summarizing the statistical findings a designation of "N.S." (i.e., not significant) represents a probability value larger than .10, usually considerably larger.

by the main participants in the persisting debate, though they continue to disagree (see the contributions of Janis, Carlsmith, Collins, Aronson, and Rosenberg in Abelson, *et al.*, 1968) about the nature and provenance of those conditions.

Of greater pertinence at the moment are two points that have nothing to do with counterattitudinal advocacy as such, though they are grounded upon the Rose Bowl counterattitudinal advocacy study. The results of the altered replication can be taken as at least an indirect demonstration of the possibility that evaluation apprehension is capable of inducing systematic bias in experimental responding, and thus of generating undetected Type I or Type II errors (in the sense of invalid confirmations and disconfirmations of hypotheses). The second point is that such bias effects need not remain undetected, nor need they be left in the realm of the merely suspected. Variations of the altered replication strategy could probably be designed in most instances where an evaluation apprehension artifact is suspected to have induced systematic bias in the array of dependent variable data.

Inventiveness and care in the design of altered replications, and a readiness to resort to them frequently could probably do much to improve the reliability of the data that experimental psychologists collect to test hypotheses and in reaction to which they often develop new hypotheses.

Evaluation apprehension is by no means the only conceivable source of systematic biasing of data, nor is it an equally threatening possibility in all realms of psychological research. But whenever our experiments are heavy on surprise and whenever the experimenter's purposes are likely to seem mysterious to subjects (or whenever subjects are likely to sense disingenuousness in the experimenter's explanatory communication) we would do well to adopt the cautionary stance of obsessive concern over the evaluation apprehension problem. And having adopted this stance, we would do well to go beyond mere obsession or mere disputatiousness and get back to the laboratory where we can put our suspicions to test by conducting the relevantly redesigned altered replications.

Anyone who resorts to this strategy, however, had better be prepared to find himself at the receiving end of the ironic justice process. For the criticized and their partisans can reverse the tactic on the aspiring critic. An altered replication designed to remove a suspected evaluation apprehension contaminant from some previously reported experiment can, in itself, be interpreted as having been contaminated by evaluation apprehension or by some other biasing force (e.g. experimenter expectancy, demand characteristics, subject presensitization).

The mind reels, and one's strength does quaver a bit, at the conceivable prospect of an infinite regress in which a study is designed to take systematic bias out of a study that was designed to take systematic bias out of a study that was . . . but in all likelihood, even fully consensual devotion to the expunging of evaluation apprehension effects will stop far short of such total, unlimited doubt. At some point it should become clear that particular experimental paradigms and particular substantive areas of experimental inquiry have been pretty thoroughly "debugged." And meanwhile, whatever temporary disruption, confusion, and outraged pride may result, the ultimate outcome can be trusted to be beneficial—not only in that it will probably elevate the trustworthiness of data in the contested area, but also because there is nothing more restorative of the scientific temper than an occasional encounter with the hard, intractable fact that one has made, and remains capable of making, mistakes.

III. DEMONSTRATION THROUGH MANIPULATED
AROUSAL AND CUEING

The construct validation strategy, useful as it has been in theory testing generally and in our own research program, is really a version of the Platonic analogy of the cave. The shadows that are projected across the wall (i.e. our data) denote that something is passing between us and the sun—but we are still tantalizingly out of direct contact with its substance.

Thus, the foregoing study, and others of similar design, though they seem to confirm the reality of the evaluation apprehension dynamic, do not bring us into direct contact with it. To look more closely at that process it appeared necessary to *arouse* it, rather than reduce it as was done in the Rose Bowl study.

My first effort in this direction was undertaken in an experiment in which I had valuable collaboration from Dr. Raymond Mulry who was, at that time, one of my graduate students. Our working plan was simple, perhaps even crude.

Through a printed "Background Information Sheet" we conveyed to two separate experimental groups the following points: They were about to participate in a study of social perception, in which they were to judge how much they liked or disliked various pictured persons. Past research by others, they were informed, had shown that liking-disliking reactions to strangers were correlated with personality, particularly with whether the rater was psychologically "mature" or "immature." To one experimental group it was disclosed further that the main burden of the past research (various invented journal articles were cited) was that psychologically mature and healthy people show greater liking for strangers than do immature people. To a second experimental group the printed communication conveyed the opposite: past research had shown that it was psychologically immature and comparatively unhealthy persons who showed greater liking for strangers.

Beyond this crucial point of difference the two forms of the manipulative communication again converged. All of the past research, it was asserted, had been done with subjects in face-to-face contact with real strangers. Would the same relationship between psychological maturity and liking hold for mere photographs of unknown people? This, the subjects were told, was a question that we planned to pursue in further research. But first it was necessary to "standardize" a set of photographs; to determine how much, on the average, they elicited liking or disliking reactions. Thus, in the present study, according to the concluding paragraph of the Background Information Sheet, we were not testing the personalities of our subjects; rather, we were simply establishing normative data against which we would later compare the liking-disliking ratings elicited from subjects whose personality qualities had already been assessed.

The simplicity and directness of this manipulation make clear its intended purpose. We were attempting to arouse evaluation apprehension by confirming, for our subjects, the sort of expectancy that subjects often bring to experiments; namely, in the present instance, that as researchers we were ordinarily interested, among other things, in personality assessment. And furthermore we were cueing our subjects about what past research had shown (and thus about the likely content of our own expectations) concerning the ways in which "mature" and "immature" people tended to react to strangers. Why did we add that we had no idea whether the same relationship would hold with pictures as with reactions to directly encountered real persons? Partly to enhance the general credibility of our communication and partly to reduce what might otherwise be a too overwhelming influence upon the individual's judgments of the pictures. Also this made the present study somewhat more comparable to many others in which the common strategy (whatever has gone before) is to provide overt reassurance that the subjects' personalities are not being scrutinized.

Apart from the two experimental groups (both aroused to evaluation apprehension and cued either toward liking or disliking responses respectively) we also set up a control group. These subjects received a brief neutral communication which did nothing to arouse evaluation apprehension or to provide directional cueing. The data from this group served, then, as the baseline against which we could assess the significance of the deflections, toward the liking and disliking ends of the scale, of the experimental subjects' self-reported judgments.

I have already suggested that the Rose Bowl, altered replication study could be interpreted as providing indirect evidence that evaluation apprehension can contaminate experimental data but not that it always or usually will. The same stricture is all the more applicable in limiting the meaning of the present study. Only a failure to find significant differences between the mean liking ratings of the three groups could be taken as definitive; for this would mean that, even under optimum conditions, evaluation apprehension does not get aroused or, if aroused, does not affect experimental data.

But if significant differences were obtained just what would they tell us? Merely that the data biasing dynamic that we suspect to be unintentionally induced in certain kinds of experiments can be intentionally induced by rather direct manipulation. In essence, then, we were giving ourselves a chance to increase the pertinence of the null hypothesis or provisionally to reject it.

If the data seemed to allow the latter (i.e. if they showed that, at least by intentional amplification, evaluation apprehension can be made to affect experimental responding) we would also be in a position to carry out inquiry a few steps further. We would then be able to ask what kinds of people, situational definitions, and experimental tasks tend to facilitate or diminish the operation of the process in which data are systematically biased under the influence of evaluation apprehension.

These foregoing considerations set the context in which we can now proceed to discuss the findings of the first evaluation apprehension manipulative study; and they are equally relevant to the various other studies that followed it and employed the same basic design paradigm. Obviously I would have no claim to write this chapter if the results of this first study, and of the others that followed upon it, had failed to render the null hypothesis improbable. Thus there will be little surprise in the disclosure that in the first of these studies a large and significant difference was obtained between the two experimental groups.

For the 12 pictures of male faces (each rated on a 21 point like-dislike scale ranging from $+10$ to -10) the algebraic sums of each subject's judgments were computed. The means of these scores for separate groups of male and female subjects and the probabilities of the differences between various pairs of means, are displayed in Table I.

For male subjects in the experimental group that was cued to think that mature people like strangers the mean algebraic sum of the ratings

TABLE I

L<small>IKE</small>-D<small>ISLIKE</small> M<small>EAN</small> S<small>UMS</small> <small>FOR</small> G<small>ROUPS</small>; <small>AND</small> P<small>ROBABILITIES</small> <small>OF</small>
D<small>IFFERENCES</small> B<small>ETWEEN</small> G<small>ROUPS</small>

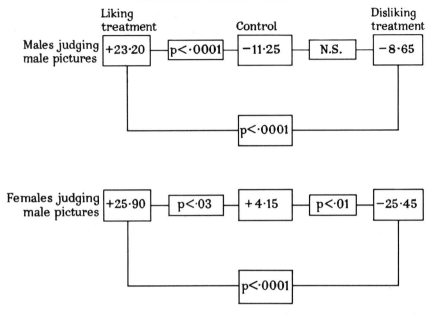

was +23.20. For the male subjects cued to think that immature people show greater liking for strangers the mean algebraic sum was —8.65. The significance of the difference between these groups (computed by the Mann–Whitney Rank Sum statistic, as are most of the other simple differences between groups that are reported in this chapter) was clearly established ($p < .0001$).

However, as reference to Table I makes clear, we also encountered an interesting complication. The disliking treatment did not, in fact, exert a significant influence upon the male subjects who received it. This is apparent from the fact that the picture ratings from the un-manipulated control group are, on the average, just as negative (the mean is —11.25) as those from the disliking group and, of course, there is no significant difference between these groups.

Does this signify that the disliking cueing that we employed was simply not credible? Or that, though credible, subjects could not bring themselves to behave in opposition to the normative standard (at least with typical middle-class Americans) that whatever our private disposition may be, strangers are to be approached with external affability?

Either of these interpretations would be plausible if it were not for various other available findings. The most striking is that with the separate groups of female subjects (judging pictures of males, it should be remembered) the disliking treatment does influence the picture ratings and they are as deviant from the control mean in the negative direction ($p < .01$) as the mean for the liking treatment is in the positive direction ($p < .03$).

Furthermore, even with the male subjects, there is evidence suggesting that a personality-linked variable has mediated the influence of the disliking treatment. For all subjects we had available their scores on the Marlowe–Crowne (1961) Social Desirability (SD) Scale which had been administered sometime before the present experiment was conducted. When the male subjects are split into high and low halves on the Social Desirability Scale distribution we find that a trend in the predicted direction is visible between the High SD subjects in the control and disliking groups respectively. But with the Low SD subjects that trend is reversed and approaches significance ($p < .10$) in the counterhypothesis direction. If the latter group had shown a trend no stronger than that obtained from the former the overall finding would have supported the predicted relationship at an acceptable level of statistical significance. Thus it is the Low SD males who, needing less approval from others (and, we may assume, from the experimenter) are not willing to respond against the normative grain and win a judgment of normality by representing themselves as disliking certain strangers more than they otherwise would.

There is a glimmer of a paradox in these last data; for generally one would expect people with a high need for approval (the High SD scorers) also to show a more persisting proclivity for representing themselves as positively disposed toward random others. In fact, passing beyond the data from the disliking condition, we find that the social desirability factor did exert the expected influence within the experimental group that was cued to believe that liking strangers is a sign of maturity. The High SD male subjects in that condition give more extreme liking scores (the mean sum of their picture ratings is $+34.77$) than do the comparable Low SD subjects (whose mean score is $+13.72$). The difference between these groups is significant ($p < .03$).

Despite the few tantalizing ambiguities that I have discussed above, the overall import of this first manipulative study seemed quite clear; with intentional arousal of evaluation apprehension the subsequent directional cueing does "take"—that is, it influences the subjects' experimental responding. Postexperimental inquiry indicated to our tentative satisfaction that these results were not due to any easy comprehension of our unrevealed purposes. The subjects usually insisted that the preliminary material that they read concerning "earlier studies" on reactions to strangers had not particularly influenced them. I do not take these reports as veridical; but neither do I think that they are due to a simple intention to deceive the experimenter. From interviewing conducted after data collection in this study and others I have formed the impression that subjects will usually obscure from themselves the extent to which they regulate their responding so as to win favorable judgments from the experimenter. And though I cannot anchor the following judgment on a base of hard data I would hazard the psychologically obvious interpretation that this sort of motivated inattention is due to the typical subject's need to conserve a positive image of himself even as he half-knowingly seeks to make a positive impression upon the experimenter.

Upon completion of this first demonstration study it would have been possible to plunge directly into studies concerned with variables that facilitate or suppress the evaluation apprehension-data biasing process. But the rating of pictures for their likeability is a rather special sort of task and, as we have seen, certain complications did arise on the dislike cueing side of the experiment. To satisfy ourselves that the process under study was a fairly general one, it seemed necessary to adapt the basic experimental paradigm to some other and quite different sorts of experimental tasks.

Two further studies of this type were successfully carried out with male undergraduate subjects at Dartmouth College. I shall describe them somewhat more briefly than the preceding study, since they are useful here only in adding some empirical weight to an assertion that I have already registered more than once: i.e. that evaluation apprehension combined with some hints about how "normal people" react (and thus implying something about how the experimenter's approval can be obtained) does exert systematic biasing influence upon experimental responding.

In one of these additional studies I was joined by two coinvestigators, Philip Corsi (who developed the basic experimental design and operations) and Edward Holmes, both of whom were advanced undergraduate students in the Psychology Department of Dartmouth College. We used an extremely simple task: the subject taps upon a key with his right and left index fingers for six separate ten-second intervals, half of these with one finger and half with the other. The number of taps is automatically registered on a Veeder Root meter. Normally there is a considerable discrepancy between the performance of the two fingers, the index finger of the dominant hand producing more taps than that of the nondominant hand.

As the subject entered the experimental room he was asked by the experimenter: "Did you take the general abilities test and the personality inventory during freshman week?" The purpose of this query was to stir some initial prompting toward evaluation apprehension.

Following the administration of three brief abilities tests focused on verbal and symbolic skills (and intended to rouse the subjects' interest in their performances) the experimenter proceeded to give a memorized, verbal explanation of the finger-tapping task. For the control subjects (eleven right handed undergraduates) this consisted only of a simple description of the task. Working with only this information these subjects did, indeed, produce more taps with their right than with their left index fingers. The mean difference between the sum of right index taps minus the sum of left index taps was 22.45 for this group.

With an experimental group of the same number of right handed subjects the preliminary communication contained some additional information designed to heighten evaluation apprehension and to turn it in a particular response direction. Thus they were told that recent research with graduate students at Yale and at the University of Michigan had turned up the surprising finding that the number of taps with the nondominant index finger was virtually equal to the number with the dominant index finger. The clear implication was that people with higher intelligence (or perhaps of higher educational attainment) performed differently than did other, more ordinary, persons.

The result was striking. The mean difference between the sums of right and left index finger taps was only 10.73 and this was quite significantly ($p < .005$) different from the comparable score of 22.45 obtained with the control group. A clear hint about the relation between performance on the experimental task and the likely evaluation that the experimenter would draw from the subject's performance had produced a "transcendence effect." The experimental subjects performed far more efficiently with the left index finger than subjects (both our own control subjects and those in many other studies) ordinarily do.

One further finding from this study is of particular interest. The control and experimental data just described were obtained under a "full feedback" condition; that is, the meter registering the cumulative number of taps was visible to each subject as he went through the separate right and left finger tapping trials. But on six other trials with these same subjects we used a "partial feedback" condition in which the meter was exposed only after the ten-second tapping interval had been completed. (For half of the subjects the partial feedback trials, and for the other half the full feedback trials, were run first.) Under the partial feedback condition the same sort of difference is obtained between the experimental and control groups but it is of lesser magnitude ($p < .03$) and the difference between the means for the two groups is correspondingly smaller. It seems clear, then, that the continuous availability of information about the quality of his performance will assist the subject in guiding that performance in the direction that he expects will bring him a favorable evaluation.

A more ambitious study was undertaken at the same time. This one followed our original experimental paradigm (as used in the picture-rating study) in all its basic details, except for using a quite different sort of experimental task.

In two basic experimental conditions and in a separate control condition the subjects (20 in each group) worked with a booklet of addition problems, each page of which had the same number of total digits. The booklet was far too lengthy for completion and the subject was free to stop whenever he chose to do so. Each fourth page in the booklet presented some scales from the Nowlis (1965) Mood Adjective Check List which the subject was to fill out before he went on to the next page of addition problems.

Again the experiment began with the subject reading a Background Information Sheet. This document, modeled after the one used in the original picture rating study, explained that past research by other investigators had revealed a relationship between personality competence and the amount of efficiency shown, and pleasure experienced, in executing dull, routine tasks. One form of the information sheet went on to report that the clear finding from many studies (again fictional citations were given) was that the mature, psychologically healthy person experienced more pleasure and was more efficient at such tasks than was the immature person.

There followed a paragraph explaining the probable psychological basis of this finding (i.e. emotionally healthy people are less prone to distraction and enjoy challenges more than emotionally handicapped persons). The text then went on to explain that all of the previous studies had dealt with "motoric and manual" tasks and there was no proof that the same relationship would hold true with clerical or other "paper and pencil" tasks. This, it was explained, was the question that would be addressed in later research that the experimenters planned, but first it was necessary to develop a standard task and to determine what the typical levels of performance would be. Thus the subject was about to participate in a pilot study focused not upon his personality but rather upon determining average performance levels for various kinds of clerical tasks—and at present the task whose utility was to be explored was arithmetic addition.

The content of the Background Information Sheet used with the other experimental group was, of course, exactly parallel in form but opposite in content. It reported that past data with routine motoric performances had shown that psychologically healthy and mature persons were less efficient at carrying out such tasks and got less pleasure from them than did psychologically immature persons. Again a brief psychological explanation of the basis for this finding was offered and this was followed by exactly the same further comments that were used with the first version of the manipulative communication.

Obviously this manipulation, just as the one used in the picture rating study, was likely to exert a strong force toward arousal of evaluation apprehension and at the same time would provide unambiguous cues that could be used to regulate experimental responding so as to maximize the chance that one would be judged "normal" by the psychological experimenter. However, despite the directness of the manipulation, post-experimental questionnaires and postexperimental interviewing with a sample of the subjects revealed little acknowledged penetration of the purpose of the experiment. Subjects did show accurate recall for the content of the Background Information Sheet but usually they insisted that they did not feel that their personalities were being scrutinized; instead, they reported that they had simply worked on the problems until they got bored or fatigued.

But, though evaluation apprehension or concern for performing in the "normal" way typically was not acknowledged to the interviewer (and, possibly, not fully acknowledged to the self) it did clearly influence the actual performances of the subjects on the arithmetic addition task.

That this is the case is clear from the findings presented in Table II. The means reported there are from the two experimental groups. The table also displays means from a control group whose members worked on the addition problems without any previous arousal of evaluation apprehension, thus establishing the baseline performance levels against which the experimental groups can be judged.

It is clear that the two experimental groups differ from one another in the predicted direction. On the average, the subjects who were led to believe that mature people tend to be comparatively dysphoric and inept toward routine tasks completed ten less addition problems than did the opposite experimental group ($p < .03$). Similarly, they correctly solved eleven fewer problems than did the other experimental group ($p < .003$).

However, examination of Table II will quickly suggest that the treatment emphasizing that mature people do not perform well on dull tasks was a far stronger influence upon the performance than was the opposite treatment. While the former experimental group differs significantly from the control group on both the number of problems completed and the

TABLE II

PERFORMANCE MEANS FOR GROUPS; AND PROBABILITIES OF
DIFFERENCES BETWEEN GROUPS

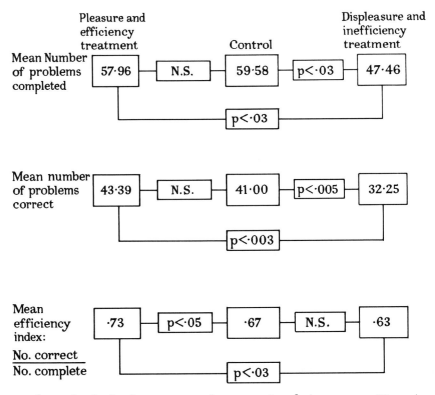

number solved, the latter group does not. An obvious proposition virtually suggests itself and it is one that may well deserve an important place in the general theory of evaluation apprehension processes that is emerging as we pursue our experimental program. Simply stated it is this: cues suggesting a response pattern that is likely to bring approval from the experimenter will have stronger influence upon actual responding when that pattern is also less effortful in execution.

There is, of course, an alternative interpretation that is quite plausible in the present instance: the "displeasure and inefficiency" version of the Background Information Sheet may simply have been more credible, more in accord with the initial expectations of the subjects. After all it does seem likely, at a common sense level, that only "odd" people will enjoy routine, repetitive tasks. But this interpretation is weakened by the fact that, by a somewhat subtler analysis, we find that the subjects in the opposite experimental group were also influenced in their performances on the addition task. Apart from comparing the groups on the total number of problems completed and correctly completed we went on to compute for each subject an index based upon the ratio between these two separate scores. Dividing the number of problems correctly solved by the number completed we obtain a meaningful estimate of the quality of the subject's performance in relation to the scope of that performance.

As Table II shows, on this index the experimental groups are again significantly different ($p < .03$) from one another in the predicted direction. However in this instance the group cued to the expectation that mature people perform poorly does not differ from the control group. Though they are completing fewer problems, the percent of these that are correctly completed is the same as with the control group. But the opposite experimental group does differ from the control group. On the average the subjects in this experimental group complete a few less problems and solve a few more. In consequence the difference between the control group and the "pleasure and efficiency" cued group attains significance ($p < .05$). Clearly these experimental subjects have been putting somewhat more effort into the task; they have been concentrating more closely on the truly tiresome task of adding columns of digits, and in consequence they have attained somewhat greater accuracy.

Equally interesting and meaningful in the light of the finding just reported, are some additional findings obtained with the Mood Adjective Check List.

Avoiding the task of describing the scoring or analytical procedures, I shall content myself here with simply reporting that on some of the subscales of this instrument we find the experimental groups differing either significantly or at borderline levels from one another and, in some instances, from the control group as well. The subjects in the group cued to think that normal people enjoy routine tasks characterize themselves as feeling less dysphoric while doing the addition problems than those cued to think that normal people do not enjoy them. And these characterizations tend to persist across the various intervals (every fourth page in the addition problem booklet) at which the subjects were required to report upon their mood states.

I have reviewed three manipulative studies each of which successfully demonstrated our basic point: that systematic bias in experimental responding can be produced through the arousal of evaluation apprehension and the cueing of particular response patterns as likely to foster positive evaluation.

However, two defects of this group of studies are apparent and they should be noted here. The first is, simply, that they do not cover as broad a range of experimental tasks as could be desired. Suspecting that virtually any type of experimental performance could be systematically biased by the evaluation apprehension process, we might well have gone on to similar studies in such diverse areas as conditioning and other learning phenomena, psychophysical judgment, impression formation, concept formation, and many other areas. Particularly I should have liked to test the proposition that the degree of attitude change shown by subjects (in their responses to questionnaires administered after a persuasive communication has been received) will be influenced by the prior suggestion that attitude change reflects a mature quality of "openmindedness" or an immature quality of "inconstancy."

Further work along some of these lines is planned. But, happily, the task of demonstrating the broad relevance of evaluation apprehension as a data biasing process has now been taken up by some other investigators. By rather different experimental techniques than those that I have employed, Silverman (1968; Silverman and Regula, 1968) has been providing some evidence that could be easily fitted to the general picture developed here. And Sigall, Aronson, and Van Hoose (1968) have recently reported a study in which subjects are exposed to evaluation apprehension cueing and also to the "demand characteristic" of the experimenter's expectancy about their performances, the latter ostensibly based upon the scientific hypothesis he is testing. With subjects for whom both forces converge, suggesting that a certain mode of responding will prove the experimenter's hypothesis and also make the subject appear a competent and adequate personality, strong influence on experimental responding is obtained. With another group of subjects these forces are made to diverge, so that the subject must violate the experimenter's hypothesis if, as he sees it, he is to appear competent and psychologically adequate. The typical subject yields to the latter rather than the former force. Thus, even with a strong demand characteristic opposing it, the evaluation apprehension dynamic is found to exert a statistically significant influence upon the experimental responding of the subjects.

Interesting and heartening as such studies are, much more experimental exploration will be required before we can take as established the claim that the systematic biasing of data through the evaluation apprehension dynamic is a *general* phenomenon, one that can be made to occur over the vast range of response dimensions with which modern experimental psychology is concerned. My expectation is that such a program of "parametric" exploratory studies would in fact reveal considerable generality of this sort. At the same time it would probably disclose that certain types of experimental responding are more prone, and others more resistant, to this type of systematic biasing. Indeed, I think it likely that one would also find that, within a given behaviorial realm, certain directions of responding are more easily affected by evaluation apprehension pressures than are others. This has already become apparent through our discoveries that liking of strangers or inefficient performance on routine tasks are more readily inducible response patterns than are their opposites.

A momentary lapse into unrestrained programmatic fantasy (an easy indulgence if one puts aside the fact that someone must actually undertake the vast labors that are contemplated) suggests the desirability of constructing, through empirical techniques, a sort of evaluation apprehension atlas of response dimensions. The hundreds of types of elicited behaviors which now serve as dependent variables in psychological research could be separately submitted to evaluation apprehension cueing of the sort employed in our demonstration experiments. The degree of influenceability of each particular response pattern (and of separate response directions) could then be assessed. Ideally, this would need to be done with systematic variation in types of subjects, types of evaluation apprehension arousal, and types of directional cueing. The result would probably have high payoff in terms of increasing our ability to do uncontaminated, bias-free research—or at least to come closer in approaching that utopian state of affairs.

I said earlier that I perceive two main defects in the group of demonstration studies described here. The first, as discussed above, can be handled only by doing more demonstration (and parametric exploration) studies over the broad range of common dependent variables employed in psychological research. The second defect is one that bears upon the *way* in which such further studies might be conducted. What I have in mind is the fact that in all of the foregoing studies the manipulation had two separate components: evaluation apprehension was aroused or heightened by our telling the subjects, in a fairly direct way, that the responses they were about to make would have some revelatory significance concerning their own personalities; then, in a separate and subsequent portion of the communication, some hints (usually rather strong ones) were given concerning the response differences that might be expected as between normal and abnormal or "mature" and "immature" persons.

Are both portions of the induction required? For that matter, can subtler inductions be used without the loss of the systematic bias effects? These questions point up a basic limit in the group of demonstration studies so far reviewed: namely, that they have not featured enough cross experiment systematic variation in ways of inducing evaluation apprehension. When such variation is attempted what are we likely to find? Both through speculative rumination and also in the light of some of the data from additional studies that I shall shortly discuss, I am willing to hazard some informed guesses. The first is that the evaluation apprehension biasing effect does not depend upon providing the subjects with an initial statement defining the experimenter as one who is interested in the study of personality or who is otherwise sensitive to the personality revealing implications of the data he is collecting. When this is done it probably does boost the data biasing process, but the same sort of process is likely to be set in motion merely by providing some cues suggesting that one mode of responding as compared to another is more "normal" or "competent" or "mature." The latter strategy was the one employed by Sigall, Aronson, and Van Hoose (1968) and it was sufficient to induce significant systematic bias.

However, what of the situation in which no direct cueing toward the "normal" pattern of response is provided? Surely this is the typical state of affairs in experiments in which evaluation apprehension is an inadvertent rather than an intended influence upon subjects' responding. Theoretical analysis has rather persuaded me (and some studies, reported later, on the mediation of the experimenter expectancy effect have turned persuasion toward conviction) of this basic point: arousing the subject to the general expectancy that his personality competence will be available for judgment by the psychological experimenter sets him examining salient aspects of the situation for what they might reveal about "the way a normal person would respond." In other words, when a general state of evaluation apprehension has been aroused by intention (as we attempt to do with the first portion of the Background Information Sheet communication) or unintentionally, direct cueing of the normality-revealing behavioral model is not required. Subtler hints will be picked up and private hypotheses will be formulated by the subjects—and, to the extent that the separate subjects attend to the same hints and draw the same interpretations, systematic biasing of response data will be likely to occur. An implied methodological corrective is lurking in these last comments. Though I shall return to it at a later point it deserves bold preliminary iteration here: techniques for reducing any stirrings of evaluation apprehension that subjects bring into an experimental situation, for disconfirming any initial concern that their psychological adequacy or inadequacy will be open to judgment, are bound to improve the trustworthiness of the data collected in that experiment.

In setting the stage for the foregoing discussion of the limits of our manipulation techniques I asked: can subtler inductions be used without loss of the systematic bias effects? By "subtler" I mean communications which do the work of our Background Information Sheet (i.e. arousing general evaluation apprehension, or cueing the subject in a particular response direction, or both) far less explicitly, with more "natural" indirectness. I am fairly sure that the answer is yes—that such subtler manipulation will induce systematic bias in experimental responding. To this purpose, a number of further demonstration studies have been planned, but not yet executed. If their results are successful they will give us a stronger empirical basis than we have yet established, for the claim that the evaluation apprehension dynamic does often operate where it is usually unsuspected: e.g. in experiments undertaken to test substantive issues and hypotheses relevant to important matters of psychological theory. But, if this point is not yet fully established through our demonstration efforts I must, nevertheless, confess that the studies we have already completed (both those described above and those that follow in the next sections) have considerably strengthened my own original suspicion, namely: Evaluation apprehension does contaminate a fair portion of the experimental work now being conducted over the broad range from social psychology to psychophysics.

To be sure, as I make this declaration I am mindful of various limiting considerations: some of my readers will certainly think it a considerable leap beyond the data—and they are right; but scientific inquiry, like other more muscular pursuits, is advanced by the judicious use of audacity. Also I am mindful that this sort of *j'accuse*, as it concerns any experiment in which one suspects that evaluation apprehension has distorted the data, cannot be sustained by a hundred, let alone three, demonstration experiments; instead the logic of inquiry forces us back to the necessity for undertaking carefully designed altered replication studies.

However, the more we can learn about evaluation apprehension through intentionally arousing it, the better equipped we will be to search it out and bring it to heel through the altered replication strategy. Thus, in further research I and my colleagues have gone on creating evaluation apprehension and expanding our inquiry to encompass subsidiary variables which may work to heighten or reduce its influence upon experimental responding. I shall now turn to a review and discussion of some of these further studies.

IV. VARIABLES INFLUENCING THE EVALUATION APPREHENSION PROCESS

Though all of our original demonstration studies showed clear main effects, there was a fair degree of intersubject variance within, as well as between, conditions. This suggested that uncontrolled factors relating to the subjects' personalities, their sensitivities to aspects of the situation, and their patterns of past experience as subjects might be affecting how much evaluation apprehension they felt and how they were acting to reduce it.

Clearly a host of variables might be found to influence the evaluation apprehension data biasing process—and the direction of such influence might be either to facilitate or subdue the overall operation of the process. I found it useful to conceive such "booster" and "suppressor" variables as falling into five major categories. They could be: personality attributes (or overall personality patterns) of the subject; aspects of the subject's recent, preexperimental experience; aspects or attributes of the experimenter; or of the experimental setting; or of the experimental task. We need not think of this taxonomy as the most logical of all possible ones, nor need we assert that it would incorporate all relevant variables. Its main value was, simply, that it was enough to get us started.

But we are just *barely* started on this line of inquiry. While many relevant variables are easily conceivable, only four major ones have been investigated in specific experiments. The results which I shall shortly present have been quite informative both in confirming our initial hypotheses and also, in two of these studies, by disclosing certain more complex interactions which have, in turn, suggested some new lines of theoretical speculation.

The four variables upon which this work has so far focused are: the need for approval as an attribute of personality, the salience of the "clinical" orientation as an attribute of the experimenter or of the experimental setting, the experimenter's "gate-keeper" power over the subject, and the ambiguity of the experimental stimulus materials.

I have already reported that the need for approval (as indexed by scores on the Social Desirability Scale) seemed to play a response affecting role in the first of our demonstration studies. The same appeared to be true in the study reported above in which "efficient" and "inefficient" performance on routine addition problems were separately cued as reflecting personality competence. In this instance we found that under the cueing treatment suggesting that bored and inefficient performance on routine tasks is a correlate of "maturity," subjects with high (upper 50 per cent) Social Desirability scores did not differ from the control group. However those with low Social Desirability scores completed and correctly solved significantly fewer problems. This finding though unexpected is a meaningful one, in the sense that hindsight suggests some hypotheses that deserve further experimental testing: perhaps those with strong approval need have in the past been more concerned with (and, thus, more rewarded for) seeking social acceptance through overt display of competence; or perhaps, because of their greater general concern with techniques of ingratiation, they find the cueing communication less credible than do the subjects who are comparatively low in the need for social approval.

The personality attribute of need for approval, as indexed by SD scores, was studied within the context of our original demonstration studies. Our more directly focused work on booster and suppressor effects began with two studies dealing with another variable: the definition of the experimenter or the experimental situation as high or comparatively low in clinical interest. In effect this can be viewed as a simple "additive" variable: i.e., another direct force making for evaluation apprehension in the subject and thus, in our typical experimental situation, adding to the weight of forces that have already served to create that motivating state.

In the first of our studies on the clinical interest variable, the same sort of Background Information Sheet that was used in our earlier studies was read by all experimental subjects. Once again its first portion was designed to rouse general evaluation apprehension while its second portion conveyed the clear hint for one group that mature people are comparatively high, on liking for strangers, and for the other group, on disliking for strangers. Control subjects received no such preliminary communication. So far this study is essentially a replication of our original demonstration experiment. The additional variable was introduced through a few memorized sentences which the experimenter addressed to the subject.

The experimenters (senior students in an advanced experimental psychology course at Dartmouth College) each ran six subjects: two who had received the liking cueing, two the disliking cueing, and two control subjects. To one subject from each of these three categories the experimenter represented himself as having a "clinical" orientation. He did this by saying, just before presenting the instructions for the picture rating task, that he was quite fascinated by the experiment as, indeed, he was by psychology generally. "I guess," he continued, "that's because I'm always thinking about what makes people tick. That's why I'm hoping to go into psychiatry after I finish medical school."

In the opposite "nonclinical" role that he played with his three other subjects each experimenter said that he did not particularly see the importance of the present experiment. He continued: "For that matter I'm not sure what I'm doing in this course but they said, at the School of Engineering, that I had to take it."

The purpose of this manipulation was, then, simply to convey that the experimenter either had or lacked interest in understanding and judging the personalities of others. At the same time, for the "clinical" role, it was clear that the experimenter was not yet professionally trained or skilled in this direction. As he alternated between these two roles the experimenter ran his subjects without any knowledge of whether they were in the control group or in the groups that had been respectively cued to the suggestion that liking or disliking for strangers was characteristic of psychologically mature persons.

One hundred and fifty subjects gave their liking-disliking ratings for 15 photographs of male faces and the data from 130 of these were analyzed. (The data from the 20 other subjects were discarded because postexperimental questionnaire data showed that they had not understood or retained the content of the like-dislike portion of the communication.)

The data clearly indicate that the definition of the experimenter as either having or lacking a clinical orientation does, as predicted, have some influence upon the amount of systematically biased responding by the subjects. Under both the clinical and nonclinical experimenter conditions the control subjects (who received neither evaluation apprehension arousal nor directional cueing) lean toward an overall liking response pattern; and there is no difference between the mean algebraic sums of the ratings for the control subjects run by clinical and nonclinical experimenters. For the former the mean of the algebraic sums is +25.20 and for the latter +23.00. In the clinical experimenter condition the subjects who received the "disliking is mature" cueing have a mean sum of +.13 while under the nonclinical experimenter condition the mean sum is +5.80. Apparently somewhat greater deflections away from the control group basal levels are occurring under the clinical condition. However in both instances the differences from the relevant control groups are quite significant ($p < .00005$ and $p < .0003$, respectively).

A more clear-cut booster effect is obtained with the subjects who received the "liking is mature" cueing. The subgroup run by nonclinical experimenters has a mean sum of +20.80; and this is not significantly different from the mean for the nonclinical, control group. However, the liking subgroup run by clinical experimenters shows a mean of +39.12. This differs significantly both from the means of the clinical control group ($p < .01$) and the nonclinical, liking-cued group ($p < .003$).

The following conclusions seem reasonable: In this subject population there was some tendency, as indicated by the control group data, to give moderately positive judgments of the pictured persons. Thus, for the liking-cued groups, the information that liking of strangers is a sign of maturity was congruent with their initial response disposition. But the identification of the experimenter as having a special interest in "what makes people tick" and in "psychiatry" operated to raise the stakes for the subjects run by the clinical experimenter. To guarantee the winning of a positive evaluation from him the typical subject in this group strives to give extreme, and thus unambiguous, proof that he possesses the defined hallmark of the mature, psychologically healthy person.

These are, then, unexceptional data. They seem to confirm the obvious and predicted relationship between the aroused strength of evaluation apprehension (the clinical definition having served to increase it, and the nonclinical definition to decrease it) and the degree to which the subject relies upon a response style he believes to be indicative of normal or attractive personality.

But, persisting in the mood of parametric exploration rather than theoretical expansion, the following simple question might be asked: Must the experimenter directly define himself as having a special interest or ability in evaluating personalities? Or can the same sort of evaluation atmosphere be induced by other means? One additional experiment seemed to confirm the latter possibility.

In this study we employed the same Background Information Sheet as in the previous one. By this means we again provided both for arousal of evaluation apprehension and directional cueing of responses in the "liking" and "disliking" directions respectively. And again we attempted to strengthen the evaluation apprehension dynamic by introducing an additional clinical implication into the experimental situation. Thus, before they read the Background Information Sheet the subjects in one main treatment read a printed announcement concerning an impending study. This told them that "Dr. P. J. Schroeder," a clinical psychologist from another institution, had asked our cooperation in recruiting subjects for a large study on "student personality and adjustment in college life." This study was being conducted on various different campuses. Participation in it would involve the subject's being interviewed by Dr. Schroeder and allowing him to administer various "projective tests of personality." Dr. Schroeder, it was made clear, would treat the findings as completely confidential and, specifically, he would not disclose them to the experimenter. The subjects were asked to sign for appointments "for this other, unrelated project" if they were so inclined. Virtually all the subjects did sign.

When we compare the subjects in this treatment to others who were not exposed to it we find the former showing stronger directional bias effects than the latter. Under the "Schroeder is coming" condition the difference in ratings between subjects cued in the liking and disliking directions respectively is clearly significant ($p < .02$). Under the standard condition comparable to the prior experiment, but lacking any extra clinical implication, the comparable finding is $p < .10$. (Smaller samples were used in this study than in the previous one; and with variances of about the same magnitude the overall probabilities are, as would be expected, somewhat larger.)

As I have already suggested, these are studies of limited import and they offer no major surprises. Essentially, their value lies in lending support to this basic point: any aspect of the experimenter (or of the situation or setting in which he is encountered) that adds some further implication of interest in psychological evaluation will tend to increase the influence of the evaluation apprehension dynamic upon the subject's experimental responding. This statement assumes, of course, that some other provocations toward evaluation apprehension are also acting upon the subjects as, for example, the information that we conveyed through the Background Information Sheet. However, it would seem quite likely that our *additional* factors (i.e., the undergraduate experimenter's confessed clinical interest or the subject's elicited commitment to participate in a later personality evaluative study) could operate as *sufficient* factors in and of themselves. Further research would be required to confirm this rather obvious speculation.

But obvious relationships (even when they raise questions about the underlying and somewhat obscure sequences of events that mediate them) are less compelling than findings that raise new and unexpected issues. Therefore, rather than linger over the findings reviewed above, I shall turn now to some further preliminary studies concerning other variables. In both of these studies the major hypotheses were confirmed, but certain unexpected relationships were also encountered; and they are of a type that promises to deepen our inquiry into the operation of the evaluation apprehension dynamic.

In one of these studies we attempted to examine the consequences of making the experimenter a "gatekeeper" for the subjects. By this we meant, simply, that the experimenter was to be perceived by the subjects as likely to allow some, but not all of them into some rewarding activity area. In addition to setting up gatekeeper and nongatekeeper conditions we also treated the manipulation of evaluation apprehension in a new way. In previous studies our Background Information Sheet had been designed to arouse (or confirm and amplify) evaluation apprehension; and control subjects who did not receive the Background Information Sheet provided the necessary baseline data. However, in the present study we used two forms of the Background Information Sheet, one intended to confirm and strengthen original promptings toward evaluation apprehension and the other to disconfirm and weaken them.

To convey fully the nature of this experiment I must linger briefly over the actual operations employed to establish the gatekeeper and nongatekeeper and high and low evaluation apprehension variables.

The gatekeeper manipulation consisted of the experimenter (myself) reading aloud a letter that, as he explained it, he had recently received from the executive director of the "National Policy Foundation" on whose advisory board, as the letter made clear, the experimenter himself had served. The letter invited the experimenter to nominate some forty undergraduate students to participate in a "regional collegiate council" that would be discussing, as part of a funded national study, college student experiences and views on general issues concerning campus life and educational practices. These students, the letter made clear, would be well paid and through their participation they would "help to educate the experts and, hopefully, the academic and governmental heirarchs who will be receiving the progress reports and the final report of the total study."

Having read this letter the experimenter said he had decided not to choose from among his own students but rather from the many subjects who were participating in "this week's experimental sessions," and that he would be "contacting some of you about this within the next week or so." In the nongatekeeper portion of the study we elected to say nothing along these lines, rather than to provide some contrasting or filler material.

The communication designed to arouse and suppress general evaluation apprehension explained that the study the subject was about to participate in was being conducted by the Personality Assessment Project (high evaluation apprehension) or the Mathematical Psychology Project (low evaluation apprehension). The low evaluation apprehension communication stressed that we were "interested in integrating the various dimensions or factors involved in social perceptual processes into a more simplified model by a method which statisticians term 'stochastic-inferential mathematical modeling'." With these, and similar comments, we intended to create in the subject the reassurance that we were studying some rather obscure and technical issues and had no interest in his unique personality. Thus, a further paragraph informed the subject that: "the photo ratings of all participants will be considered as a group and an overall average score and statistical estimate of distribution variance will be obtained for this set of photographs."

The high evaluation apprehension communication informed the subjects that "these photographs comprise a recently developed *Test of*

Psychological Maturity. The pattern of responses given to these photographs by psychologically mature undergraduate students has been shown to be significantly different from the responses of those manifesting psychological maladjustment." The communication went on to assert that our research was pointed toward further development of the picture rating personality test as an "instrument for picking out from the large college population those students who would be judged inadequate in their emotional adjustment or generally prone to psychological disorders."

Postexperimental questionnaire data established that the low evaluation apprehension communication did significantly "reassure" those who read it while the high evaluation apprehension communication did increase anxiety and set the person toward concern over what impression he would make upon the experimenter.

The contrast with our earlier uses of the Background Information Sheet should be clear. Not only were we attempting to remove evaluation apprehension in some subjects while strengthening it in others, but we were also providing no cueing that directly reported that liking or disliking for strangers had been found to be characteristic of psychologically mature persons. Instead, a more limited, or one might say, less obvious and intrusive form of directional cueing was employed. Each experimental subject, after he had been exposed to the gatekeeper or nongatekeeper and high or low evaluation apprehension manipulations, read a two-paragraph communication which simply reported that previous research with the pictures he was about to rate had shown that most people judged them positively (liking) or negatively (disliking). While one third of the total subject population of 148 males received this form of the liking cueing, and another third the disliking cueing, the remaining third received no directional cueing and thus served as a control group.

In the actual administration of this experiment we were able to achieve a high level of efficiency by use of the language laboratory at the University of Chicago. Subjects were run in groups of eight to twelve. Each subject occupied a separate work booth. Seated in the booth he first heard the experimenter deliver the gatekeeper "pitch" or, for the nongatekeeper subjects, a brief and quite neutral introductory statement. The subject then read the high or low evaluation apprehension manipulation which, under instruction, he had removed from an envelope placed on the table within his booth. He then went on, unless a cueing control subject, to read the directional cueing communication. Following this he gave, on a rating sheet, his liking-disliking judgments for each of the 15 pictured faces as they were projected on a screen easily visible to all subjects. After this rating sheet had been completed the sequence of pictures was presented again while the subject rated each of the pictured persons for "how successful" they had been. A third exposure of the pictures was then given while the subjects rated the pictured persons for "how intelligent" they appeared.* All pictures were exposed for ten seconds each, with a following ten second interval during which the subject wrote his rating on a scale from -10 to $+10$. Two postexperimental questionnaires, administered both before and after a thorough debriefing, provided strong evidence that the manipulations had been successful and that very little suspicion had been aroused as to our real purpose.

I have so far described the procedures of this study without any direct reference to the hypotheses that guided it. However, they are probably already apparent. The gatekeeper manipulation was intended to increase the desirability of winning a positive evaluation from the experimenter; for this would now have the additional payoff value of increasing the probability of being chosen for membership in the interesting and remunerative student discussion group that was being set up by the "National Policy Foundation." Thus we predicted that response dependence upon the directional cueing would be greater for subjects in the gatekeeper condition than for those in the nongatekeeper condition.

Similarly we expected that subjects receiving the high evaluation apprehension manipulation would show stronger response bias effects than those receiving the communication that was designed to reduce evaluation apprehension. And, of course, we were interested in the possibility of a meaningful interaction between the two major variables, and also their respective and combined interactions with the like-dislike cueing variable.

This rather complex study, with 12 separate cells in a $2 \times 2 \times 3$ design, and with considerable data drawn from postexperimental questionnaires and inquiry, yielded a great deal of information; and full presentation and analysis can only be attempted in a lengthy, separate article. Thus I shall dwell here only upon some of the major findings and their probable meaning.

---

* It should be clear that the subjects had not received any directional cueing concerning the personality revealing relevance of judgments that others have been successful or are intelligent. However, judging another as possessing these qualities would represent a positive evaluation of him. Thus we expected some generalization from the subjects' judgments on the like-dislike dimension onto these two other judgmental scales. Also, evidence of such generalization (or of such indirect cueing effects) could be taken as an additional measure of the degree to which the directional cueing was utilized by the subject.

Table III presents the mean algebraic sums of the liking ratings for the six cells that received the gatekeeper treatment and, separately, for the six cells in the nongatekeeper treatment. The probabilities of the differences between relevant pairs of cells are also presented. Reference to these tables will help to illuminate the findings from the separate analyses of variance that were carried out for both the gatekeeper and nongatekeeper conditions.

TABLE III

LIKE-DISLIKE MEAN SUMS FOR GROUPS; AND PROBABILITIES OF
DIFFERENCES BETWEEN GROUPS

A. Non-gatekeeper condition

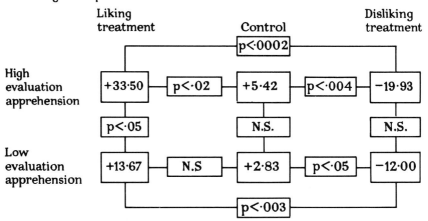

B. Gatekeeper condition

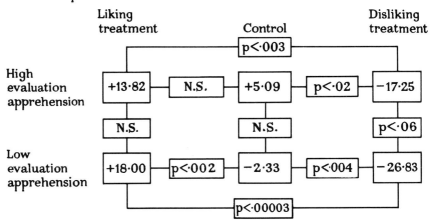

In both analyses we obtained clear evidence of a cueing effect. The algebraic sums of the subjects' ratings on the like-dislike dimension strongly reflect the cueing that was received: those who got positive cueing gave more positive ratings than those who got no cueing and these, in turn, gave more positive ratings than those who got negative cueing. In the nongatekeeper half of the experiment the p value for this effect is less than .0001. Also the effect does appear to generalize to the ratings of "success" ($p < .05$) and "intelligence" ($p < .006$).

Considering only the four groups that received cueing in either the positive or negative direction (i.e. eliminating the two no cueing, control groups) our other major prediction was confirmed. In the nongatekeeper portion of the study a significant interaction is obtained between cueing and evaluation apprehension level as regards the liking ratings ($p < .03$). This is due to the fact that when subjects have been roused to a state of evaluation apprehension their picture ratings are more extremely influenced by either the positive or negative cueing than when they are at a low or suppressed level of evaluation apprehension. Thus, the mean of the algebraic sums for the high evaluation apprehension subjects who received positive cueing is some 53 points more positive than the mean for the high evaluation apprehension subjects who received negative cueing. For the low evaluation apprehension group the comparable discrepancy, while in the same direction, is only 25 points.

Similar effects of lesser magnitude and statistical significance are obtained when we compare the two evaluation apprehension groups on their ratings of the pictures for success and intelligence. The probabilities for the overall evaluation apprehension by cueing interactions on these two dependent variables are less than .12 and .19, respectively.

In passing, it is worth noting that within the high evaluation apprehension condition the differences between the scores from the positively and negatively cued subjects are significant at probabilities of .008 or less for each of the three dependent variables; while the parallel analysis with the low evaluation apprehension subjects yields a significant probability only on the liking ratings.

I have dwelt upon these results because they suggest a point of particular interest both as concerns an emerging theory of the self-presentation process and also as they bear upon an important methodological issue. The kind of directional cueing intentionally provided in this study is often unintentionally present in other research situations, both of experimental and survey form (e.g. the respondent in the typical public affairs study often has a fairly clear idea, whether accurate or not, of "how most people would probably answer" on some of the more salient issues). More "valid" data (i.e. more accurate self-representations) are likely to be obtained when we attempt to reduce evaluation apprehension through some preliminary communication which disconfirms the subject's or respondent's concern that his psychological maturity (or, for that matter, his "public spiritedness" or "patriotism") may be open to assessment and evaluative judgment.

Yet the fact is that even with an apparently successful reduction of evaluation apprehension (judging by the postexperimental questionnaire data from the low evaluation apprehension subjects) the directional cueing still exerts some influence. Probably this indicates some residuum of persisting evaluation apprehension and, if so interpreted, it points up the necessity for developing even more effective techniques for giving subjects or respondents the sort of reassurance which allows them to be their typical selves (i.e. uninfluenced by situational and inadvertent cueing factors) when reporting on their own judgmental or attitudinal processes.

So far the discussion has been restricted to the findings from the nongatekeeper portion of the experiment. With the data from the gatekeeper portion of this study we encounter a number of interesting patterns, particularly when they are viewed in relation to the comparable nongatekeeper experimental groups. Whereas the positively and negatively cued groups in the nongatekeeper, low evaluation apprehension condition differed significantly only on their liking ratings of the pictures, but not on the success or intelligence ratings, the low evaluation apprehension groups who received the gatekeeper manipulation show significant cueing effects on the liking, success, and intelligence ratings (respectively, $p < .00003$, $p < .0002$, $p < .0005$).

This is further reflected in the difference between the liking means for the positively and negatively cued, low evaluation apprehension groups. Under the nongatekeeper condition this difference is 25.67, while the comparable difference under the gatekeeper condition is 44.83. For the success ratings the differences between the means for the two cueing groups are 3.60 for the low evaluation apprehension nongatekeeper condition and 37.34 for the low evaluation apprehension gatekeeper condition. With the ratings of intelligence the respective difference scores are 10.80 and 38.73.

It is clear that when we make the subject dependent upon the experimenter's judgment of him we restore something like evaluation apprehension. The subject, knowing that the experimenter is a psychologist and probably desiring that he "let him through the gate" to a rewarding experience, regulates his responding by reference to the cues that tell him how "most others" respond.

So far the results from the gatekeeper condition confirm our original

hypotheses. However, where we examine the data from the high evaluation apprehension gatekeeper subjects, one major surprise is encountered: Unlike the results with the low evaluation apprehension subjects,
the introduction of the gatekeeper condition (which was intended as
an extra force compelling the subject toward reliance upon the directional cueing) seems in fact to *reduce* such reliance for the positively,
but not negatively, cued group. In the high evaluation apprehension
nongatekeeper and gatekeeper conditions the mean algebraic sums for
the liking ratings in the absence of any directional cueing are 5.42 and
5.09, respectively. But whereas the liking sums for the positively cued
subjects in the former group have a mean of 33.50 (and thus the difference between the control and positively cued subjects is 28.08), in the
latter group the positively cued subjects yield a mean sum of only 13.82
(making the difference between the control and positively cued subjects
only 8.73). Similar findings are obtained with the dependent variables
of success ratings and intelligence ratings.

A possible interpretation is that the combination of the high evaluation
apprehension and gatekeeper treatments strains the subjects' credulity
or, perhaps, puts them under a degree of tension which inhibits or
otherwise disrupts their readiness to be influenced by the directional
cueing. But the absence of the same pattern with the negatively cued
groups limits the applicability of this interpretation. Subtler possibilities
have occurred to us, but their explication had best await the results
of further data analyses that are yet to be executed. These last findings
comprise one of the valuable surprises of which I spoke earlier; and
I must confess considerable interest in further experimental investigation
in this particular realm as well as considerable frustration over the
tantalizing ambiguity that presently beclouds the issue.

Among many further subsidiary findings obtained in this experiment
I shall mention only one other. A postexperimental index of the "anxiety"
aroused by the high evaluation apprehension communication is strongly
correlated with the degree to which the subjects in the experimental
groups were influenced by the directional cueing that they received.
This serves to reinforce our general theoretical view while also suggesting the importance of apprehension-proneness as a mediating, personality-linked variable.

While I have not here attempted a full description of the procedures
of this complex study or of all the available analyses, enough has been
presented to make clear the basis for the following conclusions: Evaluation apprehension has again been shown to be a factor, or process,
that mediates systematic biasing of the sort that is due to cueing (in
this study, somewhat more indirect cueing than in our previous work)

of the preferred pattern of experimental responding. A second variable, namely the perception of the experimenter as a "gatekeeper" (i.e., as one who controls access to further reward or ego-enhancement) has been shown to facilitate yielding to directional cueing, particularly when evaluation apprehension has been brought to a low, or inoperative, level. But the combination of high evaluation apprehension and the gatekeeper variables has not, as we thought it would, worked to maximize the degree of influence upon experimental responding that is exerted by directional cueing. Whether this is due to some artifactual considerations (or to some unintended and subtler pattern of evaluation apprehension that has, in turn, generated a more obscure response strategy) or whether it is our first encounter with a truly general effect, remains to be determined through further research.

In general this study does appear to add force to the claim that evaluation apprehension can contaminate the data gathering process, and it directs us toward a more complex consideration of other variables that interact with evaluation apprehension.

The last study that I shall treat in this section was, in all but two respects, a close duplicate of the one just described. Thus, its design and procedures can be outlined in short compass. Subjects were again exposed to the high and low evaluation apprehension treatments and then to either positive or negative directional cueing or to no cueing at all. Again the experiment was conducted in the language laboratory setting with each subject working in a separate booth and all viewing and rating the projected pictures at the same time.

The two major differences between this study and the previous one were: All subjects were female undergraduates; in place of the gate-keeper manipulation we attempted a systematic, two-stage variation in which the pictures to be rated were presented under conditions of high and low ambiguity. Operationally, this meant that under the nonambiguity condition each successive picture was exposed in sharp focus for ten full seconds and the subject was to give her rating only after the exposure was completed. In the ambiguity condition a stable level of poor focus (low resolution) was employed and the picture was exposed for only three seconds.

The basic hypothesis which led us toward this study on the evaluation apprehension × cueing × ambiguity interaction was that biased experimental responding due to evaluation apprehension (in interaction with directional cueing) will be a direct partial function of the degree of ambiguity in the stimulus materials to which such responding is coordinated. Basic to this prediction was the notion that the stimulus attributes of the particular pictures do, in interaction with the subject's own judgmental standards, exert some influence upon his ratings. This is likely to be true even when a larger part of the variance in the ratings is controlled by the arousal and directional channeling of evaluation apprehension. To make the pictures more ambiguous is to make the stimulus attributes less readily available. This, in turn, should foster a further intensification of the subject's reliance upon such cueing as he may have received and thus the bias effects should be intensified.

Table IV presents the mean algebraic sums of the liking ratings for

TABLE IV

Like-Dislike Mean Sums for Groups; and Probabilities of
Differences Between Groups

A. Non-ambiguity condition

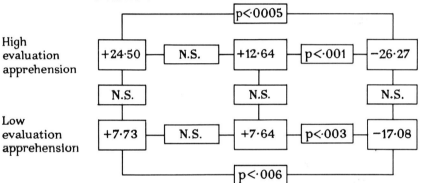

B. Ambiguity condition

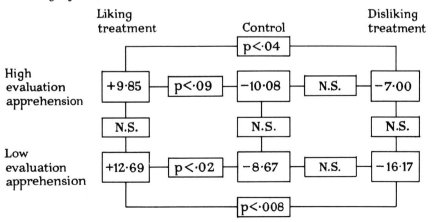

the six cells in the ambiguity treatment and, separately, for the six cells in the nonambiguity treatment. The significant differences reported in the table help to make clear the findings from the analyses of variance that we carried out for both the ambiguity and nonambiguity conditions.

Analysis of variance of the ratings from the half of the study in which the subjects rated the unambiguous photographs reveals comparatively strong cueing effects. On the liking ratings the cueing effect is highly significant ($p < .0001$); and for the success and intelligence ratings they are of borderline significance ($p < .15$, $p < .07$ respectively).

Analysis of variance of the ratings from the half of the study run under the condition of stimulus ambiguity also reveals a significant main effect for the liking ratings ($p < .002$), but no effect for the success ratings ($p < .68$), and a borderline effect for the intelligence ratings ($p < .14$).

However, while the like-dislike directional cueing exerts the predicted influence, we find that two other expectations are not directly confirmed: Within the separate ambiguity conditions we do not find that the high evaluation apprehension subjects are significantly more influenced by both types of directional cueing than are the low evaluation apprehension subjects; nor do we find significantly more biasing of responses in the cued directions in the ambiguous as compared to the nonambiguous treatments. Instead, what stands out is a complex interaction between direction of cueing, low and high evaluation apprehension and the ambiguity-nonambiguity variable. This significant interaction can best be described in these terms: Under the ambiguity condition the positive directional cueing has greater influence upon the liking ratings than does the negative directional cueing; under the nonambiguity condition the negative directional cueing has greater influence than the positive directional cueing; and while this pattern is visible with both high evaluation apprehension and low evaluation apprehension subjects, it is somewhat stronger with the former under the nonambiguity condition and with the latter under the ambiguity condition.

Further and more complex analysis of these data, and of related data gathered with an extensive postexperimental questionnaire, carries us partway toward unraveling the meaning of the triple interaction reported above. But all such interpretation remains uncertain without recourse to further, replicative study. At this point the speculative path that seems most accessible is one which highlights the interaction between our independent variables and the special meaning of the experimental task. This speculative path begins with the assumption that most (American middle class) persons take it to be socially desirable to show openness and liking toward others. Those subjects who have received cueing suggesting that most persons in past research have rated the pictures negatively face a conflict between their own expectations or half-shaped hypothesis and the directional cueing that has been addressed to them. With stimulus ambiguity high they may, in the resultant state of uncertainty, fall back upon their own, original expectations; and thus the positive cueing works more effectively upon them than does the negative cueing. However, with high clarity and detail in the photographs, typical subjects may be able to find evidence in facial and expressive characteristics onto which they can more readily impose the negative judgments that, according to the negative directional cueing, are typically made by "most people" who view these particular photographs.

That the yielding to the negative cueing under the nonambiguous condition is greater for high evaluation apprehension than low evaluation apprehension subjects (the difference between control and dislike group means being 38.91 for the former and 24.72 for the latter) suggests the further pertinence of the interpretation offered here: for the high evaluation apprehension subjects, believing they are undergoing indirect personality assessment, have a greater stake in regulating their responses in the cued direction. In effect, our interpretation, reduced to its simplest form, suggests this further hypothesis: to yield to directional cueing that endorses an unpracticed response style, the person needs "something to work with," i.e. some supporting aspects in the experimental situation or in the profferred stimulus material which will enable him to view his yielding to the directional cueing as having some basis in "reality" rather than solely in his need to win a positive evaluation.

Clearly this line of speculation, if strengthened by later research, moves our inquiry into self-presentation processes toward a subtler and more difficult kind of theorizing; one which will have to give fuller representation than heretofore to the limits and lures that the total experimental context provides for the subject who is attempting to regulate his experimental responding in a way that serves both his need for approval from others and, at the same time, from himself.

As I said in opening this section, "we are just barely started on this line of inquiry." Having now reviewed our completed studies on variables that strengthen or reduce the data biasing influence of evaluation apprehension I am all the more sensitive to the fact that this work has a decidedly preliminary air about it. Much more inquiry is required and as it proceeds we must get beyond our present and too simple classificatory taxonomy of variables and into the construction of a process or systems model of the flow of the evaluation apprehension dynamic. Further work along these lines, both experimental and theoretical, is contemplated. But for now we can, I think, conclude that at least this much has been established: Between the initial arousal of evaluation apprehension and the ultimate tilting of experimental responses in the direction that, as the subject sees it, will maximize positive evaluation, there is scope for influence through many intervening and subsidiary variables. The few we have so far investigated appear to me to derive their influence in either or both of two ways: they may directly affect the subject's perceptions of *how* his responses will be judged; or they may affect his estimate of the *importance* of winning a positive evaluation from the particular experimenter in his particular experimental setting.

V. EVALUATION APPREHENSION AND THE EXPERIMENTER EXPECTANCY EFFECT

Three research strategies have been featured in the work I have already reported: altered replication, demonstration experiments and experiments on intervening or additive variables. Yet one other related research approach has figured in our recent work on the evaluation apprehension process. Simply described, this involves manipulating evaluation apprehension (by arousing or confirming it for some groups and suppressing or disconfirming it for others) and then examining the consequences for some other phenomenon or relationship of psychological interest. In general this strategy would appear to be relevant whenever one suspects that evaluation apprehension operates as a mediating or facilitating condition for an already established relationship between other variables.

Directly illustrative of my meaning is the possibility that evaluation apprehension may well be involved in the experimenter expectancy effect: i.e. a state of concern over whether the experimenter will judge him as "normal" or "abnormal" may affect the way in which the subject perceives the experimenter's meanings, preferences, and aspirations within the experimental situation. To be specific: if, as the work of Rosenthal (1966) and Friedman (1967) suggests, the experimenter's expectancy is subtly communicated by aspects of his expressive style, the subject who is possessed of a concern over evaluation may well be more closely and accurately attuned to such indirect communication; or he may be more motivated to act upon the basis of what has been indirectly communicated.

To investigate such a possibility, then, one would attempt to replicate a standard experimenter expectancy study with at least two groups of subjects—one aroused to a high level of evaluation apprehension and one in which all tendencies toward this pattern of concern have been effectively diminished.

In a sense this research strategy can be viewed not as a fourth and new one, but as a variant of the altered replication approach described in the first section of this chapter; but in this variant, instead of eliminating evaluation apprehension we attempt also to arouse it. However one wishes to classify it, this strategy has proved effective in the one realm in which it has already been employed. As the title of this section and the illustration offered above have already suggested, that realm has been the further study of the mediation of the experimenter expectancy effect.

Before I turn to an account of our studies in this area I should like to comment briefly upon the relationship between my own preoccupation with the evaluation apprehension process and the work of other investigators of the "social psychology of the psychological experiment." From the record of research (much of which is summarized in other chapters in its volume) on demand characteristics, subject presensitization, volunteer effects, and experimenter expectancy effects, it seems abundantly clear that there are a number of sources of systematic bias in experimental data. For a long time these went unsuspected and, it can be assumed, contributed considerable nonrandom error to the data through which theoretical propositions were tested or inspired.

In the main I am persuaded by the work of others that the various processes that have been conceived as making for systematic bias do, in fact, have considerable operative force. And, obviously, I think and have tried to show that the same is true of the evaluation apprehension process.

We have then developed an empirically verified catalogue of data-biasing variables and processes. So far so good. But it seems apparent to me that we have now reached a stage at which we need not be content with a mere catalogue. Some larger, more integrative theory of the experimental-transactional process is required. The development of such a theory will afford intellectual satisfaction in itself; but, equally important, it will probably also contribute to a richer understanding of the role of self-representational dynamics in nonexperimental, interaction situations; and, of course, it will promise considerable further advance in improving the methods of research design and execution in all those disciplines (psychology is only one) whose data are gathered through interaction between the investigator and other, investigated persons.

I shall not presume to suggest the possible shape of a full and general integrative theory of the experimental process, though in the concluding section I shall risk a few preliminary speculations upon some aspects of such a theory. However, at this point I want only to register this obvious point: the development of this sort of theory will be advanced by—indeed, it may require—the prior investigation of the interaction and overlap between the biasing processes that are now separately delineated in our catalogue. A few investigations of this type have already been attempted; the study by Sigall, Aronson, and Van Hoose (1968) discussed above, is one. The three studies I shall now describe represent another such contribution. They are all focused upon the interaction between evaluation apprehension and experimenter expectancy. More particularly they are attempts to test the proposition already advanced: i.e. that the experimenter expectancy effect is mediated or facilitated by evaluation apprehension. At the same time, the last of these studies also bears upon another important aspect of the experimenter expectancy effect; namely, the paralinguistic content of the experimenter's communications to the subject.

In our first effort in this realm my coinvestigator was Marshall Minor and a portion of this study served as his doctoral dissertation (Minor, 1967). We had two basic purposes: to replicate Rosenthal's finding that the expectancy held by an experimenter can introduce "experimenter bias" into the research situation so that the expectancy is confirmed by the response data elicited from subjects; and, as I have already indicated, to show that the experimenter bias effect is mediated by evaluation apprehension. Particularly we hypothesized that the experimenter bias effect will be intensified when subjects believe that their experimental responses may be utilized to evaluate their psychological adequacy, and that the effect will be diminished when they define the situation as one in which their psychological adequacy is not likely to be evaluated. The design of this study called for 16 naive male experimenters (eight given the +5 expectancy and eight the −5 expectancy) to separately run four subjects (two male and two female) through the Rosenthal picture rating task. (In this standardized task the subject rates each of a series of pictured persons on a scale from −10 to +10 for "whether the person pictured has been experiencing success or failure.") Half of all subjects would have already been roused to a high level of evaluation apprehension and the other half to a low or "suppressed" level of evaluation apprehension. Balancing in the assignment of subjects to experimenters was to be arranged so as to enable a statistical control for sequence effects, sex differences, and other possible unintended influences upon the response data.

Difficulties in recruiting the full complement of subjects during the University of Chicago summer quarter of 1966, and the failure of one experimenter to keep his scheduled appointment, reduced the actual situation to one in which 15 experimenters ran 23 male and 16 female subjects. However, it was possible to maintain partial balance in subject assignment and to effect statistical analytic controls for the "holes" in the matrix of experimenter-subject pairs that were actually completed. The latter type of control was made possible by use of the University of Chicago MESA 95 computer program (we are indebted to Professor Darrel Bock for introducing us to this program and for helping us to fit it to our needs) in which, as each mean square for an effect is determined, a transformation is made on the model by eliminating previously estimated effects from the succeeding mean squares. This made it possible for us to get an estimate of the expectancy × evaluation apprehension interaction which estimate was independent of sex and sequence variables. (A full account of the handling of this and other analytic problems is found in Minor, 1967 and the special analysis of variance program employed is described in Bock, 1965.)

Some words about procedures and operations are required before we review the basic findings of this study.

The naive experimenters, all male graduate students in the school of education, reported individually for the scheduled experiment in whose execution they had promised to assist. After receiving a standardized background introduction to the experimental task each experimenter read a document giving further instructions. These expectancy-establishing instructions comprised a modified version of one of the methods used by Rosenthal (1966). The crucial content was in the last paragraph:

"For your information, we have found from past research that certain types of people tend to rate these pictures in very particular ways. On the basis of personality test data that we collected earlier this quarter from the subjects you will be running, you should expect them to give an overall average rating of +5 (−5). This is because our earlier testing has shown that all of the subjects whom you will be running are in the category that we are calling 'success perceivers' ('failure perceivers'). Thus if you will follow instructions and use proper experimental procedure, they will rate the pictures more extremely positive (extremely negative)—thus obtaining an average of about +5 (−5)—than would be the case if your subjects had simply been selected at random."

Each subject, before being introduced to the experimenter who was to administer the experimental task, was asked to "please read this sheet which will give you a brief description of the purpose of today's experiment." Half of the subjects read an explanation intended to arouse a high and stable magnitude of evaluation apprehension. The other half read an explanation designed to reduce and, hopefully, eliminate any tendency toward evaluation apprehension that the subjects might have brought with them into the experimental situation. The full logic that lay behind the construction of these two communications (which are similar to the ones used in our earlier studies on the gatekeeper and ambiguity variables) will not be traced here. However, much of it should be apparent from the content of the high and low evaluation apprehension communications which are fully reproduced below.

HIGH EVALUATION APPREHENSION COMMUNICATION

"Today, you will be participating in a psychological experiment; and shortly you will be assigned to an experimenter who will explain the task to you. Although we are not able to answer any questions until after the experiment is over, we do want to give you a brief description of the purpose of the experiment. This should make participating more interesting and meaningful for you. Also, a growing number of psychological researchers are beginning to realize that they have an ethical responsibility to make the purpose of their experiments known to the individuals who are helping them out by participating in their research.

"We are interested in studying social perception (i.e. how people perceive other people). More specifically, we want to find the factors which increase or decrease the accuracy of an individual's perception of other people. Certainly, with the lack of understanding in the world today, we do need to find out as much as we can about the reasons for inaccurate social judgment.

"Prior research by ourselves and others indicates that, typically, poor social perception is associated with psychopathology. That is, people who are not able to accurately perceive how other people are feeling, or what they are experiencing, usually are found to be psychologically maladjusted. Much of our initial research in this area indicates that on the basis of performance on the social perception task, we can pick out from a college population those students who would be judged clinically to be maladjusted.

"Several other researchers have presented data which support the preceding findings. Morgan and Provino (J. of Abnormal and Social Psychology, 1963) for example, report that in a college setting, the Social Perception Test could make rather subtle discriminations between varying degrees of emotional maladjustment and normalcy.

"The purpose of today's experiment, therefore, is to replicate the previous results, and thus to test further the generality of the finding that people who cannot accurately judge what other people are experiencing tend to be psychologically maladjusted."

Low Evaluation Apprehension Communication

"Today, you will be helping us to collect some preliminary data which we will use in setting up a subsequent research project. Shortly, you will be assigned to an experimenter who will explain the task to you. Time does not permit us to answer any questions, but we are able to give you a brief description of the purpose of the study. This should make participating more interesting and meaningful for you.

"We are interested in studying social perception (i.e. how people perceive other people). More specifically, we want to find the factors (e.g., fatigue, practice, etc.) which increase or decrease the accuracy of an individual's perception of other people.

"Before we can investigate these different factors, however, we have to know how people perceive the feelings and experiences of others when these experimental factors are not present.

That is, we need a control, or standardization, group to use as a baseline against which we can judge the effects that our experimental factors have on social perception. This is the reason for your participation today.

We intend to average the performance of all of the students participating today, so that we will have a measure of how subjects perform on the task when such experimental variables as fatigue and prior practice are not present. This information will allow us to judge the effects which our experimental variables have when they are used with a subsequent group of students.

In other words, today's group will help us to find out how subjects typically perform on the task. Later, we can use the data we receive here to judge the performances of subsequent experimental groups of subjects."

As in the typical Rosenthal experiment, interaction between experimenter and subject was held to a minimum level in which the experimenter read the picture rating instructions to the subject and collected his ratings for each of the ten pictures. Upon completion of this phase the subject, no longer in contact with the experimenter, filled out an extensive postexperimental questionnaire and was thoroughly interviewed. The same was done with each experimenter after he had completed running all of his assigned subjects. In a last phase experimenters and subjects were brought together for a full "debriefing" and for extended discussion, considerable care being taken to alleviate any lingering concern that might be felt by subjects who had been assigned to the high evaluation condition.

From the full analysis of variance three significant findings were obtained: Between experimenters, the expectancy variable (+5 versus −5 experimenter expectancy) controls a significant portion of the variance in their subjects' ratings of how successful the pictured persons have been ($p < .05$). In the "within experimenters" analysis the sex of the subjects operates significantly ($p < .03$) reflecting a general tendency for females in either the +5 or −5 expectancy groups to rate the pictured persons as less successful than the respective male subjects in the same expectancy treatments. Most relevant to our major interest is the finding of a rather strong interaction between expectancy and evaluation apprehension ($p < .02$).

The basis for this significant interaction is clearly revealed by a comparison of the mean photo ratings obtained from the +5 and −5 expectancy groups under both the high and low evaluation apprehension conditions respectively. (The male-female proportions are roughly equivalent in each of these four groups.) With evaluation apprehension reduced or suppressed (i.e. under the low evaluation apprehension treatment) the mean picture ratings for the +5 and −5 expectancy groups are −.78 and −.59 respectively. The difference between these means is not significant. Under the high evaluation apprehension condition the +5 and −5 expectancy group means are +.16 and −1.06 respectively. This difference is significant at a probability lower than .002.

Figure 1 provides a graphic representation of our basic finding that the experimenter expectancy effect is obtained, as predicted, when evaluation apprehension has been aroused and is not obtained when evaluation apprehension has been reduced or eliminated.

Many additional aspects of the data analysis serve to develop further detail on the picture sketched here and to further strengthen our overall conclusions. These matters will be more fully reported in a separate publication. However, one particular subsidiary finding is worth noting here. An index reflecting the degree to which each experimenter was successful in inducing bias under the high evaluation apprehension condition was computed. This index was separately correlated with the scores from various questionnaires that were administered to the experimenters after they had run all their subjects. The two strongest correlations obtained were those with the Marlowe–Crowne Social Desirability scale ($r = .40$, $p < .06$) and the Sarason Test Anxiety Scale ($r = .57$, $p < .01$). This suggests the possibility that something like evaluation apprehension is involved not only in mediating the responsiveness of the subject to the experimenter's bias-inducing cues but perhaps also in setting the experimenter to emit such cues. At any rate, these findings suggest an empirical hypothesis worthy of further and more direct study, namely: that assigned expectancies will have a greater influence upon

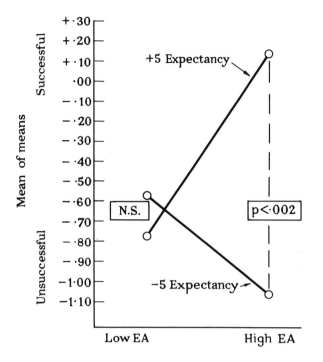

Predicted order of means	High EA +5 EE	Low EA +5 EE	Low EA −5 EE	High EA −5 EE
Obtained means	+·16	−·78	−·59	−1·06

FIGURE 1

RESPONSE TO EXPERIMENTER EXPECTANCY AS A FUNCTION OF
EVALUATION APPREHENSION LEVEL

subject performance when the experimenters to whom these expectancies have been assigned have a high need for approval and a tendency to be apprehensive over the evaluation of their own competence.

Upon completion of the analysis of this study we decided to attempt an altered and expanded replication. The major intended changes were these: to completely fill the matrix of required experimenter-subject combinations and thus handle the problem of sequence effects without recourse to the sort of statistical corrections that were required in the previous study; to run an "evaluation apprehension control" condition in which we would attempt neither to increase nor diminish the subjects' original, nonmanipulated, evaluation apprehension level; to run a "zero expectancy" as well as a +5 and —5 expectancy condition. A further purpose was to try out a way of staging the study which combined some features of mass administration (e.g. subjects reading the initial evaluation apprehension communications while waiting in a large reception room) with the individual running of subjects on the picture rating task. Our hope in this last regard was to increase the efficiency of our own experimental procedures and those employed earlier by the Rosenthal group.

In this study, then, each of 33 male experimenters (11 each having been given the +5, 0, or —5 expectancies respectively) ran 3 male subjects on the Rosenthal picture rating task (one each having first received the high, low, or control evaluation apprehension communication respectively). The first two of these communications were slightly modified versions of the ones used in the earlier study and the last was a simpler one that merely advised the subject that he would shortly be assigned to an experimenter and asking him to wait until called upon.

The main results of this study can be quickly told. We failed to replicate the basic experimenter expectancy effect.

Analysis of postexperimental questionnaire and interview data from both subjects and experimenters suggests that this was due to our having failed to provide a credible experimental staging. In attempting to maximize efficiency in the routing of subjects and experimenters we seem to have aroused considerable suspicion about our own unrevealed purposes and about the actual contents of the communications intended to manipulate evaluation apprehension.

Without going further into the details of our post-hoc analysis of the suspicion-arousing aspects of the experimental procedures used, it may be said that a number of valuable cautionary points became clear to us and that we have profited from these in our further attempts at experimental investigation of experimenter bias, evaluation apprehension and kindred processes. In fact, on the basis of our first attempt at running a partially group-administered experiment in this realm, we were able to develop a different approach which was used in our next study in this sequence. This approach is just as efficient or more so, and yet seems to keep suspicion and other intrusive artifacts at a very low level.

Before turning to a description of the major study just referred to it will be necessary to briefly describe a study that was stimulated by our earlier work but was not undertaken as part of our research program.

Starkey Duncan, a clinical psychologist who had been working on paralinguistic aspects of communication within the psychotherapeutic situation, became interested in our work on experimenter bias effects. Through our joint consultations he came to the conclusion that the mediation of biasing cues in the Rosenthal paradigmatic situation might largely depend upon variations in the nonlinguistic aspects of the experimenter's spoken communications to the subject. Particularly, he conjectured that the way in which the experimenter varied the intensity, intonation, pitch, and rhythm aspects of his reading of the instructions for the picture rating task might convey to the subject an extra-linguistic (or, more properly, a "paralinguistic") indication of the experimenter's expectancy regarding the responses the subject was about to make.

Duncan and Rosenthal proceeded to design a preliminary study to test this hypothesis. From films provided by Rosenthal, Duncan transcribed sound tapes of vocal readings of the instructions; three from each of two comparatively high biasing experimenters and four from a third high biasing experimenter. Together with the films from which the tapes were made, Rosenthal also provided the picture rating data obtained from the respective subjects who had received these separate vocal readings of the instructions. The taped readings were blindly coded on a number of different paralinguistic dimensions. The coding procedure used was based upon Duncan's earlier work. This procedure is extremely detailed and, with trained coders, yields high inter-judge reliability scores.

While the coding method will not be further described here, the results of this preliminary study can be simply summarized. Based only upon the coding of the instruction-reading tapes, Duncan was able to demonstrate that a large amount of the variance in the mean picture ratings given by the subjects could be accounted for by reference to the "Differential Emphasis Score" for each of the separate instruction readings that the respective subjects had received.

The Differential Emphasis score is a single index which reflects the degree to which the experimenter, in his vocal reading, has emphasized (through variations in volume, pitch, rhythm, etc.) either "success" or "failure" and either the positive or negative ends of the rating scale. The correlation between differential vocal emphasis and the subjects' subsequent picture ratings was $+.72$ $(p < .01)$; and all subjects who had heard greater emphasis on the rating alternatives associated with success subsequently rated the photos as being of more successful people than the subjects who heard readings that placed greater emphasis on the failure alternatives $(p < .001)$.

An additional finding of considerable interest was that the correlation between experimenters' assigned expectancies and the Differential Emphasis scores was only .24. This suggests that though the pattern of emphasis used by the experimenters is influenced by the assigned expectancy it often varies from that expectancy either in the direction of giving greater or lesser than average emphasis to it. It suggests further that even where the relation between assigned expectancy and the subjects' picture ratings is low, the experimenter may actually be influencing the subject (through his deviant pattern of vocal emphasis) a good deal more than has previously been suspected.

From this preliminary study it seemed clear that with paralinguistic analysis considerable further progress could be achieved in pursuit of the difficult question of just how experimenter expectancy effects are mediated. Since the Duncan–Rosenthal study had used a variant of the method of postdiction it seemed especially desirable to attempt a more ambitious and more fully controlled study. We would reverse the procedure, moving from postdiction to prediction; this would be accomplished by exposing subjects to vocal readings selected for their paralinguistic direction (i.e. "success" or "failure") and the degree of differential paralinguistic emphasis. Thus by experimental manipulation we could gain a closer and more stringent test of the hypothesis that in the typical experimenter bias study (and also in studies that may be inadvertently contaminated by bias effects) the subject's responses are influenced through paralinguistic aspects of the experimenter's communication to him.

At the same time we planned to extend our earlier inquiry into the way in which the experimenter expectancy effect is mediated by the subject's state of evaluation apprehension. Thus the next study (in which I was joined by Duncan and Jonathan Finkelstein) was an experimental, manipulative investigation of the separate and interacting influences upon subjects' response patterns of both paralinguistic emphasis and evaluation apprehension.

In the first phase we obtained from a number of colleagues and graduate students taped readings of the basic instructions for the Rosenthal picture rating task. Our request was that the first reading be given in an "objective and balanced" manner and that subsequent readings be "slightly shaded" in either a positive (i.e. "success" stressing) or negative (i.e. "failure" stressing) direction. None of these "experimenters" heard the readings of any other and each went about his "balancing" and "shading" in strictly his own manner.

After all the resulting speech samples were transcribed and scored for paralinguistic Differential Emphasis we were able to select a set of nine readings (three from each of three readers) to be used in the study. The three instruction readings taken from one of these experimenters were scored as balanced (i.e. no differential emphasis), moderate positive (i.e. intermediate bias toward an emphasis on perceiving the pictured persons as successful), and strong positive, respectively. From a second reader we had balanced, moderate negative, and strong negative readings; and from a third we had balanced, moderate positive, and moderate negative readings.

In the basic design of this study each of the nine instruction tapes was combined with each of three evaluation apprehension conditions, thus yielding a 27 cell design. The evaluation apprehension conditions employed were High, Control, and Low. As in our earlier studies the evaluation apprehension manipulations were effected through a "Background Information Sheet" read by the subject. The evaluation apprehension bolstering and suppressing communications were similar to those used in earlier studies. The control evaluation apprehension group received no Background Information Sheet and was given no advance "explanation of the experiment."

The subjects were 216 female undergraduates (eight per cell) who had volunteered in response to telephone calls requesting their participation in a study of person-perception. No payment or other rewards were offered. All experimental sessions were run in the University of Chicago language laboratory. In this facility the separate listening booths with multi-channel receivers could be easily adapted to a basic requirement of our design: namely, that within each administration group (N varied from 8 to 12 for the successive groups) each of the three thirds would respectively hear one of the three different readings of the instructions recorded by a single experimenter.

At the beginning of the experimental session, after all subjects were seated in their randomly assigned booths, they first heard a taped message thanking them for coming and, for the high and low evaluation apprehension groups, directing them to read the Background Information Sheet which was in a packet in front of the subject. After a five-minute pause for this purpose (control subjects were run in separate groups and had no such pause) each subject heard one of the taped readings of the Rosenthal instructions. Immediately following this the photographs to be rated for degree of "success" or "failure" were projected onto a screen in front of the booths, each for ten seconds. The subjects recorded their own ratings on a standardized rating sheet which they were also required to sign. After the rating sheets had been collected a postexperimental questionnaire was distributed and following its completion and collection all subjects went through a thorough debriefing and were pledged to keep the purpose and design of the study confidential.

Before data analysis was undertaken 35 subjects were eliminated on the basis of important manipulation validation items from the post-experimental questionnaire. Thirteen were eliminated because they indicated that they had been aware of the purpose of the experiment; and 22 were eliminated either because they were in the low evaluation apprehension conditions and rated the Background Information Sheet as "anxiety arousing" or in the high evaluation apprehension condition and rated the Background Information Sheet "reassuring."

Analysis of the data was based on the mean picture rating for each subject. Because comparisons between experimenters were not made in transcribing or scoring the readings of the instructions, and thus were not reflected in the Differential Emphasis scores, it was necessary to adjust the subject means to take into account any differences among the experimenters. For each experimenter, therefore, the mean of all subjects in his control condition (i.e. the mean of the picture rating means from the subjects who heard his "balanced" reading of the instructions and had not received evaluation apprehension manipulation) was subtracted from the separate means of all his other subjects (i.e. those who heard his "biased" readings). These adjusted scores were used in our basic analysis.

Preliminary analysis indicated no significant difference in bias induction between the subjects who heard the moderate and strong positive readings from one of the experimenters or between the subjects who heard the moderate and strong negative readings from another of the experimenters. However, on inspection, clear differences were visible between those who heard positive and negative readings respectively, while those who heard "balanced" readings occupied an intermediate position. It was apparent, then, that somewhat subtler shadings of volume, pitch, and rhythm were just as effective as more pronounced ones in conveying a differential emphasis which influenced subject response patterns. In our further analysis we combined the data from subjects who had heard the moderate and strong positive readings of the instructions and, separately, from those who heard the moderate and strong negative readings.

When we tested the difference in scores between all subjects who had received the positive differential emphasis and those who had received the negative differential emphasis, the predicted main effect was confirmed ($p < .02$).

In a further and more detailed analysis the mean scores from the six separate cells were arranged in the ascending order that could be predicted from the assumption that the effects of differential emphasis would be facilitated to the degree that evaluation apprehension was experienced. That predicted order was: high EA, negative differential emphasis; control EA, negative emphasis; low EA, negative emphasis; low EA, positive emphasis; control EA, positive emphasis; high EA, positive emphasis. An analysis of variance was executed to determine whether the predicted order did, in fact, obtain. The resultant linear trend was found to be significant ($p < .02$).

Figure 2 reveals the basis for this summary statistic and reports further probabilities obtained through application of the Mann–Whitney Rank Sum Test. Thus subjects who had first read the Background Information Sheet designed to remove or reduce evaluation apprehension were ap-

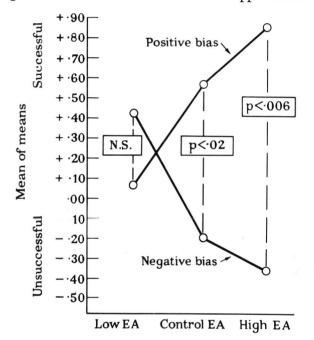

Predicted order of means	High EA Positive	Control EA Positive	Low EA Positive	Low EA Negative	Control EA Negative	High EA Negative
Obtained means	+·84	+·57	+·07	+·42	−·20	−·39

FIGURE 2

RESPONSE TO PARALINGUISTIC DIFFERENTIAL EMPHASIS AS A FUNCTION OF EVALUATION APPREHENSION LEVEL

parently uninfluenced by the differential emphases conveyed in the various instruction tapes that they heard; no significant difference is found between the scores of the low evaluation apprehension groups that respectively heard positively and negatively biased readings of the instructions. On the other hand, when subjects have read a communication designed to confirm and heighten evaluation apprehension their picture ratings are very strongly influenced by the paralinguistic shading of the instruction tapes in either positive or negative directions ($p < .006$).

Similarly we find that when evaluation apprehension is not manipulated (i.e. when, in the evaluation apprehension control condition, it is allowed to operate at a level that we may assume to be set by the interaction between the experimental task and the subject's personality) we obtain a smaller, but still significant, difference between subjects exposed to positively and negatively shaded readings of the instructions. The scope of this difference ($p < .02$) is roughly the same as that reported in typical successful experiments by the Rosenthal group.

Further and more detailed analysis of these data remains to be carried out—particularly an analysis program that will draw upon material gathered through an open-ended postexperimental questionnaire. But on the basis of the main findings reported above we feel that we can now more clearly discern the nature and dynamics of the experimenter bias effect. Loosely stated, the process appears to be one in which subtle paralinguistic shadings in the experimenter's communications do convey his expectancies or preferences as regards the response choices that the subject must make.* Whether the subject will be attuned to these paralinguistic cues or, if attuned, whether he will allow them to influence his experimental responding, may depend upon a number of things; but we are now in a position to conclude that one of these considerations, and probably an extremely important one, is whether the subject has come to perceive the experiment as one in which the experimenter is likely to form judgments about the subject's psychological adequacy or attractiveness.

---

* Of course, we cannot logically rule out the possibility that still other modes of mediation such as "kinesic" cueing may play a role in conveying the experimenter's expectancy to the subject. What is clear is that no such additional channel of indirect communication was open in the present study since the only experienced differences between the three separate instruction readings contributed by any single "experimenter" lay in their differential paralinguistic emphases. Also relevant in this connection is this further fact: In the present study, the magnitude of the experimenter expectancy effect under both the control and high evaluation apprehension conditions was as great, or greater than, that obtained in most experiments concerned with this type of bias. This strongly suggests that differential paralinguistic emphasis is the main, if not the only, process through which the direction of the experimenter's expectancy is transmitted to the subject.

VI. SOME RECOMMENDATIONS AND OPEN ISSUES

In bringing to conclusion a chapter that has already probably taxed the reader by its length and detail I shall resist the temptation to elaborate further upon my basic argument and its supporting evidence. By way of general summary it shall suffice to say that I have tried to explicate a conceptualization of the evaluation apprehension process and that all of the present studies appear to show that this process does induce systematic bias in experimental responding. Some of the research studies that have been reviewed have served an additional purpose: they have delineated and examined certain variables that appear to facilitate or restrict the operation of the evaluation apprehension biasing process. On the basis of the present studies I think it reasonable to put the seal of provisional validation (and the judgment that they are worthy of further experimental study) upon the following propositions:

The biasing influence of evaluation apprehension upon response data will be reduced if those data are collected by an experimenter other than the one whose evaluative judgment was the original focus of the subject's concern.

When a response pattern cued as likely to bring positive evaluation is also counternormative, subjects high on the need for approval will be more likely to produce that response pattern than subjects low on the need for approval.

The availability of continuous feedback about the quality of a subject's performance will facilitate his shaping that performance in the direction he thinks likely to earn him a favorable evaluation from the experimenter.

The less effortful the response direction that has been cued as likely to bring positive evaluation, the more will the subject go in that direction.

When the experimenter is perceived by the subject as having "power" over him (in the sense of controlling his access to some goal region or activity) this will foster the biasing of his responses in cued directions; and this will be particularly likely in the absence of other conditions that directly arouse evaluation apprehension.

When the subject expects that a particular type of judgmental response will earn him positive evaluation from the experimenter, and when that type of response is also counternormative or unpracticed, his adoption of it will be facilitated by clarity in the stimuli to be judged.

Still other propositions supported or suggested by the research reviewed in this chapter could be summarized. But the past work is prologue to present and future concerns. Thus, my main purpose in this concluding section will be to address some interesting implications and open issues that seem to be suggested by the studies that have been reported here.

The first of these is the question of whether one can draw from the present research and analysis any clear prescription concerning the conduct of psychological and related forms of research. A number of fairly obvious recommendations do come easily to mind. One of these I have already suggested: the altered replication approach does seem to afford a way of testing reinterpretations of experiments whenever it is suspected that the original data were influenced by inadvertent arousal of evaluation apprehension. This strategy can and should be more widely employed. Disputatious reinterpretation of the other man's research is easier than research itself; but the later legitimates the former and assesses its relevance. Thus, whenever possible, these activities should be joined.

Another prescription follows rather obviously from our studies, described in the previous section, which demonstrated that evaluation apprehension mediates the experimenter-expectancy effect. These studies do seem to show that evaluation apprehension and its data distorting effects can be reduced (or, at least, minimized) if one defines the experimental situation in a certain way for the subject. Whatever the particular details of such preliminary communications, they should lead the subject to perceive at least two things about the experimenter and his experiment: that his interest is focused not so much upon individuals in their uniqueness as upon aggregates of persons in their normative or nomothetic aspect; that some purpose far more technical (and perhaps more "dry") than personality study is being prosecuted by the experimenter.*

Credible messages to this effect, or "accidental" revelations of the same order, can probably be rather easily developed and almost as easily pretested. Undoubtedly, content and style will need to be varied with types of subjects and types of experimental situations; but if interest in handling this problem became widespread we would soon develop a technology of evaluation apprehension control that would, I think, contribute significantly to improving the quality and trustworthiness of psychological research.

---

* At the same time it woud probably be necessary to guard against making the experiment seem so empty of purpose or relevance as to destroy the subject's motivation to remain psychologically involved in it. Clearly, some art (and some validation of its products) will be required in the further development of techniques for limiting and reducing evaluation apprehension.

However such a change in standard procedure would raise an important problem concerning an aspect of experimental method that has, in recent years, become quite ritualized. Should the postexperimental "debriefing" include an explanation of the evaluation apprehension problem and of the way it was brought under control? Recently, some commentators have argued that debriefing should not be conducted unless it is required to reduce anxieties or ego-injuries directly due to the experiment, and unless it is also clear that the debriefing itself will not embarrass the subject or diminish his self-esteem by demonstrating his gullibility.

Against these considerations I would give great weight to the notion that experimenters have an ethical obligation to be as frank as possible with their subjects, even though full, disingenuous revelation must be deferred until all data are collected. Nor do I think that such revelation need be degrading. Whether the subject comes out of the debriefing feeling tricked, and exposed as an "easy mark," or whether he comes out with a sense of having participated in a useful endeavor in which he played an important part and was honorably treated would, I think, depend largely upon the secret motives and visible style of the experimenter. Surely, as Kenneth Ring (1968) has suggested, the "fun and games" approach to experimental social psychology degrades subjects, trivializes research and, I would add, quite probably activates the evaluation apprehension dynamic so as to induce unsuspected but sizeable systematic bias in resultant data.

Candid and thorough debriefing, unmarred by any proclivity towards gloating, can do much for the experimenter's self-image and probably it also serves the enrichment of the subject's experience and knowledge. However it does generate a further problem—as much for experimenters who may employ evaluation apprehension control procedures as for experimenters pursuing other approaches. I refer, of course, to the risk that, despite the elicitation from the subject of a pledge to say nothing about the experiment to other potential subjects, the vessel of secrecy may spring leaks. This, in turn, may spoil the host culture of the naive subject pool without the experimenter knowing that anything of the sort has happened. It is my impression that the pledge to postexperimental secrecy is usually internalized when a bond of mutual trust has been woven; and I am not aware of anything that works better to insure that bond than full and candid postexperimental debriefing.

Furthermore, the postexperimental discussion that can be opened up by mutual debriefing tends to free the subject to reveal much of his own recent, subjective experience in the experimental situation. The information thereby gleaned can be of considerable help in determining whether evaluation apprehension or other contaminating processes may have been operating during the experimental transaction. Such discussion also provides the experimenter with a fairly comfortable occasion for asking whether "you had heard anything about this experiment from a previous subject," just as it provides a facilitating context in which subjects are likely to respond to that query with candor.

I am aware, of course, that I am dealing here in lore and impressions. Clearly, more systematic research is required on the effects of the debriefing strategy upon the subject's self-esteem, upon his maintenance of the secrecy pledge and, for that matter, upon the value of his introspections about his experiences in the experiment. But until such a body of research has been undertaken and reported I do think it reasonable to hew to the general standard favoring postexperimental revelation of all deceptions and of all major experimental purposes; and this should include discussion of the evaluation apprehension problem and of the techniques that have been used to bring that problem under control.

I shall turn now to a second major matter that requires some discussion. Among various other issues heretofore unattended is a question that any thoughtful reader must have already conceived as he has worked through these pages: Is the desire to win the experimenter's approval, and his judgment that one is psychologically adequate, the only motive of interpersonal relevance activated in the subject during the experimental transaction?

Assuredly the case cannot be that simple. Even if we reduce our range of conjectural scan to patterns of motivational arousal that directly affect the subject's way of relating to the experimenter (and, thus, how he responds in the latter's experimental situation) a number of other possibilities come easily to mind. Though they are probably far less common than the process upon which this chapter has focussed they do require discussion. At least one of these additional data-biasing processes is quite familiar to all psychological experimenters of sufficient experience and sensitivity. There are some subjects who most of the time (and many subjects who some of the time) are likely to want to confound the experimenter, to disconfirm what they perceive as his expectations, to violate what they construe as his apparent scientific hypothesis.

I am mindful that this observation partially contradicts the view elaborated by Martin Orne (1962). For him the experimenter's hypothesis is a "demand characteristic" to which subjects, by the very nature of their role, are prone to yield. This may often happen though, as I shall argue later in this section, when it does it is probably mediated less by a general role-based standard of cooperativeness than by the evaluation apprehension dynamic.

Under what sorts of circumstances, or with what kinds of persons, does the opposite tend to occur; i.e. what accounts for the not uncommon instance in which the subject's purpose seems to be to "screw up the works"?

With an ease and haste that may bespeak defensiveness, psychologists are often prone to interpret such behavior as due to general hostility, to character-based "anality," or to lingering reverberations of the oedipal revolt against authority figures. Such may indeed be the case with occasional subjects. But another dynamic process seems to me to be far more common. Evaluation apprehension, when strongly experienced, may sometimes generate a sort of reactive anger toward the experimenter; or it may be so intolerable as to require immediate "distancing" from the experimental situation and its evaluative implications. Either of these purposes, and yet other comparably defensive ones, can be served by turning the tables on the experimenter and giving indirect expression to a negative evaluation of him. Given the constraints of the usual experimental situation, the most effective way of doing this may often be to disrupt the experimenter's enterprise by emitting just those responses which will, as the subject sees it, confound or disappoint him. Also if this can be done with a "light" style, with some visibly amused irresponsibility, a further defensive stratagem is brought into operation. The subject may then be able to believe that he has destroyed the evaluative significance of the experimental transaction; for, if he is clearly not taking the situation seriously his behavior cannot be meaningfully interpreted as saying much about his true psychological nature or competence.

From the viewpoint of the experimenter, the problem posed by this sort of process is not so much that it may occur as that it may not be easily or reliably discerned. While skillful postexperimental inquiry may be of some use in reducing this problem, there is, I think, another important alternative. There may well be some personality patterns and some foci of regnant conflict that tend to heighten the likelihood that subjects will take recourse to the "confound the experimenter" strategy. The question begs for early investigation and psychologists interested in the social psychology of the experiment will need to turn their investigative skills in this direction.

Equally compelling and probably even more readily open to systematic investigation, is the question of what attributes of the experimenter and of his instructions and preliminary explanations work toward the same effect. It is my untested impression that experimenters who are perceived by subjects as rather severe and unrevealing while, at the same time, intrusively "nosy," are the ones most likely to arouse special data biasing patterns of resistance in some of their subjects.

And obviously, it could be hypothesized also that the same is true of experiments that are perceived (or misperceived) as probing too deeply into anxiety-laden or low self-esteem areas of the private self.

At least one other rather obvious bias-inducing pattern requires discussion in the present context even though, as far as I know, it has not been submitted to any systematic study whatever. I have in mind the occasional sounding of the "cry for help" by a genuinely troubled or unhappy subject who thinks he ought to be, but presently is not, a patient.

Undoubtedly, this is far less common than the aspiration to appear "normal" and win a positive evaluation, but just how uncommon it is I do not know. From my own experience and that of colleagues with whom I have discussed the matter I would hazard this judgment: with some small number of undergraduate subjects (and, perhaps, most often with freshmen at times of situational stress) contact with a "psychologist" does activate the regressive longing for some show of support and sympathy from a wise, compassionate parent surrogate.

When this does occur a number of problems arise. The most important, in the light of our methodological concern, is that out of this background there may issue a pattern of experimental responding opposite to that with which this chapter has been most concerned, but just as troublesome for its data biasing consequences. Where involvement in the experimental situation fosters the tendency to emit the "cry for help" the subject, utilizing the same directional cues as are available to other subjects and either with or without fully conscious intent, may shape his experimental responding so as to make himself appear "abnormal" or troubled or anxious. In consequence, his pattern of experimental responding will lack valid bearing upon the hypotheses that are being put to experimental test.

The obvious corrective, again, is to submit the problem to systematic scrutiny through further research. A paradigm experimental situation such as the picture rating task used in some of our studies can be employed, and to it there can be attached fairly clear implications of "normal" and "abnormal" response patterns. Response deflection in the "abnormal" direction could be taken as an index of the motivation toward negative or "needful" self-representation. And variations in such an index could be examined against coordinate variation in personality indices, in systematic manipulations of the experimenter's style, the experimental script, and prior inductions of psychological stress. Out of some such research program there would probably emerge a set of useful cautionary strictures that would help to further reduce the problem of systematic bias in psychological and kindred types of research data.

My purpose in these last few pages has been to note that, in addition to the subject's striving toward positive self-representation as a way of reducing evaluation apprehension, there are some other, related trends which may also induce systematic bias in response data. Returning to our main focus upon the former process, I should now like to address an issue that has haunted the discussion at a number of points but has not yet been fully confronted: What is the relationship between the evaluation apprehension dynamic and such other sources of systematic bias as the experimenter expectancy and demand characteristic processes?

The answer that I think most acceptable, though only in a provisional way, is already implicit in my earlier discussion of the two experiments in which we found that the activation of evaluation apprehension facilitated, and its reduction obliterated, Rosenthal's experimenter expectancy effect.

In their separate research and theorizing Rosenthal and, to a lesser degree, Orne have both emphasized the experimenter side of the experimenter-subject interaction: that is, they have delineated and demonstrated that experimenters do indirectly reveal what sorts of responses they would welcome from their subjects and they have also shown that this does, somehow, affect the responses of those subjects. However they have had far less to say about the subject's side of the transaction; about the patterns of concern, apprehension, and ego-defensiveness which move him toward acting out, or at least coordinating to, the experimenter's implicit demands.

It is, of course, true that Rosenthal has addressed this issue in some of his fascinating side-excursions (Rosenthal, 1966) into the personality attributes of comparatively biasable and unbiasable subjects. But what has been required as well is a narrower or more process-oriented focus upon the actual psychological events that carry the subject through the experiment and up to the point at which he "delivers" the elicited gift of his responses.*

* While it has been insufficiently developed, this sort of concern has not been totally ignored during the short period in which the social psychology of the experiment has commanded intellectual interest. Some usefully provocative beginnings in this direction were elaborated by Riecken in his seminal article (1962); and Orne, despite the experimenter-oriented nature of the demand characteristic concept, has also been somewhat sensitive to these matters.

However, while the focus upon subject processes has not been totally absent in earlier speculative writing, it has lagged in development. Perhaps this is due to its having been obscured by the deserved figural prominence of the work on experimenter expectancy and demand phenomena. The proper corrective lies not in abandoning the latter interest but in restoring and expanding our concern with the former.

The evaluation apprehension process as defined in this chapter and as exemplified in our various studies appears now to be an important part of the subject side of the total experimental transaction. In the emerging general theory of the "social psychology of the experiment" it does not replace the account of experimenter expectancy effects developed by Rosenthal. Rather it extends it and perhaps also deepens that account by adding further clarity about the conditions under which experimenter bias is likely to be induced. As regards the demand characteristic process posited by Orne, the present approach does inevitably raise some difficulties and disposes me toward one note of disagreement. This concerns the motivational-perceptual pattern which facilitates the subject's yielding to the "experimenter's scientific hypothesis." Where the experimenter's true hypothesis is clear to the subject (and I would think that usually it is not) yielding to it would most likely be mediated by the expectation that this will somehow bring approval or other immediate social rewards from the experimenter. To be sure Orne might be interpreted as saying that positive self-evaluation is being sought by the subject, particularly in that he may take pleasure in viewing himself as an accommodating and helpful person. But the present studies, coupled with the very pertinent one by Segall, Aronson, and Van Hoose (1968), suggest that evaluation apprehension focused upon the experimenter is a more potent and more basic pattern of subject sensitivity. Thus, I would hazard the hypothesis that the subject's readiness to help the experimenter make his scientific point, if experienced at all, is an instrumental stage in his search for reassuring evidence that the experimenter judges him as an acceptable or even attractively "normal" person.

My basic argument, then, is that our focus on evaluation apprehension adds to the picture developed by Rosenthal and other major contributors. By carrying us beyond the kind of biasing processes which can be traced to variability in the experimenter's behavior it directs us toward those which may be due to the figural highlights and ambiguities of the *experiment* itself.

While they do not logically require it, the experimenter-oriented theories sometimes tend to view the subject as a comparatively passive recipient of implicit "messages" or "cues" from the experimenter. This would suggest that where such cues are absent or imperceptible systematic bias would be unlikely to occur. In distinction, a subject-oriented theory of the experimental transaction views the subject as seeking something from the experimental experience. In the present theoretical view that "something" is the experimenter's judgmental validation of the subject's psychological adequacy and on this basis, the ultimate maintenance or enhancement of the subject's self-esteem.

However, whether this or some other private purpose animates the typical subject is of less importance for the moment than the altered perspective that is opened to us when we lay basic stress upon the subject as seeker. From this emphasis there follows the necessary recognition that even when there is no direct cueing conveyed through the experimenter's behavior, the subject may be prone to construct some personal interpretation of the "true meaning" of the experiment. More often than not, he will speculatively examine the instructions he has received, the overall rationale that has been provided, the procedures and measuring devices to which he has been exposed; and out of the questions these raise for him and the hints they convey to him he will, if at all possible, draw some meaning, some guiding hypothesis about what is really being investigated and how he can best display himself to the investigator.

In this view, then, the experimental situation and, for that matter nonexperimental research situations as well, can activate the subject to search for their meaning. Whether the meaning found is often focused upon the evaluation theme, as I have argued, or upon yet other themes, there ensues a consequence as intellectually fascinating as it is methodologically troublesome. The subject's final "definition of the situation" will affect his responding and thus will be reflected in the dependent variable data.

To turn again to the problem of improving research procedures, the foregoing argument clearly suggests a further caution. The danger of inadvertent systematic bias in response data cannot be fully reduced by effective elimination of the experimenter expectancy and demand characteristic problems. We must remain sensitive to the possibility that the subject, no matter how acquiescent or calm he appears, may be actively processing his impressions toward the development of some interpretive hypothesis, one that will lead him to adopt a response strategy that may distort the resulting data.

An analogue for this whole process is provided by the larger number of our present studies, excepting those focused upon the experimenter expectancy phenomenon. In the former group of studies the systematic biasing of the subject's response patterns was not demonstrably due to any intraexperimenter or interexperimenter variations in behavioral style. Rather, the differences in subjects' performances could be directly traced to the fact that the preparatory materials they read contained hints that they could then rather easily shape into hypotheses about the purpose, or the indirect revelatory significance, of the experiment.

In substantive research focused upon other psychological issues and conducted by experimenters who do not *intend* their experimental procedures to induce systematic bias, the suspicions aroused and the hints conveyed by the instructions, manipulations, and measures may be of more obscure origin and less certain import. Yet "seeking" subjects are prone to pick up whatever cues may be available in the structural and procedural detail of the experiment itself.

The more figural and prominent are the cues of this type, the more likely that separate subjects will come to the same or similar interpretive hypotheses about how to assure positive evaluation for themselves, or, for that matter, about how to reach still other social goals that they may be seeking. In consequence, it will be more likely that a systematic bias in one or another response direction will result. In contrast, the more obscure and the more numerous such provocations toward suspicion and interpretation, the more likely that subjects will reach comparatively unique interpretive hypotheses; and this will tend to foster "random" rather than systematic bias.

Either way, the consequence is an increase in the possibility that intrinsically valid hypotheses will be "disconfirmed" and intrinsically invalid ones "confirmed." Thus it becomes imperative that we submit to far closer scrutiny the processes by which subjects engage in active information seeking, ambiguity reduction and the development of interpretive hypotheses.

Whether subjects engage in such activities with full "consciousness" (i.e., with purposive self-direction and ratiocinative clarity) or, as I think more likely, with intersubject and intrasubject variability in motivation, effort, and attentiveness, is an interesting issue but not a crucial one. At the present stage what is most important is that we translate our research interest in such processes into the more specific questions that will make possible their controlled investigation. In my view the most useful focus of the required further research effort would be to ask just what variables determine when and how subjects go about formulating hypotheses; and what other variables influence the content and certainty of those hypotheses and the ways in which they are transformed into actual, data-yielding responses.

Equally important, of course, is the search for conditions which reduce the likelihood that such activities will take place at all. The reduction or elimination of evaluation apprehension (or the structuring of an experiment so that evaluation apprehension never arises) appears to be one such important condition. But there are probably others and their discovery would be a great boon to the whole experimental enterprise.

Until all these matters have been more fully clarified through further research it is necessary that experimenters strive to abandon the image of the "average" subject as a passive and patient human component within a total experimental system; a component that, by processing imputs into outputs, somehow automatically reveals immutable psychological laws.

Having said this much I must hasten to add that I do believe that such laws exist in nature, and that the experimental method has been and will remain essential to the task of apprehending and confirming them.

Those psychologists who have responded to recent research on the social psychology of the experiment with despair over the prospects of the experimental method itself are, I think, guilty of unjustifiable reactive depression and are casting out the baby with the bath. When they call for renewed recourse to "field studies," to "natural observation" with "non-reactive measures," and to phenomenological inquiry they are doing the behavioral disciplines a useful service. Those ways of gathering data (though equally open to systematic bias effects) can do a great deal to enrich inquiry into the regularities that govern man's psychological development and his functioning in relation to the persons and institutions that define his existence.

However, when such critics suggest that the experimental God is dead, they appear to have missed the point implicit in all research on the social psychology of the experiment. That point is that the experimental method can readily be used to perfect, or at least to significantly improve, itself. Any experimental demonstration of some source of systematic bias and of the process by which it operates immediately suggests procedures for the control and elimination of that source of bias. Another heartening consideration is, simply, that on the basis of present knowledge a great deal is already known about how to reduce the dangers of contamination and systematic bias. Such knowledge can also inform the critical evaluation of the worth of particular experiments as these are reported. The wheat, then, can even now often be separated from the chaff—and the yield is not a grossly unfavorable one.

A truly exciting and optimistic prospect has been opened by a decade of work on the social psychology of the experiment and I hope that it has been further advanced by the present inquiry into the evaluation apprehension process. We are approaching the point at which we may achieve a practical (if not philosophically perfected) solution to the classic epistemological problem of detaching the knower from the known; of allowing the order inherent in behavioral and social processes to tell us its own true story without any distortion due to promptings from the listener or failings of his listening device.

The velocity of further advance toward the improvement of both experimental and nonexperimental investigative procedures is likely to increase as research on the social psychology of social inquiry is vigorously prosecuted. And if, on occasion, one is troubled by the ostensible paradox that the processes inducing systematic bias may operate in our very investigations of systematic bias, there are at least two types of reassurance available. The lesser one is that every investigation in this realm profits the succeeding one; error should fall away as we continue to "zero in" toward the goal of bias-free research. The greater reassurance is that paradox itself is a goad toward intellectual and scientific adventurousness; the more closed off and ostensibly circular the problem, the more deserving it is of assault and solution.

REFERENCES

Abelson, R. P., Aronson, E., McGuire, W. J., Newcomb, T. M., Rosenberg, M. J., and Tannenbaum, P. H. (Eds.) *Theories of Cognitive Consistency: A Sourcebook.* Chicago: Rand McNally, 1968.

Aronson, E. The psychology of insufficient justification: an analysis of some conflicting data. *In* S. Feldman (Ed.) *Cognitive Consistency.* New York: Academic Press, 1966.

Bock, R. D. A computer program for univariate and multivariate analysis of variance. *Proceedings of the I.B.M. Computer Symposium on Statistics.* White Plains, New York: I.B.M. Data Processing Division, 1965, 69–111.

Brehm, J. W., and Cohen, A. R. *Explorations in Cognitive Dissonance.* New York: Wiley, 1962.

Brown, R. Models of attitude change. *In* R. Brown, E. Galanter, E. Hess, and G. Mandler. *New Directions in Psychology.* New York: Holt, Rinehart and Winston, 1962, 1–85.

Carlsmith, J. M., Collins, B. C., and Helmreich, R. L. Studies in forced compliance: I. The effect of pressure for compliance on attitude change produced by face-to-face role-playing and anonymous essay writing. *Journal of Personality and Social Psychology,* 1966, **4,** 1–13.

Chapanis, N., and Chapanis, A. Cognitive dissonance: five years later. *Psychology Bulletin,* 1964, **61,** 1–22.

Crowne, D. P., and Marlowe, D. A new scale of social desirability independent of psychopathology. *Journal of Consulting Psychology,* 1960, **24,** 349–354.

Crowne, D. P., and Marlowe, D. *The Approval Motive.* New York: Wiley, 1964.

Edwards, A. L. *The Social Desirability Variable in Personality Assessment and Research.* New York: Dryden, 1957.

Festinger, L., and Carlsmith, J. M. Cognitive consequence of forced compliance. *Journal of Abnormal and Social Psychology,* 1959, **58,** 203–210.

Friedman, N. *The Social Nature of Psychological Research: The Psychological Experiment as a Social Inter-action.* New York: Basic Books, 1967.

Minor, M. W. *Experimenter Expectancy Effect as a Function of Evaluation Apprehension.* Unpublished doctoral dissertation, University of Chicago, 1967.

Nowlis, V. Research with the Mood Adjective Check List. *In* S. S. Tomkins and C. E. Izard (Eds.), *Affect, Cognition, and Personality.* New York: Springer, 1965.

Orne, M. On the social psychology of the psychological experiment: with particular reference to demand characteristics and their implication. *American Psychologist,* 1962, **17**, 776–783.

Riecken, H. W. A program for research on experiments in social psychology. *In* N. F. Washburne (Ed.), *Decisions, Values, and Groups.* Vol. 2. New York: Pergamon Press, 1962.

Ring, K. Experimental social psychology: some sober questions about some frivolous values. *Journal of Experimental Social Psychology,* 1967, **2**, 113–123.

Rosenberg, M. J. Cognitive structure and attitudinal affect. *Journal of Abnormal and Social Psychology,* 1956, **53**, 367–372.

Rosenberg, M. J. An analysis of affective-cognitive consistency. *In* Rosenberg, M. J., Hovland, C. I. *et al., Attitude Organization and Change.* New Haven: Yale University Press, 1960. (a)

Rosenberg, M. J. Cognitive reorganization in response to the hypnotic reversal of attitudinal affect. *Journal of Personality,* 1960, **28**, 39–63. (b)

Rosenberg, M. J. When dissonance fails: on eliminating evaluation apprehension from attitude measurement. *Journal of Personality and Social Psychology,* 1965, **1**, 18–42.

Rosenberg, M. J. Some limits of dissonance: toward a differentiated view of counter-attitudinal performance. *In* S. Feldman (Ed.) *Cognitive Consistency.* New York: Academic Press, 1966.

Rosenberg, M. J. Hedonism, inauthenticity, and other goads toward expansion of a consistency theory. *In* R. P. Abelson, E. Aronson, W. J. McGuire, T. M. Newcomb, M. J. Rosenberg, and P. H. Tannenbaum (Ed.) *Theories of Cognitive Consistency: A Sourcebook.* Chicago: Rand McNally, 1968.

Rosenberg, M. J., Hovland, C. I., McGuire, W. J., Abelson, R. P., and Brehm, J. W. *Attitude Organization and Change.* New Haven: Yale University Press, 1960.

Rosenthal, R. *Experimenter Effects in Behavioral Research.* New York: Appleton-Century Crofts, 1966.

Sigall, H., Aronson, E., and Van Hoose, T. *The Cooperative Subject: Myth or Reality?* Dept. of Psychology, University of Texas, 1968 (mimeographed).

Silverman, I. Role-related behavior of subjects in laboratory studies of attitude change. *Journal of Personality and Social Psychology,* 1968, **8**, 343–348.

Silverman, I., and Regula, C. R. Evaluation apprehension, demand characteristics, and the effects of distraction on persuasibility. *Journal of Social Psychology,* 1968, **75**, 273–281.

Chapter 8

PROSPECTIVE:
Artifact and Control*

Donald T. Campbell

Northwestern University

I. LOGIC OF INFERENCE

If we had remained with the definitional operationism of our recent past, we would not have known the problems with which this volume deals. Our experimental setups and our measurement procedures would have been treated as *definitional* of our theoretical concepts. Conceptualizing them as definitions would have excluded recognizing them as biased, as systematically imperfect as well as randomly errorful.

Definitional operationism did indeed lull some into an uncritical complacency and reification of test scores, but fortunately the major practitioners of science had too little contact with or too little faith in philosophy of science to be misled. While logical positivists were defining intelligence in terms of the Stanford Binet, 1916 edition, Terman was already initiating revisions designed to make it a less biased and more accurate measure of intelligence, a goal which clearly showed that for him, his test was *not* the definition. Similarly, ever physicist working with a measurement device such as the galvanometer knows that in

* Supported in part by National Science Foundation Grant GS1309X. This paper was written while Fulbright Lecturer in Social Psychology at the University of Oxford. I am indebted to my host Michael Argyle both for generous hospitality and for help with this paper.

practice it fails of perfect reflection of electrical potential differences because of the effects of gravity, friction, inertia, field forces, etc. (e.g., Wilson, 1952). While compensated and corrected design may minimize these sources of error, on *theoretical* grounds the galvanometer is known to be subject to systematic biases, the elucidation of which is itself a history of cumulative scientific achievement rather than of logical revelation.

If definitional operationism and other accoutrements of logical positivism now are recognized as misleading, how are we to understand our predicament as knowers, and in such a way as to make philosophical sense out of the prototypic activities of this book? For me, the orientation of Karl Popper (1959; 1963; Campbell, in press) and that partial common denominator shared with Polanyi (1958), Toulmin (1953; 1961), Kuhn (1962), and Quine (1953) although they might be the last to acknowledge any such, seems most appropriate. I shall try to present an aspect of this orientation, albeit through metaphors that are perhaps unorthodox.

Following Popper, I honor Hume as a logician and reject him as an inductivist psychologist. Hume called attention to the scandal of induction, to the fact that scientific generalizations are not logically proven or provable. While most modern philosophers take this to be a mere technicality, a mere statement of the inappropriateness of analytic logic to contingent truth, it is Popper's strength to recognize this as a fundamental limitation. Not only are scientific truths *logically* unproven, they also lack certainty in any other sense—inductive, empirical, scientific, or implicative. Yet they are in some sense "established." The best of theories if not "confirmed" are at least "corroborated."

Logic is relevant to the statement of the situation. The "scandal of induction" can be expressed by noting that science makes use of an invalid logical argument, making the error of the "undistributed middle," or of "affirming the consequent." But while *invalid*, the argument is not *useless*.

The logical argument of science has this form:

> If Newton's theory A is true, then it should be observed that the tides have period B, the path of Mars shape C, the trajectory of a cannonball form D.
> Observation confirms B, C, & D.
> Therefore Newton's theory A is true.

We can see the fallacy of this argument by viewing it as an Euler diagram:

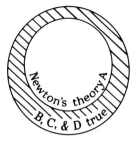

The invalidity comes from the existence of the cross-hatched area, i.e., other possible explanations for B, C, and D being observed. But the syllogism is not useless. If observations inconsistent with B, C, and D are found, these validly reject the truth of Newton's theory A. The argument is thus highly relevant to a winnowing process, in which predictions and observations serve to weed out the most inadequate theories. Furthermore, if the predictions are confirmed, the theory remains one of the possible true explanations. This asymmetry between logically valid rejection and logically inconclusive confirmation is the main thrust of Popper's emphasis on falsifiability.

The truism is now safely ensconced in elementary presentations of inductive logic, without the necessity of citations to Popper (e.g., Hempel, 1966; Salmon, 1963). There is another decision locus in the process upon which Popper's critics have focused: do the observations in fact confirm the predictions. It was assumed in the above that this decision could be and had been made. At this level, falsifiability and confirmability are more logically symmetrical. And at this level, observations *always* falsify a quantified prediction if carried out with sufficient precision. At this level the tolerance for accuracy which scientists actually allow is a social system function, determined by the degree of development of the science, the degree of experimental control achieved, and the sharpness of competition from other theories. Thus for Einstein's prediction of the bending of starlight passing the sun, as in the 1919 eclipse, a predicted value of 1.745 seconds of arc has been "confirmed" by values of 1.61″, 1.98″, 1.72″, 2.2″, and 2.0″.

Let us look in more detail at the Euler circles and the relation of confirmed predictions to the truth or credibility of a theory. It is our inescapable predicament that we cannot prove the theory. We must work within the limitations there diagrammed. What we as scientists do is to try in some *practical* way to "empty" the cross-hatched area, to make it as small as possible. We do this by expanding as greatly as possible the number, range, and precision of confirmed predictions. The larger and more precise the set, the fewer possible alternative singular explanations, even though this number still remains in some sense infinite.

More important, we in fact pay little or no attention to the mere logical possibility of alternate theories, to the merely logical existence of a cross-hatched area. Toulmin has stated the point well:

"Again, philosophers sometimes assert that a finite set of empirical observations can always be explained in terms of an infinite number of hypotheses. The basis for this remark is the simple observation that through any finite set of points an infinite number of mathematical curves can be constructed. If there were no more to 'explanation' than curve-fitting, this doctrine would have some bearing on scientific practice. In fact, the scientist's problem is very different: in an intellectual situation which presents a variety of demands, his task is—typically—to accommodate some new discovery to his inherited ideas, without needlessly jeopardizing the intellectual gains of his predecessors. This kind of problem has an order of complexity quite different from that of simple curve-fitting: far from his having an infinite number of possibilities to choose between, it may be a stroke of genius for him to imagine even a single one." (Toulmin, 1961, 113–115)

It is only when there exist actually developed alternative explanations, that is when there are known contents to the cross-hatched area, that validity questions arise for theories whose predictions have been confirmed. It was because there were no actually developed rivals that Newton's theory was regarded as certainly true for 200 years, even by such critical epistemologists as Kant. The cross-hatched area was empty in any practical sense. But the logical correctness of Hume's analysis of scientific truth is brought home as a relevant problem for scientific induction by the fact of the subsequent overthrow of Newton's theory for that of Einstein.

The situation is in fact even sloppier than this. When a theory such as Newton's has, in current fact, no near rivals at all, and when it predicts exquisitely well an enormous range of phenomena, we tend to forgive it a few mispredictions. Thus, as Kuhn (1962) emphasizes, there were known in Newton's day systematic errors of prediction, as of the precision of the perihelion of Mercury, which would have invalidated it at that time had Einstein's theory then been available. The truer picture is one of a competition between developed and preponderantly corroborated theories for an overall superiority in pattern matching (Campbell, 1966).

Thus the only process available for establishing a scientific theory is one of "eliminating plausible rival hypotheses." Since these are never enumerable in advance, or at all, and since these are usually quite particular and require quite unique modes of elimination, this is inevitably a rather unsatisfactory and inconclusive procedure. But the logical analysis of our predicament as scientific knowers, from Hume to Popper, convinces us that this is the best we can do, that this is our labor of Hercules, if not our task of Sisyphus.

II. METHODOLOGY AND PLAUSIBLE RIVAL HYPOTHESES

Many of the potentially invalidating plausible rival hypotheses come from other well developed theories. These are not our particular concern here. Other plausible rival hypotheses are concomitants of the specific apparatus of the experiment. These become the subject of "methodology." The hypotheses involved are often very specific, unelaborated, and unintegrated with wide-ranging theory. Nonetheless, they are hypothesized empirical laws relating two or more variables. To the extent that they become methodological essentials, they are well-established, and hence plausible, empirical regularities. This, rather than logical requiredness, is the source of their authority. This is not to deny that they are also in some sense logical (Petrie, 1968). But there are so infinitely many logically required controls that it would be impossible to incorporate them all. The cross-hatched area is infinite, logically. It is only at a practical level that we approach emptying it.

This empirical status of methodological requirements seems to me an important point too little noted. Too frequently we teach scientific method as though it were a dispensation from logic, prior to and external to science. In an early advocacy of experimental designs lacking pretests (Campbell, 1957, 302), I wrote as though it were a matter of obvious logic that if one had only experimented with pretested populations, one had no basis for generalizing to unpretested ones. This now seems to me quite wrong in emphasis. The authority came not from the logic, but from the empirical plausibility, the probable law-like character, of pretest interactions. Following logic alone, it was equally illogical to try to generalize to other groups of human beings, to other dates past and future, or to other settings varying in any detail from those explored in the original experiment. In this vast array of logical restrictions, this one was persuasive because of its empirical appeal. The hypothetical laws involved, as reviewed by Lana in this volume, do not now seem at all as plausible as they seemed then, and as a result, we will no doubt see less emphasis upon experimental designs doing without the pretest, or will see these justified on other grounds. Furthermore, when interaction effects are present, they are of a dampening nature, leading to an underestimation of the other law under investigation. They are not of the sensitization type that would produce pseudo effects utterly untypical of the natural situation.

In this case, the "plausibility" of the rival hypothesis as stated in 1957 was based partly upon an appeal to common-sense knowledge of psychological processes. However, my presentation did contain what now appears to have been an erroneous pseudo-citation, and one of considerable persuasive power. It will add to the manifest uniformity of Lana's review of empirical findings if I take space here to set the record straight. What I reported was that in the "Cincinnati looks at the United Nations" study, it was only the pretested panel that showed any awareness of, or effects from, a very intensive public communications effort. The study involved two parts. The main one compared two separate but randomly equivalent samples of 1000, one taken before the campaign, one after, finding essentially no differences. The results of this had been published in the paper I cited. By oral report from one of the authors of that paper I learned of the subsidiary study done for Columbia's Bureau of Applied Social Research, which involved reinterviewing the pretest sample. By this oral report I learned, or thought I learned, of the outcome of that still unpublished study, and this is what I reported. It seemed a most apt illustration, just what was needed to make the point. Years later, Claire Selltiz, in the process of revising *Research Methods in Social Relations* (Selltiz, Jahoda, Deutsch, and Cook, 1959) spent a great deal of effort trying to track down a more precise reference, but without success, and therefore presented the retest study as a hypothetical possibility. Eventually there turned up a duplicated report by Glock (1958) presenting quite different findings: there were no significant differences between the pretested and unpretested posttest samples and not even trends in the direction of a sensitization or communication-enhancement effect. (A later presentation in Campbell and Stanley [1963] set the facts straight but did not give the detailed apology here presented.) This anecdote illustrates, I hope, the dependence of the argument upon the hypothesized laws, hypothesized empricial regularities, and therefore, the relevance of empirical fact to the establishment of a "necessary" scientific control. One important implication of this argument is that it is not failure-to-control in general that bothers us, but only those failures of control which permit *truly plausible* rival hypotheses, laws with a degree of scientific establishment comparable to or exceeding that of the law our experiment is designed to test.

Thus our current standards of experimental design represent a *scien-*

tific achievement, an *empirical* product, not a logical dispensation. They represent generally verified hypothetical laws—in the philosophers' terms, contingent, descriptive, synthetic, and therefore corrigible "truths," rather than logical or analytic truths. The "control group" is a feature we psychologists are taught as axiomatically required. It is seldom noted that it, or its analogue, is totally missing from most of the 19th century physics, chemistry, and physiology from which we took our methodological models. As Boring (1954) documents, it was invented as recently as 1907 to control for a plausible rival hypothesis quite specific to psychology, namely that pretests would produce gains in performance even in the absence of experimental treatments (that is what we can call a main effect of testing in contrast to the interaction effect of testing described above). Were it regularly to be found that there were no practice effects, this reason for the control group would be eliminated. This is not likely to be so for much of experimental psychology, but might be for persuasion studies, as Lana has noted. Our typical synchronous pretest-posttest-control group design also controls for other hypothetical rival explanations of change (Campbell, 1957). But for an experimental psychologist studying the learning of nonsense syllables, none of these are plausible enough explanations for a gain in memory so that he typically does without. Even in the most primitive one-group pretest-posttest design, the need for a pretest would not be there if it were not for the empirical facts that test-retest correlations are greater than zero and that individuals are not all equal.

Superimposed upon the simple control group are other required control groups whose empirical justification remains more obvious. Thus in cortical ablation studies, the sham-operation control group reflects the empirical fact of surgical shock. With accumulating evidence about the nature of surgical shock, it becomes an utterly implausible explanation for many ablation and electrode-stimulation effects, and as a result is dropping out of use. The placebo control group reflects the very well established law as to the therapeutic effects of believing one has received a curative treatment (see Orne, Chapter 5). Where pharmaceutical research is being tested in terms of the very general variable of illness-health, it still remains essential. For much more specific effects, it can often be skipped. The double-blind placebo control group reflects the further empirical law of the effect of experimenter faith when administering the pill, and gets us into the realm of facts which Rosenthal has so well documented (1966; and Chapter 6).

A major way in which this volume contributes to the science of psychological method is thus in establishing the need for new control groups. From Orne come "demand character" control groups. From Rosenthal come the high expectancy and low expectancy treatment replications. From Rosenberg come the evaluation apprehension control groups, and the recommendation of experimental arrangements disguising the administrative relation between treatment and posttest. McGuire's and Rosenthal's chapters in this volume provide confirmation of the law-like character of threats to validity, in showing how such variables can shift from being control problems to being focal.

III. A TYPOLOGY OF ARTIFACTS, BIASES, OR THREATS TO VALID INFERENCE

While threats to validity or artifacts can come from any aspect of the experimental process, and while a complete typology is not possible, it may help to lay out some recurrent types of artifact.

A. Confounded Aspects of the Experimental Treatment: Main Effects

For this purpose, we can regard as aspects of the experimental treatment *all* features which differ between experimental and control groups. Inevitably many of these are irrelevant to the theoretical variable we are manipulating. They are "instrumental incidentals." Such features are arbitrary, in that there might have been other implementations, but are unavoidable in that had there not been these incidentals, there would have had to have been others. No "pure treatments" are possible.

Each one of these irrelevant details is a potential rival explanation of an effect. A major class of artifacts is of this type. In this volume, it is exemplified by Rosenberg's specific claim that the relevant manipulation was not cognitive dissonance but evaluation apprehension. A still more general one is Rosenthal's criticism of a vast array of experiments, to the effect that differential experimenter expectation, rather than more specific treatment details, was the essential treatment variable.

Two ways of controlling a specific exemplar of this type of confound emerge. First, there is the way of the new control group, or the expanded-content control group. That is, the control group treatment is modified to include more of what was previously only experienced by the experimental group. The sham operation and the placebo control groups are of this sort. Thus a control group given equivalent evaluation apprehension, or demand-character, or experimenter expectancy is created, increasing the common denominator so that experimental and control groups no longer differ on this feature. Second, there is the opportunistic search for new modes of implementation in which the theoretical variable is exemplified without this particular rival variable, that is, through a modification of the experimental group. As a control, this involves an *a priori* preference for parsimony, for it is always possible that two separate irrelevancies, a different one in each setting, explain the superficially consistent results. Again, we must disregard this possibility except insofar as specific versions are developed and plausible.

B. Confounded Aspects of the Treatment: Interaction Effects

There may be a genuine effect of the theoretical variable that is specific to (or inhibited by) particular vehicular components. Again, the potentialities are so numerous that we pay attention only to explicitly elaborated and plausible hypotheses of this nature. More than that, we are even more likely to disregard or judge implausible an interaction effect than a main effect. Perhaps part of the reason for this is that main effects are more easily handled. Probably more important is the very general inferential generalization that main effects are more probable than interaction effects. This would be analogous to, or perhaps even a part of, Mill's inductive presupposition that nature is orderly. Such a generalization might be descriptively true, and it would seem to me worth an actuarial survey of analyses-of-variance in Ph.D. dissertations (a less biased sample than published research). But even if this is not descriptive of nature as we find her, it is descriptive of the knowable aspects of nature, a biased sample upon which science and simpler knowledge processes necessarily focus (Campbell, in press). By knowledge we mean, in part, usable reidentifiable samenesses in settings that are not identical. If the highest order interactions with the specifics of space, time, and attributes are always significant, then no generalization is possible, and hence no knowledge and no science. A successfully established main effect is a much more general generalization than is an interaction effect. Much of the basis for the recalibration of measurement dimensions is the search for that option of quantification which turns the most regularities into main effects.

Rival hypotheses in this class are *not* controlled by the expanded content control group approach, but would usually be by the altered experimental treatment. Note that this latter as a control here too involves the *a priori* preference for parsimony and the presumptive bias in favor of main effects. For it would always be possible that the apparent general confirmation of the law in two settings was in fact a coincidence of two separate specific interaction effects.

C. Background Interactions

Background here refers to those common features shared by both experimental and control groups. Inevitably these involved many features unspecified in theory, probably even more numerous in the social sciences than in the physical. All of these are potential sources of interaction effects with the theoretically relevant aspect of the treatment or, to be sure, with an irrelevant one of the aspects confounded with the treatment. Again, these are so numerous that we can only pay attention to the plausible and well developed rival hypotheses.

Hypotheses of interaction in this category, in the prior category, and in several to come below (as on subject selection) are in some sense not as serious threats as those in the first category. They represent only potential *limitations* on the generality of a law already established in one setting. It is only when that one setting is "artificial" and when we are interested primarily in applying our generalizations to other settings than that artificial laboratory, that such threats to validity worry us. The possible pretest sensitization in persuasion studies, discussed above, is of this nature. It should be recognized that an elegant science of persuasion restricted to pretested audiences would be a quite worthy scientific achievement, even if of little practical value, and that, by and large, the physical sciences have been preoccupied with predicting exclusively in laboratory settings, although, to be sure, in their truly impressive achievements they predict from one artificial laboratory to others of quite different structure.

In this case too, the expanded-content control group approach will not work, and a changed experimental treatment provides a general control.

D. Interactions with Population Characteristics

This paper is written in the context of "true experiments," not "quasi-experiments" (Campbell and Stanley, 1963), and hence population differences do not appear as spurious sources of main effects, i.e., as differences between experimental and control groups, but instead as potential limitations on the generality of laws observed in a study done with a specific population. We in social psychology may inherit a misleading super-ego ideal from sociology, to the effect that this should be solved by representative sampling from some universe of theoretical relevance, perhaps of all mankind. (Our emphasis on randomization to achieve equivalence between quite parochial experimental and control groups should not be confused with the sociologists' emphasis upon randomization to achieve representativeness of some specified population [Campbell and Stanley, 1963, 23].)

This is to be sure an unpracticed ideal. But it is so out of keeping with what we know of science that it should be removed even from our philosophy of science. A consideration of the time dimension will help show its utter unreasonableness. In the physical sciences, the presumption that there are no interactions with time (except those of daily, lunar, seasonal, and other cycles) has proved to be a reasonable one. But for the social sciences, a consideration of the potentially relevant population characteristics shows that changes over time (e.g., a 30-year comparison of college students) produce differences fully as large as synchronous social class and sub-cultural differences. To representatively sample from our intended universe of generalization would require representative sampling in time, an obvious impossibility.

More typical of science is the case of Nicholson and Carlisle. Taking in May, 1800, a very parochial and idiochronic sample of Soho water, inserting into it a very biased sample of copper wire, into which flowed a very local electrical current, they obtained hydrogen gas at one electrode, oxygen at the other, and uninhibitedly generalized to all the water in the world for all eternity. It was a hypothetical generalization, to be sure, rather than a proven fact. There have been by now many studies of the effect of "impurities" in the water upon hydrolysis, but these too have been done on very biased samples. The idea of a representative sampling of all the waters of the world, or of England, never occurred even as an ideal. The very concept of "impurities," of segregating the contents of water into the "pure" stuff and the alien contents, is one which would never have emerged had a representative sampling approach to water been employed. In the successful sciences, generalizations have never been "inductive" in the sense of summarizing what had been observed within the bounds of the generalization, but instead have always been presumptive, albeit guided by prior laws. The limitations to the generalization have emerged from checking in nonrepresentative ways on an initial bold generalization. Scientists assumed that hydrolysis held true universally until it was shown otherwise.

In this light, had we achieved one, there would be no need to apologize for a successful psychology of college sophomores, or even of Northwestern University coeds, or of Wistar strain white rats. Exciting and powerful laws would then be presumed to hold for all men or all vertebrates at all times, until specific applications of that presumption proved wrong. We already are at this latter stage, but even here a representative sampling of species or school populations is not the answer. Theory-guided, dimensional explorations, as in comparing primates widely varying in evolutionary development, are in the typical path of science.

Thus it would be a fine achievement, even though not science of proven universality, to have a lawful psychology of volunteer subjects (e.g., Rosenthal and Rosnow, Chapter 3). However, here too, when a specific plausible hypothesis has been developed, predicting restrictions on a generalization we very much want to make as to nonvolunteering populations, we attempt to control it. Not only would we want to generalize to such nonlaboratory populations for reasons of applied science, we in experimental social psychology also aspire on pure science grounds to bridging generalizations to the unavoidably nonexperimental social sciences. Also to be noted in the volunteer subject problem is the fact that the plausible interaction hypothesis affects not just one treatment variable, but a very large class of them, e.g., to the effect that volunteer subjects will show the results they believe the experimenter wants in *any* experiment. Such a hypothesis is indeed threatening enough, so that if empirically justified, it would make us want to shift populations for our basic exploratory studies.

E. Confounded Aspects of Measurement: Main Effects

Every measuring device, like every treatment, is dimensionally complex with many theoretically irrelevant vehicular components. The measured effects of the treatment could be due to one of these irrelevancies.

Such artifacts in measurement have generated a vast literature. There are no doubt hundreds of studies of response-sets in questionnaires, attitude tests, personality tests, etc. (e.g., Cronbach, 1946; 1950; Rorer, 1965; Campbell, Siegman, and Rees, 1967). Social desirability provides another vast literature (Edwards, 1957; Block, 1965). For ratings, there are halo effects and implicit rater theories of personality. There are artifacts in scores of dyadic discrepancy, inter-personal perception, and pattern similarity (Cronbach, 1958; Corsini, 1956; Silverman, 1959). Other measures, including observations, traces, and actuarial records, have analogous problems (Webb, *et al.*, 1966).

So far, such artifacts have been used in the literature in criticism of the interpretation of correlations and group differences, rather than in criticism of experiments. Thus social class differences in *F*-Scale authoritarianism have been criticized as due to the intelligence (Christie, 1954) or acquiescent response-set component of the measure rather than the authoritarian component, but similar criticisms of attitude change studies involving the *F*-Scale have not appeared. It is perhaps for this reason that this large segment of the research artifact literature is not represented in this volume.

Control for these problems is through the use of multiple measures differing in vehicular or method components (Campbell and Fiske, 1959; Campbell, 1960). In most laboratory experimentation more of this could be done than usually is, and with much less addition to research cost than would be involved in methodological replication of treatments. Probably more is done than is reported, because having multiple measures generates the jeopardy of discrepant results which are a great embarrassment to write up.

F. Confounded Aspects of Measurement: Interactions with Treatments

Even when the measured change is due to the theoretically relevant aspects of the measure, the irrelevant method components can condition the reaction—the observed reaction thus may be specific to this particular mode of measurement. Again, control of such a plausible rival hypothesis lies in alternative measurement devices. (Note that the interaction of the *relevant* aspects of pretest measurement with the treatment have been discussed above.)

IV. CONTROLLING ARTIFACTS

In the previous section, several distinguishable modes of control have been presented. There are: 1. Expanded-content control groups, in the tradition of sham operations and placebos; 2. Treatment replication with altered methods, and 3. Multiple methods in measurement. The present section continues this discussion with three additional points more general in nature.

A. Controlling Plausible Rival Hypotheses through Supplementary Variation

This heading refers to a very general technique of partial or inferential control useable for many settings in which direct or complete control is not possible. While its primary application has been in quasi-experimental settings, it is available also in experimental ones. One noteworthy implication is that clarity of inference sometimes may be improved by deliberately reducing the quality of part of the data collected. Let us begin with such an illustration.

In our study of cultural differences in susceptibility to optical illusion (Segall, *et al.*, 1966) one of the plausible rival explanations of the differences obtained was in terms of variations in the administration of the visual tasks by the various anthropologists involved. To control this, we made what seems to me now to have been the amazingly brave decision to deliberately debase half of our best controlled data collection. Instructions were for the test pages to be held vertically at four feet from the respondents' eyes, not the easiest position to achieve if the same person is also to record results. In our Evanston sample of 200, collected on a door-to-door survey sample basis, half were done correctly, and the other half were administered as in table-top presentation, at one and one half feet from the eyes with the booklet in a horizontal position. The latter was thought to be more slovenly than any actual administration, but in the likely direction of deviation. These two conditions did produce differences, but small ones, not at all sufficient to explain the cultural differences which were five to seven times larger. Our resultant power of inferences was greater than had all of the Evanston data been of the best quality.

The study also provides a second illustration. After the major body of data had been collected, published research appeared indicating that inspection time differences were a possible plausible rival explanation. These we "controlled" by collecting a new Evanston sample in which two exposure times were used, one very brief, the other much larger than was likely to have occurred in any sample. Here again, while there were differences, they were of much too small a magnitude to explain the major cultural differences.

In his book on data quality control, Naroll (1962) divides ethnographies used in quantitive cross-cultural comparisons into two or more levels of quality. For example, if the ethnographer lived in the area for two or more years, and if he learned the local language, the ethnography would be classed as of high quality. Variables such as belief in witchcraft and non-European positions in childbirth turn out to be correlated with data quality, being more apt to be noted by those with better acquaintance. Any two such variables will as a result show a spurious correlation with each other. By introducing the variation in data quality, Naroll is able to rule out or confirm the existence of such spurious correlation.

Bitterman (1965), working in the quite different laboratory of comparative psychology, has arrived at the more general methodological percept of which these quality variations are one illustration:

"I do not, of course, know how to arrange a set of conditions for the fish which will make sensory and motor demands exactly equal to those which are made upon the rat in some given experimental situation. Nor do I know how to equate drive level or reward value in the two animals. Fortunately, however, meaningful comparisons still are possible, because for *control by equation* we may substitute what I call *control by systematic variation*. Consider, for example, the hypothesis that the difference between the curves which you see here is due to a difference, not in learning, but in degree of hunger. The hypothesis implies that there is a level of hunger at which the fish will show progressive improvement, and put in this way, the hypothesis becomes easy to test. We have only to vary level of hunger widely in different groups of fish, which we know well how to do. If, despite the widest possible variation in hunger, progressive improvement fails to appear in the fish, we may reject the hunger hypothesis. Hypotheses about other variables also may be tested by systematic variation. With regard to the question of reversal learning, I shall simply say here that progressive improvement has appeared in the rat under a wide variety of experimental conditions—it is difficult, in fact, to find a set of conditions under which the rat does not show improvement. In the fish, by contrast, reliable evidence of improvement has failed to appear under a variety of conditions." (Bitterman, 1965, 396–410)

As applied for the control of artifacts, two types can be distinguished. On the one hand there is *interpolating* or *bracketing variation,* in which the supplementary variation includes the whole likely range or more. The two illustrations from the optical illusions study are of that nature. As controls, these assume linearity or monotonicity of laws, i.e., that intermediate values would have intermediate effect. This is usually a reasonable enough assumption to render the threat implausible if the extreme bracketing values find it so.

Second, there is *extrapolating variation,* in which we do not have full access to all values of the dimension, and to achieve our control must extrapolate outside the range of explored values to unobtainable values. The problem of volunteer respondents might be such. What we would like to do is to extrapolate to the nonvolunteering population, but in even the best we can do, some degree of volunteering is required. A degree of control is introduced if one adds a much more extremely voluntary situation, more voluntary than would normally be used. If these two degrees of voluntarism show the same laws, we extrapolate, assuming monotonicity, to the condition of no voluntarism at all. Here the assumptions involved seem intuitively less plausible than in the bracketing case, but are still plausible enough to make such a control worth adding. In this case too we have added a body of deliberately poorer data.

A widespread utilization of supplementary variation as a control is in the common practice of classifying respondents on the basis of postsession interviews as to degree of awareness of the experimenter's purpose, and checking the replication of the same laws in such subgroups. McGuire's research, in this volume, has extended this by deliberately introducing more extreme degrees of awareness on an experimental basis.

B. Heteromethod Replication

The reiterated history in research on artifacts is for an exciting original one-treatment, one-measure experiment to be criticized with specific plausible rival hypotheses, and to be followed up by a series of experiments with expanded control groups or changed treatment method, or changed measurement method, until the original finding is doubly confirmed or rejected in favor of some rival interpretation. Even where the field is active and research is cheap, this cycle takes a good ten years or more, as illustrated by Rosenberg's work on the dissonance experiments, reported in this volume. Any strategy which would cut down on this wasteful procedure would seem at first glance to be worth introducing.

If one reviews the control comments in the previous section on types of artifact, one notes a very general utility to varied experimental implementation. Multiple methods of measurement have a parallel value. There emerges the suggestion of routinely programming heteromethod replication in the initial research phase. Each Ph.D. research would, for example, be required to induce the treatment variable in two methodologically independent ways, and for each implementation to measure the effects by two independent methods. If an hypothesized law was initially confirmed in all of the four heteromethod replications thus generated, most of the probably plausible rival hypotheses would have been ruled out in advance (without having ever been explicitly formulated). If all four were not consistent, but if there were several strong effects, the candidate would be left with a challenging empirical puzzle upon which to work, but without the temptation to over-strong theoretical claims which he would have had if he had only seen one part of the puzzle.

This methodological precept is, however, not recommended. If I judge our present theoretical successes and experimental skills properly, full confirmation would almost never be found. The process would in general be much more discouraging than present practice, so much more so that many would cease research altogether. Journal editors would almost certainly reject an honest presentation, under current standards against publishing negative results on novel hypotheses, and these standards are probably correct from the point of view of optimal collective information processing (Campbell, 1959, 168–170). The social system of science requires sufficient motivation to produce scientific investigations in redundant number. That motivation is much higher when each investigator believes that he has the optimal method, and, when his expectations are confirmed, believes that he has proven a true theory. Some degree of over-optimism may be necessary, both in anticipation and in retrospect upon accomplished research. So too with a perspective on artifacts in general, perhaps it is motivationally best not to anticipate these as an overwhelmingly likely aspect of all research, but instead to close our eyes to their general possibility, and to regard each such challenge as it appears as a specific local anomaly in an otherwise straight-forward scientific quest.

If we are indeed in an extremely difficult arena, then there is even a motivational utility in the regular occurrence of exciting findings which later are discounted as artifacts. These provide exciting rewards to the would-be discoverers, and exciting rewards to the successful critics (the more exciting the greater the reputation of the false claims). These are rewards and motivation for experimental work and empirical explora-tion. Both would be lost under a procedure that effectively screened out over-optimistic pseudo-confirmations of exciting theories.

C. Disguised Experiments in Natural Settings

While the formalism of the previous section provided a useful general perspective on possible artifacts, it serves to fragment a central class of plausible rival hypotheses with which this volume deals. This we can call *awareness of experimentation*, or as I once labeled it in 1957, *reactive arrangements*:

"In any of the experimental designs, the respondents can become aware that they are participating in an experiment, and this awareness can have an interactive effect, in creating reactions to X [experimental treatment] which would not occur had X been encountered without this 'I'm a guinea pig' attitude. Lazarsfeld (1948), Kerr (1945), and Rosen-thal and Frank (1956), all have provided valuable discussions of this problem. Such effects limit generalizations to respondents having this awareness, and preclude generalization to the population encountering X with nonexperimental attitudes. The direction of the effect may be one of negativism, such as an unwillingness to admit to any persuasion or change. This would be comparable to the absence of any immediate effect from discredited communicators, as found by Hovland (1953). The result is probably more often a cooperative responsiveness, in which the respondent accepts the experimenter's expectations and provides pseudoconfirmation. Particularly is this positive response likely when the respondents are self-selected seekers after the cure that X may offer. The Hawthorne studies (Roethlisberger and Dickson, 1939), illustrate such sympathetic changes due to awareness of the experimentation rather than to the specific nature of X.

"The problem of reactive arrangements is distributed over all features of the experiment which can draw the attention of the respondent to the fact of experimentation and its purposes. The conspicuous or reactive pretest is particularly vulnerable, inasmuch as it signals the topics and purposes of the experimenter. For communications of obviously persuasive aim, the experimenter's topical intent is signaled by the X itself, if the communication does not seem a part of the natural environment. Even for the posttest-only groups, the occurrence of the posttest may create a reactive effect. The respondent may say to himself, 'Aha, now I see why we got that movie.' This consideration justifies the practice of disguising the connection between O [observation or measurement] and X . . . as through having different experimental personnel involved, using different façades, separating the settings and times, and embedding the X-relevant content of O among a disguising variety of other topics." (Campbell, 1957, 308–309)

Many, although not all, of the artifacts covered in the previous chapters are subsumable under the hypothesis that the results are what they are only because the subjects were aware that they were being experimented with, including the possibility of differential awareness on the part of the experimental group. Orne's demand characteristics (Chapter 5) are entirely of this nature, although the placebo effects which he also reviews are not, inasmuch as they no doubt are also characteristic of nonexperimental medical applications of drugs. Pretest sensitization (Chapter 4), had it been empirically established, would have been in this class, and possibly the commitment effect of pretest is also due to awareness that one's pretest and posttest scores will be experimentally compared. Volunteering for an experiment (Chapter 3) implies awareness of an experiment to be volunteered for. Experimenter effects (Chapter 6) are not in general of this nature (indeed, the Pygmalion effects occur with neither teacher nor pupil aware of the experiment) but those aspects of them due to respondent cooperation with the perceived goal of the experiment are. Suspiciousness of experimenter's intent (Chapter 2) is a near synonym of the category head here used, and McGuire's measures and experimental manipulations are specific illustrations of it. Evaluation apprehension (Chapter 7) is entirely a matter of awareness of experimentation, at least in the illustrations Rosenberg provides. The interaction effects of measurement which have led to efforts at indirect attitude measurement (Campbell, 1950; Kidder and Campbell, in press) and unobtrusive measurement (Webb, et al., 1966) are of this nature. The issue of "experimental realism" versus "mundane realism" (Aronson and Carlsmith, 1968) is to a large extent a matter of awareness. While much of the research reported in this volume is reassuring, much of it is not. The alternative of simulation (e.g., Brown, 1962; Kelman, 1967; Orne, Chapter 5) is clearly useful as an auxiliary, but unappealing as a substitute because it carries awareness of experiment to an extreme.

The obvious cure for all these artifacts is the disguised experiment in which the respondents (if not the experimenters) are unaware of participating in an experiment, are unaware that they are "being experimented with." Such experiments are best done in natural rather than laboratory settings, not because natural settings are more representative of the target of generalization, but rather because in natural settings respondents do not suspect they are being experimented with. Laboratories, in general, are perceived as just that, i.e., as settings for experiments.

The force of the argument may be strengthened if we note that most of the laboratory studies with dramatic "experimental realism" achieve this by distracting the respondent with some plausible façade or cover story while introducing the treatment as an incidental or accidental event. Thus French (1944) assembled groups for discussion purposes and then used smoke seeping under the door as an experimental treatment. Orne (Chapter 5) uses an "accidental" power failure, Darley and Latané (1968) an epileptic seizure. For some, the real experiment is among the respondents waiting to serve in the experiment. For the innumerable experiments using a confederate, the treatment is the performance of a fellow respondent. The incidental fact that one experimenter was Negro, the other Caucasian has been used (Rankin and Campbell, 1955). The respondent has frequently been led to believe that he is the experimenter (e.g., Festinger and Carlsmith, 1959; Milgram, 1963), and so forth. All of these are efforts to use the natural aspects of the setting, to evade the effects of awareness of experimentation. The utility of these deceptions is being lost through publicity, but can be regained for a while by moving out of the laboratory entirely.

Social psychology has had by now enough experience with disguised experiments in natural settings to provide the basis of a mature taxonomy and methodology. Webb and his associates (1966) have provided very useful beginnings, although their focus is on measurement rather than experimental treatments. Aronson and Carlsmith (1968) provide another part of the framework. The projected book by Gross, Collins, and Bryan (in preparation) may fill the bill as also may Rosenblatt and Miller (in preparation), but the task has not yet been done, nor will this chapter do it. However, a few paragraphs and illustrations are in order. Preparatory to the illustrations, two general issues will be raised that provide perspectives for evaluation.

1. Content restrictions. What are needed for a fully disguised natural setting experiment are a natural mode of contact to persons (or to social units small enough and numerous enough so that random assignment to treatments achieves effective equation) with the mode of contact being private enough so that there is no awareness that other units are getting different treatments, and with a natural response available in the same setting relevant as a measure of effect. If they are to retain naturalness, such settings cannot be created at will for all possible treatments and with all possible measures. Instead, they must be opportunistically hit upon. Any given setting will inevitably impose great restrictions on the kinds of problems that can be studied in it. These restrictions will be upon the kinds of experimental variables that can be implemented and upon the modes of measurement available.

2. *Deceit, debriefing, and other ethical issues.* Disguised experiments obviously involve deceit at some level, and as McGuire (Chapter 2, part 5) and Kelman (1967) make clear, this is an undersirable feature only justified by more important considerations. One of these considerations is the moral value of producing a nontrivial social science. In any such comparative weighing of competing values, the degree of each becomes relevant, for example the magnitude of the deceit. In terms of pain to the liar (the experimenter), white lies are less painful than black ones (McGuire's "active deceit"), and while they may be equally damaging to the recipient, he would likewise judge them less immoral, due to our linguistic legalism. Lying of either sort is less painful and less immoral when occurring in a setting where it is both expected and justified by convention. In terms of debasing language and our communal ability to depend upon the verbal reports of others (Asch, 1952; Campbell, 1965), the effect is greater the more that lying is conspicuously exhibited by high prestige models. For all of these, the adaptation-level created by other segments of social practice provides a relativistic comparison base. A flagrant lie is less immoral introduced into a language community where such lies are frequent than when it is a novelty.

In these terms, disguised naturalistic experiments vary greatly, and probably in balance present no greater problems than do laboratory ones. They probably depend more on nonverbal or white lies, less on direct deceit. They operate typically in arenas of discourse already more debased by deceit than are the halls of learning. If lying is revealed, the modeling impact is presumably less than it is in the professor-student relationship. But natural settings generally lack the implicit convention of acceptable lying which the psychology laboratory may be achieving.[*]

[*] Indeed, one practical way of avoiding the ethical problem on campus would be to announce to all members of the subject pool at the beginning of the term, "In about half of the experiments you will be participating in this semester, it will be necessary for the validity of the experiment for the experimenter to deceive you in whole or in part as to his exact purpose. Nor will we be able to inform you as to which experiments these were or as to what their real purpose was, until after all the data for the experiment have been collected. We give you our guarantee that no possible danger or invasion of privacy will be involved, and that your responses will be held in complete anonymity and privacy. We ask you at this time to sign the required permission form, agreeing to participate in experiments under these conditions." This would merely be making explicit what is now generally understood, and probably would not worsen the problem of awareness and suspicion that now exists.

A separate problem is that of obtaining the respondent's permission, a problem which has become of great practical importance now that half of our research support requires it. This is obviously an impossibility in the experimental setups to be described here, if disguise and unawareness is to be maintained. On the other hand, in those settings using means and ranges of communication that are within the public domain, and which nonexperimenters are using freely without such permission, this becomes an utterly unreasonable requirement.

Another ethical problem is that of invasion of privacy. This is not a necessary aspect of disguised naturalistic experiments, and indeed is an impossibility in some. Anonymity of records is an aspect of the problem. However, when potentially embarrassing material is collected in a manner that makes possible linking it with the person's name, the threat to the invasion of privacy is made worse by the disguise and the lack of permission. Injury, including humiliation and insult, is a problem no greater in degree than in laboratory experiments.

Debriefing, explaining to the respondent the true nature of the experiment, apologizing for the deception, and if possible, providing feedback of the results are procedures characteristic of the self-announced campus laboratory and generally omitted from the disguised field experiment. While such debriefing has come to be a standard part of deception experiments in the laboratory, it has many ethical disadvantages. It is many times more of a comfort to the experimenter for his pain at deceiving than to the respondent who may learn in the process of his own gullibility, conformity, cruelty, or bias. It provides modeling and publicity for deceit and thus serves to debase language for the respondent as well as for the experimenter. It reduces the credibility of the laboratory and undermines the utility of deceit in future experiments.* Argyle (1962), Milton Rokeach (personal communications), Stollak (1967), McGuire (Chapter 2), and Aronson and Carlsmith (1968) have called attention to these disadvantages, and they are strong enough to justify elimination of debriefing in those cases where the experimental treatment falls within the range of the respondent's ordinary experience, merely being an experimental rearrangement of normal-level communications. This normal range is certainly exceeded in the Asch (1956) studies that present eight fellow Swarthmore students in solid contradiction of what would ordinarily have been a simple perceptual judgment, or the Milgram (1963) studies in which the respondent had to administer strong electrical shocks to a fellow student. It is probably exceeded in persuasive

* The gleeful reporting of deception experiments in introductory psychology texts and lectures is probably still more important in regard to these last two points.

communications containing fictitious facts on important topics, but is probably not exceeded in most persuasion studies. In experimental social psychology, we are doomed to wear out our laboratories. For this reason we are already leaving the college in favor of the high school, the grammar school, and the street. Publicity will eventually contaminate these laboratories too, but this process will be greatly increased, and public anger over the deception not reduced, by debriefing in disguised naturalistic experiments.

3. *A range of classic studies.* Gosnell (1927) sent persuasive messages to registered voters urging them to vote, and used precinct records to later determine whether or not the member of different experimental and control groups had voted, achieving an entirely inconspicuous experiment using a range of communications well within normal limits. While today there would be distrust of Chicago's precinct records, other cities' are still useable. Here is a laboratory which should have been reused a hundred times by now, but so far as I know, it has not been reused even once. While the topic is very narrow, the persuasive messages could vary along a wide range of the experimental dimensions utilized in laboratory persuasion studies. The value of this laboratory would greatly increase if one could use how the person voted as well as whether he voted. While this information is not public for individuals, it is public for precincts as a whole, and this became the sampling unit for Hartmann's (1936) classic study of rational versus emotional political leaflets. Used in a state like California in which voters get to vote on issues as well as persons, a very wide range of persuasion theories could be tested. Again, Hartmann's laboratory has not been reused. In these studies, permission and debriefing would seem totally unwarranted, unless the content of the communications contained libel or falsehood, and if so, debriefing after the election would certainly raise a storm of justified protest. Thus the range of experimental stimuli is certainly limited—but could still cover one-sided versus two-sided communications, extremity of position advocated, or degree of adulatory vocabulary. Gosnell and Hartmann were both advocating sides they genuinely believed in. (Hartmann was himself running for mayor on the Socialist ticket.) This sincerity, and the related nondeception, would be lost in primacy-recency studies in which both of opposing alternatives are advocated, unless experimenters of opposing advocacies collaborated, or unless an experimenter got endorsements for the appropriate messages from the opposing sides. This is moving into the white-lie area, but on the other hand all that need be manipulated is the when and to-whom of messages that are going to get partial and haphazard distribution anyway. (In such studies one would often give disproportionate pub-

licity to minor issues, just because of the relative absence of other communications on the same topic.) Using this laboratory for conformity studies (Campbell, 1951) one would abstain from feedback of falsified public opinion poll results, so readily used in the college laboratory, and limit one's comparisons to the presence or absence of feedback, and the source (precinct, state, or nation) from which the feedback came. This limitation would in some cases represent a very real sacrifice in clarity of experimental inference, but to present falsified poll results would be an intolerable tampering with the ballot, quite different in kind than had not the action of voting been involved.

Most disguised field experiments provide more limited laboratories than this, and are opportunistically hit upon for very specific purposes. Thus in a conformity study Lefkowitz, Blake, and Mouton (1955) modeled walking across an intersection against the light, in high-status or low-status clothing, and observed the effect upon an observer's tendency to violate the traffic light. Schwartz and Skolnick (1962) manipulated the contents of applicant briefs sent to employers of temporary summer resort help, studying the effect of a criminal record upon employability. Schwartz and Orleans (1967) used income tax returns to measure aroused fear of legal sanctions. Bryan and Test (1966) created the altruism opportunity of helping a woman with a flat tire: with and without a prior helping model. Page (1958) randomly applied motivating comments on student papers and measured impressive effects on later classroom tests. Doob and Gross (1968) used the horn-honking response of the car behind and the experimental treatments of failing to go when the light went green, in high-status versus low-status cars.

While some of these are such restricted laboratories that one can hardly imagine any other problem being studied in them, some could be more broadly used. Thus the Schwartz and Skolnick setting could be used for a wide variety of topics in impression formation or the presentation of self, albeit with a very impoverished dimensionality of effect measures. Even a technique seemingly so narrowly focused on honesty as the lost letter technique (Merritt and Fowler, 1948) lends itself to the addition of many other variables. By addressing envelopes to attitude-relevant groups, Milgram (Milgram, Mann, and Harter, 1965; Milgram, 1969) has obtained performance measures of attitude of seemingly high validity. By leaving the envelopes unsealed, Gross (1968) has been able to use variations in letter content to manipulate a variety of variables.

4. Employment. Essential to experimentation is arbitrary control over some segment of a person's time. It is this arbitrariness which cuts the causal links between past conditions and experimental treatments and which makes possible randomly assigning equivalent samples to different treatments. The greater this arbitrary control, the greater the multipurpose experimental utility. One such setting is provided by the employment situation. I will neglect here its use in applied experiments focused on the employer's problems and administrative options (e.g., Feldman, 1937; Kerr, 1945), and focus instead on the uses of employment for research in theoretical social psychology. Adams (1963) has set an outstanding example in his studies of pay inequity and work produced. Typical is his use of short term part-time employees, in which the wages paid represent a research cost of the same order of magnitude as paying subjects in the manifest laboratory. Stuart Cook (1964) has used this setting in his classic study (as yet unpublished) of the effect of equal-status contact on race attitudes.

The admirable study of Rokeach and Mezei (1966) used a related setting, the employment agency, in replicating a finding already demonstrated in more artificial laboratories. (Close inspection of their results, however, suggests some degree of leaning-over-backwards in the direction of fair-play in interracial contacts, a trend possibly symptomatic of reactive arrangements.)

In these illustrative studies, no extreme or damaging treatments were involved, there being merely a scheduling of experiences that some would have been, or might well have been, exposed to anyway. For these studies, debriefing would seem unnecessary, if not unwise, and the ethical problems of deception minimal. But this is of course a matter of the nature of the treatments. Consider in contrast the use of military assignment power to create a realistic threat of imminent death (Berkun, Bialek, Kern, and Yagi, 1962; Daily Palo Alto Times, 1959; Argyle, 1960), a landmark in unethical excess of scientific zeal.

5. *Encounters in public places.* There are a considerable range of experimental stimuli that can be administered in the chance encounters of strangers. Bryan and Test (1967) set up a Salvation Army kettle on the sidewalk and varied the ethnicity of the Salvation Army member and the presence or absence of a model giving. Feldman (1968) had locals and foreigners ask for directions, ask for help in mailing a letter, and ask if the respondent had dropped the dollar bill just found. Cook, Bean, Cialdini, Krovetz, and Ray (submitted) have done an interesting study in which a somewhat unusually forward but nonthreatening stranger complimented a woman walking on a campus, the effects being measured by a charity appeal set up farther along the path (and by interviewers who were posing as survey takers and who asked the women questions about their reactions to the different kinds of compliment). Milgram, Bickman and Berkowitz (submitted) set up experimental seed-crowds

of varying size and noted the number of passers-by who were thereby attracted. Sommer's (1959) approach to interpersonal space lends itself to such settings, through asking strangers questions, sitting next to them on public conveyances, at cafeteria tables, etc. The possibilities are wide in range, including the ethically unacceptable. Rumors already provide reports of epileptic seizures enacted on streets, of experimental taxi drivers introducing unexplained delays to frustrate anxious passengers, and the like.

6. *Sample solicitation.* For persuasion studies, a broadly flexible disguised laboratory is provided by all those settings in which custom sanctions make appeals to strangers. Intrinsically, a response measure is made available in the natural response to the appeal. Selling, fund raising, and petition circulating exemplify the sanctioned goals; direct mail, telephone, and door-to-door contacts, the sanctioned means. Survey research establishments provide a readily transferable sampling technology and staff (and what more poetic reversal than to have public opinion surveyors pose as salesmen). Door-to-door or letter-to-letter variations in the persuasive appeal provide an elegant opportunity for random equivalence without respondents being aware of experimentation. (Spatial separation of comparison groups receiving different appeals would often be desirable to avoid suspicion through respondents comparing experiences.) It is a commentary on the ethics of white lies that the experimenter and the door-bell-ringers would feel better about the deception if a genuine interest in the fund collection or the product promotion could be incorporated, as it often could be by offering one's services to the relevant causes. Note here an additional financial advantage, in that costs-of-collection are legitimately deductible from the proceeds in much charitable fund raising. Salesmen's commissions would have a similar role. These "sincere" façades would also expedite getting the solicitation permits that most police departments now require. One can envisage primacy-recency studies in which funds were solicited alternately for the White Citizen's League and the Black Power Coalition. One could study the effect of degrees of fear arousing appeals for nuclear disarmament on the sales of air-raid-shelter construction plans.

For fund raising, the amount given provides a relevant quantification, and the comments of even the noncontributors can be graded in favorableness. For sales, the dichotomous sale-no-sale can be enriched by a series of Guttman scale steps, through offering postcards which can be used for postponed purchase decisions, booklets with additional information, etc. For petitions, the natural measure is dichotomous, but not unuseable on that account, and comments are codeable as in opinion surveys, (although face-to-face recording of comments would be out).

In some settings, a mild and a strong version of the petition could be offered without reducing plausibility.

Blake and his associates (Blake, Mouton, and Hain, 1956; Helson, Blake, and Mouton, 1958) have pioneered the use of petitions in nonlaboratory campus studies, as have also Gore and Rotter (1963). In the advertising industry there are some highly applied experiments with direct mail advertising. Cook and Insko (1968) have used mailed letters of differing contents as experimental treatments. Brock (1965) has used a salesman in a store to administer varying experimental treatments. It is probable that door-to-door sales companies have done some deliberate experimentation in techniques. But by and large, this vast range of possibilities has not been utilized for the purposes of science.

While opinion surveys would seem apt to invoke a "guinea pig" effect, they have become enough a part of the public scene so that several theoretically oriented experimenters have used them to present varied treatments in disguised field experiments (e.g., Abelson and Miller, 1967; Freedman and Fraser, 1966; Miller and Levy, 1967). They are less disguised than sample solicitations in general. Artifices have to be added to introduce persuasive content or other treatment, while solicitation provides the occasion for persuasion. On the other hand they offer the special advantage of justifying verbal attitude measures.

Customers as well as salesmen may be experimenters. The old civil-rights approach of "test cases" provides such an experimental paradigm for field experimentation on the effect of race on access to housing, overnight lodging (La Piere, 1934), service in restaurants (Kutner, Wilkins, and Yarrow, 1952), etc. Franzen (1950) experimentally varied customer's behavior in scaling the willingness of druggists to give medical advice. Jung (1959) experimented by presenting automobile dealers with customers of varying degrees of gullibility. Feldman (1968) varied the ethnicity customers and studied merchants' acceptance of inadvertant overpayment and taxi drivers overcharges. E. Schaps* is studying helping behavior among shoe salesmen as a function of customer dependency (e.g., a woman with or without a broken heel on the shoe she is wearing), costs or comparison level for alternatives (other customers waiting for service or not), and visibility (the experimental customer has a friend with her or not). The main dependent variable is the number of shoes shown the customer, although codings of verbal responses are also available. Ethical issues in the design of the study include whether or not to debrief the salesman and remunerate him for his time. Arguing against these procedures are the following considerations. The treatment does

---

* "Some determinants of helping and exploitative behaviors in a field situation," Ph.d. dissertation, in preparation. (Northwestern University.)

not exceed the frustratingness of the regular range of female customers, some 30 per cent of whom do not make purchases in any given visit. Given sufficient budget and the use of a large number of experimental customers, a desirable feature in any event (Hammond, 1954; Brunswik, 1956), a final purchase could be included without social waste. The setting is one in which the social norms for deceit have already been debased not only through deceit in salesmanship, but also through the use of pseudo-customers to check on employee courtesy, effectiveness, and honesty, entrapments which also invade privacy by attaching the acts to the salesman's name. In contrast, the research customer provides complete privacy and anonymity. Debriefing would probably not reduce the salesman's frustration, but merely change its target. For a professional proud of his sophistication and cynicism, it would be painful to learn he'd been had. Some damage to the future utility of natural settings would result even from the salesman's private communications, and the possibility of journalistic publicity would be greatly enhanced. The nature of the experimental treatment is the crucial factor, and those treatments requiring debriefing should probably not be used anyway without the respondent's permission. On the other hand there are the ethical values of a relevant and dependable social science, and our desperate shortage of appropriate laboratories.

7. *Artifacts.* A spirit of advocacy has slipped in to the presentation of the previous paragraphs, but this must not be allowed to blind us to the fact that disguised field experiments share the epistemological predicament described so pessimistically in the earlier sections of this paper. It is only the one family of artifacts related to awareness of participating in an experiment that is controlled. Of the artifacts treated in this volume, it is obvious that experimenter effects will be likely in most of the natural settings here described, aggravated in some by the experimenter having to record verbal reactions after having left the respondent. For each of them, the treatment variable and the response measure will turn out to be conceptually complex, with irrelevant aspects frequently responsible for the results, either as main effects or as modifying interactions. For the natural response measures involved, Webb and associates (1966), in spite of their generally optimistic tone, have provided detailed grounds for pessimism. In the end, expanded-content control groups or replication with varied treatments and measures will be required just as they have been for laboratory studies.

V. SUMMARY

The logic of scientific inference indicates that experiments cannot prove theories, but only probe them. For every theory-corroborating experimental result there are an infinity of rival explanations potentially available, a few of which we must attend to because they are both explicitly advocated and have a plausibility comparable to that of the theory corroborated. A major class of these plausible rival hypotheses are methodological artifacts introduced through irrelevant vehicular aspects of the experimental treatment or the measuring device, either as main effects or interactions.

Control can never be complete in ruling out all plausible rival hypotheses in advance. As a rule, research must seek out ways of controlling each artifact as it is developing, through means that are specific to each combination of artifact hypothesis and theoretical variable. But general-purpose controls are discovered for recurrent classes of artifacts, and these become the empirically developed methodological requirements of a field. General strategies of control include expanding the content of the control group, varying the vehicular irrelevancies of the treatment variable, varying the method of measurement, and supplementary variation in data quality.

Because most of the important artifact hypotheses in laboratory social psychology are made possible by the respondent's awareness that he is participating in an experiment, attention is given to the techniques and ethics of disguised experiments in natural, nonlaboratory settings. Such experiments do not avoid the general artifact problem, but just this one type.

REFERENCES

Abelson, R. P., and Miller, J. C. Negative persuasion via personal insult. *Journal of Experimental and Social Psychology,* 1967, **3,** 321–333.

Adams, J. S. Toward an understanding of inequity. *Journal of Abnormal and Social Psychology,* 1963, **67,** 422–436.

Argyle, M. Report to the Council of the British Psychological Society on my dealings with the APA Committee on Scientific and Professional Ethics and Conduct. June 24, 1960. (Mimeo)

Argyle, M. Experimental studies of small social groups. *In* A. T. Welford, M. Argyle, O. V. Glass, and J. N. Morris, (Eds.), *Society: Problems and methods of study,* London: Routledge and Kegan Paul, 1962, 77–89.

Aronson, E., and Carlsmith, J. M. Experimentation in social psychology. *Handbook of Social Psychology,* (2nd ed.), Volume 2, Reading, Massachusetts: 1968, 1–79.

Asch, S. E. *Social Psychology,* Englewood Cliffs, New Jersey: Prentice Hall, 1952.

Asch, S. E. Studies of independence and conformity: I. A. minority of one against a unanimous majority. *Psychological Monographs,* 1956, **70,** No. 9 (whole number 416).

Berkun, M., Bialek, H. M., Kern, R. P., and Yagi, K. Experimental studies of psychological stress in man. *Psychological Monographs,* 1962, **76** (15, whole number 534) 39.

Bitterman, M. E. Phyletic differences in learning. *American Psychologist,* 1965, **20**, 396–410.

Blake, R. R., Mouton, J. S., and Hain, J. D. Social forces in petition signing. *Southwest Social Science Quarterly,* 1956, **36**, 385–390.

Block, J. *The challenge of response sets.* New York: Appleton-Century-Crofts, 1965.

Boring, E. G. The nature and history of experimental control. *American Journal of Psychology,* 1954, **67**, 573–589.

Brock, T. C. Communicator-recipient similarity and decision change. *Journal of Personality and Social Psychology,* 1965, **1**, 650–654.

Brown, R. Models of attitude change. *In* R. Brown, E. Galanter, E. H. Hess, & G. Mandler, *New directions in psychology.* New York: Holt, Rinehart & Winston, 1962.

Brunswik, E. *Perception and the representative design of psychological experiments.* (2nd ed.) Berkeley: University of California Press, 1956.

Bryan, J., and Test, M. A. Models and helping: naturalistic studies of aiding behavior. *Journal of Psychology and Social Psychology,* 1967, **6**, 400–407.

Campbell, D. T. The indirect assessment of social attitudes. *Psychological Bulletin,* 1950, **47** (1), 15–38.

Campbell, D. T. On the possibility of experimenting with the "bandwagon" effect. *International Journal of Opinion and Attitude Research,* 1951, **5** (2), 251–260. Reprinted in H. Hyman and E. Singer (Eds.), *Readings in Reference Group Theory and Research.* New York: The Free Press, 1968, 452–460.

Campbell, D. T. Factors relevant to the validity of experiments in social settings. *Psychological Bulletin,* 1957, **54** (4), 297–312.

Campbell, D. T. Methodological suggestions from a comparative psychology of knowledge processes. *Inquiry* (University of Oslo Press), 1959, **2**, 152–182.

Campbell, D. T. Recommendations for APA test standards regarding construct, trait, or discriminant validity. *American Psychologist,* 1960, **15**, 546–553.

Campbell, D. T. Variation and selective retention in socio-cultural evolution. *In* H. R. Barringer, G. I. Blanksten, and R. W. Mack, (Eds.), *Social change in developing areas: a reinterpretation of evolutionary theory.* Cambridge, Massachusetts: Schenkman, 1965, 19–49.

Campbell, D. T. Pattern matching as an essential in distal knowing. *In* K. R. Hammond, (Ed.), *Egon Brunswik's Psychology.* New York: Holt, Rinehart and Winston, 1966, 81–106.

Campbell, D. T. Evolutionary Epistemology. *In* P. A. Schilpp (Ed.) *The philosophy of Karl R. Popper. In: The library of living philosophers.* La Salle, Illinois: The Open Court Publishing Co., (volume in press).

Campbell, D. T., and Fiske, D. W. Convergent and discriminant validation by the multitrait-multimethod matrix. *Psychological Bulletin,* 1959, **56** (2), 81–105.

Campbell, D. T., and Stanley, J. C. Experimental and quasi-experimental designs for research on teaching. *In* N. L. Gage (Ed.), *Handbook of research on teaching.* Chicago: Rand McNally, 1963, 171–246. Reprinted as *Experimental and quasi-experimental design for research.* Chicago: Rand McNally, 1966.

Campbell, D. T., Siegman, C. R., and Rees, M. B. Direction-of-wording effects in the relationships between scales. *Psychological Bulletin,* 1967, **68**, 293–303.

Christie, R. Authoritarianism reexamined. *In* R. Christie and M. Jahoda (Eds.), *Studies in the scope and the method of the authoritarian personality.* New York: The Free Press, 1954, 123–196.

Corsini, R. J. Understanding and similarity in marriage. *Journal of Abnormal and Social Psychology*, 1956, **52**, 327–332.

Cook, S. W. Desegregation and attitude change. Address to the Southeastern Psychological Association, 1964. (Mimeo)

Cook, T. D., Bean, J. R., Cialdini, R. B., Krovetz, M. L., and Ray, A. A. Three contexts of ingratiation, and their effects on attributions, affect, and donating to charity: Two field experiments. (Submitted for publication).

Cook, T. D., and Insko, C. A. Persistence of attitude change as a function of conclusion reexposure: A laboratory-field experiment. *Journal of Personality and Social Psychology*, 1968, **9**, 322–328.

Cronbach, L. J. Response sets and test validity. *Educational and Psychological Measurement*, 1946, **6**, 475–494.

Cronbach, L. J. Further evidence on response sets and test design. *Educational and Psychological Measurement*, 1950, **10**, 3–31.

Cronbach, L. J. Proposals leading to analytic treatment of social perception scores. In R. Tagiuri and L. Petrullo (Eds.), *Person perception and interpersonal behavior*. Stanford: Stanford University Press, 1958, 353–379.

Daily Palo Alto Times, Psychologists protest tests by Army to see recruits reaction to danger. Thursday, August 13, 1959, p. 5.

Darley, J. M., and Latané, B. Bystander intervention in emergencies: Diffusion of responsibility. *Journal of Personality and Social Psychology*, 1968, **8**, 377–383.

Doob, A. N., and Gross, A. E. Status of frustrator as an inhibitor of horn-honking responses. *Journal of Social Psychology*, 1968, **76**, 213–218.

Edwards, A. L. *The social desirability variable in personality assessment and research.* New York: Dryden, 1957.

Feldman, H. *Problems in labor relations.* New York: Macmillan, 1937.

Feldman, R. E. Response to compatriot and foreigner who seek assistance. *Journal of personality and social psychology*, 1968, **10**, 202–214.

Festinger, L., and Carlsmith, J. M. Cognitive consequences of forced compliance. *Journal of Abnormal and Social Psychology*, 1959, **58**, 203, 210.

Franzen, R. Scaling responses to graded opportunities. *Public Opinion Quarterly*, 1950, **14**, 484–490.

Freedman, J. L, and Fraser, S. C. Compliance without pressure: The foot-in-the-door technique. *Journal of Personality and Social Psychology*, 1966, **4**, 195–202.

French, J. R. P. Organized and unorganized groups under fear and frustration. *University of Iowa Studies in Child Welfare*, 1944, **20**, 229–309.

Glock, C. Y. The effects of reinterviewing in panel research. 1958. Multilith of a chapter to appear in P. F. Lazarsfeld (Ed.), *The study of short run social change*, in preparation.

Gore, P. M., and Rotter, J. B. A personality correlate of social action. *Journal of Personality*, 1963, **31**, 58–64.

Gosnell, H. F. *Getting out the vote: an experiment in the stimulation of voting.* Chicago: University of Chicago Press, 1927.

Gross, A. E. Some determinants of honesty in a naturalistic situation. Talk presented at the Western Psychological Association, San Diego, California, March, 1968.

Gross, A. E., Collins, B., and Byran, J. *Experiments in social psychology.* New York: Wiley (in preparation).

Hammond, K. R. Representative vs. systematic design in clinical psychology. *Psychological Bulletin*, 1954, **51**, 150–159.

Hartmann, G. W. A field experiment on the comparative effectiveness of "emotional" and "rational" political leaflets in determining election results. *Journal of Abnormal and Social Psychology*, 1936, **31**, 99–114.

Helson, H., Blake, R. R., and Mouton, J. S. Petition-signing as adjustment to situational and personal factors. *Journal of Social Psychology*, 1958, **48**, 3–10.

Hempel, C. G. *Philosophy of natural science*. Englewood Cliffs, New Jersey: Prentice Hall, 1966.

Hovland, C. E., Janis, I. L., and Kelley, H. H. *Communication and persuasion*. New Haven: Yale University Press, 1953.

Jung, A. F. Price variations among automobile dealers in Chicago, Illinois. *Journal of Business*, 1959, **32**, 315–326.

Kelman, H. C. The human use of human subjects. *Psychological Bulletin*, 1967, **67**, 1–11, reprinted in Kelman, H. C. *A time to speak: On human values and social research*. San Francisco: Jossey-Bass, 1968.

Kerr, W. A. Experiments on the effect of music on factory production. *Applied Psychological Monographs*, 1945, No. 5.

Kidder, L., and Campbell, D. T. The indirect testing of social attitudes. *In* G. Summers (Ed.), (to be a chapter in book on Attitude Theory and Measurement, in press).

Kuhn, T. *The structure of scientific revolutions*. Chicago: University of Chicago Press, 1962.

Kutner, B., Wilkins, C., and Yarrow, P. R. Verbal attitudes and overt behavior involving racial prejudice. *Journal of Abnormal and Social Psychology*, 1952, **47**, 649–652.

La Piere, R. T. Actions versus actions. *Social Forces*, 1934, **13**, 230–237.

Lazarsfeld, P. F. Training guide on the controlled experiment in social research. Columbia University, Bureau of Applied Social Research, 1948. (Mimeo)

Lefkowitz, M., Blake, R. R., and Mouton, J. S. Status factors in pedestrian violation of traffic signals. *Journal of Abnormal and Social Psychology*, 1955, **51**, 704–706.

Merritt, C. B., and Fowler, R. G. The pecuniary honesty of the public at large. *Journal of Abnormal and Social Psychology*, 1948, **43**, 90–93.

Milgram, S. Behavioral study of obedience. *Journal of Abnormal and Social Psychology*, 1963, **67**, 371–378.

Milgram, S. The lost-letter technique: An unusual way to predict the outcome of elections, sentiments on integration, the strength of communist influence in Hong Kong, and the orientation of Americans to communists and fascists. *Psychology Today*, 1969, June (in press).

Milgram, S., Bickman, L., and Berkowitz, L. Note on the drawing power of crowds. (Submitted for publication, 1968).

Milgram, S., Mann, L., and Harter, S. The lost-letter technique: A tool of social research. *Public Opinion Quarterly*, 1965, **29**, 437–438.

Miller, N., and Levy, B. H. Defaming and agreeing with the communication as a function of emotional arousal, communication extremity, and evaluative set. *Sociometry*, 1967, **30**, 158–175.

Naroll, R. *Data quality control*. New York: The Free Press, 1962.

Page, E. B. Teacher comments and student performance: A seventy-four classroom experiment in school motivation. *Journal of Educational Psychology*, 1958, **49**, 173–181.

Petrie, H. G. The strategy sense of "methodology." *Philosophy of Science*, 1968, **35**, 248–257.

Polanyi, M. *Personal knowledge: Toward a post-critical philosophy.* London: Routledge and Kegan Paul, 1958.

Popper, K. R. *The Logic of Scientific Discovery.* London: Hutchinson, or New York: Basic Books, 1959.

Popper, K. R. *Conjectures and Refutations.* London: Routledge and Kegan Paul, New York: Basic Books, 1963.

Quine, W. V. *From a logical point of view.* Cambridge, Massachusetts: Harvard University Press, 1953.

Rankin, R. E., and Campbell, D. T. Galvanic skin response to Negro and white experimenters. *Journal of Abnormal and Social Psychology,* 1955, **51**(1), 30–33.

Roethlisberger, F. J., and Dickson, W. J. *Management and the worker.* Cambridge, Massachusetts: Harvard University Press, 1939.

Rokeach, M., and Mezei, L. Race and shared belief as factors in social choice. *Science,* 1966, **151**, 167–172.

Rorer, L. G. The great response-style myth. *Psychological Bulletin,* 1965, **65**, 129–156.

Rosenblatt, P. C., and Miller, N. Experimental method. *In* C. G. McClintock, (Ed.), *Experimental Social Psychology.* (To be published by Holt, Rinehart, and Winston, in preparation.)

Rosenthal, D., and Frank, J. O. Psychotherapy and the placebo effect. *Psychological Bulletin,* 1956, **53**, 294–302.

Rosenthal, R. *Experimenter effects in behavioral research.* New York: Appleton-Century-Crofts, 1966.

Salmon, W. *Logic.* Englewood Cliffs, New Jersey: Prentice Hall, 1963.

Schwartz, R. D., and Skolnick, J. H. Two studies of legal stigma. *Social Problems,* 1962, **10**, 133–142.

Schwartz, R. D., and Orleans, S. On legal sanctions. *University of Chicago Law Review,* 1967, **34**(2), 274–300.

Segall, M. H., Campbell, D. T., and Herskovits, M. J. *The influence of culture on visual perception.* Indianapolis: Bobbs-Merrill, 1966.

Selltiz, C., Jahoda, M., Deutsch, M., and Cook, S. W. *Research methods in social relations.* (Rev. ed.) New York: Holt-Dryden, 1959.

Silverman, L. H. A Q-sort study of the validity of evaluations made from projective techniques. *Psychological Monographs,* 1959, **73**(7, Whole No. 477).

Sommer, R. Studies in personal space. *Sociometry,* 1959, **22**, 247–260.

Stollak, G. E. Obedience and deception research. *American Psychologist,* 1967, **22**, 678.

Toulmin, S. *The philosophy of science.* London: Hutchinson, 1953.

Toulmin, S. *Foresight and understanding: An inquiry into the aims of science.* Bloomington: Indiana University Press, 1961.

Webb, E. J., Campbell, D. T., Schwartz, R. D., and Sechrest, L. B. *Unobtrusive measures: nonreactive research in the social sciences.* Chicago: Rand McNally, 1966.

Wilson, E. B. *An introduction to scientific research.* New York: McGraw-Hill, 1952.

AUTHOR INDEX

Numbers in italics refer to the pages on which the complete references are listed.

SUBJECT INDEX

A

Abreaction, 27
AB variable, 258 *ff*.
ACE, 87, *see also* Tests
Acquaintanceship, 66
After-only design, 33, 122 *ff*., *see also* Pretest effects
American Telephone and Telegraph, 25
Amphetamine, 166
Animal learning, 199 *ff*.
Animal spirits, 6
Anxiety, 81 *ff*., 188 *f*., *see also* Evaluation apprehension, Sarason Test Anxiety Scale, Taylor MAS
Approval need, 74 *ff*., 189, 295 *ff*., 306 *f*., 328, 362
Arousal seeking, 79 *ff*.
Artifact, *see also* Meta-artifacts
  background interactions, 359 *f*.
  confounded aspects of measurement, 362 *f*.
  confounded aspects of the treatment, 358 *f*.
  constancy of conditions and, 3
  control and, 351 *ff*.
  controlling, 363 *ff*.
  social influence research and, 23 *ff*., 101 *ff*., 132 *ff*., 143 *ff*., 181 *ff*., 284 *ff*.
  sources of,
    demand characteristics 143 *ff*.
    evaluation apprehension, 145, 279 *ff*.
    experimenter effects, 147 *ff*., 181 *ff*.
    experimenter's expectancy, 195 *ff*., 322 *ff*.
    pretest sensitization, 119 *ff*.
    response sets, 13 *ff*.
  role demands, 159 *ff*.
  suspiciousness of intent, 13 *ff*.
  volunteerism, 59 *ff*.
  stages in the life of, 15 *ff*.
    coping, 18 *ff*.
    exploitation, 20 *ff*.
    ignorance, 16 *ff*.
  typology, 358 *ff*.
Astronomy, observer error in, 182 *f*.
Authoritarianism, 77 *f*., 132
Awareness, 122, 144 *ff*., 222
  deception of, 160

B

Background Information Sheet, 292, 299 *f*., 304 *f*., 309 *ff*., 334 *f*.
Before-after design, 33, 122 *ff*., *see also* Pretest effects
Berlin, 197
"Best foot forward," 67, 280
Birth control, 137
Birth order, 71 *f*.
Black Power Coalition, 375
Boomerang effect, 35
Boston University, 105, 109
Bracketing variation, 365
British Columbia, 231
Buffalo, SUNY, 231
Bureau of Applied Social Research, 356

C

Caffeine, 79 *f*.
California, 372
California Psychological Inventory, 73, 90, *see also* Tests

393